Strategic Management for Nonprofit Organizations

STRATEGIC MANAGEMENT FOR NONPROFIT ORGANIZATIONS
Theory and Cases

SHARON M. OSTER

New York   Oxford
OXFORD UNIVERSITY PRESS
1995

Oxford University Press

Oxford   New York   Toronto
Delhi   Bombay   Calcutta   Madras   Karachi
Kuala Lumpur   Singapore   Hong Kong   Tokyo
Nairobi   Dar es Salaam   Cape Town
Melbourne   Auckland   Madrid

and associated companies in
Berlin   Ibadan

Copyright © 1995 by Oxford University Press, Inc.

Published by Oxford University Press, Inc.,
200 Madison Avenue, New York, New York 10016

Oxford is a registered trademark of Oxford University Press

Library of Congress Cataloging-in-Publication Data

Oster, Sharon M.
Strategic management for nonprofit organizations : theory and cases /
by Sharon M. Oster.
p.   cm.
Includes bibliographical references and index.
ISBN 0-19-508503-5
1. Nonprofit organization—Management.   2. Strategic planning.
I. Title.
HD62.6.O87   1995
658.4'012—dc20   94-21405

2 4 6 8 7 5 3 2 1

Printed in the United States of America
on acid-free paper

Preface

The world of the nonprofit organization has grown increasingly complex. Competition—both among nonprofits and between nonprofit and for-profit or public organizations—has increased. Both the clients of and donors to the nonprofit have intensified their demands for professional, efficient provision of goods and services. Tax and accounting rules and standards are changing. In this environment, many nonprofit organizations have turned to the managerial tools of the for-profit sector for help. But the nonprofit sector is not exactly like the for-profit and thus the diffusion of ideas across the sectors does not always proceed smoothly. This book is designed to fill in this gap: to help nonprofit managers select those tools and ideas from the for-profit sector that will be most helpful to them and to adapt those tools to the demands of the nonprofit sector.

Many of the ideas in this book come from the discipline of economics. The tools of economics—supply and demand, marginal analysis, the idea of trade-offs and opportunity cost—are, of course, sector-neutral. Nevertheless, in the past, many of the examples of economics have been in the private or public sector. One of the themes of this book is that economic tools are equally applicable in the nonprofit world and, indeed, the resource scarcity of the sector may actually accentuate their utility.

This book also draws heavily from the management literature. Understanding human resource management, dealing with staff, volunteers, and the board, require us to look at ideas from organizational theory. The areas of managerial control and evaluation lead us to the accounting and tax literature. Product choice and pricing are discussed using literature from marketing, strategy, and economics. Nonprofit management, in the modern age, can benefit from the lessons of a number of fields.

The analytical material in this book is supplemented by a number of examples, drawn from varied markets and from both large and small organizations. The perspective taken in this book, I would argue, is as useful for a small art museum as it is for a large relief organization or an economic development group.

The last section of the book consists of a series of cases. These cases are designed to be used as teaching tools in a course on nonprofits, either in a management curriculum or a public policy program. While many of the cases deal with issues that cut across functional areas, several are targeted to be taught in conjunction with particular chapters. Teaching notes are available from the author for each of the cases.

I was drawn into research on nonprofit organizations by students at the Yale School of Management (SOM). SOM was founded on the principle that analytical management techniques could be brought to bear on problem-solving in all three sectors and, indeed, that managing in any one sector required an understanding of all three. This book, and all my research on nonprofit organizations have benefited enormously from the students I have taught over the years at SOM, and I thank them for their interest and prodding.

As I progressed on this manuscript I benefited from the close readings of many of the chapters by colleagues at Yale and elsewhere. Paul Dimaggio, Melissa Middleton Stone, Robert Augsberger, Charles Perrow, Stan Garstka, Jonathan Feinstein, Barry O'Neill, and Ray Fair were all very helpful. Robert Augsberger, in particular, shared his excellent Stanford class materials with me, much to my benefit. I also appreciate the help given to my case writers by the many people at the organizations we turned into cases for this book. It is not always either easy or gratifying to be the subject of such close scrutiny!

Contents

1. Introduction, 3

   The Emergence of Nonprofits, 4
   A Look at the Field Today, 4
   A Look at Diversity in the Nonprofit Sector, 8
   Internal Revenue Service Distinctions, 10
   The Management Process: A Road Map of the Book, 11

2. The Mission of the Nonprofit Organization, 17

   Why Do we have Nonprofits?, 17
   The Role of the Mission Statement, 22
   The Process of Mission-Setting, 24
   How Broad or Narrow Should the Mission Statement Be?, 27
   Conclusion, 28

3. Structural Analysis of a Nonprofit Industry, 29

   Competitive Analysis for the Nonprofit: The Industry Level, 29
   Market Definition, 30
   Description of Current Industry Participants, 31
   Entry Conditions, 32
   Competition from Substitute Products, 36
   The Demand Side, 37
   Users, 38
   Donor Power, 40
   Supply, 40
   Industry Structure: Sources of Advantage, 42
   Summary, 45

4. Competition and Cooperation Among Nonprofits, 47

Game Theory, 48
Simultaneous versus Sequential Games, 50
Cooperation among Nonprofits: Beyond Games, 57
Strategies for Cooperation, 60
Competing with For-Profit Organizations and Public Agencies, 61
A Few Thoughts on the Balance Between Competition and Cooperation, 63

5. Human Resource Management, 65

Attracting and Motivating Staff, 65
Centralization versus Decentralization, 69
Managing Volunteers, 73
Conclusion, 74

6. The Nonprofit Board of Directors, 75

A Review of the Stylized Facts About Nonprofits, 75
Function of the Board: The Theory, 76
Functions of the Board: In Practice, 80
Increasing Board Effectiveness, 83
Conclusion, 85

7. Product Mix and Pricing, 87

Why Broaden the Product Portfolio?, 87
The Product Portfolio: Balancing Ventures, 92
Combining for Profit and Nonprofit Ventures, 93
Tax Issues, 94
Strategic Management Issues, 96
Pricing in the Nonprofit World, 98
Pricing in the Nonprofit Sector: How Much Do We Charge?, 102
Conclusion, 105

8. Fundraising for Nonprofits, 107

Charitable Contributions: Magnitude and Sources, 107
The Optimal Level of Fundraising Effort, 111
Determinants of Giving: The Individual Level, 114
Corporate Giving: Trends and Determinants, 118
Cooperation versus Competition in Fundraising, 119
Conclusion, 121

9. Managerial Control, 123

Why do we have Financial Reports?, 123
The Budget Process, 127

The Problems of Inadequate Budget Control: Using Variance Analysis, 132
Conclusions, 138

10. Program Evaluation, 139

    Effectiveness versus Efficiency: A Few Definitions, 140
    For Whom are we Evaluating Programs?, 141
    The Mechanics of Program Evaluation, 143
    Concluding Thoughts on Performance Evaluations, 146

11. The Potential for Change, 149

    The Adaptability of the Nonprofit, 149
    Sources of Change, 151
    Experiencing Change, 154
    Concluding Thoughts, 155

    Appendix: Guide to the Cases, 157

    A. *People for the American Way, 160*
    B. *United Hmong Association, 176*
    C. *Public Broadcasting System, 197*
    D. *American Red Cross, 218*
    E. *The Good Faith Fund, 233*
    F. *Classical Jazz at Lincoln Center, 251*
    G. *The Future of Donor Choice at United Way, 272*
    H. *Guggenheim Museum, 287*
    I. *Leeway, Inc., 310*

Notes, 333

Index, 345

Strategic Management for Nonprofit Organizations

1

Introduction

Nonprofit organizations earn more than $100 billion in revenue in the United States each year, in more than 1 million different organizations.[1] In some sectors—like religion and the arts—nonprofits are the dominant organizational form. In other areas, nonprofits share the market with for-profit corporations and public agencies. In almost all markets, however, nonprofits face increasing competition, competition that has intensified the pressure these organizations face to find effective management methods.

In this book, we explore strategic management in the nonprofit. In the last several decades, the management of nonprofit organizations has become an increasingly rich terrain for academic work in the social sciences. As our knowledge of these organizations has deepened, so has our sense of both the applicability of management principles developed in the for-profit sector and the limitations of those principles for nonprofit management. At the same time, we have seen managers in the nonprofit sector reaching out for new ideas to improve their operations. Many nonprofit managers—especially those in large nonprofits—have adopted the managerial techniques and systems of the for-profit corporations as a way to try to improve their operations. For example, in the Roman Catholic Archdiocese of Boston, Archbishop Bernard Law hired a professor of business administration from Boston to be the chancellor of the diocese. The new chancellor created a new budget system, instituted planning, and redesigned the organizational structure, bringing many of the tools of management to bear on the religious organization.[2] There are substantial areas of overlap between nonprofit and for-profit management. Running the American Red Cross, however, is not exactly like running IBM, and it is important to keep in mind the differences between the two organizations as well as their similarities as we proceed to develop tools for strategic management.

3

The Emergence of Nonprofits

Early colonists in the United States were, on the whole, hostile to corporations of any sort, either private or nonprofit. Hence, in the United States at least, it was not until the early to mid-nineteenth century that private charitable corporations were firmly established.[3] Harvard College, for example, was widely regarded as a public institution in its early life. It was governed by state-appointed ministers, and state officials; its funding came largely from public appropriations.

The nineteenth century saw rapid growth among nonprofits in the United States coming from several diverse sources. Hall argues that the rise of the large private corporation in the nineteenth-century United States created a demand for education that was then served by nonprofit colleges. These colleges were, in this period, supported and, to some extent, directed by business. In the same period, social reformism stimulated growth of social service nonprofits, while the well-to-do began to support new cultural activities, the museums, and symphony orchestras. Thus, the nonprofit sector grew both in scope and size.

In this abbreviated history we see several themes that will recur in our discussion of nonprofits. First, the lines between nonprofits, business, and the public sector have been, from the beginning, somewhat blurry. Nonprofits have historically shared territory with public organizations and been funded and influenced by for-profit businesses. We see further that, again from the beginning, the nonprofit sector has shown considerable diversity, in terms of what is being produced and for whom. Finally, we see nonprofits concentrated in the service sector and, in particular, in activities with at least some public character.

A Look at the Field Today

What makes an organization a nonprofit? Perhaps the easiest way to distinguish a nonprofit organization is by virtue of its tax and regulatory designation. Organizations that are designated nonprofits are put in a special category in terms of tax, legal, and regulatory rules. In many countries and in most states of the United States, laws governing contracts, labor, securities, antitrust, and the like all distinguish between for-profit and nonprofit corporations, typically treating the latter more leniently.[4] The most prominent difference between for-profits and nonprofits is, of course, their tax status. In most countries, nonprofits are exempt from federal income taxes, and many are exempt from other regional and local taxes as well. These organizations are, simultaneously and in part as a consequence of this tax relief, subject to some governmental limits on how their revenues can be used. In particular, any financial surplus that may result from operations cannot be distributed to those in control of the corporation, its directors,

staff, or members. This provision of nonprofit corporate governance law is known as the *nondistribution constraint.*

The nondistribution constraint is a provision of the law of nonprofits preventing such organizations from distributing their net earnings to those in control of the corporations.

The differential treatment of nonprofits under the law has quite substantial effects for the management process. The favorable tax and legal treatment of the nonprofit may enable it to pursue activities that are difficult to sustain in the for-profit arena. Legal scholars have been particularly interested in the effect of the nondistribution constraint. Because they are subject to a nondistribution constraint nonprofit organizations cannot have shareholders, or owners, in the same way that for-profit corporations do. As a consequence, in the nonprofit sector, we have more questions about what the governance structure should be. The limitation creates questions about what the financial goals of the organization should be, about how managers can be motivated, and about whose views about the structure and operation of the organization should prevail. In this text we will explore at some length the ways in which the special legal and tax treatment of the nonprofit influence management.

The definition of a nonprofit organization, however, goes beyond the formal legal designation. When we think of nonprofit organizations, we normally think of a constellation of particular characteristics. These characteristics, in turn, help to define the management problems of the nonprofit and help to distinguish them from those of the typical for-profit firm. Tables 1.1–1.3 contain data describing the scope of the nonprofit sector in the United States and selected other countries. Perhaps the first thing one is struck by as we look at the nonprofit world both in the United States and abroad is that this form of organization appears principally in certain kinds of industries. Social services, religion, health, and cultural activities are all common venues for nonprofit operations, while we rarely see the non-profit form in heavy manufacturing, for example. In part, this concentration of the nonprofit form comes from tax rules; not every kind of business

Table 1.1. Composition of the Non-profit Sector, United States

	Percentage
Social Service	9.4%
Community, civic	3.9
Education, research	17.9
Health Care	49.9
Arts and Culture	1.9
Religious	17.0

Source: James and Rose-Ackerman, 1986, 6 and 14.

Strategic Management for Nonprofit Organizations

Table 1.2. Distribution of Nonprofit Activity in Sweden, 1979

	Share of Nonprofit Expenditures (%)
Education	35
Culture and Recreation	37
Health	—
Religion	14
Other	14
Total	100

Source: Estelle James cited in Estelle James and Susan Rose-Ackerman, the *Nonprofit Enterprise in Market Economics,* Hawood, New York, 1986, p. 14.

is eligible for nonprofit status. This is not the entire explanation, however, for patterns of nonprofit activity. Nonprofit corporations, under law, can serve private as well as public purposes, and often carry on their operations side by side with for-profits. Moreover, there are differences across countries, even among the three represented here. The United States and Japan organize their health sectors at least in part through the nonprofit form; in Sweden, all health care comes through the governmental sector. One of the puzzles we will explore in this book is why certain goods and services are well suited to nonprofit production and why others are not. In some cases we will discover that the push to nonprofit form operates across countries with rather different institutional regimes; in other cases, we will see more cross-county differences. In general, the rationale for nonprofit production will turn out to have substantial implications for the way in which those nonprofit organizations should be managed.

Table 1.3. Distribution of Nonprofit Activity in Japan, 1981

	Share of Nonprofit Organization (%)
Education and Culture	33
Health, Welfare, and Environment	33
Aid to Private Industry	26
Quasi-Government	8
Total	100

Source: Minoru Tanaka and Takako Ameniya, *Philanthropy in Japan 1983: Private Nonprofit Activities in Japan,* Tokyo: Japan Association of Charitable Organizations, 1983, p. 26.

Nonprofit organizations are typically quite labor intense, with a heavy use of both professional and volunteer labor. Table 1.4 provides data on both the paid staff and the value of volunteer services in the nonprofit sector in the United States. Nonprofits as a whole comprise more than 8.5% of the total U.S. employment, but only 6.8% of national income, indicating the labor intensity of the sector. Every other adult works as a volunteer for one of the many nonprofit organizations in the United States, giving on average five hours per week.[5] Nonprofit organizations have been called the "natural locus" for professional staff because of the kinds of fields they occupy and the kinds of working conditions they typically supply.[6] The labor intensity of the nonprofit sector highlights the importance of human resources management for these firms, while the presence of a supplemental, unpaid labor force in the form of volunteers and the concentration of professionals make questions of motivation and control of staff all the more complex. It has been argued, for example, that the staff in nonprofit organizations have their principal allegiance to a profession or a cause rather than to an organization.[7]

A final common characteristic of nonprofits is their reliance at least to some extent on donations as a revenue source. Table 1.5 documents the revenue sources for U.S. nonprofits. On average, in the United States, twenty percent of the revenues of private nonprofits comes from donations. The use of donations sets these organizations apart from their for-profit colleagues. As Table 1.5 suggests, many nonprofits also realize earned revenues, through the sale of goods and services. Nevertheless, in our discussion of the revenue side of management, we will need to add a discussion of fundraising to the more common treatment of product pricing. Moreover, the existence of fundraising as a revenue source compli-

Table 1.4. U.S. Work Force in Nonprofits

	Percentage of Workers by Sector; 1990
Nonprofit	8.5
Business (For-Profit)	74.9
Government	16.6

	Percentage of Population 18+ Volunteering by Area
Arts	7.3
Education	16.3
Environment	6.3
Health	11.9
Human Services	14.0
Informal	25.7
Religious organizations	28.6
Youth development	15.8

Source: Hodgkinson, et al., *Nonprofit Almanac,* 69, 119.

Table 1.5. Source of Revenues U.S. Nonprofits, 1987

	Dollars (billions)
Private Contributions	36.3
Government Grants	25.4
Program Revenues*	211.9
Other	37.2
Total revenue	310.8

Source: Hodgkinsone, et al., *Nonprofit Almanac,* 69, 157.

*Includes Medicare/Medicaid.

cates our discussion of organizational governance, product choice, and accounting systems. Here, too, some of the differences between the for-profit and nonprofit will become salient.

Nonprofits are distinguished by their mix of goods and services, the character of their labor forces, and their source of revenues.

A Look at Diversity in the Nonprofit Sector

We have thus far concentrated on common characteristics of nonprofits, those characteristics that set them apart from for-profit counterparts. Within the nonprofit sector, however, we also see enormous variety. As I begin in this book to develop some theory and techniques that we can use to understand management concerns in this sector, the existence of these large organizational differences will come into play as well. We will explore ways in which the ideas we develop will be helpful for organizations as disparate as the Santa Fe Opera Company, the Salvation Army, and the National Football League.

Consider three nonprofit organizations as an example of the complexity of the nonprofit landscape: The United Negro College Fund, the Guggenheim Museum, and the Dixwell Community House. These three organizations clearly differ substantially in the populations they serve and in the services they provide. The United Negro College Fund, with revenues of $40 million per year, raises funds to support a consortium of black colleges. The Guggenheim is one of the finest modern museums of fine arts in the world, with sites in New York, Italy, and Spain, with an annual operating budget of $10 million. The Dixwell Community House is a recreational and social service organization, serving a small neighborhood in New Haven, Connecticut, on a budget of less than $500,000. These differences in the missions and the size and scope of the three organizations

clearly influence the kinds of management issues they will confront. Chapters 2 and 3 explore these issues.

When we probe further into these three organizations, we see still other differences among them. Consider the level and composition of competition each of these three organizations faces. The College Fund competes principally with other, nationally based, nonprofit organizations, similarly engaged in fundraising. For the College Fund, one strategic decision it faces is whether to compete at all with other fundraisers, or whether cooperation among similar fundraisers would be a better strategy. The Guggenheim competes with other organizations along at least three different dimensions—admissions, art acquisition, and fundraising—and the nature of competition it faces differs substantially along these axes. Thus, in terms of attracting admissions, the Guggenheim competes with local attractions, including, of course, other New York and Venetian museums. There is cooperation among museums as well, as they share artwork through exchanges and traveling shows. In the acquisitions area, the Guggenheim's competition comes not only from other nonprofit museums, but from public museums, for-profit museums and galleries and private collections. Moreover, in the acquisition of art, the scope of competition is global, not local. The Dixwell Community House has essentially no competition for its clients, and works very closely with the other major provider of social services in the area, the city. On the other hand, it competes broadly with other nonprofit organizations for donations within New Haven and Connecticut. Thus, even across these three examples, we can see quite substantial differences in terms of how much competition there is and on the complexion of that competition. We will clearly need to take these differences into account when we look at the nonprofit strategy for dealing with competitors in Chapter 4.

Where do each of our three sample organizations get their funds for operations? We noted earlier that almost all nonprofits rely at least to some extent on donations; however, the extent of that reliance is quite different. The United Negro College Fund relies principally on current contributions, generated from individuals and corporations. The Guggenheim earns about 20% of its revenues from its endowment, approximately 25% from current grants and gifts, and the rest from admissions and gift-shop sales. The Dixwell Community House depends on the City of New Haven and on individual donations to support its current operations. These differences will influence not only fundraising strategies, but the design of accounting systems, the structure of management control, and the choice of product mix.

We also see differences in the cost side of the budget. As we suggested, on average, nonprofits are more labor intensive than for-profit firms. Nevertheless, the extent of the use of labor and type of worker employed clearly differs among types of nonprofits. The United Negro College Fund relies on a mix of well-educated paid staff and corporate and individual volunteers to run its fundraising campaigns. The Guggenheim uses relatively little labor, given its revenues, and much of that staff is highly specialized and trained. The Dixwell Community House is almost entirely run by volunteers, individuals with interests in working with children, but often little formal training.

Within the nonprofit sector, there is considerable diversity in terms of both mission and structure.

Internal Revenue Service Distinctions

I have given only three examples of organizations in the nonprofit sector to illustrate the variety within the sector. In the preceding discussion, I have focused on many of the structural differences among nonprofits. The Internal Revenue Service (I.R.S.) has another method of classifying nonprofits, which points us to other distinctions among them. Nonprofit organizations are exempt from federal income taxes under section 501 of the Internal Revenue code. Within this class, however, there are several subcategories. In Figure 1.1, I have reproduced the ring chart of nonprofits that Simon[8] developed to sort the differing 501 organizations. Ring 1 represents the

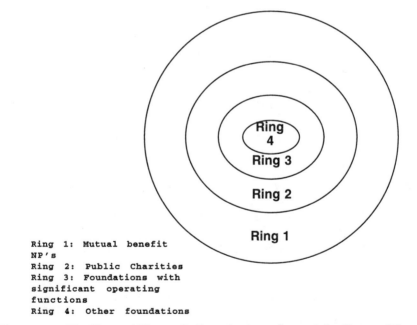

Ring 1: Mutual benefit
NP's
Ring 2: Public Charities
Ring 3: Foundations with
significant operating
functions
Ring 4: Other foundations

Figure 1.1. The Rings of Nonprofit Organizations. *Source:* John Simon, "The tax treatment of nonprofit organizations: A review of federal and state policies" in W. W. Powell, *The Nonprofit Sector*, New Haven: Yale University Press, 1989. p. 68.

Mutual Benefit nonprofits, covered under sections 501(c) (4)–(21) of the I.R.S. code. These are the social clubs, fraternal organizations, clubs that are organized in order to provide mutual benefits to the members. These are the least regulated of the nonprofits. While they are, along with the other nonprofits, exempt from corporate taxes, contributions to these organizations are not exempt.

Rings 2–4 include the charitable nonprofits, the 501(c) (3) organizations. Ring 2 includes the public charities that most people think of when they think of nonprofits. Approximately one third of the nonprofit organizations in the United States are in this category. Here are the charities, schools, churches, hospitals, and the like. The tax privileges of this class extend to charitable deductions and include exemption from most property taxes. Rings 3 and 4 include the foundations, both with and without substantial operating functions. This group has tax privileges, but is probably the most highly regulated of the nonprofits. Thus, we see in this taxonomy, differences within the sector in terms of purpose of the nonprofit, tax status and regulatory oversight. As we develop an approach to strategic management in this book, we will use this variety to enrich our discussion.

The Management Process: A Road Map of the Book

This book describes the strategic management of nonprofits. It takes us from setting the mission of the organization all the way to evaluating how well the organization is carrying out that mission. Before we begin this exploration, it is useful to lay out the pieces of the management process and see how those pieces are connected.

Figure 1.2 is a summary schematic of the process of strategic management as it might be used by a nonprofit organization. In the large box on the left-hand side of the figure, I have represented the first task of management: setting the goals of the organization. The central strategic question facing an organization—any organization—is to decide what its goals are and what business it wants to be in to accomplish those goals. Perhaps the most fundamental "fact" about any nonprofit organization is what business it is in and what it hopes to accomplish in that business, questions that, for most nonprofit organizations, are answered in their *mission statement*. General Motors is in the business of producing cars, Coca-Cola in the business of producing soft drinks. Both explicitly seek to maximize shareholder value of the firm as they go about their businesses. In a similar way, the Guggenheim is in the business of acquiring, preserving, and presenting art, while the United Negro College Fund is in the business of fundraising for black colleges, though clearly neither organization carries on its business with the goals of a shareholder in mind.

We will begin our exploration of nonprofit management with the mission statement in Chapter 2. How do a group of individuals, at the start of an organization's life, decide and make concrete what that organization

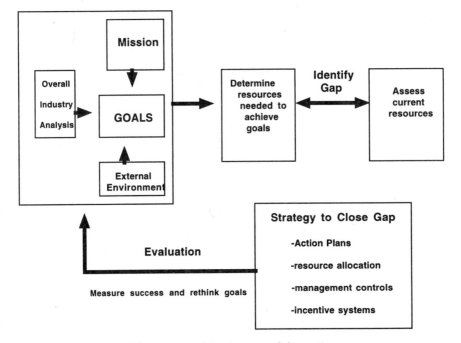

Figure 1.2.   Management Schematic.

should be doing? In the absence of shareholders, whose goals should the nonprofit be serving? For a nonprofit organization, the question of values is often quite central to management in the way that it is often not in the corporate world. Drucker quotes one CEO who serves on many nonprofit boards on this point: "The businesses I work with start their planning with financial returns. The nonprofits start with the performance of their mission."[9]

Questions of mission go beyond the early life of an organization. Organizations at times change direction as they mature. The current YMCA, with its focus on health and community service, has clearly left the religious part of its original mission behind. How do organizations change direction? Are nonprofits more or less adaptable than their for-profit counterparts? Do mission statements lead in the change process or are they simply an articulation of change made in the past? These are the kinds of questions we will explore in Chapter 2 of this text.

As an organization begins to think about what it is it wishes to do, one element in that decision is clearly the vision and values of its founders and constituents. Mission statements and the vision they embrace in terms of the business of an organization, however, have an economic base as well as an ideological one. In particular, organizations need to consider not only what they want to do, but what they can do, given the constraints imposed on them by their environment and by the economic, political, and social characteristics of the market in which they conduct their business. In the schematic, I represent these two elements by the boxes labeled external environment and industry analysis. The techniques a nonprofit organization can use to analyze its environment and industry are the focus of Chapter 3 of this book. The discussion will cover the way in which organizations learn about the *key success factors* in their business, those characteristics that are essential to function in a particular market. Here, we will particularly focus on the major sources of change for organizations, for it is change that brings with it the major opportunities and threats that enliven the management process and feed into the evolution of goals of the organization.

In the for-profit world, one of the major factors that influences the likelihood of an organization's success is the behavior of its rivals. By and large, in the for-profit world, firms prosper in situations in which the goods and services they produce cannot be produced at equal costs by other competitors. Thus, strategic management in the for-profit emphasizes speed in exploiting competitive advantages and secrecy in developing those advantages. This is not to say that cooperation among firms is unheard of in the corporate world, but it remains the exception rather than the rule. In the nonprofit world, the balance between competition and cooperation is more even and perhaps more complicated as some of our examples have already suggested. Chapter 4 will deal with these issues of rivalry and cooperation among firms.

The first chapters of this book, just described, concern themselves with the strategic aspects of management: What should we be doing, for whom and what constraints will we face in getting there? The nonprofit manager also faces operational tasks, and these are represented in the right-hand side of Figure 1.1. Logically, though not always in practice, the first operational task of the manager is to identify the gaps between the current resources of the organization and those needed to accomplish its goals. These gaps may well involve financial assets, human resource imbalances, and organizational and control inadequacies. This task involves a hard form of organizational self-scrutiny and is often a particularly difficult task in a nonprofit where vision plays such a central role.

The next step for the organization is to develop a strategy to close the gaps identified by its analysis or to adjust its goals to the realities of the resources available. Here the firm will need to develop plans that will typically involve resource allocation decisions, and often include management control and incentive systems. At this point strategy moves well beyond lofty vision to concrete plans for implementation. Chapters 5–10 cover these operational tasks of management, organized by major functional area. We begin in Chapter 5 with human resource management, including in our discussion both staff and volunteer development. Here we will use work in economics and organizational behavior to explore issues like performance evaluation, organizational structure, and compensation. It will turn out that because nonprofits often produce goods and services that are difficult to judge and because they rely for the production of these goods and services on a largely professional and volunteer staff, much of the current new work in labor and information economics will be especially pertinent.

Chapter 6 introduces another part of the nonprofit management team, the board of trustees. Interestingly, nonprofit organizations have traditionally had much more active boards than have for-profit organizations. Indeed, Drucker has argued that if you were in search of a truly effective board, you would be much better off looking in the nonprofit sector than among public corporations.[10] Despite Drucker's enthusiasm, most executive directors of nonprofit organizations will list more effective board involvement as one of their prime management priorities. We will look at the structure of the typical nonprofit board, and try to understand how it functions both in the ideal and in practice. In terms of our schematic, we will explore the ways in which the nonprofit board is active not only in the strategic decisions we normally associate with boards in the for-profit sector, but also with many of the operational tasks on the right-hand side of our figure. Part of our discussion will focus on special problems and opportunities created by this multistage involvement by trustees.

Nonprofit organizations raise revenues through a combination of fundraising and sale of goods and services. The typical strategy developed by a nonprofit will thus have initiatives in both of these areas. In Chapters 7 and 8, we discuss revenue generation. First, we will consider the goods and services side in Chapter 7. How should a nonprofit decide what its mix of goods and services should be? If a public corporation produces a product that fails to cover variable costs on a continuing basis, we normally expect that company to abandon the product. Indeed, the stockholders of the firm might well wish to replace a management team that persevered in the production of goods and services that were losing money. In the nonprofit sector, the right answer is more complicated. Many nonprofits continue to produce goods and services that lose money and do so with the continuing, conscious support of their boards, cross-subsidizing those activities with net revenues from other services. Planned Parenthood, for example, uses revenues from clinics in affluent areas to support those in poorer areas, and fees from affluent patients to help support procedures on the less advantaged. This cross-subsidization is built into the Planned Parenthood operation. On the other hand, at times nonprofits have and should follow their corporate sisters in abandoning losing operations. In Chapter 7, we consider the related questions of product choice and pricing.

Chapter 8 moves to the second revenue source of nonprofits, fundraising. As the nonprofit sector has grown in the last few decades, the competition among organizations in the fundraising area has increased dramatically. In Chapter 8, we explore issues like how much cooperation should we have in fundraising across different nonprofits. Here the issues of cooperation and competition that we discuss in Chapter 4 will emerge in a quite pragmatic context.

Management control systems and financial reporting systems play a role throughout the bottom half of our schematic. In order to implement any strategy, an organization clearly needs some kind of management control system to help insure that the people inside the organization are each doing what he or she is supposed to do. Such systems need not be highly bureaucratized or formal to be effective; indeed, loose systems are preferred for some organizations. Control systems as well as evaluation and appraisal systems depend, to one degree or another, on some financial reporting system. In some ways, precisely because the nonprofit organization is not being constantly judged by its shareholders on its financial performance, the organization itself may be even more needful of an informative financial reporting system than would be a for-profit organization. Yet, in practice nonprofits often neglect their financial reporting systems. For publicly traded companies, the Financial Accounting Standards Board (FASB) has established a set of rules governing the kinds of information that must regularly be reported. There is surely leeway in the rules, and much of modern accounting literature has concentrated on the way in which reported information can be manipulated. Nevertheless, there are considerable guidelines available. In the case of nonprofits fewer uniform standards exist.[11] As a consequence, nonprofits in different sectors have developed their own sets of rules, rules that are followed at best by a small fraction of the organizations within a sector. In Chapter 9, we will take a look at some of the issues surrounding financial reporting and provide some guidelines to creating a reporting system that will actually help the management of the nonprofit to make more reasoned decisions.

Perhaps the most neglected task of either for-profit or nonprofit managers is the last task on our schematic; the evaluation task. What little evaluation nonprofit managers do is often at the behest of funding agencies and is little more than a pro forma exercise. In Chapter 10, we will look at the process of evaluation and performance appraisal in the nonprofit organization.

2

The Mission of the Nonprofit Organization

It is difficult even to begin to discuss nonprofit organizations without almost immediately ending up in a discussion of the *mission* of that organization. Consider the following description of the process of reorganization at the Girl Scouts of America from Frances Hesselbein, former executive director:

> We kept asking ourselves very simple questions. What is our business? Who is the customer: And what does the customer consider value? If you're the Girl Scouts, IBM, or AT&T, you have to manage for a mission.

While Hesselbein is doubtless correct that for-profit companies must ultimately manage with some mission in mind, for a nonprofit, the role of the mission and its articulation is typically larger than it is for the for-profit corporation. This augmented role comes from the particular nature of nonprofit operations. In this chapter, we examine the function of nonprofits in the economy and the way in which nonprofit structure and function enlarge the role of the mission statement. We then turn to a more detailed discussion of how nonprofits develop and change their missions.

Why Do We Have Nonprofits?

I begin from the position that organizational form affects the ability of an organization to survive in the marketplace.[2] In some markets, large well-integrated, highly diversified corporations are most successful. In others, small, flexible entrepreneurial operations can best meet the changing needs of the marketplace. In still other markets, nonprofit organizations or public institutions are the most efficient producers of goods and services. Because different forms are more or less able to meet the technological, social, and economic demands of a market, as we look at a market over time, the environmental forces in that market will tend to weed out some of those organizational forms and allow others to proliferate. When we see a particular organizational form dominating a marketplace, we are led to ask what it is about that form that has helped it to survive in that market.

Thus, we ask, as a way to understand why we have nonprofits: What advantages does the nonprofit form have over its for-profit and public counterparts? In designing a mission, nonprofits should be considering how their advantages can be best used. If the nonprofit's advantage is in its flexibility or its ability to motivate staff, then all else equal it should specialize in markets in which these two advantages are important. In other words, our knowledge about the advantages of nonprofit organizations will influence our view of the kind of mission that a nonprofit can best serve and the way it should go about defining and changing that mission. This discussion has particular relevance as more nonprofits look outside their traditional markets toward activities that can help to improve the financial stability of the organization or its growth.

As we indicated in Chapter 1, nonprofit organizations are concentrated in particular segments of the economy: health, education, social services, and the arts. Why is it that we see this concentration? In particular, is there some reason the nonprofit form most suits these markets?

The first group of theories used to explain patterns of nonprofit organization emphasize the role of *contract failure*. Work in this area comes principally from social scientists and lawyers who have surveyed patterns of nonprofit activity such as the ones we described in Chapter 1 and noted the contrast between the kinds of goods and services produced in the nonprofit sector and those typically described in our models of economic behavior.[3] In the traditional markets that form the stuff of economics models, products are assumed to be easily judged in terms of quality by consumers who both pay for the good and then use it. Under these conditions, products that are a bad value are ultimately forced out of the marketplace by consumers who eschew their purchase and use. In the nonprofit sector, the typical good looks rather different. Many nonprofits produce goods or services that are complex, difficult for a user to judge in terms of quality. Much health care falls in this category. Moreover, many of the goods and services produced in this sector are paid for by people who do not ultimately benefit from the good or service. For example, a donor to Save the Children is typically an affluent North American, while the beneficiary of the donation is most often an impoverished Asian, African, or South American. As a consequence of this profile of the typical nonprofit product, the usual story about bad value products being forced out of the marketplace is less compelling. Indeed, firms will have an incentive to "cheat" customers by producing goods of lower quality than they claim to be producing, since customers have no way to monitor such claims, and cheap production would typically save the firm money. In situations in which goods and services are not easily judged by purchasers, these purchasers will begin to look to other ways to guarantee that firms are delivering on their claims.

What is the competitive advantage of the nonprofit in markets in which *reputation* and *trust* are important? The hallmark of a nonprofit organization is that it cannot redistribute its profits; it operates under the nondistribution constraint, as we described earlier. Thus, such organizations have a reduced incentive to cheat on the quality of their products, since this cheating will not result in an appropriable surplus. As a consequence, consumers tend to trust nonprofit organizations because they recognize that the managers in these firms have different incentives than the managers of their for-profit counterparts. Thus, nonprofits have an advantage over for-profits under conditions of contract failure.

Contract failure theories emphasize the development of nonprofits in sectors in which trust and reputations are important.

Another way that customers can assure that they are receiving high-quality products under the circumstances described here is by exerting more direct control over the organization itself. Consumer cooperatives and mutual nonprofits are both subtypes of the nonprofit form that allow for such improved control and thus these forms will have advantages in markets of this type.[4]

The contract failure arguments could equally well be thought of as an explanation for public provision of goods. When monitoring of products or services is difficult, public production and provision is often used. Similarly, when we have goods that exhibit joint consumption (i.e., the usual "public good"), like environmental quality, public and nonprofit provision are both plausible alternatives. The public sector supports these activities with taxation and creates trust with the ideology of government. The nonprofit sector uses donations and creates trust with its ideological staff.

Weisbrod argues that nonprofit production serves in many circumstances as a complement to public production, supplementing or replacing public goods when individuals are unsatisfied with the level or quality of those goods or services.[5] Thus, private education is a response to the failure of public education; private charity is a response to the inadequacy of redistribution, and so on. Contract failure creates a need for public or nonprofit production, and the existence of diversity in tastes among the population leads to a system in which the public sector provides a level of service consistent with the average voter, while the nonprofit sector serves specialized needs of the population. Douglas notes that by playing this role, nonprofit organizations can serve as important political stabilizers.[6] This is a competitive advantage of nonprofits that transcends the individual marketplace.

Nonprofits operate in many of the same areas as the public sector, and act as partial substitutes for public provision.

There are other advantages nonprofits have over public provision. In some cases, nonprofits may have lower labor costs, in part due to the rules and bureaucracy of the public sector. Moreover, nonprofits can often charge fees for service when public fees run into political barriers.[7]

The view that nonprofits in part substitute for public provision also helps us to understand some of the comparative data on nonprofits presented in Chapter 1. Throughout the world, education is provided outside the for-profit sector. Some countries use the nonprofit sector heavily; others use the public sector. Sweden, with its homogeneous population, relies almost entirely on public education, for example, while in nearby Holland, where religious differences split the population, nonprofit education is quite common.[8]

In general, we expect nonprofits to specialize in the part of the public good spectrum that is most controversial; nonprofit production allows outliers in the population to receive goods and services not likely to come from a public sector aimed at the median voter. Thus, religious and military education are nonprofit; Planned Parenthood remains committed to producing abortions; the A.C.L.U. defends everyone from the Nazis to the Communist Party.

While the discussion, thus far, focuses on the choice of public versus nonprofit production, in practice, nonprofits and public agencies often operate as partners in the delivery of public services.[9] Federal and local governments in the United States have often contracted with nonprofits for delivery of public services. In this case, the nonprofit serves as the *mechanism* for delivering public services, rather than a substitute for the public sector. Krashinsky notes the same tendency in Canada, where nonprofits often receive a substantial fraction of their revenues from the government.[10]

In the discussion thus far, contract failure has emerged as the prime mover in our theory of nonprofits. An alternative explanation finds the explanation for the nonprofit form in the preferences of the people who work in the nonprofit sector.[11] Nonprofits are often ideological organizations; in fact, religion has been called "the godmother of nonprofits."[12] A substantial number of nonprofits have an ideological origin, religious or secular, and their continuing ideological focus serves to attract workers. Indeed, there is some evidence that workers give up salary and benefits in order to take nonprofit jobs.[13] Thus, potential workers sort themselves out; those principally interested in and motivated by economic rewards will gravitate to the for-profit sector, while those interested in noneconomic incentives will move into the nonprofit sector. In much the same way, having some jobs in the for-profit sector that compensate workers via a commission helps those organizations to attract the most aggressive salespeople, since they expect to thrive under this organizational form. This explanation focuses not so much on the nature of the goods and services being produced in the nonprofit sector, but on the nature of those working in that sector. Young has found some evidence for this worker sorting story in his case histories of organizational change from the for-profit to the nonprofit form.

Nonprofits are well-suited to production of hard-to-evaluate goods and services, collective goods, and goods and services with ideological content.

Figure 2.1 illustrates the three forces that give rise to the nonprofit organizational form. As we examine particular nonprofit organizations, an argument can be made for the importance of each of the three forces. Organizations like Save the Children, with its focus on the economic development and relief abroad, and local child-care centers are good examples of nonprofits in which contract failure seems a cogent explanation. These organizations produce services that are quite hard to evaluate, and delivered to someone other than the purchaser. Trust seems to be an important part of the nonprofit status in these organizations. Education and the arts seem to be good exemplars of areas in which the public/nonprofit sharing model seems most powerful. These are collective goods, in which nonprofit production has concentrated on the more specialized and controversial niches. Finally, organizations like the Girl Scouts, churches, and the Red Cross clearly represent organizations that are staffed by people especially attracted to the idea of a nonprofit and thus represent the ideological, worker-sorting model.

What are the implications of this story of the genesis of nonprofits for the setting of the mission? I would argue that the niche occupied by the nonprofit accentuates the role of the mission for these organizations. Because so many nonprofits are born out of monitoring and trust problems in hard-to-evaluate services, a clear mission is essential to create focus and trust among clients and donors. For nonprofits supplying collective goods—environmental quality, the arts—a clear mission statement is needed to raise revenues. For nonprofits producing goods and services with an ideological position, a clear mission statement will help attract the right staff. Thus, the *centrality* of the mission flows directly from the kind of markets nonprofits serve.

The centrality of the nonprofit mission comes from the kinds of markets these organizations serve.

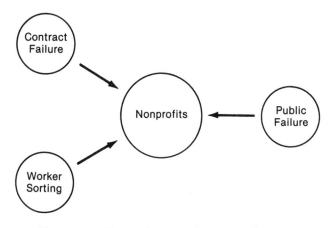

Figure 2.1. Forces Creating the Nonprofit Form.

Our discussion also suggests that some kinds of missions are more suitable to nonprofit production than are others. As nonprofits consider broadening their missions, they might do well to consider ways in which they can exploit their reputational advantage over other organizational forms. Organizations will often find their mission in their critiques of public institutions. Under such circumstances, the public sector will often play the dual role of competitor and funder for the nonprofit. Recent growth in the nonprofit sector has been attributed by some to the shrinking of the public sector, for example. Finally, the proposition that nonprofits choose their form to attract a particular kind of staff also creates some imperatives for the mission. Missions with at least some ideological content will likely be most attractive to the nonprofit.

We have now described the reasons the mission is so important in nonprofits and made some broad observations about the types of mission we expect nonprofits to embrace. We turn now to look more closely at the pragmatic business of setting a mission.

The Role of the Mission Statement

What do we mean when we talk about an organization's mission? In the business world, an organization's mission is generally defined as the broadly stated identification of the basic business scope and operations that distinguish it from other organizations.[14] Among nonprofits, mission statements typically identify both the audience and product or service being offered. They answer the twin questions: What are we producing and for whom? In addition, we typically find, in a nonprofit mission statement, some either explicit or implicit reference to the core values of that organization.

Mission statements potentially serve three functions for an organization:

Mission statements serve boundary functions, act to motivate both staff and donors, and help in the process of evaluation of the organization.

As it turns out, the nature of the nonprofit sector enhances the importance of each of these three roles, and this in turn helps to explain why mission statements are so hotly debated within many nonprofits.

We begin with the *boundary* function. A mission statement describes the bounds of the business of the organization. The boundary function is important as a way to provide focus for all organizations, but for nonprofits it is particularly so given the ambiguity of control and criteria for success in this sector. A for-profit enterprise interested in a new project will typically make its decision by looking at the effect of that decision on profits, however difficult that may be to measure. For nonprofits, which are often producing either collective, or hard-to-evaluate goods, the profitability of a venture is often not the right criteria for success. Consistency with the mission is a partial substitute for profitability in the management of the nonprofit and this in part explains its augmented role.

The nonprofit also lacks clarity in ownership. Absent a class of share-holders, staff, clients, volunteers, and the board all vie for control at one time or another. Discussions of the mission statement often form part of the battleground for these deeper struggles for control. A clear mission statement can often limit struggle within an organization, both because it attracts people with similar ideas and because it makes clearer the basis on which decisions will be made. Thus, a clear mission statement, by resolv-ing some of the boundary issues for the organization, call allow organiza-tions with many competing stakeholders to move forward.

The second function of the mission statement is to *motivate* the staff, board, volunteers, and donors of an organization. This role, too, is partic-ularly important in the nonprofit sector. Mission statements help to carry the ideology of the organization, to serve as a flag around which the orga-nization can rally.

The final function of the mission statement is to help in the *evaluation* function. In this role as well, the mission statement often substitutes for profits as a criteria for success.

Just as there are three functions served by the mission statement, there are also three constituencies the statement will affect: the staff, the donors—including volunteers—and the users of the service. As a bound-ary mechanism, the mission statement serves all three groups. It helps attract donors, focus the staff, and identify clients. The motivational func-tion of the mission operates principally on staff while the evaluation func-tion is a staff–donor domain.

All three stakeholders in the nonprofit—the donor, staff, and client—are affected by the mission statement.

Figure 2.2 gives some examples of mission statements for several nonprofits. Consider the first mission statement given. The New York Children's Health Project is a van-based health program directed at poor children. The mission statement answers the question, What do we provide —medical care; and For whom?—"the homeless, housing vulnerable, and medically undeserved child." The boundary function and basis for evalua-tion are served clearly and well. The core values of the organization—belief in the rights of all children to medical care—are left implicit, and thus the motivational portion of the mission statement is less salient.

For a contrast, look at the mission statement for Girls, Inc. Here, the core values are emphasized, with a strong motivational focus, but the boundary and evaluation functions are less well served given the breadth of the statement. In general, as we examine a range of mission statements, we often see stress on either the boundary, evaluation, or motivational functions of the mission.

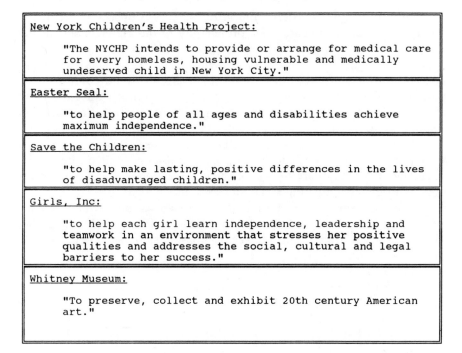

New York Children's Health Project:

   "The NYCHP intends to provide or arrange for medical care
   for every homeless, housing vulnerable and medically
   undeserved child in New York City."

Easter Seal:

   "to help people of all ages and disabilities achieve
   maximum independence."

Save the Children:

   "to help make lasting, positive differences in the lives
   of disadvantaged children."

Girls, Inc:

   "to help each girl learn independence, leadership and
   teamwork in an environment that stresses her positive
   qualities and addresses the social, cultural and legal
   barriers to her success."

Whitney Museum:

   "To preserve, collect and exhibit 20th century American
   art."

Figure 2.2. Nonprofit Mission Statements.

The Process of Mission-Setting

How did the various mission statements listed in Figure 2.2 come about? In the nonprofit world, just as in the for-profit world, the typical organization begins with an individual or group of individuals with an idea. That idea sometimes involves the production of a good or service not currently in the marketplace. The Polaroid Company grew up and developed in response to Edwin Land's ideas about instant photography and polarized light, technologies unknown before Land's work. Eli Whitney began one of his first companies with the plans for a Cotton Gin, an idea that revolutionized Southern agriculture, but generated few financial rewards for Whitney. The Federal Express Company began with an idea in a Yale senior thesis to provide overnight mail service using a fleet of planes. The Church of the Latter Day Saints began with a religious vision to Joseph Smith, a vision that embodied a new idea about the way in which a religious experience should be structured. Margaret Sanger began Planned Parenthood in the early part of the century to provide a forum for distributing information on child spacing and contraception. In each of these cases, nonprofit and for-profit, it was a new idea that precipitated the development of the new organization. In each of these cases, it was a founder or small group of founders who brought the new idea to the table. What we see in each of these instances is an *entrepreneur* in the classic Schumpeterian sense of an individual who carries out "new combinations of means of production."[15] Companies are not, for the most part, started by a group of arm's-length stockholders, nor nonprofit organizations by anonymous, uninvolved donors. Such outsiders play an important role in the development and growth of the organization, but they are generally not the prime movers.

In the cases in this book, we will see the prominence of the founder quite clearly in the discussions of Catherine Kennedy and her proposed New Haven home for AIDS patients, and with Norman Lear and his Washington-based organization, the People for the American Way. In these cases, as well as in the other examples given, it is the entrepreneur who defines the first statement of mission of the organization; indeed, the initial mission of the organization can be viewed as the articulation of the entrepreneurship.

The mission statement of a new organization is the embodiment of an entrepreneurial idea.

Of course, not all new organizations are based on completely new ideas. Some organizations crop up in response to other organizations, imitative of those other organizations. The success of MacDonalds in the fast food market surely spawned numerous imitators who jumped in trying to earn a share of the profits with modest changes in the product or service offered. Many of the Protestant denominations are appropriately viewed as derivative of each other. The Good Faith Fund, an organization designed to strengthen the economy of rural Arkansas through a program of lending highlighted in a case in this book, is clearly based on the model of the Grameen Fund in rural India. In these instances as well, however, the initial impetus to the formation of the organization is a single individual or small group, an entrepreneur.

The originating mission of the organization, whether it is articulated or not, thus comes from its founding entrepreneur. The *function*, however, of that early articulation of the mission extends far beyond the originator, as we indicated earlier. For the mission, if it is to be viable in the marketplace, must be able to attract staff, donors, and volunteers.

Mission statements serve functions for each of the constituencies of the nonprofit organization—the staff, the donors and volunteers, and the service users. In designing and revising the mission statement, all constituencies must be kept in mind.

The early mission statement will be the flag around which new staff is recruited, new donors and volunteers are created, and a user group is identified. In this marketplace, some ideas will fall by the wayside, the nonprofit entrepreneurs having failed to inspire others with their vision. Other ideas form the seeds from which large organizations will grow. At this stage in the development of the mission, however, the donors, staff, volunteers, and users are playing largely a passive role, responding to the entrepreneur's mission, and not, in most cases, working to modify that mission.

Once the organization moves beyond this early period, the role of these other agents in the refining or even radical changing of the mission of the organization becomes considerably more active. As we indicated earlier, nonprofits have advantages in markets in which ideology plays a role. Staff and donor attracted by ideological causes, however, will often wish to play a role in articulating that ideology, and thus be concerned with the evolution of the mission of the organization. The interest in mission is heightened in community level nonprofits in which the process of organization often becomes as important as the good or service produced by the organization. Sociologists have argued, for example, that local nonprofits serve the function of community building and that this function is really only served if individuals engage the organization at the level of the mission.[16] In most of the strategic planning work I have done for nonprofits, work on the mission statement involves the joint efforts of staff, volunteers, the executive director, and large donors. Such discussions are typically much broader in terms of the participants than we would expect to see at the typical corporate meeting at which the organizational mission might be discussed, although recent work by Stone suggests that significant differences exist even within the nonprofit sector in terms of how wide involvement is in the mission-setting process.[17]

To see the way in which mission statements change over time, consider the following example. The Creative Arts Workshop is a nonprofit community art school located in New Haven, Connecticut. In 1961, when the school began, its mission statement read as follows:

> To provide instruction and facilities for the study and practice of the visual arts in both elementary and advanced artistic creation.

This mission was developed by a small group of women artists who were interested in creating a joint working space, and cooperating in providing instruction out of that space. This group was the founding entrepreneurs and their vision was embodied in the first statement of mission.

The 1990 Strategic Plan of the Creative Arts Workshop provides a rather different statement:

> To be a cultural resource, accessible to a broad and diverse population, devoted to fostering creativity through participation in and appreciation of the visual arts.

This statement came from an elaborate strategic planning process that included the executive director, all of the faculty and staff, the board of trustees, and a group of volunteers. The later statement clearly broadens the articulated mission of the school both in terms of product and audience. Art appreciation is now included as part of the mission, in addition to the study and practice of art. The later mission might well encompass, for example, the use of a gallery or art lectures for a general audience. The organization is intended to be accessible to a broad and diverse audience. In part the new mission is a reflection of the changing conditions in New Haven, changing demographics, and economic conditions. In part, the changes reflect the needs of present-day faculty and volunteers. Even the views of large donors—here funding agencies—played a role in helping to broaden the audience focus of the school. Thus, we can see the way in which the various constituencies have played a role in the evolution of the mission statement. This pattern is typical in the nonprofit sector.

How Broad or Narrow Should the Mission Statement Be?

When we look back at the two mission statements for the Creative Arts Workshop, we see a real broadening of the mission over time. One of the constant issues in designing a mission statement involves just how broad one should make it, and we see considerable differences as we look back on the mission statements given in 2.2. In the corporate world, there has emerged a general view that broader mission statements may be more helpful to an organization than more narrow statements.[18] Theodore Levitt noted this point in his query about the railroad industry, an industry with extraordinarily poor performance in the postwar period: "Would the railroad industry be better off today if its management had thought of their business as being not just railroads but transportation?"[19] In the nonprofit sector, given the multiple and critical roles played by the mission statement, I am less convinced of the advantages of very broad missions.

A broad mission statement can direct an organization toward new opportunities; broadly drawn boundaries are thus sometimes useful. For a nonprofit that relies on fundraisers, a more general mission statement can allow it to appeal to a range of donors as well. Overly broad statements, however, have substantial dangers, particularly around the functions of motivation and evaluation. The narrower the mission, the less dissension you are likely to see among stakeholders and the easier it will be to evaluate programs. For nonprofits, with their multiple constituencies and hard-to-measure products, this may be a considerable advantage. Moreover, there may be times at which organizations wish to tie their own hands in terms of committing themselves to not pursuing particular opportunities; a narrower statement can help in this venture.

In this light, consider the mission statement of the United Negro College Fund:

> To raise and distribute funds to the colleges and universities of the United Negro College Fund, and to provide program services to its UNCF member institutions.

This mission statement is relatively narrow, but at the same time has served the College Fund well. In order to keep the support of the member colleges of the Fund, it may well be important for the UNCF to keep its mission statement this narrow, to explicitly prevent themselves, for example, from soliciting for other Black colleges, currently not among the members. Milofsky has argued that nonprofit organizations with stable, narrow goals will find it easier to recruit individuals to articulate and support those goals to the broader community.[20] These observations, of course, bring us back to the key point articulated earlier:

The mission statement has a function for each of the organizations' constituents. Changes in that mission come about because either the environment changes or the needs of one or more of the constituents change.

In one of the cases in this book, People for the American Way, the question of when and how a mission should be broadened is raised. The question is a difficult one for all evolving organizations.

Conclusion

In this chapter, we have considered the ways in which the mission of a nonprofit organization comes from its core competitive advantages. I have argued that nonprofits tend to focus on their missions because of several characteristics of their structure. We typically think of this emphasis on mission as a plus; indeed, the Drucker quote cited in Chapter 1 is quite laudatory on this point. The focus on mission in the nonprofit sector, however, can also have a dark side. For some organizations, discussions of mission are used to cloak inefficiency, or a job poorly done. Nonprofits that are in financial trouble often retreat to discussions of the mission when discussions of management control systems, fundraising, and accounting systems might well be more useful. We sometimes see an organization creating a kind of cocoon of its mission, clinging to an outdated mission, even in the face of radical environmental upheaval.

Thus far, we have depicted the mission statement largely as a visionary document. To succeed, however, an organization needs a set of goals that not only embody the vision of the constituents, but make some sense in terms of the realities of the economic marketplace and the political and social environment. In the next chapter, we will consider some of the tools that an organization in the nonprofit area can use to understand its environment.

3

Structural Analysis
of a Nonprofit Industry

Nonprofit organizations often begin with a vision. To survive, however, organizations must also understand the economic and political markets in which they operate. The importance of hard-headed market analysis and good management in running a nonprofit is made well by Franklin Thomas, president of the Ford Foundation, the largest philanthropic foundation in the world: "People think of (nonprofits) as soft, imprecise, and touchy-feely. That's just malarkey. Invariably when businessmen come over to this side, they say they never imagined it to be so hard."[1]

In this chapter, we will focus on an analysis of nonprofit markets. What are the salient characteristics of markets that help determine the success or failure of a nonprofit venture? How do we analyze demand and supply in nonprofit markets? What are the key success factors for organizations in those markets? As we answer these questions, we will begin to form a picture of the markets in which nonprofit organizations operate, and the tools available to help nonprofits manage in those markets.

Competitive Analysis for the Nonprofit: The Industry Level

We begin our analysis by looking at the market in which a sample nonprofit organization currently operates. Is it a market with fierce competition from other organizations? Are there good substitutes from other public or private-sector products or services? Are the donors to this organization powerful or diffuse? How likely is it that new firms will enter this market? The answer to these questions help to determine how easy it is for an organization to succeed in its market.

One helpful way to organize our discussion of the current condition of the industry is by using a *Six Forces Diagram*, adapted from a similar diagram developed by Michael Porter for the corporate sector.[2] Figure 3.1 is a

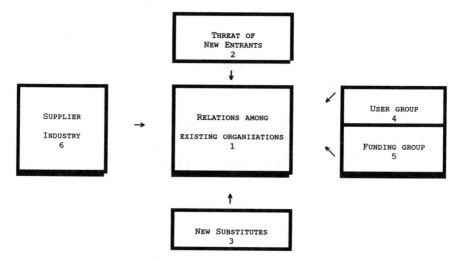

Figure 3.1.   Six Force Chart for Nonprofit Industry Analysis.

schematic of the Six Forces analysis. In the discussion that follows, I have applied this model to the United Way to give some flavor for the way in which it might be used by a nonprofit.

Market Definition

Before we analyze the industry an organization is in, we must know what that industry is. Saloner has argued that the first element in any organization's strategy is a statement of the *scope* of that organization, a description of the activities it is engaged in and the market in which those activities are embedded.[3] In the corporate world, we call this the *market definition* task. Is Bumble Bee in the tuna market, the canned goods market, or in the food market? Is the Santa Fe Opera House in the classical opera market, the music market, or the tourist trade? Is the YMCA in the business of character development or athletics? Often, we will look to the mission statement to get a first cut on the way an organization sees its industry. It is a first cut only, however, and many organizations spend considerable time trying to decide just what their market definition should be.

In the case of the United Way, we will take their mission statement as a guide to market definition in order to apply the Six Forces analysis. The United Way is a collection of more than 2,000 local affiliated operations designed to organize workplace solicitation and distribute funds raised in the workplace to local charitable organizations. In many regions of the country, the United Way grew from the Community Chest operations. Its stated mission is "to serve as a single, communitywide, voluntary fundraising or planning agency; to increase a community's organized capacity to give." The primary method of fundraising used by United Way throughout the country has been workplace solicitation. Thus, at least for now, we will define the industry of United Way as "fundraising in the workplace for community-based agencies."

Description of Current Industry Participants

Once we identify the market, as we have done for the United Way, the next task in an industry analysis is to describe the existing relations among organizations in that market. This area is covered in box 1 of Fig. 3.1, in the center of our picture. Are there a great many organizations that share the market or are you more-or-less alone? If there are other organizations in the market, can you identify them, either individually or as types?

The first task of an industry analysis is to develop an inventory of the other organizations currently in the market and the characteristics of those organizations.

In general, market attractiveness decreases with the number of competitors. Diversity among competitors increases market attractiveness.

Competition for donors, clients, and staff are all reduced in markets with few rivals. Moreover, these markets provide more coordination opportunities than do denser markets, and coordination typically improves a firm's ability to survive. Diversity allows organizations to specialize in particular niches and also avoid head-to-head competition.

In the corporate world, our normal expectation is that organizations that share the same industry will be competitive vis-à-vis one another. Thus, in looking at the central box in Fig. 3.1 we can largely confine ourselves to a structural analysis of the number, size, and character of the industry participants. In the nonprofit area, the analysis is more complicated for we often see more cooperation among firms. Thus, in addition to the structural analysis of how many and what kind of organizations are in the industry, in nonprofit markets we will typically also want to know something about the nature of relations among those organizations. Museums, for example, share parts of their collections through traveling exhibits. It is not uncommon for administrators of schools to meet regularly to discuss both pedagogic and business issues, though as we will discuss in the later chapters, some attention must be paid to antitrust laws governing these areas. Relief and development organizations like Save the Children and Oxfam often cooperate in programs involving airlifts of food. In Chapter 4, we will pursue further the question of cooperation versus competition among nonprofits. For now, I simply want to indicate that even if there were a considerable number of organizations within an industry, the level of competition need not be intense and our analysis should probably go beyond the structural level to indicate something about the level of cooperation, if any, in the market.

Task 1 of an industry analysis is to create an inventory of competitors, and a characterization of any existing cooperation among those competitors.

In the United Way example, this first task is relatively easy. In the past, the United Way has had virtually a monopoly on workplace solicitation, and it still maintains this monopoly in many areas. Thus, in the central box of our United Way Six Forces diagram I would characterize existing rivalry in the industry as *modest*, although I would note that even now in some areas of the United States, the level of competition is growing.

Entry Conditions

Consider now the top box of Figure 3.1, box 2, marked *threat of new entrants*. Here we turn in our analysis to look at the future. How many new competitors are lining up around the industry and what are their characteristics? What are the major *barriers to entry* into the industry? How high are those barriers? If barriers are high, the organization can expect little change from new entrants; with low barriers we often see considerable volatility in a market. Knowing about entry barriers helps nonprofit managers gauge the amount of change they can expect in an industry.

The idea of entry barriers comes directly from the for-profit sector and requires some adaptation if it is to be useful here. An *entry barrier* is defined as any "phenomenon which permits incumbents to earn supra normal profits on the whole process of getting into the market and continuing to act, without inducing others to enter and bid those profits away."[4] Typical entry barriers in the corporate sector include economies of scale, sunk costs, marketing and/or research experience, and reputational affects. The presence of one or more of these phenomenon can protect a firm from new competition, competition that will eventually reduce prices and erode profits.

We clearly cannot rely precisely on this definition of entry barriers with its focus on supranormal profits when we think about the nonprofit sector. Nevertheless, it is clearly important in the nonprofit sector to get some measure of how protected the organization will be from other organizations trying to enter the same market. I would propose the following definition of entry barriers for use in the nonprofit sector:

An entry barrier in the nonprofit sector is any phenomenon that prevents new organizations from entering the market and serving that market in an economically viable way.

In identifying entry barriers, we look for features of the market that allow existing firms to survive but keep other firms out. Note the reference to "economically viable" in the definition. In the nonprofit sector, such viability is created by revenues generated from fees, grants, or donations. We are thus looking for factors that make a particular venture viable for one organization and yet leave no room for rival organizations.

A second important feature of the entry barrier definition is the focus on the *differential* impact of a given factor. For example, the fact that a particular activity is hard to sell via a fee is not in itself an entry barrier. This feature of the market is certainly a problem, but it is one that potentially affects existing firms as well as new firms. On the other hand, if existing firms have long-term contracts to supply that service for a fee, then this contract is an entry barrier, inasmuch as it hurts new entrants but not old. This distinction should become clearer as we examine particular examples of entry barriers.

What are the principal entry barriers we see in the nonprofit area? If we consider for a moment the kinds of goods and services produced in the nonprofit sector, then it is clear that a major entry barrier in many of these markets is *reputation*. Indeed, as we argued in the last chapter, nonprofit organizations arise in many sectors because they engender trust in either donors, government agencies, or clients. Well-established nonprofits, however, are typically more able to engender trust than would newcomers to the field. In markets in which fundraising is important, this entry barrier is likely to be most important.

The importance of reputation as an entry barrier helps to explain some of the organizational patterns we see in the nonprofit area. In the nonprofit area, geographical expansion of a good or service typically occurs through a kind of franchise system, in which a national organization lends its name to a network of local affiliates.[5] This pattern occurs because of the high value that the brand name has in the nonprofit area. It also suggests that nonprofits may need to be more concerned about rumors of misbehavior than the for-profit sector. Nonprofits are held to higher standards precisely because reputation plays such a central role in the allocation process.

Reputation is the major entry barrier in most nonprofit markets.

A second entry barrier we see in some parts of the nonprofit world is *access to distribution channels*. For organizations that do workplace solicitation—like the United Way—privileged access to corporation payrolls is a formidable barrier. Relief projects that work through religious organizations have a similar advantage in fundraising because they can use the distributional network of the Church. In some areas of the world, Catholic Relief Services, for example, has advantages over other relief operations because it can tap church connections to administer its programs as well as for fundraising.

Access to distribution is an important entry barrier for many nonprofit markets.

Scale Economies are one of the most important entry barriers in the for-profit world, and they sometimes play a role in the nonprofit as well. Economies of scale exist whenever unit costs fall as an organization expands its scale of operation. When economies of scale are substantial, the size of the investment required of a new entrant increases. This, in turn, raises the risk of entry and thus discourages new entry. In this way, an entry barrier is created.

In manufacturing operations, scale economies come principally from the opportunity to use more advanced technologies as scale increases. In service industries, scale economies come from increased opportunities for labor specialization. A large museum can employ a specialist in many different periods; a smaller one may need to meld together curatorial functions and business functions. Being able to use specialists may allow the museum to mount the kind of show which will attract both audience and donors, a show that is beyond the abilities of the smaller operation, even if it has extensive gallery space. Blau et al., in their analysis of performing arts organizations, argue that the ability of large arts organizations to attract volunteers and unpaid artists lead to an economy of scale in the paid staff.[6] Large schools can spread the costs of a library, gym, school nurse, and the like over more students and thus achieve lower costs in this way. Large community-based hospitals can have advantages over small rivals because of their ability to efficiently spread costs of specialized personnel and equipment. The Centers of Excellence run by Humana Hospitals in which a facility is devoted to a particular specialty and patients come from far and wide to be treated in that facility is another example of an organizational structure designed to exploit scale economies.

Scale economies are another entry barrier in some markets.

A fourth source of entry barriers is *government regulations*. In a number of industries, entry is controlled by government. Liquor stores in many states, for instance, require state or local licenses to sell their wares. In a number of cities in the United States, taxicabs require medallions as a prerequisite to operation. Patents often prevent firms from copying product or process innovations developed by their rivals and thus reduce entry. In the nonprofit world, government regulation via licenses and certification often play a role in deterring entry. Hospitals must obtain certificates of need in order to invest in certain specialized capital equipment. In most states, nursing homes and day-care centers require licenses in order to operate. In the case of LEEWAY, the hospice for AIDS patients in this text, we see some of the effects of these licensing regulations on entry. In some regions of the country, fundraising is subject to various restrictions. The American Red Cross in many localities has been granted monopoly control over blood collection. In each of these areas, state, local, or federal government rules influence entry.

Government regulation controls entry in many markets.

The last entry barrier I will discuss is the presence of *specific assets* in the conduct of business. Every firm considering entry into an industry must simultaneously consider the costs of exiting that industry. For small businesses probabilities of exit are extremely high. In 1985, for example, half as many small businesses failed as started.[7] Mortality rates for nonprofits are also quite high, again particularly for smaller ones. Forty percent of the nonprofit organizations currently in operation were started in the last twenty years. If failure is possible, however, then new entrants into a market will need to consider the costs of that failure. The higher are the costs of failure, the less likely new entry will be. It is here that specific assets play a role.

An asset is specific to market if it cannot be used to increase value or reduce costs when applied to another market. Large specific assets increase entry barriers.

If I have to invest in a specific asset in order to enter a market and that venture fails, then my full investment is wasted. This is clearly a less-attractive market than one in which I can move my assets from one failed market to a second, more promising one.

What are examples of specific assets? Production facilities are often quite specific. Thus, an oil pipeline from Prudhoe Bay, Alaska, to Valdez is a very specific asset. Once the oil is gone, the pipeline will have no use. Church buildings and university facilities are often thought of as quite specific assets; thus, it is often difficult to raise capital using these facilities as collateral. Banks recognize that if the church fails, then its building will not be worth very much. Nonprofit organizations that carry most of their balance sheet operations in their buildings and plant account are typically quite vulnerable, precisely because the specificity of these assets makes them difficult to liquidate in hard times. Very specific knowledge, networks, and relationships developed by the principals in an organization are also often specific assets, not very useful in other ventures. Decisions to invest in these assets are not made casually.

The existence of specific assets discourages entry by raising exit costs.

I have now described the five main entry barriers seen in the nonprofit world. They are summarized in Figure 3.2. Let us turn to the United Way and examine entry threats in its market.

For the United Way, analysis of the entry conditions is quite revealing. In 1980, less than $1 million was raised in workplace solicitation outside of

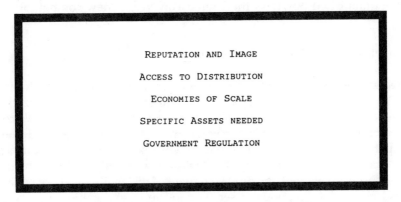

REPUTATION AND IMAGE

ACCESS TO DISTRIBUTION

ECONOMIES OF SCALE

SPECIFIC ASSETS NEEDED

GOVERNMENT REGULATION

Figure 3.2. Barriers to Entry for Nonprofits.

United Way auspices. By 1990, the figure was close to $10 million, and rapidly growing. In many parts of the country, the Combined Health Appeal—a fund raising unit for most of the disease research funds—has launched a major challenge to United Way. In other parts of the country, organizations, including many state agencies, are allowing their employees to designate any nonprofit to receive workplace contributions, effectively overriding the United Way role. What were the factors that historically protected the United Way so effectively and what is eroding those barriers?

In the workplace solicitation market, the three principal entry barriers are access to distributional channels, reputation, and specific assets in the form of network building. While each of these barriers remains substantial, there has clearly been some erosion in their overall magnitude.

In this market, the major change has been in the importance of distributional access, or more precisely in the difficulty of gaining such access. With the increased sophistication of corporations in their information systems, firms can now essentially conduct their own campaigns, in which employees have wide latitude on designation of recipient charity. Large firms like Xerox and state government organizations have led the way in this area, and it is a trend that is likely to continue.

The role of reputation in the workplace solicitation market, on the other hand, seems undiminished. Thus, most of the competition in the area has come from other organizations—like the Combined Health Appeal—that also have substantial reputational assets. Unfortunately, the United Way's own reputation suffered substantially in 1992, with the widespread discussion of the high salary of William Aramony, the head of the national organization, and allegations of misuse of power.

There have also been changes in the power of the United Way networks. For most United Ways, the strength of the networks has been in the manufacturing area. In many parts of the United States, however, manufacturing is losing employment. Thus, while the importance of networks as entry barriers remains, the value of the specific networks developed by many local United Ways is beginning to crumble. This, too, has contributed to the diminished power of the United Way versus new competitors.

Competition from Substitute Products

Thus far, we have described the threat to existing organizations from current rivals in the same market and from potential entrants. Organizations, however, are also affected by competition from related markets. We cover this area in box 3 of the Six Forces diagram, *substitutes*. Air conditioners compete with fans, disposable diapers with cloth, opera with musicals, and dramatic theater and public television with videos. In all of these cases, the availability of substitutes influences the ability of an organization to charge fees for its goods or services and to raise donations to cover its costs.

Readily available substitutes reduce an organization's ability to attract either donors or clients.

How do we identify those products and services that are substitutes for our own? In part, this returns us to the market definition task we discussed earlier. Here, we wish to identify products and services that serve more-or-less the same function to more-or-less the same people as our own. This process of identification can clearly be a subtle task and one that requires both analysis and imagination.

In some cases, it is possible to use statistical analysis to shed some light on the degree of substitution among goods or services. Gapinski, for example, uses data from London to examine how attendance at theater, opera, symphony, and dance events are influenced by the prices of one another.[8] How does the price of opera tickets, for example, influence theater attendance, holding all else constant? This effect is known as the *cross elasticity of demand*, and is a measure of substitutability across entertainment types. For Gapinski's sample, symphony and dance attendance appear to be very sensitive to theater and opera prices, while the patrons of theater and opera are less influenced by prices in the other lively arts. Thus, dance and symphony companies may need to track the prices of the other arts quite carefully, where theater and opera companies appear to compete primarily within their own niches.

What are the substitute products in the case of the United Way? Solicitation at home, via direct mail or other appeals, is clearly an important competitor to the workplace solicitation done by the United Way. Indeed, as direct mail fundraising has become more common, it has become more of a threat to the United Way's efforts.

The Demand Side

The right-hand side of the Six Forces diagram contains the "customer" part of the picture, what economists might call the *demand side*. For nonprofits that depend on fundraising, there are two classes of customer. First, there are the users of the good or service. We cover this in box 4 of Figure 3.1. For many nonprofits, these users will be one revenue source, through collection of fees-for-service. As we indicated, however, most nonprofits are not strictly fee-based and thus the nonprofit must look to the second "customer," the donor, in box 5 of the picture. To this customer, the nonprofit is selling the peace of mind that goes with giving to a good cause, or the prestige of having one's name on a patron list, or whatever service these donors are seeking. In doing its competitive analysis, the nonprofit needs to assess the power of both its users and its donors.

For the "donative" nonprofit, like Save the Children or Greenpeace, which rely principally on donors, box 5 will be paramount. For commercial nonprofits, like the Educational Testing service and most hospitals, box 4 will dominate.[9]

Users

All businesses—for-profit or not-for-profit—need to pay attention to what their customers want. Nevertheless, there are considerable differences among organizations in terms of how powerful buyers are, on just how much attention they need. What are the factors that increase the power of the buyer group?

First, we look at the *number* of buyers and the distribution of their purchases. For the local Red Cross, which sells blood to hospitals, the individual hospital may have considerable control, particularly in areas served by only one hospital. This is a very different situation from that facing the Chicago Art Institute as it considers the power of its customers, art visitors, and art students. For the Art Institute, while it cares about its audience as a whole, no one or two particular customers wield much influence.

> The more concentrated are the clients or customers of a nonprofit, the more control they will wield. A measure of concentration is the fraction of services used by the top three or four clients of the nonprofit.

The second major consideration in determining the power of the buyer is whether the buyer can produce the good or service himself or herself or turn to other suppliers. We have already covered the importance of substitute producers in boxes 1, 2, and 3 of our diagram. In some cases, however, even with no substitutes available, buyers can create their own substitute by *vertically integrating*. Individuals who want to learn emergency water safety cannot do this themselves; they need an intermediary like the YWCA or the Red Cross. On the other hand, the hospitals to which the Red Cross supplies blood may have a plausible threat that they could integrate backward into the blood collection function. In the late 1980's, the then-president of the United Negro College Fund, Christopher Edley, acknowledged that several of the Fund's strongest member schools had threatened to withdraw from the consortium to raise money on their own.[10] This threat clearly influences the strategy of the Fund vis-à-vis its members. One might argue that the Catholic Church developed more power than the typical Protestant denomination because the individual is less able to produce his or her own religious experience in the former case than in the latter. In this sense, Martin Luther challenged the power of the Church in a quite profound way by augmenting the power of the buyer by increasing his or her ability to vertically integrate.

> Customers gain power when substitutes for the service are available, or self-production is possible.

The last element to look at in evaluating the power of the buyer is how important the good or service is to that buyer. The more important the good or service, the more the buyer will invest in making sure he or she is

well treated. Hence, the more power the buyer appears to have. As education becomes more important to parents, for example, they become more powerful buyers in the private school market. It is not uncommon these days to hear private school administrators in areas that service highly academic parents to describe parental attitudes as "consumerism." Here, administrators are clearly responding to the power of the involved buyer.

> **Customers are more powerful when the product or service they consume is very important to them.**

This latter point is particularly important given the political nature of many nonprofit operations. One way customers gain power in the nonprofit sector, even when they are relatively diffuse, is by banding together. The costs of collective action, however, are typically relatively high, and thus such action will only be taken in selective cases.

For the United Way, the users are the many local organizations that depend on it for their fundraising. These users provide no funds directly to United Way, but they are nevertheless quite important from a fundraising perspective because, at least to some extent, it is the composition of this user group that determines the strength of the United Way's pull to donors. Understanding this group, and the alternatives they have for coordinated fundraising, is thus essential for the United Way.

How much power do these groups have? In most communities, the number of groups served by the United Way is large; the pattern is one of many small users, rather than one or two large ones. In general, organizations served by the United Way have had limited ability to integrate backward and do workplace solicitation themselves. Here, too, we see limited buyer power. On the value dimension, the assessment is mixed. Some organizations do rely heavily on the United Way. It is interesting to note, however, that at least some local United Ways have policies that limit the share of an organization's revenues that can come from United Way. The effect of this policy—however disinterested its cause—would clearly be to limit buyer power.

Thus, in the past, organizations served by the United Way—especially the smaller ones—have had relatively little power vis-à-vis United Way. Given United Way's current monopoly in the workplace, most of these groups have no place else to turn should United Way offer an unappealing bargain. The picture, however, is not all good for the United Way, for while no one organization can integrate backward into workplace solicitation, groups of organizations, united by area of concern, can serve themselves and increasingly seem to be doing so. For some organizations, the importance of workplace solicitation has been large enough to induce collective action to challenge the United Way. The Combined Health Appeal, for example, is an umbrella organization serving the American Heart Association, the American Cancer Society, and so on, that has entered the workplace market in a very powerful way. The Black United Fund similarly pulls together organizations and allows them to jointly pose a threat that none

could mount on its own. In sum, while the power of buyers has historically been low for the United Way, it is growing.

Donor Power

For the typical nonprofit organization, there is a second group on the demand side of the market, the donors. Here, too, we can do a structural analysis to determine how much power is held by this group. We begin by asking: Who gives to the organization? Are there many small donors or a few large ones? Are they concentrated regionally? Are donors corporate, individual, or the state? How much power does each have? As with the user groups, the more numerous the donors and the less the average gift, the less power each donor has.

The power of the donor typically increases with his or her share of revenues.

We see this effect clearly in the museum market. For museums like the Whitney Museum in New York and the Getty Museum in the Southwest, much of the business revolves around the collections, resources, and views of a few important donors. At the Guggenheim Museum, the original connection with the Guggenheim family stifled gifts from other potential patrons for some time. For these organizations, donors have considerably more power than the typical small donor at Save the Children or the Girl Scouts.

One substantial donor for many organizations is the government. In 1989, approximately 25% of the revenues of the typical nonprofit in the U.S. was provided by the government.[11] In health, social, and legal services, the contribution of the government is even larger. In these sectors, as Salomon suggests, the government becomes a partner to the nonprofit.[12] As with all partnerships, the result is some loss of control.

Consider the example of arts organizations. Direct federal support of nonprofits arts organizations started with the creation, in 1965, of the National Endowment for the Arts (NEA). In the late 1980s and early 1990s, this partnership faltered, for two reasons. First, the funding levels from NEA dropped precipitously. The 1985 grants for dance, for example, were 22% less than they had been in 1975, despite the considerable increase in inflation during the period.[13] Moreover, some claimed that the agency was exerting considerable pressure on arts organization to alter their mix of activities. Here, we see a clear example of the dangers of concentrated donors.

In most cases, nonprofits have little power relative to the government, but this is not always the case. In particular, in cases in which government agencies are using nonprofits to provide services as substitutes for government activities, those nonprofits can wield considerable power. In this case, the government is a client—not a donor— and may be less power-

ful. Consider the following quote from the former executive director of Brooklyn's Catholic Charities, Auxiliary Bishop Joseph M. Sullivan:

> We are constantly being asked to take on new projects that no one else will handle—and we've had to learn to refuse some of them. However, when we do take on a new project, we do so on the condition that we receive 100% funding from the governmental agency concerned.

What kind of donor power do we see at the United Way? For the United Way, the corporation that serves as the site for the fund drives and provides corporate sponsorship is the main donor of interest. The power of this group is substantial and, indeed, much of United Way's efforts are directed toward this group. In a 1989 meeting of Connecticut United Way executives, for example, Andrew Sigler, CEO of Champion International, one of the largest manufacturing operations in Connecticut, referred to himself and other CEO's as the "gorillas in the corner," in terms of their power over United Ways; it is an apt metaphor. For individual United Ways, it will be important to understand just which gorillas are about to emerge from the corner.

Supply

On the left of the Six Forces diagram, in box 6, we look at the supply part of the picture. Suppliers can exert bargaining power over an organization by raising their prices, or by reducing the quantity of the good or service supplied. The kinds of questions one would want to ask about suppliers focus on the level of competition in their industry: How many alternative suppliers are there? The more alternatives there are, the less is the power of any one supplier. Does the supplier sell to other markets and, if so, how important are they to the supplier industry as opposed to you? When suppliers sell in a number of different markets, they can often exert more power over any one of those markets. All of these questions go the issue of how much power each supplier has: How important are you to the supplier versus the supplier to you?

The power of the supplier is determined by the concentration of the supplier's industry and the availability of good substitutes.

Who are the typical supplier industries for the nonprofit? In the case of a manufacturing operation, nonprofit or for-profit, the analysis of suppliers typically involves a discussion of other firms. For example, an analysis of General Motors would include, under this box, a discussion of the structure of the auto parts industry. Lack of competition in the auto parts industry would be expected to squeeze profitability from General Motors because auto parts manufacturers could raise their prices to General Motors. We see similar patterns in some nonprofit activities. Understanding the structure of the art market is surely essential to running a museum like the Getty, engaged in an ambitious acquisition program. Similarly, increased concentration in the hospital equipment market would be expected to increase costs for hospitals and thus reduce their profit.

For most nonprofits, a more typical concern on the supply side is changes in the power of the labor force. On average, approximately one half of the operating expenses of the typical charitable organization consists of labor expenses. Moreover, a substantial fraction of the nonprofit is typically professional, and these professionals often wield more power because of their alternative opportunities. An excellent example of this is in the area of teaching. For most elementary schools, private and public, women have historically made up the bulk of the teaching staff. In the 1950s and 1960s, alternative opportunities for these women were relatively modest and, as a consequence, teaching salaries were low, reflecting the low bargaining power of these women. In the 1980s, under pressure from competition for this labor force from other sectors of the economy, teachers' salaries increased rapidly. The consequence has been considerable pressure both on private school tuition levels and on public school budgets.

Return again to the United Way example. Much of the United Way labor force is volunteer, corporate leaders who are responsible for campaigns in their offices. For the United Way, the task is to understand what motivates these volunteers. In the past, at least in some firms, United Way corporate coordinators were almost conscripted by their employers. If United Way's power inside the corporation drops somewhat as new competitors come into the market, the United Way may find itself having to motivate corporate volunteers more.

Industry Structure: Sources of Advantage

Once we have gone through the Six Forces schematic, we should have some sense of the level and character of competition facing the nonprofit both from firms within its own market and from firms in related markets. This analysis will also provide us with some sense of where new axes of cooperation may prove most fruitful.

A second task in deepening our understanding of the market is to take a more microlook inside the industry and seek out the *key success factors* inside that market.

> **The key success factors in an industry are those characteristics that are essential to successful performance in that industry.**

Once we understand the key success factors in an industry, we can use these to develop an inventory of our own organization—for-profit or nonprofit—comparing our own traits with what we believe to be important in the industry. The key to sustained success in a market is clearly to run an organization that is good at all the things that really matter in that industry.

There are a number of techniques that have been developed in the for-profit world of strategic planning to try to identify the key success factors in a market. We will review the several that seem most helpful in the non-profit context.

Strategy 1: Survey Expert Opinion Inside and Outside the Organization

The obvious first place to begin in trying to identify those characteristics that are essential to surviving in a market is to survey the views of field experts, both inside and outside the organization. What do the people inside your own organization think is essential? Is there a literature in the field, either academic or business? If so, what does it say?

Some of the information you wish to know will already have come up in a discussion of the entry barriers into your market. By saying that scale economies are an important entry barrier in a market, for example, we are saying that size is a key success factor. If distributional access is an entry barrier, then a good distribution network is clearly critical. And so on. Only some of the key success factors, however, will typically be pinpointed through the competitive analysis. The task now is to refine and supplement this initial list.

In conducting this first survey, it is essential to look at the differences between what insiders and outsiders say. Consider the following several examples. Levi Strauss & Company produces clothes, principally denim jeans. It is a company well known for its progressive labor policy; benefits are good, wages are above industry standards, and lay-offs are rare. If we asked Levi Strauss & Co. executives to give us the key success factors in their market—jeans—many would say a stable labor force. Yet, the nature of production in this industry—uses unskilled labor, repetitive work—indicates that stability in the labor force is not critical to low costs. Most of the firm's rivals do quite well with rather high labor turnover. Levi Strauss, *because it is successful and it has a stable labor force, may believe such a labor force is essential to success.* There is a difference, however, between those traits that a successful firm has and those that are *necessarily needed* to be a success. Only by looking rather broadly at an industry can we begin to identify the latter.

Another example of the kind of perspective generated by comparing inside and outside opinion comes from the educational field. In doing its planning for the future, a middle-sized, private school in the Northeast was trying to decide whether to continue its practice of running for only half day on Wednesday, a common private-school practice. The school addressed the wisdom of this policy by running a survey of its parent body. By and large, the parent body favored the current practice. These parents, however, are certainly not a representative body of potential customers for the school; these people chose the school, *knowing it had a half-day Wednesday policy.* Thus, this group is likely to have a biased view, compared to the general population from which the school might hope to draw future students. This is not to say that current parents ought not to be consulted. The opinions of insiders are critical, but such views need to be weighed along with the views of outsiders as well if an organization is to grow over time.

Strategy 2: Analysis of Market Survivors

In private industry, one way economists use to try to identify key success factors is by examining common characteristics of those firms that have survived in that industry. Thus, one way we might estimate the minimum size needed in an industry (sometimes called the *minimum efficient scale*) is to look at Census data and see what is the minimum size category of firm that has either maintained or increased its share of the market over time. In another area, we might examine whether all of the growing firms in an industry invest heavily in marketing, or research and development. And so on. This approach has been called the *Survivor Technique*.[14] Its usefulness rests heavily on the basic economic proposition that inefficient operations will be weeded out by the rigors of the marketplace. Thus, if a number of firms of a given size survive for a substantial period of time, that size cannot be an inefficient one. If only some organizations advertise their brands, then this is probably not essential to operations. And so on.

I would also argue that in the nonprofit world, over time, inefficient firms are weeded out. This is not to say that all long-lived nonprofits can support themselves; most require infusions from generous donors or government. One of the skills that helps the nonprofit to serve may be its political acumen. Unless these organizations are skilled at raising funds and parsimonious in spending them, however, they will not survive in the long run. Thus, in the nonprofit world as well as in the for-profit world, we can learn much from examining the characteristics of stable firms in a market.

Consider, for example, the market for extracurricular services to disadvantaged children. What are the key success factors in this market? The Boys and Girls Club of America is one example of a stable participant in this market. It is a national organization that works through local affiliates to "provide support for children from disadvantaged circumstances." What can we learn about the market from looking at publicly available data about their operations?

Looking at the Annual Report of the Boys and Girls Club, we see that in 1990, 49% of their budget was spent on salaries, while 1% went to supplies. Even this simple information from the budget suggests that labor relations are likely to be considerably more important in this market than is inventory control. The allowance for depreciation is also rather modest, suggesting that this organization manages its operations without enormous building expense. Indeed, further investigation suggests that many of the programs run by this organization operate through schools, churches and public housing facilities. Again, good staff seems to be key; independent facilities appear not to be. On the revenue side there is also information to be gleaned. We see that just over 50% of the revenues of the Boys and Girls

Club comes from public support, while less than 1% comes from United Way. Here, too, is information about the importance of individual fundraising efforts as opposed to United Way networks.

Ideally, one would want to do this analysis for several years and several different organizations. One would also want to investigate information beyond that contained in the financial reports. Nevertheless, even a cursory review gives us a start on the key success factors and helps us to begin to distinguish idiosyncratic organizational characteristics from key success factors common to a market.

There are several caveats to using either of the two methods described here, surveys of experts or analysis of success stories. Both methods really address the question, What have been the key success factors so far in this market? If the market is rapidly changing, so, too, will the key success factors be changing. Some organizations will be made obsolete; others, with quite different structures and strategies, may come to dominate. Trying to figure out what will succeed in the future is clearly much harder than identifying the commonalities of the past. Second, many organizations— for profit and nonprofit—operate within distinctive niches in an industry, and key success factors may differ substantially across niches. Surviving as a Midwestern military academy may require quite a different set of assets than surviving as a New England Friend's school.

Summary

In this chapter, we have looked at ways in which the market in which nonprofit organizations operate can be analyzed. We focused on the importance of understanding the structure and dynamics of the marketplace and on anticipating the changes that are likely to occur. In a sense, the chapter reflects the recent observation by John Garrison, president of National Easter Seal Society, on the importance of good management: "Commitment isn't enough anymore. You also have to have professionalism or you're going to go out of business."[15] Part of that professionalism involves a deep understanding of the market.

4

Competition and Cooperation Among Nonprofits

Quite often the results of our decisions—both managerial and personal—depend not only on what we do, but on what everyone else does. The success of my bunt in a baseball game depends in part on whether the third baseman and catcher have successfully anticipated the bunt and moved accordingly. The success of a bluffing strategy in poker depends on whether you fold your cards or recognize my bluff and stay in the game. Coca-Cola's profits from a new diet drink depend in part on whether Pepsi-Cola produces a copy-cat brand. The success of a Walk-A-Thon run by the Muscular Dystrophy Association depends in part on whether the March of Dimes is running a similar event at the same time in the same city. In each of these situations, if we wish to make the right decisions ourselves, we clearly need to anticipate the decisions of others. The central theme of this chapter is that nonprofits are highly interdependent and, as a consequence, understanding the likely actions of both their partners and competitors is very important.

In trying to model interdependence among for-profit organizations, we typically assume self-interested behavior on the part of individual organizations and treat competition as the predominant mode of interaction. The nonprofit situation is more complex, both in terms of motives of the individual organization and the nature of the interorganizational interaction. Many nonprofit managers are focused on missions that transcend the interests of the individual organization, and the traditional value orientation of nonprofits has been cooperative, or interorganizational, in nature.[1] On the other hand, competition among nonprofits also clearly exists and organizations are often quite self-interested. Work on British voluntary organizations suggests, for example, that tight resources have increased the level of competition among British nonprofits.[2] Thus, in this chapter, we will be continually moving across situations in which cooperation versus competition are stressed, and in which local versus societal goals are paramount.

In many ways, the position of the nonprofit organization is not unlike that of a tennis player, engaged in a somewhat quirky tournament. At times, in this tournament, individuals face each other as singles opponents. At other times, they are doubles partners, and, at still other times they switch partners and become doubles opponents. So, too, in the nonprofit world organizations may be both cooperaters and competitors, either sequentially, or even simultaneously, within different functions. Just as in the tennis game, however, anticipating what the other players are likely to do is important whether they are your partners or your rivals.

> **Nonprofits often serve interests that transcend their own local self-interest, and are typically both cooperative and competitive vis-à-vis other organizations in their field.**

An example will help make the point. In the middle 1980s when famine problems in mid-Africa began to accelerate, there were a number of instances of nonprofit organizations, like Save the Children and Foster Parent Plan, using strategies that were designed to combat famine, without much regard for whether those strategies left their own organizations vulnerable. At the same time these organizations were cooperating on programmatic initiatives, they were vigorously competing for donations, imitating each other's successful marketing ideas, handling their own donor lists, and so on. For nonprofit organizations like these, one of the challenges of management is working with the ambiguity involved with acting both competitively and cooperatively.

In this area, nonprofits may have much to teach the for-profit world. In the 1990s, we have seen the rapid growth of joint ventures among previously competitive for-profit firms.[3] One of the challenges of managing these joint ventures has been maintaining a balance between cooperation and competition among entities that are neither completely partners, nor completely opponents. Of course, this is the classic situation facing the nonprofit.

In the next section, we look at some of the techniques that are available to help understand the way different people and organizations interact. The primary focus of this section will be game theory. We then turn to look at some of the specific ways nonprofits have used both to cooperate and to compete.

Game Theory

Game theory is the formal analysis of conflict and cooperation among intelligent and goal-directed decision makers, and is an especially useful way to trace the likely reactions of organizations to the moves of other organizations. Applications of game theory in the areas of managerial strategy, defense, and public policy are large and rapidly growing; thus far, applications to nonprofits have been relatively few. Nevertheless, I think the theory has much to offer the nonprofit manager.

When we use game theory, as is the case with most formal modeling, we end up boiling down the complex phenomenon we are interested in to a simpler, structured characterization. In the case of game theory, we begin by identifying the organizations in whose activities we are interested. These organizations are called the "players." For each of these players, we identify a set of actions or "moves." Finally, we will be interested in the outcomes or "payoffs" from each possible sequence of actions. Generally, when we stylize an interaction in this way, we lose something in the translation. The test of the usefulness of the ideas of game theory we will introduce in this chapter is whether this stylization captures the essence of the problem we are studying and allows us to see things we would not see otherwise. I believe that in some situations game theory will be helpful in this way, while in others we will need to find other ways of understanding what is going on.

In many of the games commonly described in game theory, the players in the game follow strategies that serve their own narrow ends. There is nothing in the theory, however, that requires that players be self interested. Indeed, one of the classic games discussed in the literature on game theory is a representation of the famous O. Henry story, "Gift of the Maji," in which altruism dominates. These kinds of games are especially pertinent as we look at nonprofits.

Game theory is a very general structure that allows us to characterize and react to interdependencies. It allows us to model and thus to anticipate the way other people's actions affect us and the way in which what we do calls forth a particular response from others. Such anticipation is at the heart of strategic analysis: An organization's strategy is a plan of action that describes what it will do conditioned on the past sequence of actions taken by itself and the other players in its market. Thus, strategy uses game theory, though it often does so only implicitly.

In their 1990 Annual Report, the Boys and Girls Club of America describes its current strategy of growth and expansion. This strategy reflects the Club's past actions: development of a stronger local network, past growth, an outreach program. It also reflects the actions of others in their market, or their inaction, as the annual report tells us:

> Our determination to grow is in direct response to the critical failure of society to protect the safety, health and well being of our nation's children (p. 6).

Of course, this strategy is a very broad one, and one that will need to be supported by more focused initiatives. Nevertheless, even here, we see a strategy based explicitly on the actions of the other players in the market. By using some of the tools of game theory, we hope to make this strategic analysis even more useful.

Simultaneous Versus Sequential Games

A central first distinction among types of games we might analyze is the structure of the players' moves. In particular, do the two or more players in the interaction move *sequentially* or *simultaneously?* Chess is a sequential game; players move one at a time and observe each other's moves. Good chess players, thinking ahead, will have to make some judgments about what their opponents will do. These judgments will be updated each time the opponent makes a new move. The children's game, 1–2–3 Shoot is a simultaneous game, in which children choose, *at the same time*, whether to put out one or two fingers to create an odd or even sum. Simultaneous does not necessarily mean temporally simultaneous. The critical question is whether one person has information from the others' move before moving. I will start with sequential games and move on to simultaneous games.

Sequential Games The main rule of strategy in a situation of sequential moves has been succinctly summarized by Dixit and Nalebuff and is well known to chess players:

Look ahead and reason back.[4]

In choosing whether to move my bishop or my knight in a game of chess, I must look forward at what my opponent will do in subsequent moves in response to my move. I then go through a familiar thought experiment: "If I do this, he will do that, then I will do this," and so on. Based on this analysis, I decide what to do now. Similarly, in deciding a product strategy or a fundraising strategy, the manager needs to look forward to what others in the market will do and then *based on that information* decide what it is best for him or her to do.

This rule, while simple to articulate, is not so easy to use in practice. The difficulty comes because in most situations there are a large number of possible responses that could be made to each of my moves and analyzing each of them or even thinking of each of them is not always possible. It is here that some of the formal structure of game theory are helpful for they allow us to systematically set out the possibilities and give us some clues about which possibilities need to be further examined and which can safely be ignored.

The central piece of apparatus used in game theory in analyzing sequential move interactions is the *decision tree* or *game tree*.

A game tree is a pictorial representation of the sequence of moves or choices available to the agents in a particular situation and the outcomes associated with those moves. A decision tree spells out the options of a particular decision maker at various junctions.

We can look at a simple interaction to see how the game tree would work. Last week, I made a small apple pie to be split between two of my three children, Emily and Stephen. Stephen was asked to cut the pie into two pieces, one for each of them. Our family rule is that if one person cuts the pie, the other person gets first choice on which piece he or she wants. Now, what strategy should Stephen use for cutting the pie?

To make the problem simple to picture, we assume that Stephen has only two cutting choices; even division or grossly uneven. The game tree associated with this simple interaction is shown in Figure 4.1. Stephen has the first move. He can do his best to make the pieces even, represented by the first branch, or he can cut them into one large piece and one little one, a choice represented by the bottom branch of the tree. The next move is Emily's. If Stephen has cut the pieces evenly, she can choose either of the two pieces. For this choice the payoffs are the same: Each child receives an equal amount of pie. Along the bottom branch, should Stephen choose this route, Emily would then have a choice of taking the big piece, with nine tenths of the pie, or the tiny piece, with one tenth of the pie. This exhausts all of the moves of the game, and provides the payoffs.

What would Stephen conclude from representing the game this way? At this point, Stephen needs to think about Emily's preferences and motives. Let us suppose that he knows she likes pie, and that, at least in this kind of decision, she is entirely self-interested. Then, Stephen should note that if he chose the bottom branch of the tree and made an uneven cut, Emily would inevitably select the big piece of pie. Stephen could therefore "prune off" the bottom branch of the lower part of the tree, since Emily will never choose that option. Therefore, Stephen's real choices are between the one tenth of the pie resulting from an uneven cutting and the larger pie coming from an even division. The best strategy for Stephen is clearly to take the top branch and cut the pie as evenly as possible.

There are several features to note in this simple game. First, in constructing the game, Stephen did not need to know anything about Emily's preferences or motives. It was only in pruning the tree and finding his optimal strategy that Stephen needed to learn more about Emily's motives. Second, Stephen arrived at the even division strategy not because he had a fundamental concern for fairness, but because he wished to get as much pie for himself as possible! Representing the game in this way shows us

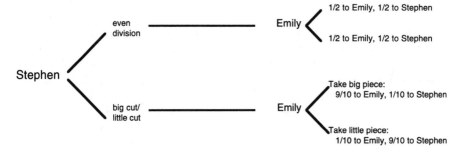

Figure 4.1. Game Tree for Splitting the Pie.

that the simple rule, well known to parents, of "You cut, I choose" is the simplest plan for achieving equity among children, without imposing it directly. The rule is a pretty good one for other bargaining situations as well!

In the homey example just given, we have shown the way in which laying out the moves of a game would help Stephen to make a decision. One of the ways in which the tree is helpful is that it allows him to rule out certain outcomes based on his knowledge about Emily's self-interest motives. Game trees sometimes allow you to eliminate future possibilities from consideration and thus can actually simplify decision making. We can see this advantage again in the example given next, taken from the management world.

In many cities in the United States, the YMCA and the YWCA are located close to one another, and each have substantial investments in physical facilities. Historically, they have divided the market by gender. In the 1980's, however, a new market for recreational and athletic services has emerged—the "family" market—and this market has been a lure for both organizations. This institutional situation makes a nice setting for an example of the use of game trees to reduce complexity in decision making.

Let us suppose we are in the position of a local YWCA, considering whether to introduce a new program for the family market. Perhaps the program might consist of a set of athletic offerings for men and women, coupled with a simultaneous children's sports and games program and a nursery program for any toddlers in the family. Setting up such a program clearly has some fixed costs and would be viable only if a certain number of families would be expected to use the program. In most organizations like the YWCA, part of the analysis of this situation would involve a calculation of the "break-even" number of patrons and an assessment of whether, given the market, this customer volume is likely. The complication in this situation is that next door to us there is a YMCA, which also has some excess capacity. If the YMCA copies our program, then fewer people will come to ours. Thus, a program that looks like a money-maker when we have a monopoly may well lose money under competitive conditions. Can we model this situation in a way that will help the YWCA decide what to do?

Suppose the YWCA and YMCA are each currently exactly breaking even. Suppose further that a family program would tap an entirely new market and, if the YWCA can offer this program unchallenged, it would earn an annual revenue in excess of costs of $30,000. On the other hand, if the YMCA copies the program, both will run under capacity and the net effect will be to leave each with an operating deficit of $10,000. At first blush, under these circumstances, introducing a family program may look like a risky decision for the YWCA, one in which it could either earn $30,000 or lose $10,000. It turns out, however, if we play out the tree, the decision facing the YWCA is less risky than one might think.

In the tree represented in Figure 4.2, we have modeled this situation.

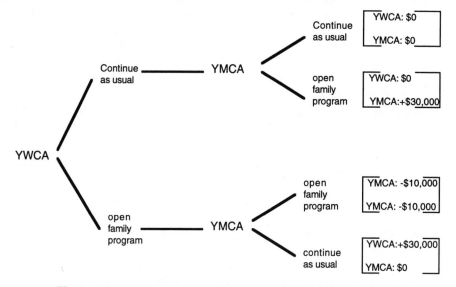

Figure 4.2. Game Tree for YMCA and YWCA Program Choice.

The first move in the game is the YWCA's and they can choose to continue current program offerings or to create a new family offering. With the former choice, both of the Ys continue with operating surpluses of $0. If the YWCA chooses to expand into this market, the YMCA then has two choices. It can continue its business as usual, in which case the YWCA earns $30,000 and the YMCA earns $0, or the YMCA can open a rival program, in which case both organizations lose money. We are assuming in this example that the YMCA managers are not clever enough to think about a family program first, but can only imitate one at the YWCA. Again, in looking at its decision the YWCA can do some pruning of the tree to reduce the complexity. In particular, if the YWCA decides to open a new program, the YMCA is faced with a choice of losing money by competing, or remaining whole by continuing business as usual. Given the characterization of the program here, it is clear that the YMCA will not choose to compete; the YWCA can prune this branch and, when it does so, its choice becomes obvious: open the new program.

Suppose in the preceding example that the YMCA moved first; that is, the YMCA was the clever innovator and introduced its family program first. Under those conditions, it would be in the enviable position of earning $30,000. Here, we see an example of a phenomenon relatively common in markets: the *first mover advantage*. Under the circumstances described here, the YWCA reaps the benefits of having had the idea of family programs first.

In both of the examples just given, the outcomes of each branch of the tree were known. In many circumstances, you will not know with certainty the payoffs to the other players. In the preceding example, the YWCA is unlikely to know exactly how much the YMCA stands to lose or gain from imitating their program. What do we do under these circumstances? The usual method used in the game theory is to assign probabilities to the various outcomes that would result along a given branch and then calculate the *expected value* of a set of actions. For example, suppose we believe that if the YMCA imitates the YWCA strategy there will be a 50% probability it will lose $20,000, a 25% probability it will lose $10,000, and a 25% probability it will gain $10,000. The expected value of this outcome is then −$10,000, calculated as .5 (−$20,000) + .25 (−$10,000) + .25 ($10,000).

To calculate the expected value of a strategy, multiply the value of each outcome by the probability it will occur.

Of course, we understand in all of this that it is unlikely we will have a precise probability associated with particular financial results. The intention here is to simply encourage decision makers to be concrete about their expectations. However, because there is uncertainty, decision makers will wish to look at a range of possible probability assignments to answer the question, Under what conditions does my strategic conclusion change? This is a form of *sensitivity analysis* and is a very important part of the exercise described here.

In both the examples just given we have ended up with what appear to be noncompetitive outcomes without either any explicit coordination or any concern by one player for the welfare of the other. Of course, this is not always the case. In a game described later in this chapter, some of the losses from independent, uncoordinated behavior will be described.

Simultaneous Moves Thus far, we have looked at situations in which the players in the market alternate their moves. Under these circumstances, we have seen that using a game tree can help you outline the possible reactions to each of your moves and the consequences of those actions and reactions. In other situations, players move without knowledge of what the other player is doing; under these circumstances we will often find the device of the *payoff matrix* quite helpful as a way to organize our understanding of the player interaction.

A payoff matrix summarizes the results of simultaneous game moves to each of the players.

Consider the following hypothetical situation. Two private schools, Prime and Best, operate in a particular city. These two schools are the only private schools in the area. At present they each enroll 250 children and charge a yearly tuition of $7,000 per child. The two schools are quite similar in terms of the programs offered and the kinds of families served by the schools.

Prime is considering a tuition increase. The finance committee of Prime believes that if it raises tuition to $7,500 and *Best maintains its current tuition levels*, a number of parents will withdraw their children and switch to Best.

In fact, the Finance Committee has estimated that twenty-five children will be moved under these circumstances. On the other hand, if both schools raise their tuition, only ten children, five from each school, will be withdrawn from the private school system. We will assume in this example that this movement of children is small enough so that costs of operating the schools are not affected. Prime must decide whether to raise tuition or not.

There are four possible scenarios represented in the payoff matrix given in Figure 4.3. Each of the players has a "strategy space" consisting of two actions: raise tuition or hold it constant. The numbers in the square are the gross revenues in millions associated with each pair of choices. Prime's revenues are given at the top right and Best's at the lower left in each cell. The first possibility is in the top left-hand box; here both schools raise tuition to $7,500. At these levels each will attract 245 children and thus earn $1.84 million. A second possibility shown in the bottom right cell is that both Prime and Best will continue to charge $7,000 and each attract 250 children. Revenues in this case are equal at $1.75 million. The more interesting possibilities come in the off-diagonals. If Prime raises tuition to $7,500 while Best remains at $7,000 (bottom left box), students will flow from Prime to Best. Prime will now attract only 225 children, each paying $7,500, for a revenue of $1.688 million, while Best will be filled to capacity, serving 275 children at $7,000 each for a gross revenue of $1.925 million. The reverse situation is given in the top right cell.

We have clearly simplified the problem greatly here. School administrators are sure to object at this point that the shift of students would have revenue consequences beyond the first year and that such shifts would likely affect costs. Nevertheless, by simplifying the problem this way we will be able to see some interesting effects that characterize the real world of independent school rivalry.

Note, from the matrix, that both schools would be better off by raising tuition. In terms of the discussion in Chapter 3, public schools in this example are not a good substitute for private schools, and the *simultaneous* tuition increase has only a modest effect on attendance. On the other hand,

	Prime	
	Raise Tuition	Stabilize Tuition
Best Raise Tuition	$1.84 (top right) / $1.84 (lower left)	1.925 (top right) / 1.688 (lower left)
Best Stabilize Tuition	1.688 (top right) / 1.925 (lower left)	1.75 (top right) / 1.75 (lower left)

Figure 4.3. Payoff Matrix for Tuition Increase Example.

the cross-elasticity of demand between Prime and Best is high; a tuition increase by one encourages substantial migration. What would we expect Prime and Best to do?

To answer this question, to use the game structure, we must now consider the motives of Prime and Best. Suppose the two schools act without cooperation, each seeking only to maximize its own revenues. Assume that each must set tuition at the same time—in the context of acceptance letters for example. What would each school find it in its own best interest to do?

Begin by looking at the problem from Best's perspective. If Prime raises its tuition, then Best's optimal move is to keep its own tuition steady, earning $1.925 million as opposed to the $1.84 it would earn from a matching increase. What if Prime holds its tuition steady? Then, too, Best would be well advised to hold tuition steady and avoid ending up in the low revenue scenario of $1.688 million. In short, *regardless of what Prime does*, Best is better off holding tuition down. The same can be told for Prime. Thus, we will end up, under these conditions, absent cooperation, with both schools holding down tuition and earning $1.75 million. The solution, in which both schools hold tuition down, is a *dominant strategy* for each of the two schools.

A dominant strategy is one which is preferable regardless of the actions of other players.

In a noncooperative game, the dominant strategy solution typically results. Notice that stable tuition occurs despite the fact that both schools would be better off by raising tuition, if only each could be sure that the other would follow suit!

This case is an example of a well-known problem in game theory, the *Prisoner's Dilemma.* In this problem, two prisoners are held in separate cells and confessions are extracted from the two because each is afraid the other will confess. In the school example, each school holds tuition down because it is afraid that the other school will hold down its tuition. As a result, both are worse off. In the example, unlike the case of the YMCA, independent action does not achieve the optimal solution for the individual organization.

We see examples of nonprofit organizations caught in Prisoner Dilemma situations all the time. Organizations overspend on fundraising in part to counteract the fundraising efforts of other charitable organizations. All would be better off scaling down such activities, if only they could be sure that other charities would do the same. Colleges stretch their rules on payments to athletes, caught in a competition that ultimately hurts all schools and so on. In many of these cases, lack of coordination hurts society as a whole as well as the individual organizations. In other cases, society is well-served by the competition among nonprofits, even when individual organizations might prefer cooperation. We turn next to look at some examples of cooperation to explore both when cooperation occurs and when it is socially beneficial.

Cooperation Among Nonprofits: Beyond Games

The United Negro College Fund was founded in 1943 by Dr. Frederick D. Patterson of Tuskegee Institute and twenty-seven other college presidents who believed that private, historically black colleges should work together on fundraising. In this case, cooperation to avoid excessive fundraising costs, was done through creating an institution—a joint fundraising organization. Similar *joint ventures* for fundraising have been accomplished through the United Way, the Black United Fund, the Combined Health Appeal, and numerous other interorganizational institutions. In Tennessee, agencies serving the homeless have banded together into an umbrella organization called the Tennessee Coalition for the Homeless; this umbrella group coordinates both programs and fundraising.[5] The practice of lending paintings among museums to create coherent exhibits of a particular painter's work is a long-standing example of cooperation. Indeed, I would argue that joint ventures, which are just recently emerging as a new corporate practice in the United States, are a common practice in the nonprofit world and have been for some time.

Why do we see so many nonprofit joint ventures, both formal and informal? In the for-profit sector, joint ventures arise for one of two reasons. First, companies coordinate in order to exploit differential resources. A standard example given here is of a small, innovative firm establishing a joint venture with a large, experienced firm to market a new product. The joint ventures allow for temporary and partial integration. A second reason for joint ventures among corporations is the presence of externalities. Organizations band together in joint ventures to produce in ways that would benefit all but from which no single organization could capture those benefits. Joint ventures on basic research and development (R & D) are one example of this; the creation of a new operating system for computers is a second; product category marketing ("Drink Milk") is a third. For nonprofits, this second motive for joint ventures is also quite important. Externalities are ubiquitous among nonprofits, particularly in the area of fundraising. These externalities manifest themselves in the kinds of Prisoners Dilemmas we covered earlier; coordination allows organizations like Prime and Best schools to avoid costly competition. As a result, there are substantial pressures toward joint ventures.

There is still another force encouraging cooperation among nonprofits. Many nonprofits manage for a mission that transcends the boundaries of their particular organizations. For individual nonprofits, commonality of interests in social issues with their counterparts lead to what Laufer has called "commonualistic independence . . . common behavior and shared goods."[6] Thus, nonprofits at times band together not because collective effort necessarily helps each individual operation, but because collective action serves the greater good. Thus, nonprofits may, at times, be altruistic not only toward their clients, but toward their ostensible rivals.

A final force in encouraging cooperation among nonprofits has historically been efforts of donors. In many cases, organizations write joint grant proposals at the direction of funders. In the example given of the Tennessee Coalition for the Homeless, it was the state legislature that encouraged such coordination.[7] Throughout the United States, the United Way has recently stressed interorganizational cooperation, as have other large foundations. This has been a very powerful force indeed.

Nonprofit cooperation is encouraged by the existence of differential resources among organizations, externalities across groups, commonality of mission, and pressures by government and funders.

What are the problems of managing cooperative ventures among nonprofits? In many for-profit joint ventures, the principal problem is preventing the partners from "cheating" on the venture. In a joint research project, for example, results must be shared in a proscribed way to prevent either party from gaining unfair advantage. In joint production efforts, profit splitting is normally carefully monitored. In nonprofit joint ventures, particularly those inspired by commonality of interests, self-interested behavior is mitigated somewhat, but some typically survives. For joint fundraising activities, in particular, we typically impose some conditions to reduce self-interested behavior.

An example of mechanisms used to reduce self-interested behavior can be found in the United Negro College Fund. For this fund to be successful individual colleges must eschew independent fundraising, at least beyond their own alumni base. How could these colleges guarantee they would do so, since monitoring behavior would be costly? In this situation the black colleges dismantled much of their independent fund raising apparatus, thus making a *credible commitment* to letting the College Fund do the bulk of their fund raising for them. In this way, the college fund can help avoid the Prisoner's Dilemma. All players publicly tie their own hands, so that each is confident that the other will cooperate, and hold down joint fundraising costs. In another example, research suggests that the tying together of contributions by United Fund actually increases overall donations over what the individual organizations could raise themselves.[8] Here, too, we see gains from cooperation to all organizations.

Another way to ensure cooperation, when monitoring is somewhat easier, is to threaten eviction from the joint venture if organizations do not cooperate adequately. If the cost of losing cooperation is large enough, then even a modest probability of detection will deter potential cheaters. The United Way, for example, assures cooperation by using the threat of eviction against organizations that do not cooperate by reducing their own fundraising efforts. Given the excellent access it as in the workplace, this threat is a considerable one.

Thus far, we have discussed nonprofits using institutions to manage the coordination process. Cooperation, however, also occurs informally, particularly in situations in which organizations interact repeatedly, as most do in the nonprofit sector. Robert Axelrod, a political scientist, argues that a strategy of Tit-for-Tat often moves organizations out of the Prisoners' Dilemma when they repeatedly face one another.[9] In a Tit-for-Tat strategy, players cooperate in the beginning, but then imitate other players' action in later periods. Thus, in the school example given earlier, the Tit-for-Tat strategy for Best would be to start by raising tuition, but if Prime does not raise its tuition, Best cuts tuition in the next period. Axelrod, trying this strategy in a large tournament of game theorists, found it outperformed a wide class of alternative strategies.

Few managers in practice are likely to follow a Tit-for-Tat strategy in a formal way. Nevertheless, we do see patterns in industries in which cooperation is the norm, and when we talk to such managers, pointing out how they could do better by not cooperating, many allude to a future in which the other player will retaliate. On an informal basis, then, cooperation is often sustained by the knowledge that all of the players will be in this market for a long time together.

Cooperation among nonprofits is also facilitated by the prevalence of networks, formal and informal, among these organizations.[10] In part these networks come from shared volunteers; most people who do volunteer work in a community do so for multiple organizations. This sharing of staff would be quite unusual in the for profit setting and allows for close monitoring and shared ideology. Both of these features of a market promote cooperation. Board membership is another network link, although this link exists in the for-profit arena as well. Finally, nonprofit organizations—especially small ones—often exchange information in ways that promote cooperation.

Figure 4.4 summarizes the characteristics that encourage cooperation among nonprofit organizations. Some of these features—ability to credibly commit to cooperation, ease of monitoring, the existence of other shared lines of activity, repeated encounters—operate to encourage cooperation in

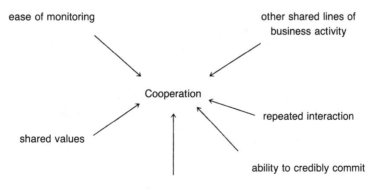

Figure 4.4. Factors That Encourage Cooperation.

both for profit and nonprofit sectors. In addition, among nonprofits common ideology also plays a central role in many situations in encouraging collective action.

Strategies for Cooperation

We have explored some of the formal ways nonprofits work together to avoid destructive competition. There are also some strategies that nonprofits pursue more or less independently to move in a cooperative spirit. One interesting recipe for cooperation among nonprofits comes from Macmillan.[11] Macmillan asks: On what basis should nonprofits decide whether to expand, or contract their activities? He suggests the use of an adaptation of the corporate product matrix, where the adaptation clearly reflects the unique cooperative values of the sector.

Resources in nonprofit organizations are typically quite limited, and thus decisions about which program or activities should be curtailed and which encouraged are critical. It is in the context of this decision that organizations often think hardest about their relationships with other nonprofits. Macmillan pulls together a prescription for deciding among competing activities in a three-dimensional product matrix, depicted in Fig. 4.5.

All programs are dichotomized along three dimensions: program attractiveness, competitive position, and alternative coverage. Decisions about whether to expand, contract, or abandon programs are based on how they rank on these three criteria.

Programs are first calibrated on their attractiveness, measured by a mix of congruence with the organization's mission and resources and its capacity for generating revenues and creating benefits for clients. Macmillan argues that goal congruence is key here.

The second axis of the matrix is the organization's competitive position. How well does the organization serve its clients relative to competitors? Organizations should be wary about expanding programs in which they do not have a clear comparative advantage.

The third criteria along which activities should be judged is alternative coverage. Alternative coverage is a measure of whether other organizations provide the good or service in question.

The conclusions drawn by Macmillan clearly show the influence of ideology in the nonprofit world, and illustrate our earlier proposition about the simultaneous existence of cooperation and competition among nonprofits. Cell 1 contains programs in which the organization is strong, the market is attractive and the level of coverage high. The advice here is to compete vigorously, and to try to ease out other organizations who are dissipating social resources by trying to share this market. The contrast here is with Cell 3, in which the market is again attractive, but your organization is in a weak position. Here, social goals require that you abandon the field to more efficient competitors even if, for the moment, it is an

		Program Attractiveness			
		High		Low	
		Alternative Coverage		Alternative Coverage	
		High	Low	High	Low
Competitive Position	Strong	I	II	V	VI
	Weak	III	IV	VII	VIII

Figure 4.5. Macmillan Product Matrix Eight Basic Program Categories. *Source:* I. Macmillan, "Competitive Strategies for Not-for-Profit Agencies," *Advance in Strategic Management*, Vol. 1, 1983, p. 65.

attractive and lucrative one. In this sense lines of business are judged not necessarily by whether they are lucrative, but by how much they contribute to the social surplus. Organizations decide whether to compete or not based not on self-interest, but on social benefits.

Another contrast between the for-profit and nonprofit sector comes in Cell 6, where there is strong position and low alternative coverage, but low program attractiveness. On economic grounds, one would often wish to abandon these product lines. On the other hand, in the nonprofit sector these programs are often the "soul" of the organization. Cell 6 contains the goods or service the organization provides efficiently, creating social value, but are hard to fund. Private businesses avoid these markets; nonprofits need to figure out how to continue them. As James and Rose-Ackerman note: "A tension between financial viability and principle is one of the distinguishing characteristics of many NPOs."[12]

Competing With For-Profit Organizations and Public Agencies

In the discussion thus far, we have focused on situations in which nonprofits share the market with other nonprofits. As we indicated in an earlier chapter, however, nonprofits both in the United States and around the world often share their markets with for-profit and public organizations. We see this pattern particularly distinctly in the areas of medical care, child care, and education, but the practice occurs in other nonprofit areas as well. How does the fact that ownership structure differs among providers in an area influence the nature of competition in a sector?

Consider first the situation in which nonprofits compete with for-profit firms. The child-care industry is a good example here. At present approximately 45–60% of the child care produced outside the home in the United States comes from nonprofits, with the remainder coming from for-profits.[13] Several of the larger chains, like Kinder Care, for example, are run on a for-profit basis. Other for-profits, like Bright Horizons, organize child care using corporate facilities. In both cases, these organizations typically compete with child-care centers that are run out of schools, churches, and other organizations on a nonprofit basis.

Under these circumstances we typically see several patterns emerging, indicating differences reflecting ownership structure. First, when we look more closely at these markets, we often see substantial differences in the market niches occupied by the nonprofit and the for-profit. It is not surprising that for-profits are more common in the part of the market in which fees can be charged to cover costs. Thus, in the child-care market, we see for-profits in the middle to upper end of the income scale, and in the suburbs rather than in the central cities. In part, this occurs because for-profits are at a competitive disadvantage relative to nonprofits in raising funds to supplement those fees, and in their tax position.

For-profits might also be expected to run their businesses somewhat differently than nonprofits, wherever they are located. Expansion and contraction decisions are more likely to be economically driven than are comparable decisions in the nonprofit sector. Rose-Ackerman argues that the better access of for-profits to capital accounts in part for the larger scale and more rapid growth of for-profits in the child care field.[14] For-profits may also need to spend more of their resources creating trust in consumers than do nonprofits, who earn the trust more easily due to their ownership status. Thus, we might expect for-profit child-care centers to worry more about tangibles like quality of the site and materials, while nonprofits might focus their attention on less-tangible contributors to quality child care. Again, the two organizations are exploiting their competitive advantages.

We can also expect to see differences in the structure and operation of organizations in the public versus nonprofit sector. Nonprofits emerge in part to supplement the public sector in areas in which tastes over the public good are highly diverse.[15] As a result, we would expect nonprofits and public agencies to be providing somewhat different-looking menus of services, even within the same sector. Education provides a good example of this situation. A substantial portion of the private education provided in the United States is religious. The education provided in these schools is different from that provided in the typical public school. Those are the differences that attract people to the schools and give them their unique missions. In general, independent schools seek to provide education that is in some way or another distinct from public education.

What does this imply about the nature of competition for nonprofits in mixed markets? I would argue that the kind of interaction we typically see is more like "monopolistic competition" than it is like perfect competition. In these markets, organizations are providing goods and services that are related, but are by no means identical. Therefore, the form that competition takes often involves product competition rather than pure price competition. Indeed, in the case of public provision/nonprofit provision, competing on price is clearly a losing proposition for the nonprofits! In pursuing these kinds of markets, the central message for nonprofits is to make sure you are in a part of the market in which your own competitive advantages are favored. In this way, nonprofits can often act to complement their private and public rivals rather than to compete directly with them.

A Few Thoughts on the Balance Between Competition and Cooperation

There is considerable disagreement in the nonprofit field on the role of competition and cooperation, both as a normative and a descriptive matter. Many of those who come to nonprofits from a study of management among for-profits emphasize the importance of competition as a way to stimulate increased efficiency.[16] Economists, in particular, extoll the virtues of competition. In nonprofit markets, just like in other markets, competition can help to make organizations more responsive to the communities they serve. Competition can serve to weed out the inefficient organizations and act as a prod to encourage diffusion of innovations throughout the industry. In addition, there is considerable evidence that competition among nonprofits is substantial and growing.

Alan Houghton, the minister of Manhattan's Episcopal Church of the Heavenly Rest, described the situation facing New York churches: "In New York city, churches are like restaurants—there's one on every block. If you don't like the menu, you can walk down the street to eat somewhere else."[17] Houghton's solution: To make his church responsive enough to the community and distinct enough that people will want to join. Here competition has increased the church's responsiveness.

There is much argument on the other side as well, testifying to both the pervasiveness of cooperation and its advantages. Jon Van Til, one of the leading scholars in the nonprofit field, has argued, "while [the philanthropic organization] cannot fully escape the temptations of individualism and commercialism so rampant in society, it should nevertheless struggle bravely to preserve altruism and solidarity as core values."[18] Competition, in areas like fundraising and program initiatives, can dissipate resources much needed by society. Alliances among nonprofits reduce costs and risks of developing new programs (consider the YMCA–YWCA example), and expand an organization's ability to act on a larger scale.[19] A recent large-scale study of human services organizations suggested that approximately two thirds of managers saw their environments as cooperative rather than competitive, and in many areas cooperation plays a vital role.[20]

In this chapter, I have argued that for most nonprofits competition and cooperation co-exist. Greenpeace and the Nature Conservancy act as partners in program and advocacy efforts, while simultaneously competing for donations. Partnerships grow up, dissolve, and are later reformed. In some situations, competition among nonprofits increases efficiency and responsiveness, while at other times society is better served by cooperation. Whether organizations face each other as partners or opponents, however, the ability to understand and anticipate one another is critical to strategic management.

5

Human Resource Management

One of the hallmarks of the nonprofit organization is its high labor intensity. For charitable nonprofits as a whole, in 1987, 44% of total expenses were in the form of labor payments,[1] as shown in Table 5.1. This paid staff is supplemented by a large and active volunteer staff, the value of whose services in the United States alone has been estimated at over $150 billion.[2] For reasons of size alone, human resource management is a critical issue in most nonprofits.

There are other, more fundamental reasons, however, that human resources are so important in the nonprofit sector. For nonprofits, which lack the clear ownership properties of the for-profits, staff and volunteers are a critical *stakeholder* group.[3] They are one of the groups with a strong and legitimate claim over the resources of the organization and, in most nonprofit organizations, one of the most powerful constituencies. Moreover, the goods and services produced by the nonprofit sector are often both difficult to produce using routine tasks and thus needful of skilled personnel, and hard to evaluate. Both features of nonprofit production accentuate control issues in organizations.[4]

Human resource management increases in importance in the nonprofit sector as a result of the labor intensity of the sector, the lack of clear ownership and the complex nature of the goods and services produced.

This chapter treats three topics of particular importance to nonprofits: attracting and motivating staff, decentralization versus centralization of control within an organization, and managing volunteers. In each of these areas, we will see both how nonprofits can learn from for-profit management and ways in which nonprofits have a set of unique problems and issues.

Attracting and Motivating Staff

Consider the following puzzle: Nonprofit organizations, because of the kinds of goods and services they produce, are critically dependent on high-

Table 5.1. Labor Intensity by Sector

Nonprofit Sector	1987 Percentage of Total Expenses
Total	44
arts	40
education	47
environment	39
health	47
human services	48

quality staff. Nevertheless, there is good evidence that suggests that non-profits offer this staff less compensation than their for-profit counterparts. Why do we see this pattern and how do nonprofits continue to attract staff under these conditions?

There is considerable evidence that nonprofits do in fact pay less than their for-profit counterparts. Work by both Young and Cole have found that physicians in nonprofit hospitals receive less compensation than they would in either for-profit or public hospitals.[5] Similar evidence for university staff comes from Freeman.[6] In a quite interesting paper, Weisbrod compares wages for lawyers in for-profit versus nonprofit public interest law firms, and finds a substantial wage differential.[7] Survey data in the United States suggest that the white collar worker in the for-profit sector has a 20% wage advantage over his or her nonprofit counterpart.[8] Perhaps the best study of nonprofit and for-profit wage differences comes from Preston's careful analysis of data from a large-scale survey of managers and professionals.[9] After correcting for a wide range of differences both in the demographics of workers and the benefits associated with jobs, Preston still finds a substantial wage gap. Nonprofit jobs not only pay less for workers with comparable characteristics (gender, age, experience, education), but they offer fewer benefits. It is interesting to note, however, that in this context there is greater wage equality between men and women in the nonprofit sector than the for-profit.[10]

How can nonprofits continue to attract highly skilled workers given their wage scale? A partial answer may be found in the different nature of work in the two sectors. In her large sample, Preston found that nonprofits offer significantly more task independence and sick leave flexibility than their for-profit counterparts.[11] Mirvis and Hachett also find, in a different sample, that nonprofits frequently offer a less-controlled working environment.[12] In effect, workers may be trading off salary for working conditions.

Even after correcting for job characteristic differences, however, Preston finds that large wage differences remain. She argues that this wage differential in part reflects the willingness of nonprofit workers to "donate" part of the wages they deserve in support of the mission of their organization. Individuals are drawn to organizations for ideological reasons and are thus willing to work for lower wages. James' evidence that religious groups are the major founders of nonprofit service organizations around the world speaks to the power of ideology in staff.[13] As a result, in many nonprofits, the line between paid staff and volunteers is somewhat blurry. Young makes a similar observation based on his review of a wide range of case studies.[14]

Nonprofit wage differentials persist even when we correct for job and worker differences.

The conclusion that professional workers in nonprofits accept lower wages because they are committed ideologically to an organization has very powerful implications. In a very real sense, the status of the staff as stakeholders increases under these conditions. The importance of involving staff is accentuated when staff is donating part of its wages.

To some extent, then, the literature suggests that there are real differences between sectors in the labor force. Workers are *sorted* into sectors depending on their relative preferences for wages, working conditions, and interest in mission. These differences across work forces suggests that we may wish to use different tools to motivate and control staff; we will discuss this further later in this chapter.

Nonprofit workers may implicitly donate part of their wages to the organizational mission.

The willingness of nonprofit staff to forego wages in devotion to the mission meshes well with the overall structure of the sector. In a sector in which it is hard to evaluate either individual performance or organizational output, it is more difficult to justify large salaries. The recent public brouhaha over William Aramony's salary as the head of United Way is symptomatic. Trustees and volunteers often wish staff to demonstrate their own charitable inclinations by foregoing wages.[15]

Thus far we have focused on the way nonprofits attract workers, emphasizing the role of compensation, job structure, and ideology. We now consider the way these organizations motivate and control staff, once hired. Here, too, we will see some differences across the sectors.

Top-level managers in the for-profit sector are commonly rewarded, in some part, on the basis of measured performance. Stock options, for example, are used to encourage managers to work to improve the overall earnings capacity of firms; bonuses are paid based on divisional profits and growth and so on.[16] In these cases *incentive contracts* are designed to encourage managers to act in the best interests of company owners, in cases in which managerial effort is hard to directly observe. These contracts are a response to what economists call *agency problems.*

Incentive contracts encourage managers to work for the interests of stockholders and thus reduce agency problems.

In the nonprofit sector, incentive contracts are rare. In a survey of hospitals, for example, 31% of investor-owned hospitals used incentive contracts, but only 4% of nonprofit hospitals.[17] Yet, nonprofits, too, suffer potential agency problems. Managerial performance is generally more difficult to monitor in nonprofits than it is in for-profits, and nonprofit managers are also motivated by local concerns. Under these circumstances, one might expect incentive contracts to arise. Why do we see them so rarely and should nonprofits be encouraged to adopt such contracts in greater number?

As Steinberg notes, until the late 1980s, the nondistribution constraint of the 501 (c) (3) provision of the tax code was generally interpreted as prohibiting profit sharing.[18] By 1987, however, the IRS had more-or-less abandoned its objections to profit-sharing incentive plans as long as the plan was congruent with the overall mission of the organization.

Absent legal prohibitions, however, there are several reasons nonprofits should approach incentive contracts with some care. As Steinberg notes, performance contracts are most effective when individual effort is hard to measure, but the *result* of that effort (i.e., increased growth or profits) *is* observable. In the nonprofit world, however, neither effort nor outcomes may be easily measured. In this case, a viable, effective incentive contract may be difficult to construct. The existence of incentive contracts, particularly large contracts, may be perceived by donors as a violation of the nondistribution clause, even if IRS is more tolerant. Here the incentive contracts may threaten a nonprofits' reputation, one of its key strategic assets.[19] We can also ask how effective incentive contracts are likely to be in the nonprofit sector. In general, organizational theorists are less sanguine about the power of economic rewards to motivate workers in any sector. Pfeffer, for example, argues that "the evidence is ambiguous concerning the effect to which compensation systems based on relations to owners are actually effective in motivating managerial behavior that is in close correspondence with ownership interests."[20] In the nonprofit sector, in which staff is both more ideological and more likely to react according to strongly held professional canons,[21] incentive compensation is likely to be even less effective. Finally, incentive contracts are likely to be most effective in reducing shirking. For nonprofits, however, the central motivation/control issue may not be shirking, but the clash of local versus broad organizational goals. Thus, incentive contracts may be directed at an area that is not the principal concern of the nonprofit.

Incentive contracts in nonprofits may clash with the ideological focus of the organization and not fit as well with the character of the nonprofit.

Of course, there may well be instances in which incentive compensation is effective. Some nonprofit organizations, like hospitals, appear to be quite similar to their for-profit counterparts. Pauly, for example, in a review of the literature on hospitals argues that ownership type matters considerably less to staff outcomes than do incentive patterns.[22] Hospitals, indeed, have begun to compensate doctors financially for referrals.[23] In other nonprofits, the application of incentive contracts may work less well, and these organizations will need to turn to other instruments for motivating workers.

In part because measurement of output is difficult, many nonprofits turn to control over inputs—use of staff time and expenses, for example—as a way to reduce both shirking and the pursuit of local interests. This strategy, however, typically fits rather poorly with the highly professional, independent labor force we see in nonprofits. To the extent that Young and others are right, and nonprofit staff have traded off wages in favor of independence, trying to control their behavior is likely to create considerable ill will.[24] We consider this issue of control versus discretion in the next section as we discuss the second major issue affecting nonprofits: How much centralization versus decentralization should nonprofits use?

Centralization Versus Decentralization

Nonprofit organizations are typically professional organizations, staffed by managers trained principally in a service discipline rather than management.[25] Social service agencies are typically run by social workers, schools by former teachers or counselors, and so on. Indeed, Mintzberg has described the typical nonprofit as a *professional bureaucracy.*[26] In these bureaucracies, professional codes, developed outside the particular organization, exert strong controls on staff, and independence is a highly valued job trait. We will examine the impact of both of these organizational characteristics in the context of an issue of central concern to most nonprofits: How much centralization of authority and power should there be?

The organization hierarchy is a formalized set of authority relations and information flows.[27] It indicates who reports to whom, and carries with it information on who gets to make which kinds of decisions. One way to describe a hierarchy is by how many levels it has. This measure also indicates the typical *span of control* inside the organization: How many people are typically supervised? For a given size firm, the more layers of hierarchy, the smaller the span of control.

What kinds of considerations go into deciding how many levels the hierarchy should have? One way to exert control in a process is to reduce the span of control; as a result, the more hierarchy, all else equal, the more control we will find. As we increase the number of people under a manager, we reduce the opportunity for that manager to closely supervise. Workers thus have more autonomy and the organization less control.

Flat hierarchies increase individual control and autonomy.

Most researchers, working on nonprofits, recommend that these organizations adopt as flat a hierarchy as possible.[28] In many ways, the flat hierarchy fits the worker profile we described earlier, giving scope for the task independence and autonomy highly valued by professional workers. Flat hierarchies, with decentralized control, also accelerate the response time of organizations, and for nonprofits faced with scarce resources and inadequate buffer assets speed may be very important. Pfeffer argues that tall hierarchies tie up organizations by obfuscating information flows, in much the same way that messages become garbled in the familiar children's game of telephone.[29]

One example of the attention nonprofits themselves have paid to the motivating role of decentralized control is provided by the affiliation manual of the National Urban League.

> Because the achievement of Urban League objectives depends upon the quality of leadership available in each community and because that quality is highest where self initiative is most encouraged a certain degree of autonomy must be maintained in the conduct of affiliate affairs.

There are, however, some dangers to decentralization and these, too, come from the professionalism of the staff. For professionals, many decisions are controlled by the canons of their profession, and not the rules of the organization to which they belong. Mintzberg and others call the process of professional training *pigeon holing* in which professionals learn how to characterize needs and apply to them standard recipes.[30] Pigeon-holing controls and molds behavior, pushing staff behavior outside the scope of the local organization.

As a result of their training, professionals often see themselves as members of the profession first and of the organization only a distant second. As a result, professional staff often follows quite narrow, local concerns, rather than embracing the broader concern of the organization as a whole. Thus, the central staff problem of the nonprofit may not be reducing shirking [professional codes do that], but encouraging broad interests and coordination among largely autonomous, professional staff members. Decentralization offers scope for these managers to follow local interests and may be problematic for this reason.

It is useful to look at an example of the complex set of issues involving management in a professional nonprofit. The Waverly Community House (WCH) was formed in the early 1940s as a social-service agency focusing particularly on the needs of children in the urban Northeast. Over the years, the agency has grown, both in scope and in size. Much of this growth has occurred in the last ten years, during which time the budget of the organization has increased sixfold.

By the early 1980s, there were considerable tensions in the social-service organization. Senior staff believed that growth was putting pressure on both the facilities and staff, that growth was proceeding higgledy-piggledy, and that the agency was in danger of forgetting its mission. Finally, the staff, which had once seen itself as a close-knit family, was beginning to feel competition among themselves for resources. The parallels between the feelings of staff in this small nonprofit and those of staff in growing entrepreneurial ventures are striking.

In the early 1980s, WCH ran programs in four areas: a Children's Program; an Adult Program; TEAM, a program for the retarded; and Emergency Food. The Children's Program was a large one, the oldest and best-established division at WCH. It consisted of an after-school recreation program, a latch-key program, a summer camp, and an outreach program taking special educational and recreational sessions to the community schools. In any given year, the Children's Program served over 600 children. The after-school program was extremely popular in the community and was consistently oversubscribed. On the other hand, the Children's Program was the least well funded of WCH's four programs. In conventional economic terms, the Children's Program was a high-volume, low-margin operation.

The fastest growing part of the WCH agency was TEAM, the division responsible for programming for retarded adults. TEAM started in 1978 as a one-evening-a-week social program. In 1981 it expanded into vocational training, running a daily "school" for several dozen retarded adults. Later, TEAM opened several group homes that allow some retarded adults to live more independently than they had been able to previously. The TEAM division is funded primarily by the State Department of Mental Retardation and is the best funded of the WCH divisions. From the organization's perspective, this part of the operation was a relatively profitable high-growth opportunity.

WCH has also traditionally served as a gathering place for local adults to pursue various educational and social activities. Indeed, this is one of the fundamental services associated with traditional settlement-house agencies, of which WCH was an example. In 1984, approximately 100 adults used the WCH facilities. Fees charged for these services are set in an attempt to cover direct costs, though, as in most for-profit operations, calculating direct costs in a nonprofit is not a simple matter.

Recent public concern with the homeless led the agency in 1980 to begin an emergency food program. WCH provides food and some counseling for the indigent and homeless in the community. It serves primarily a walk-in population and coordinates with the clergy in the community. Emergency Food is the fourth and final division of WCH.

WCH is run by an executive director, who has been at the agency since 1970. The Children's Program is also run by an old-timer, a woman who has been at the agency since 1971, and who has strong ties to the local community. The other three directors have all come to WCH in the last three years and are young social workers.

This is a sketchy outline of the divisional structure at WCH, but we can already see some potential organizational tensions, tensions that highlight issues of local versus broad organizational goals. The explicit mission of the agency is to serve the *local* community. Consider, however, the following concerns. The Children's Program runs a summer camp in a lovely idyllic spot, but camp enrollment is under capacity. In recent years WCH has been accepting Fresh Air children to bring it up to capacity. Indeed, in one year, almost half of the camp population consisted of Fresh Air Fund kids. These children, however, were not from the local area; most came from another state. Many people in the community think the camp should be shut down, and the resources of WCH redeployed since relatively few local children actually use the facility. The Children's Program director, a social worker, is interested in serving children more broadly; her professional code does not distinguish among local and out-of-state children. Thus, she wants to keep the camp open. This view is reinforced by the fact that the camp constitutes a third of the program budget and the director believes that resources released by the camp closing will be allocated to another program in the agency, a program to which she is much less professionally committed.

A similar conflict played itself out in the program for retarded adults. At first, the TEAM program served local adults by providing a social evening. When the WCH introduced vocational training, the client base expanded to serve those outside the local community, in part because there are some scale economies in the provision of vocational services and there were simply not enough retarded adults in the local community to fill to capacity the program. The group-home project reaches out even more to outsiders, since the funding agency requires that half the home spaces be allocated to individuals currently in institutions, not in the community. Again, the professionals inside the agency are interested in the expansion of what they believe to be a needed and valuable service; the community in part is concerned about the agency moving away from local services. The executive director is again under pressure from both constituencies.

Cross-group tensions were also manifest in the agency, particularly around resource issues. The TEAM director in particular was very committed to the needs of the retarded and resented suggestions that resources from the well-funded retarded program cross-subsidize the rest of the agency. The executive director, on the other hand, was committed to a full-service agency and believed he needed some flexibility to move money around to accomplish this. The Department of Mental Retardation opposed cross-subsidization, but was almost helpless to find out if there was any going on, given the arcane allocation rules followed by the agency. Again, one is reminded of tensions in multidivisional private corporations in which cash flow from one operation is used to fund a start-up in another.

It is easy to explain rising stress levels in the WCH agency. As the agency grew, the subgroup structure began to take precedence over the organization itself. Directors, in part as a consequence of their professional identities, began to see themselves as committed to their particular constituencies, not to the now rather large social-service agency WCH was becoming. The agency used a flat hierarchy and the four individual directors had considerable autonomy within their programs, but there was little incentive for them to coordinate. As a consequence, only the executive director had a stake in the central organizational mission.

In decentralized organizations, local interests may come to dominate global interests. This effect is exacerbated in professional organizations.

In these decentralized operations, the creation of a strong culture that emphasizes the overall mission of the organization is vital, particularly for large and diverse organizations.

Managing Volunteers

One of the distinguishing features of the nonprofit sector is its use of volunteer labor. Table 5.2 shows the extent of volunteer labor in a number of segments in the nonprofit sector, as best we can measure it. In some sectors, like social services, the value of the volunteer labor is half of the expenditures in the sector. The American Red Cross, for example, is staffed almost entirely by volunteers. Arts organizations, community development activities, and religious organizations are all heavily dependent on volunteer labor.

Consider how the presence of a sizeable number of volunteers affects the organization. One nonprofit manager with whom I have worked characterizes the problem of volunteers as follows: "First, I have to figure out how to recruit them. Then I have to figure out how to best use them. Finally, too often, I have to figure best how to get rid of them." In the complex world of nonprofits, where authority relations are already ambiguous, and motivation and control an issue, the presence of volunteers who are outside the main hierarchy can often have profound effects, and managing these volunteers can be quite difficult.

How do we attract and motivate volunteers? Perhaps the best work in the field comes from Weisbrod. He argues based on data on volunteers that there are two classes of reasons people volunteer.[31] Some are motivated by "investment" gains (i.e., the expectation that volunteer efforts will increase their own experience and skills and thus enhance their later careers). Others volunteer for "consumption" reasons because they are interested in the mission of the organization and gain utility from helping the nonprofit accomplish its goals. Thus, volunteers have both altruistic and self-interested motives. This, of course, suggests that differences between volunteer and staff in nonprofits may be smaller than appears on the surface. While it is true that unpaid volunteers cannot, as Drucker argues, "be bossed like galley salves,"[32] neither, of course, can the oft-times underpaid

Table 5.2. Volunteers by Sector

Type of Nonprofit	Value of Volunteer Labor a Percentage of Expenditures
Social Service	50
Community Development	47
Education and Research	25
Health Care	10
Arts and Culture	45
Religious	36
Total	28

Source: B. Weisbrod, *The Not-for-Profit Sector in a Mixed Economy,* New York: Twentieth Century Fund, 1985, Table 8.7.

staff of nonprofits. Rather, for both groups, there must be considerable attention to incentives.

People volunteer both to help the organization and to gain experience.

Organizations can attract and retain volunteers by working on both the investment and consumption sides. Many organizations have a hierarchy of volunteers that is parallel to the staff hierarchy. Promoting productive volunteers into positions of more authority in the hierarchy is a valuable tool for it provides experience for those volunteers that may later generate financial rewards. Organizations that provide training for their volunteers also help on the investment side. Organizations also attract and motivate volunteers by clearly articulating an attractive mission and involving those volunteers in mission discussions. Research indicates that the desire to influence the amount and type of service provided by the nonprofit moves most volunteers.

Volunteers are attracted to organizations with compelling missions who craft their volunteer opportunities so as to both utilize existing talents of those volunteers and help add to those talents.

Training volunteers serves a function in addition to helping organizations to recruit volunteers. Many organizations extensively train their volunteers as a way to control them, in the same way that professional training helps in the control process for the paid staff. The more dependent an organization is on volunteers, the more important such training is. The American Red Cross, for example, because it does depend so heavily on volunteers, has quite careful control of the volunteer process, limiting what kinds of volunteer can do what kinds of jobs, providing training, certification, and the like. One of the cases in this book describes the Red Cross' experience with volunteers in a range of activities.

Conclusion

This chapter has explored some of the issues involved in human resource management in the nonprofit sector: attracting and motivating staff, deciding levels of centralization within the organization, and managing volunteers. In the next chapter, a related issue is discussed, the management of the board.

6

The Nonprofit Board of Directors

In the last five chapters of this book, we have identified a number of special features of nonprofit management: the centrality of the mission, the complexity associated with facing customers who are simultaneously clients and donors, the intermingling of competition and cooperation in the sector, and the problems of dealing with professional staff and volunteers. This chapter examines the role of the board in the nonprofit and argues that in both structure and function, nonprofit boards differ somewhat from their for-profit counterparts.

A Review of the Stylized Facts about Nonprofits

When we look at nonprofit boards of directors, there are a number of characteristics that distinguish these boards from their for-profit counterparts. Our first puzzle is to ask what are the sources of these differences and, in particular, whether they are functional.

One of the first things that strikes one about nonprofit boards is their average size. Nonprofit boards are much larger than is typical for the board of a for-profit corporation. The corporate board averages ten to fifteen trustees; the nonprofit board generally consists of thirty to fifty members, even in rather modest-sized corporations.[1] The United Negro College Fund has forty-six directors; Save the Children has twenty-six directors, and an even larger advisory council; The Braille Institute has twenty-nine directors. Contrast this with some organizations in the for-profit sector: Bristol Myers has fourteen directors; Humana Hospitals has nine directors; General Motors has eighteen directors. I serve as one of ten directors on the board of a publicly traded bank with assets of $2 billion; I also serve on the board of a local private school with revenues of $4 million and twenty directors.

The composition of the nonprofit board also differs from that of the for-profit in several ways. Nonprofit boards typically consist entirely of outsiders, nonemployees of the organization. The for-profit board generally combines insiders and outsiders. Four of the eighteen General Motors directors are insiders; four of the nine Humana directors are insiders; and four of the fourteen Bristol Myers directors are insiders. I will argue that there are some good reasons for this difference. For-profit boards are also typically heavily weighted in favor of people who have professional expertise in the area of business of the firm. The Humana board's five outsiders, for example, consist of one doctor and four representatives of investment firms. These people have specific knowledge about major elements of the Humana business. Nonprofit boards typically include representatives from the public sector, other nonprofits, and community representatives, as well as the more typical lawyers and business people. These boards, too, contain knowledge and expertise, but it is of a more far-ranging sort.

What about the way that the nonprofit board functions? Hirsh and Whistler argue that in the nonprofit sector, "A noisy board is normal," while such a board in the for-profit sector is typically a symptom of impending crisis.[2] Not only does the nonprofit board have more dissension on average than the for-profit, but, as Unterman and Davis point out, these boards also have considerably more operating function.[3] Boards are especially active in the fundraising area, but often supplement management in other areas as well, including finance and even programmatic functions. Boards in small nonprofits are particularly active in operating areas, as are boards in young nonprofits.

Nonprofits boards are larger, with fewer insiders, more conflicted and more involved in operations than for-profit boards.

Function of the Board: The Theory

We have listed four ways in which the typical nonprofit board differs from a for-profit board: size, composition, degree of dissension, and level of operating function. We turn now to consider some of the theoretical literature on the mandate of the board. We will see that some of the differences we see in the structure of the nonprofit board flow directly from the nature of the mandate of the nonprofit board. In this area, structure seems to follow function.

In an ideal setting, we can characterize the role of the board in a typical publicly traded corporation as follows: The stockholders own the company. They delegate the responsibility for running the company to the board and it, in turn, delegates most of that operating responsibility to the management of the company. The board, however, retains ultimate control over the management. In particular, the board typically remains active in overseeing broad policy decisions of the management, and in hiring, firing, and deciding compensation of the top management. Moreover, the board carries on these functions within the context of a market for the ownership rights of the company—the stock market—and, consequently, within a market in which takeover is possible. This market constrains the actions of the board by providing the stockholder with a "court of last resort" in the case of board failure.[4]

Now let us look at ownership and control in the nonprofit sector. As indicated earlier, nonprofits are subject to the nondistribution constraint. As a consequence there are no stockholders in the nonprofit, and there is no one with clear claims over any residuals. Thus, the usual role of the board as a protector of stockholder rights over the interests of management is absent in the nonprofit. On the other hand, the donor in the nonprofit may need some protection against the possibility of expropriation of the benefits of donations by internal management. In this sense, the board of the nonprofit can be thought of as providing protection for one of the customers of the nonprofit.[5] In a broader sense, given the tax exemption of the nonprofits, the board can be thought of as providing protection to the public who has indirectly contributed these tax savings. Indeed, most states in the United States have vested the power to enforce duties of nonprofit directors in the government, in particular, the states' attorney generals.[6] In the for-profit sector, shareholders enforce their rights over directors, while customers protect themselves through their purchasing behavior. We also note that the board of the nonprofit is not constrained by an active takeover marker, and this absence makes its role as a buffer between outside interests and management more crucial.

The work by Price in analyzing the boards of two wildlife management agencies is especially interesting in the light of this perspective on boards.[7] Price found that in these agencies the principal function of the board was to mediate between the sportsmen, who were the principal clients of the agencies, and the management of the agencies. Their function, according to Price, was a political one. This example of the nonprofit board as a "boundary-spanner" is a common characterization in the literature on nonprofits,[8] and, I would argue, that it is the peculiar nature of the way resources are allocated in this sector that intensifies the importance of this political function. Cole's findings in another set of twelve nonprofit organizations that managers of these organizations were frequently resistant to the board's role as an intervenor with external agents is also not surprising when we recognize that by adopting this role the board increases its ability to control management.[9]

In sum, the nonprofit board has a protective, supervisory role similar to that of the for profit board. Under state law, directors of business corporations have two fiduciary duties—the duty of care and the duty of loyalty. They are expected to discharge their duties with prudence and in good faith. In the nonprofit sector, directors have been held to a variety of standards, ranging from the higher standards associated with trusteeship to less stringent standards based on the voluntary, unpaid nature of nonprofit directorships. Most courts and the Revised Model Nonprofit Corporation Act adopted by the American Bar Association treat nonprofit directors much like their for-profit counterparts.[10] The nonprofit board protects donors, broadly construed, whereas its for-profit counterpart protects stockholders. Both are expected to avoid conflicts of interest and exhibit care. The nonprofit board, however, has fewer natural constraints on its behavior than does the for-profit board. There is no takeover market, and no Security Exchange Commission. These differences also contribute to the kinds of differences we see across boards in the nonprofit and for-profit sector. There are other salient differences in for-profit and nonprofit organizations, as well. In particular, as indicated earlier, nonprofits often produce hard-to-evaluate products and services and measure their performance in hard-to-quantify ways. These two features of the nonprofit also play a role in explaining the structure of the nonprofit board.

Consider first the question of the role of insiders on the board. On the one hand, insiders have the kind of detailed knowledge of the institution that is very important in helping boards to make informed decisions. On the other hand, as insiders they may not share the goals of the owners of the company. Fama and Jensen argue quite persuasively that the discipline provided by the active market for shares allows for-profit boards to include insiders.[11] Nonprofits, lacking the discipline of a takeover market, face a greater threat of capture of the board by insiders and thus typically limit the role of insiders on the board. This effect is reinforced by the amorphous quality of many of the goods and services produced in the sector and by the difficulty in evaluating successful performance. Under these circumstances, the role of the board as protector is magnified, and the reduced role of the insider on the board is to be expected. The board plays a role in preventing nonprofit managers from abusing their positions, a role normally played by shareholders. In 1991, the president of the United States Olympic Committee, a nonprofit, resigned amid reports that he had received large consulting fees from clients who were pursuing Olympic contacts.[12] These same conditions—lack of a takeover market and the amorphous goods and services—may also contribute to the pattern in which tenure on nonprofit boards is typically much shorter than on for-profit boards.[13] This shorter tenure may also protect against capture of the board by management.

Staffing nonprofit boards with outsiders with relatively short tenure reduces the probability of board capture by the executive director.

It can also be argued that the "noisy" quality of nonprofit boards and their functioning in the operations of the organization come in part from the absence of an active market for ownership. Both of these features of the nonprofit board reflect a somewhat stronger disciplining of the management of nonprofits by the board. Again, this is consistent with the lack of alternative disciplining methods. The board questions managers and looks over their shoulders because there is less market assurance that the organization is running well. Again, the absence of quantifiable performance measures exacerbates this effect.

How do we explain the large size of the typical nonprofit board and its heterogeneous composition? In part, the size of the board reflects its greater operating function. For a board to engage in active oversight and work, larger numbers are required simply to spread the work. Nonprofits rely on networks for much of the activity in which they engage, and these networks are enhanced by larger numbers.[14] Evidence suggests that larger boards increase the contact organizations have with government agencies of all types, increasing public sector opportunities and resources.[15] In addition, the diversity of interests the board wishes to protect creates pressures to increase size. The nonprofit board often has large donors serve directly on the board. The presence of large donors on the board of an organization provides a direct way for them to monitor how well their funds are being spent. Thus, a donor is put on a board not as a benefit of giving, but as insurance for giving. It is no surprise, therefore, that trustees are active in the fundraising function. By their presence, such donor-trustees implicitly promise other potential donors that their funds will not be wasted. For the same reason, nonprofits are also attracted to trustees who serve on other nonprofit boards; multiple membership enhances the reputation of the trustee and facilitates his or her ability to generate trust to new donors. A typical case is that of Mr. John Phillips of Cleveland, Ohio. Mr. Phillips is a trustee for the Cleveland Salvation Army, St. Luke's Hospital, the United Negro College Fund, and the Karami House Theater. Multiple memberships provide both information networks and credibility for organizations. Nonprofit boards also typically include trustees from the public sector, trustees who bring assurances that public tax relief and grants are being applied wisely. Trustees from the public sector encourage public giving at least in part because they provide protection against the misuse of those funds. Eugene Sturckhoff, former vice president for the Council on Foundations, clearly articulates the view that boards have a public responsibility: "Every member of a board has a duty to speak to the overall public interest and not for a single interest."[16] Finally, given the absence of insiders on the nonprofit board, such boards also need experts of their own, from outside the organization. This swells the ranks of the board as well.

The large size of nonprofit boards increases interorganizational contact, allows for more monitoring and control, and reflects the importance of donors.

Pfeffer's work on hospitals is especially pertinent in this context.[17] In this interesting study of public, religious, and private nonprofit hospitals, Pfeffer finds substantial differences in board composition by ownership type. Private nonprofit hospitals had boards that consisted principally of local business people, and their job was to provide assurance to the funding community. Religious hospitals, not dependent on local funding, had boards that were broadbased and more concerned with patient interests than with donor interests. Here, too, we see the composition of the board as a reflection of the kinds of protection it provides.

How does this view of the role of the nonprofit board comport with the ideas of such boards in the popular literature? It is common in this field to hear that boards are solicited on the basis of three criteria: Wealth, Work, and Wisdom. In a sense, I have argued here that the structure of owner-ship in the nonprofit sector along with the nature of the goods and services produced in this sector create the need for the Three Ws on nonprofit boards. Wealth is needed to safeguard the interests of the donors, in the absence of more direct protection. Work is needed to provide monitoring of the management in a market in which performance is hard to measure and markets are less informative. Wisdom is essential when the absence of a market for ownership rights makes the presence of insiders on the board difficult.

This same lack of market constraints may also contribute to differences we see in the governance of boards in the for-profit and nonprofit sectors. Members of the for-profit board are allowed to carry on transactions with the corporation as long as those transactions are made public. For example, a member of a board who runs a bank is permitted to make a loan to the company on whose board he or she serves, as long as that loan is an arms-length, public one. For nonprofits, under the Internal Revenue code, self-dealing by directors is prohibited. Section 4941 of the code lists prohibited self-dealing transactions including sales or leases, loans, and payment of compensation. Private foundations found guilty of self-dealing will be charged an excise tax on the self-dealing party equal to at least 5% of the amount involved, for each year.[18] Because the outside market is less effec-tive in disciplining directors, more formal rules are used.

As we look at the structure and functioning of the nonprofit board, we see that it flows quite naturally from the particular characteristics of non-profit production. Ownership patterns in the industry coupled with the nature of goods and services produced result in a board which is both more active, and more highly charged than is typical in the for-profit sector. These considerations make it even more important that boards in this sector work well and, yet, our evidence suggests that in many nonprofits the board is quite ineffective.[19] We turn now to this evidence and to work that suggests some ways to improve board performance.

Functions of the Board: In Practice

Thus far in this chapter, we have considered the way in which the structure of the nonprofit board supports the particular functions required of that board. Our discussions of the functions of the board, however, have re-mained relatively abstract. We can now proceed to consider in more detail what it is the typical nonprofit board does and how it operates. We will see that some of these broader themes will recur in the more nitty-gritty discus-sion.

Most discussions of the nonprofit board identify five chief tasks of the board[20]:

1. Select and evaluate the chief executive officer
2. Define and reevaluate the mission of the organization
3. Develop a plan for the organization
4. Approve budgets
5. Help get resources

Surveys of trustees include on the list of functions of a board, enlisting the support of others and balancing the organization with a different point of view.[21] Boards are boundary-spanners and organizational go-betweens.

As we look at the list of functions of the board, we see quite a large variation in the level of operations of the board. On the one hand, the board engages in activities at a very high level in the decision process; setting a mission and selecting a CEO represent tasks of this sort. These are typically thought of as functions at the *strategic level* of the organization. On the other hand, some of the activities of the board, even in the preceding list of ideal activities, are at the operating level: budget control and resource attraction. In fact, one of the difficulties some boards have is in moving between these levels.

The museum industry provides an interesting example of the multiple roles of trustees. A National Endowment of the Arts survey of museums indicated that in 16% of U.S. major museums, trustees had responsibility for major exhibits and programs.[22] In one third of the museums, trustees set staffing requirements. Both of the functions are clearly in the operating domain. At the same time, trustees were engaged in strategic planning, choice of the executive director, and other broad oversight functions.

The existence of both operating and strategic functions for the board creates some clear problems in its operations. Principal among these is the unclear authority relationship that may develop between the board and the executive management of the nonprofit. Fenn's interesting survey of 400 business executives who serve on volunteer boards suggested that there was substantial disagreement between staff and the board on what the board should be doing. This lack of clarity, in turn, contributes to tension between staff and board,[23] and increases the overall noisiness of the non-profit board, which we discussed earlier. Brian O'Connell, president of the Independent Sector, has observed: "The greatest source of friction and breakdown in voluntary organizations of all types, sizes and ages and relative degrees of sophistication and excellence relates to misunderstandings and differing perceptions between the voluntary board president and staff directors."[24] Extensive involvement with the day-to-day operations may also jeopardize the directors' ability to oversee those operations. Chait and Taylor cite the example of Arnold Edwards, a semi-retired trustee of the Wilkins Art Institute whose daily involvement with the treasurer of that Institute led him to violate board confidence and ally himself with the staff.[25]

The balance among the nonprofit board functions also seems to change over time. Wood argues that there is a dynamic pattern in the activities of nonprofit boards. Board members in new agencies focus on the mission, while veteran board members of mature organizations "become less committed to the cause around which the agency was organized and more committed to the bureaucratic procedures they believe will assure the success of the agency."[26] Robert Augsburger has developed a graphic to illustrate the change in board function over the life cycle; it is reproduced as Figure 6.1. In the early period, the board is the agency: It sets the mission, raises the funds, and often operates the organization. As the organization matures, the executive director and staff typically assume more power until, in a more mature stage, what Augsburger calls "Fortune 500–style oversight" occurs.[27]

Another problem that besets the nonprofit board is its large size and heterogeneous composition. There are profound differences in people's motives for serving on boards, differences that further contribute to the noise of the average nonprofit board. The difficult task for the board is to take its disparate members and create from them a group that is bound together by a shared commitment to the mission. In a well-functioning board, this sense of common mission is developed over time and spreads to new board members. In this setting, board differences emerge as constructive dissension and the "noise" of the board plays a vital, energizing role. Evidence suggests that this adherence to a common mission is a major determinant of board effectiveness. In an ambitious study of over 400 Canadian nonprofits, Bradshaw et al. found that boards that shared a

Figure 6.1. Changes in the Life Cycle and its Effect on the Board. *Source:* R. Augsburger, class notes, Stanford University, Autumn 1992.

common vision scored high on effectiveness.[28] In other boards, differences in motives and interests among board members are never united in a common mission, trustees are left unmotivated and unsatisfied, and the organization is ineffective.

It is important to stress again the positive role of noise in the organization. Large size and heterogeneity of board population clearly make it more difficult at times for the board to operate. Board diversity can increase tension both within the board and between the board and the executive director; however, diversity also increases the size of the area over which nonprofits can cast their nets in attracting volunteers, private donors, and government aid. Even dissension, while sometimes difficult for the nonprofit manager to live with, is not without its side benefits. Experimental work in the area of organizational theory suggests that organizations with a base level of dissension will be more likely to recognize and react to vital, strategic problems likely to beset their organizations than organizations filled with people who peacefully cooperate. Through differences often emerges change, a relationship clear as well to those who wish to avoid change. Here, an excerpt from a 1933 letter from blue blood George Apley to his son on the Harvard University board, is appropriate:

> I have heard from very good sources that there may be a vacancy in the Harvard Corporation. Certain of us are looking for a younger man and one of the right sort. There is altogether too much sentiment here lately for getting outsiders and so-called new blood into Harvard. The traditions of the place must not be spoiled . . . I think you might be fitted to take your place on the corporation. It is true you have never been a scholar but now that you are actually going to live in Boston this does not really make much difference.[29]

Increasing Board Effectiveness

Organizational effectiveness is extremely hard to measure, even in for-profit organizations. For nonprofits, with multiple goals and often-amorphous goods and services, measuring organizational effectiveness is even more difficult. Moreover, even when one can measure organizational effectiveness, disentangling the role of the board, staff, and volunteers, and measuring the contribution of each to the organization is almost impossible. In fact, in the empirical literature, we see a variety of measures of board effectiveness being used, ranging from quite objective, externally focused indices, like organizational growth, budget deficits, or outside expert rankings, to measures that are generated entirely through self-evaluation by the board.[30] Across a range of studies, there are several factors that consistently emerge as determinants of board effectiveness.

In one study, Taylor, Chait, and Holland surveyed board effectiveness in a number of private, undergraduate colleges.[31] Based on extensive interviews with trustees, Taylor et al. ranked boards based on six criteria: understands institutional context, builds capacity for learning, nurtures the board itself, recognizes complexities, respects process, and is future-oriented. The rankings based on these criteria were then compared with rankings generated by a set of outside experts who based their judgments on general reputation. The ratings were strongly consistent, suggesting that while board effectiveness may be difficult to capture on a single measure, it may be broadly identifiable. In a similar study of 400 nonprofits in Canada, Bradshaw, Murray, and Wolpin find strong correlation between self-generated effectiveness ratings and at least one outside measure of board effectiveness—the extent of budget deficits.[32]

The single, most important factor in board effectiveness that emerges from the literature is the existence of a common vision of what the organization consists of and where it is going.[33] This finding is quite consistent with the characterization of the role of ideology in motivating staff, volunteers and donors, that we described earlier in this book. Given that ideology is so important in attracting people to serve on boards and in encouraging them to work hard on those boards, it is essential that those board members have some common vision. Indeed, the Taylor study found that while both ineffective and effective board were motivated by ideology, it was only in the effective boards that the ideology was shared and directed into a concrete, common vision.[34]

How do effective boards generate a shared vision? One approach is to focus heavily on the recruitment end. In the Taylor study, the critical difference between effective and ineffective boards was in the kinds of board members recruited.[35] Members of effective boards had more connections to their institutions and stronger identification with its mission before joining the board. Members of effective boards were often alumni or people with long-standing family connections. This characterization of effective boards is very close to the picture Hall describes of the nineteenth-century nonprofit board, in which community leaders "socialized their sons to civic values."[36] Nonprofit boards historically have often facilitated the cohesion of local elites.

Developing a common vision by recruiting board members who are already committed to the institution is not without its costs. This recruitment strategy typically reduces board diversity, and may encourage conformity, and resistance to change. Evidence suggests that homogeneous boards are conflict-averse,[37] a feature that enhances board effectiveness in easy times, but may be a liability when change is needed. Bradshaw et al. find that boards with fewer intraboard conflicts also have larger deficits, suggesting they have not adapted well. The challenge for the nonprofit is to walk the narrow, middle line, encouraging diversity in membership for adaptability while striving for a sufficiently common embrace of the mission to give the organization a sense of motivation and direction.

Strategic planning builds a common vision within nonprofit boards and staff and may also help in the process of airing conflict. In the Bradshaw et al. study, strategic planning explained 37% of the variance in the board's satisfaction with its own performance.[38] Strategic planning was also associated with lower-than-average deficits. Carver argues that strategic planning is the *sine que non* of the effective board.[39]

For new board members, there are additional clear, practical ways to begin the process of developing a shared vision. Houle offers the following list of documents as a starting point in the education of the new board member: the constitution of the organization, the bylaws, a description of the programs, an annual schedule of work of the board, a board roster and list of committees, a statement of board policies, an organization chart, and a budget.[40] Board minutes for the past year are also helpful. Herman and Heivocs suggest that pairing new members with a "buddy" from among the current board members is another helpful way to communicate the board culture.[41]

Once we move past the development of a common vision, it is more difficult to identify the sources of board effectiveness. As Houle suggests, "Just as nobody can write a prescription that would make all marriages happy, so no one can suggest a formula for a universally successful board–executive partnership."[42] Board size played no role in determining effectiveness in the Bradshaw study, nor in a survey of United Ways by Fletcher,[43] for example. On the other hand, committee structure does appear to matter.

Committees allow the board to use the special talents of trustees in a focused way, to carry out some of the work of the organization without spending the time of the full board, and to permit confidential discussions made more difficult in the full board. In addition, the smaller size of the committees often allows for more fulsome discussion and thus improves both decision making at the nonprofit and morale on the board. The Bradshaw observation that the existence of a core group within the board enhances performance reinforces this point.

Effective boards have a shared vision, often developed by strategic planning efforts, a tolerance for conflict coupled with an ability to control it, a strong committee system to manage size, and a strong core working group.

Conclusion

In this chapter we have examined the role of the nonprofit board, and seen some of the reasons for its structure. We have also seen some of the management problems created by the particular structure of the nonprofit board. Nonprofit boards play an important role both for their organizations and in the overall society. Indeed, one observer of nonprofits has argued:

> There is no other way that as few people can raise the quality of the whole American society as far and as fast as can the trustees and directors of our voluntary institutions, using the strength they now have in the positions they now hold.[44]

7

Product Mix and Pricing

The typical large museum has a number of products and services that it provides. It maintains a core collection, often runs film and lecture series, hosts special exhibits and school projects, runs a museum store and restaurant, and rents out its facilities for private functions. Small social service agencies often run counseling services, recreational programs, employment-related activities, and general community services. Universities provide education for undergraduates as well as specialized professional students and continuing education for adults. In addition, they run food concessions, athletic programs, dramatic and musical shows, and a wide range of other activities. In each of these cases, some of these activities are financed through fees, while others are supported through fundraising efforts. In this chapter, we look at two related questions in the marketing of nonprofits: how do nonprofits decide what range of products and services to provide, and how do they decide whether and how to charge fees for these products and services. In this context, we will discuss a number of important topics in the nonprofit area: the relationship between core businesses and the organization as a whole, the role of for-profit activities in a nonprofit organization, and the importance of cross-subsidization of programs in nonprofits.

Why Broaden the Product Portfolio?

Most nonprofit organizations begin by focusing on a single central or *core* activity. Planned Parenthood, for example, began with a mission to provide birth control information to the population. Harvard and Yale Universities began their lives devoted to the undergraduate education of young men. Figure 7.1 summarizes the forces that lead organizations to broaden the set of products and services they provide.

Nonprofits diversify for a variety of reasons, many of which are common in the for-profit sector. Recent expansions in services at the Girl Scouts

NONPROFITS DIVERSIFY TO:

1. Meet the old mission in a changing world;

2. Take advantage of production and/or distributional complementaries;

3. Increase opportunities for cross subsidization.

Figure 7.1.   The Role of Diversification.

look remarkably like the changes at I.B.M. Consider the evolution of I.B.M. over the past several decades. I.B.M.'s core business is information processing, which at one time was defined as mainframe computing. Technological developments in the last several decades, however, have changed information processing so that it now includes a new set of products: work stations, personal computers, and minicomputers. As technology changed, so did the scope of products that I.B.M. needed to satisfy its core mission. In this instance, the mission remained focused while the ways to accomplish the mission broadened.

In a similar way, the Girl Scouts broadened its product mix because exogenous forces redefined the activities needed to support the original mission. The mission of the Girl Scouts has always been "to help a girl reach her fullest potential."[1] The change in society, however, has meant that the services required to help meet that mission have broadened. Training in business and science has supplemented more traditional efforts in homemaking skills. Other changes have occurred as well. At the Girl Scouts, just as at I.B.M., the products expanded to help meet an old mission in a new environment.

Another example of the same phenomenon comes from the religious sector. In 1983, the Archdiocese of San Diego founded a self-help work program (SHARE) in which the recipients of food packages are required to provide labor for packaging and distributing that food. The business created by the Archdiocese—food distribution—was very clearly intended as a new, secular mechanism to serve the original sacred mission of the church.[2]

Nonprofits sometimes diversify to allow them to fulfill an original mission in a more responsive way.

Diversification which occurs in this way is often easiest from an organizational perspective because it leaves unchallenged the original foundation of the organization.

Organizations also move into new areas because they see activities or products that are complementary to their core products, and which would allow them to better support those core activities either by sharing costs or by facilitating marketing and distribution. Economists refer to these situations as ones in which there are *economies of scope*. In these situations, the costs of producing two products, including their distribution and marketing costs, are less when the production is joined than when it is separate. Lovelock and Weinberg who write extensively about nonprofit marketing, call these activities the *supplementary products* of nonprofits.[3] They exist to broaden the appeal of the core product, facilitate their use, or reduce their production costs. Here it is principally reasons of efficiency that are driving the product expansion decision.

A few examples will be useful in showing how supplementary products develop. Consider a college that begins with the goal of educating undergraduates. Yale University is a good example, as are most of the other older universities in America. In order to accomplish this goal, Yale hired a number of faculty, created an administrative structure, and invested in a large physical infrastructure—housing, libraries, gym facilities, even riding stables. Once this structure was in place and these investments made, the costs of producing graduate and professional education was reduced. Many of the facilities as well as the faculty could be used to support graduate as well as undergraduate education. Thus, the university developed a set of supplementary activities around the core undergraduate program. At Yale, this model has persevered and we still see the undergraduate program at the core of the university.

We see similar economies of scope operating on the demand side of the market. As we saw in Chapter 2, the Whitney Museum in New York City has as its mission: "To preserve, collect and exhibit twentieth-century American art." These are the core activities of the museum, but it produces a number of supplementary products as well. For example, the museum also runs films and lecture series. Because the museum attracts people who are most likely to be interested in a particular kind of art film, the museum is able to provide this service more efficiently—with lower marketing costs—than would a free-standing nonprofit entrepreneur. Moreover, to the extent that these activities bring new people to the museum, they help enhance the core activity.

Nonprofits broaden their product lines to capture efficiencies in production or distribution.

We have thus far seen two explanations for a broadening of the product line of the nonprofit: a redefinition of the core resulting from changes in the environment, and the search for ways to exploit joint economies in production or distribution. The third motive for a broadening of the product line is to promote earnings stability and growth potential for the organization.

All lines of business have peaks and troughs. In the nonprofit business, these ups and downs come from movements in the fee-for-service business, and in the fundraising area. Public support may be high for the homeless in one year and the next year shift toward famine relief in Africa. Audiences may be large for classic drama in one period and shift to interest in jazz in the next. As long as the earnings for two lines of business are not perfectly correlated, combining them will reduce the variance of total earnings for the organization. Good times for one line of business can balance the lean times from the second line.

The search for budget-stabilizing activities takes one additional turn in the nonprofit case. Among for-profit organizations, operations that persistently lose money are eventually shut down. Therefore, while organizations move capital across lines of business as opportunities open up, we do not typically see very-long-term subsidization of one operation by a second. In the nonprofit sector, however, organizations will at times have elements of the core mission which are not economically viable, using either fees or fund raising. As we indicated in an earlier chapter, in some organizations, these activities are the "soul" of the organization. Under these circumstances, however, the nonprofit will need to find some way to subsidize these activities; hence the search for new profitable activities. Lovelock and Weinberg call these the *resource-attracting* activities of the nonprofit.[4] Their purpose is to earn revenues to subsidize the unprofitable activities.

Examples of nonprofit organizations that seek activities outside their core to *cross-subsidize* are numerous. In one large-scale survey of nonprofits, 65% of the surveyed organizations were found to generate substantial revenues from activities outside their normal missions.[5] The Smithsonian publishes *Smithsonian* magazine, for instance, and sells products through its mail order catalogue. The Children's Television Workshop, using the merchandising power of Sesame Street and other shows, generates substantial revenue for funding new projects.[6] Nonprofit hospitals historically often coupled unprofitable research-intensive activities with profits from routine operations,[7] a practice that has become more difficult with new health payment regulations. Museums have expanded their gift shops and used blockbuster exhibits to cross-subsidize their more serious pursuits. Undergraduate education typically cross-subsidizes graduate education.[8] The director of National Public Radio, which has moved into a variety of new ventures, has defended his interests in cross-subsidization as follows: "We're prepared to enter almost any profession except the oldest one."[9] In each of these cases, one venture is deliberately run in order to provide funds for a second. This practice has been termed *strategic piggybacking*, since the core venture rides on the back of the money-making operations.[10]

Nonprofits expand their product lines to stabilize their budgets and support unprofitable core activities.

Broadening the product portfolio, however, as a way to manage earnings variability and create opportunities for cross subsidization is not always successful. Aggressive broadening may affect the organization's ability to sell itself to donors, granting agencies, staff, and volunteers. In organizations with a broad set of programs, donors and granting agencies lose control, precisely because of the cross-subsidization possibilities described. Clark, in fact, argues that nonprofit hospitals, through the use of cross-subsidization allow staff preferences to substitute for the interests of the funding agent.[11] In large nonprofits with varied services, donor trust may be particularly misplaced, since the activity donors hope to finance may not in fact be the one actually supported.[12] In these circumstances, bundling together disparate activities to try to improve budget stability may backfire by reducing the individual appeal of each of the activities.

Bundling together programs increases the difficulty of control and may make a program less attractive to donors.

Similarly, cross-subsidization may create staff tensions, when one group's profitable venture is used to support a second "more worthy" effort. We saw some of these tensions in our discussion of the Waverly Community House in Chapter 5. In People for the American Way, one of the cases in this book, these same issues emerge.

The corporate managers who engaged in aggressive diversification programs in the for-profit world in the 1960s and 1970s learned another lesson applicable to nonprofits as well: Managers who were very able at running one kind of business often turned out to be not very good at running other, quite different lines. United Airlines, for example, found that running an airline was very different from running either a rental car agency (through Hertz) or a hotel (through the Hilton chain). Owens-Illinois, a successful container company, had much less success in the forest products area. Volvo North America discovered that marketing oil was very different from marketing the cars that used that oil. In each of these cases, the firms eventually sold off their auxiliary lines.

Nonprofits, too, may find management of a new service quite difficult. As a way to gain support for the core business, the nonprofit may be tempted to enter a line substantially different from its core business. Consider again the National Public Radio quote. The further away the new activity is from the old, however, the less the specialized assets of the core business—including the acumen of the managers—can be used in the new venture. As a result, in these kinds of far-flung ventures management may well find itself operating as an inefficient producer, unable to generate either fee-for-service business or donor support.

From an economic perspective, the most successful product extensions involve products which are close to existing products and best able to share in the core assets of the organization. In some circumstances, there are *resource attracting* activities which satisfy this condition. In the case of the Boston Symphony Orchestra and its popular Boston Pops series, for example, we see a highly successful example of product extension. The Orchestra and Pops use the same concert facilities and some of the same musicians; they share a distribution network for performance tapes, and they pool a variety of employee benefits.[13] Here, there are substantial economies of scope and they help create value that can then be in part used to subsidize the core activity of the Orchestra. The message here is clear: Cross-subsidization can occur only if the organization is successful in the supporting activity.

Of course, one of the difficulties in all of this is that it is not always easy to tell when there are strong complementarities across product lines. A good example of this problem is an entrepreneurial venture by Planned Parenthood. In 1982, in part moved by the growing AIDS epidemic in the United States, the national Planned Parenthood organization decided to sell condoms as a way of raising funds to support the core mission. Management believed that this product extension would earn revenues to help cross-subsidize the core activities of the organization and that such sales would be both socially productive and consistent with the overall goals of the organization. Indeed, Skloot, one of the advocates of profit-making ventures by nonprofits, lauded this move by Planned Parenthood and referred to the sale of the condoms as a "good choice" for the organization.[14] Nevertheless, several years later Planned Parenthood exited the condom business, donating its large inventory to clinics in South America. This failure was in part attributable to the fact that the core strategic assets of Planned Parenthood—counseling staff, reputation, political clout—were not very helpful in the private merchandise market of condom sales. Because the organization had no particular expertise in the condom business, it could not generate the revenues that would then subsidize the rest of the operation.

We have identified several reasons nonprofits seek product extensions: outside changes in the requirements for delivering on the core mission, desire to take advantage of efficiencies in the production of complementary products, and a wish to balance the budget through more lucrative and steady funding sources. The central theme of this chapter thus far has been that the most successful extensions are ones that build on the organization's preexisting strategic advantages.

The Product Portfolio: Balancing Ventures

As an organization evolves and develops new products, it is helpful to keep in mind the balance among traditional and new products. One way to do this is through a *Product Portfolio Map*. A sample is given in Figure 7.2 based on the social service agency described in Chapter 5.

The horizontal axis of the map measures economic contribution: How much does each activity contribute to the ability of the organization to generate revenues, either through fundraising or fees? The vertical axis indicates the contribution of the activity to the overall mission of the organization. The size of the various activities is given by the relative size of the circles, where size can be measured either in terms of revenues, employment, or clients served.

Putting activities together on the product portfolio serves several purposes. Most importantly, mapping helps to show the balance of programs. For example, organizations that are dominated by programs in the left side of the matrix often face serious budget problems. Programs on this side of

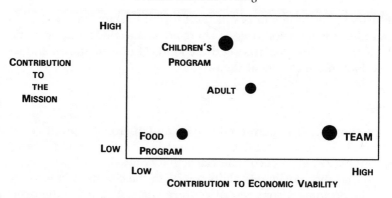

Figure 7.2. Product Portfolio Map: Waverly Community House.

the matrix do not cover costs. At the other extreme are the activities in the top right corner, which both generate resources and support the mission, but these programs are often hard to find and subject to competition from other organizations. Activities on the bottom right of the map are the "resource attracting" programs described earlier. The management issue here is to keep these circles in proportion to the rest of the activities so that the mission remains clear. Finally, organizations should try to exit programs that are in the bottom left corner contributing little to either the mission or the revenues.

Organizations should balance their mix of activities to assure a focus on the mission and economic viability.

The social service agency pictured in Figure 7.1 has several disturbing features. First, the program for the mentally retarded—TEAM—which started as a small, supplementary activity, has grown to a dominating position in the agency. Here, the supplementary activity threatens to take over the work, in an all-too-common process of goal displacement. TEAM growth has occurred in large measure in response to fund availability and despite its tangential role in serving the local mission of the agency. The food program (Fd) is also problematic, as it is low on both mission enhancement and revenue-generating ability. This program is draining agency resources but may well belong in another organization. Finally, the absence of programs in the top right corner is difficult for WCH, but quite common among nonprofits, which specialize in the production of goods and services that are difficult to fund.

Combining for Profit and Nonprofit Ventures

One of the motives nonprofits have in product line extensions is to create revenue sources to support the core mission, to look for activities in the right-hand portion of the product map. Nonprofits have increasingly sought these revenue sources in the for-profit sector, in a process some-times called *nonprofit venturing*.[15] There are some special opportunities and problems, however, that arise in these kinds of new ventures, and we turn now to look more closely at them.

Tax Issues

Exempt nonprofits are permitted to own and operate for-profit ventures in the United States and most other countries. In the United Kingdom, a nonprofit may engage in commercial activity only through a separate orga-nization that then covenants all its profits to the charity.[16] In most parts of the world, running a commercial venture will not threaten the overall tax status of the nonprofit unless the profitable side venture grows to domi-nate the organization. For example, the Mueller Macaroni Company, a rather large New York firm, was for years owned and operated by the law school at New York University. Such ownership in no way threatened the exempt status of the law school. Indeed, prior to 1950, in the United States even the income earned was tax exempt as long as it was only used to support the nonprofit's exempt function. In 1950, the tax code changed and under current law, in the United States, tax status depends not on the use of the funds, but on their source.[17] Profit-making activities that are under-taken primarily as a source of income that is otherwise *unrelated* to the principal purpose for which the nonprofit was formed will be subject to the business tax. Profit-making activities related to the exempt purpose are themselves tax exempt.

Under I.R.S. rules, in the United States, unrelated business taxable income is the "gross income derived by any organization from any unre-lated trade or business . . . regularly carried on by it, less the deduc-tions . . . directly connected with the carrying on of such trade or busi-ness."[18] Unrelated business is defined to include all activities not "substantially related" to the basis for the organization's exemption. Excep-tions to the rule include the value of volunteer work, revenue from busi-ness conducted for the convenience of the nonprofit member, sale of donated goods, certain hospital services and convention activities.[19]

Rules on the treatment of commercial earnings by nonprofits in the rest of the world vary, as Weisbrod's excellent survey indicates.[20] Hungary, for example, exempts such earnings from taxation as long as it is used for charitable purposes, using the pre-1950 U.S. model. Austria and Thailand offer reduced tax rates on such income. In many other countries, commer-cial income is taxed at standard corporate rates.

Commercial ventures may be subject to business taxation.

On the one hand, then, it seems a simple matter to marry profit-making ventures with nonprofit ventures, at least from the perspective of taxes. On more reflection, however, there are at least several difficulties that emerge. The first issue to arise is how to determine whether an activity is "unrelated" or not. A small art school runs a craft shop. Are the proceeds taxable or not? On the one hand, this venture looks like the activity of a standard retail store—clearly not a tax-exempt activity. On the other hand, to the extent that the sale serves as a display of American Crafts and promotes education in the crafts—the core mission of the school—it can be seen as a related activity. Museum gift shops face a similar dilemma. On the one hand, they seem quite like other retail operations; in other respects, museums sell products clearly related to the artwork in the museum. Modern fitness centers, supported by fees, at local YMCAs are similarly subject to challenges to their tax exempt status. Timothy Haake, speaking for a consortium of health club operators challenging the status of the YMCA fitness centers in Washington, D.C., argues, "The YMCA was not traditionally set up to have Nautilus machines for yuppies. It was set up as a charity."[21] A spokesman for the YMCA, Robert Boisture, gives the case for tax exemption: "Fitness is a fundamental part of the Y's mission in developing spirit, mind and body."[22]

In fact, the I.R.S. has up to now taken a middle ground in classification of unrelated businesses, although many local jurisdictions have been stricter in disallowing property tax exemption. In the case of museums, the I.R.S. has subjected some of the sales of large museums to the unrelated business tax, while other sales—museum reproductions, for example—have been exempt. YMCAs—even those with considerable elaborate equipment—have maintained their tax-exempt treatment of fees from their health clubs. The area is a quite volatile one, however, and nonprofits need to be sensitive to changes in it. In a 1991 ruling, the I.R.S. announced that hospitals may jeopardize their tax-exempt status by forming joint ventures with doctors involving referral fees, arguing that such arrangements violate the prohibition on private increment.[23] In many cases, it has been competitive small businesses who have most aggressively pushed for taxation of the profitable ventures of the nonprofits, showing us another way in which operating in an environment side by side with for-profit organizations can be difficult. It is not an accident that the sector that has seen the most aggressive scrutiny of unrelated business tax activity has been in health care, where the for-profit organizations play a prominent role.

A second problem in enforcing the unrelated business tax provision of the I.R.S. has been in defining the "income" on which taxes are collected. In the United States and many other countries, nonprofits can deduct the costs of running the commercial venture before calculating taxable income. Many of the most successful side ventures of the nonprofit will be ones that exploit joint economies with the mission of the organization. Save the Children is not likely to do very well opening hamburger restaurants. But the closer the profit-making venture, the more likely it is that the two will share some costs. Which costs should the nonprofit attribute to the commercial activity? Note, it is in the interest of the nonprofit to shift costs toward the commercial venture in order to minimize the "income" attributed to the venture and reduce the tax burden. From the point of view of taxing authorities, such shifting will be difficult to monitor. Even nonprofits who are doing their best to comply with the spirit as well as the letter of the I.R.S. code may well find the right cost allocation difficult to identify.

In sum, adding a for-profit venture to the product portfolio will complicate the management process somewhat. Questions about what is and is not a related activity will need to be addressed. If at least part of the new venture is unrelated, some tracking of revenues and costs will be needed. In this case, a different set of tax forms will need to be filed. In fact, in practice, small organizations faced with these complications often simply avoid the issue entirely and act as though all profitable side ventures were in related areas. Recent evidence suggests that there is widespread avoidance of the unrelated business tax by nonprofits.

Strategic Management Issues

Thus far, we have described some of the complications associated with the taxing of unrelated businesses in the nonprofit. There are, however, deeper, management issues as well when we try to marry for-profit ventures with nonprofits.

One of the themes of this book has been that nonprofits are not exactly like for-profits in terms of the management challenges that they offer. On average, the goods and services nonprofits provide are more difficult to measure; they operate subject to a nondistribution constraint; they depend on both donations and fees for service; they use more labor than most for-profits, and most of that labor is professional and often ideologically motivated. These characteristics influence the optimal management style. They affect the structure of the ideal board, the organizational structure, the way labor is hired and evaluated, and so on. Organizations that broaden to include under their wings for-profit businesses may well find that the management of those businesses requires a very different strategy and structure than they have used in their core ventures. And, it is often quite difficult to maintain one structure for one part of the business and a second structure for the rest of the business.

> **The optimal organizational structure will typically be different in for-profit and nonprofit organizations and this difference may hamper integration.**

A more insidious problem can also crop up in the marriage of the for-profit and the nonprofit. One of the characteristics of nonprofits is that performance evaluation, on either the individual or the project level, is difficult to do, in large measure because of the absence of market measures of performance. For-profit side ventures will typically have such market measures. We can tell if a museum shop is succeeding simply by looking the Profit and Loss statement. Since success in these ventures is easier to measure than it is in the core activities of the nonprofit, however, it is easy to fall into the trap of thinking that these for-profit ventures are more successful. Ventures with quantifiable success measures will tend to crowd out ventures in which success is harder to see. In these circumstances, peripheral activities sometimes threaten to take over the core. In precisely this way, it has been argued that lucrative athletic programs have had a pernicious effect on the core educational business of some universities.

For-profit ventures may crowd out activities where success is less easily measured.

Finally, there is a human relations problem associated with running profitable ventures in a nonprofit. The raison d'être of the profitable venture is to provide revenues for the core mission activities. Such ventures are, in a very real way, second class citizens in the nonprofit, but it is sometimes difficult to motivate people who work in these ventures when they know that the revenues raised will simply be transferred to another group. This is particularly true for the professional workforce of the nonprofit, who are often more attuned to the needs of their area than to broader organizational goals.[24]

Despite these problems, nonprofits continue to be attracted to commercial ventures. In a period in which competition for donations has increased, such activities clearly offer promise to the struggling nonprofit. What can the nonprofit manager do to help increase the chances that a profitable side venture will work for the nonprofit?

A first requirement for long-term success is that the side venture be kept small relative to the core activity. Large size threatens both the overall tax status of the nonprofit and exacerbates many of the management problems we have discussed. Often some of the most successful side ventures are ones run only sporadically—holiday sales or auctions, for example. Their irregular nature reinforces the secondary status of the activity, and exempts them from the tax on unrelated business income.

Finding the right people to run the for-profit venture is also essential. In particular, it is useful to find people to run the profit-making venture who have both business experience and share the social goals of the nonprofit. This will make the income transfer process easier and help make the operations of the for-profit compatible with the overarching goals of the nonprofit. Children's Television Workshop—a good example of a nonprofit that uses for-profit ventures extensively—deliberately sought business executives for their profitable ventures who shared the organization's social goals.[25] Firstenberg, a former executive vice president of Children's Television Workshop (CTW), describes a situation in which CTW spent two years trying to negotiate a computer software distribution arrangement with a for-profit computer company only to have it fail because the company's short-term profit focus was at odds the product quality concerns of CTW. For ventures located either inside or outside the firm, some agreement on the overall social goals of the core operation is essential.

Finally, it is also important in running the for-profit venture to understand that management *may* be different in the two kinds of ventures.

Managers may have to be compensated differently, and monitored differently in the two parts of the operation. Evaluation and control is likely to differ. To the extent that the senior management of the nonprofit lacks for-profit corporate experience, they may need to seek help on structuring the for-profit operation from outside the organization. For this reason, joint ventures between nonprofits and for-profit companies are often advantageous, as long as the goals of the nonprofit for the venture are clearly spelled out and protected.

Pricing in the Nonprofit World

On average, in the United States, nonprofit organizations raise 29% of their revenues through fee-for-service operations.[26] This percentage clearly varies considerably across segments of the nonprofit sector. Religious organizations receive less than 10% of their funds from fees, while educational organizations typically earn more than half their revenues. Fundraising organizations like the American Heart Association and Oxfam have almost no earned income beyond investment returns. As competition for donations and public resources intensifies, more nonprofits are likely to turn to activities that generate earned income. In this section, we examine what considerations should go into the nonprofit pricing decision.

Consider at the outset the role of price in general in the economy. Of course, charging prices for various goods and services allows organizations to earn revenues and thus to stay in business. Prices, however, play a deeper role as well. In particular, prices help to direct resources toward some activities and away from others and simultaneously to ration demand for those activities. Most of the interest in introducing pricing mechanisms into Eastern Europe, for example, is not because charging prices would enable companies to survive without government subsidies, but because prices are thought to improve the way in which resources are used in the society. It is this function of prices, their potential for altering consumption and investment decisions of individuals, on which we will focus in the discussion of nonprofit pricing.

One of the central principles of economics is that "demand curves slope down." As prices fall, people will wish to purchase more of a good or service; as they rise, less will be demanded. This principle holds at both the individual level and the market level. As the price of health care is raised, for example, there will be less use of health care by a given individual and fewer people in the market for health care services. Thus, one way that prices help to allocate resources is by choking off demand.

A second companion principle of economics is that "supply curves slope up." As prices rise, it becomes more profitable to serve a market, and under most circumstances, this results in an increase in production, at least after some period of time. Thus, the second allocational function of prices is to increase the supply of desirable goods.

Why is this allocation function of prices thought to be so desirable? Consider first the demand side. If a good or service is offered for free, the tendency will be to use that good or service until its incremental value is zero. Unless the cost of producing that good is also zero, however, this rate of usage will be excessive. In other words, offering goods and services for free creates, under many circumstances, waste; free or heavily subsidized distribution encourages people to ignore the true costs of producing the goods and services that they consume. In large measure, the current reform of health care—which has, through insurance, offered many people free or subsidized health care—is trying to cut excessive use of health care services by reintroducing prices and creating better incentives for individuals to ration their use of health care.

Prices also play an important role on the supply side. When goods and services are allocated via prices, the only kinds of goods and services that will be produced are those that, on the margin, cost less than the price people are willing to pay for them. Under these circumstances, society will not spend $20 producing an item that consumers value only at $10. Indeed, in the example of Eastern Europe, it was discovered that a considerable amount of production was occurring that resulted in products that would not be purchased once the full costs of producing them were reflected in prices. In short, prices are useful because they contain information about how valuable goods and services are to individuals consuming them and this information is then used to move resources in or out of markets.

For the nonprofit, prices can also serve allocational functions, though there may also be circumstances under which allocation by prices is inappropriate. Charging a fee can help to motivate clients to conserve on the goods or services being offered. Again, the health care example is a good one. By charging a fee that covers at least part of the costs of service, clients are encouraged to think carefully about using the service unnecessarily. Along the same lines, charging a modest fee can also help to allocate the good or service among clients, helping to identify those people who place the highest value on the good or service. It is common practice, for example, for private schools to require that even the most indigent student pay at least a small fraction of tuition. This practice helps to sort among parents and identify those families with the highest value on education. It also helps to ensure that parents have some "stake" in their children's education, so that price plays an ideological role as well. Given the extent to which education has been increasingly seen as a collaborative effort between parents and schools, some pricing may be quite important.

A second function of charging fees for service is to convey information to nonprofit managers. When clients have to pay for at least part of a service, they provide a floor on what the service is worth to them. To the extent that clients are not willing to pay such a fee, that may tell the managers that the service is worth less than those managers thought it was worth.

Charging fees can also help to create a spirit of healthy competition among programs within a nonprofit, and improve the information available to nonprofit managers. A local art school charges for its programs on a program by program basis. In this way, they can tell which programs fill up with individuals willing to pay for the services and which do not. This information can be used to plan for future courses. If the school instead charged a fixed fee and allowed people to attend classes at will, much information about the value of the various classes to clients would be lost and in turn the organization would lose some ability to monitor and motivate the staff.

In sum, charging a fee for service can have beneficial effects in a nonprofit both in terms of motivating service users and in terms of informing and motivating the staff of the nonprofit. Nevertheless, there are clearly occasions in which charging a fee is not advisable.

The advantage of charging fees on the demand side is that fees help to ration goods and services. For some goods, however, rationing is neither necessary nor desirable.

Public goods are defined as goods or services which, once provided, can simultaneously be given to others at no incremental costs. Public goods are nonrival in consumption.

The classic example of a public good is a lighthouse. When the lighthouse is lit, it helps all ships in the vicinity. If we add another ship to the area, its way is also lit with no added cost. In these cases, we would not wish to charge a price to choke off demand, since once the good is produced there is no incremental cost of serving an additional customer. It is most efficient to serve all clients who place a positive value on the good or service.

Fees should not be charged for pure public goods.

We may also wish to avoid charging fees when there are large positive externalities associated with consumption. An externality in consumption exists whenever an individual's act of consumption has a perceptible effect on other people. A classic example here is education. When a child is educated, that education benefits both the child and society as a whole through the creation of an informed and productive citizenry. If education were only available for a fee, too little education would be purchased, to society's loss. For this reason, society is provided with free, public education. Indeed, such education is not only free, but compulsory, emphasizing the advantages of not rationing this good.

Large positive externalities from consumption make fees less desireable.

Third, fees are to be avoided when the costs of collecting the fees exceed any benefits to be generated by those fees. Charging for the use of a swing in a park might well improve the allocation of swings, but the costs of collection would clearly make such an effort uneconomical.

Collection costs should be considered in setting fees.

The last consideration in deciding whether or not to set a fee for a good or service is ideological. It is clear that in some areas, charging for a service would be unacceptable to either donors or staff, regardless of how much such charges would contribute to the efficiency of the operation. Our sense of what are best kept out of the market system has changed over time, but clearly there are such categories of goods and services, and nonprofits must be careful not to violate these social and organizational norms.

Ideology also plays a role in deciding the appropriateness of fees.

A few examples will illustrate the trade-offs involved in charging fees for service. The American Red Cross has three principle activities: it collects and distributes blood, it teaches health classes of various sorts, and it provides disaster relief. For the first two activities, fees are charged, while disaster relief is provided free. Why do we see this difference? Consider first the role of fees in choking off demand. The fact that blood is not free clearly encourages hospitals to be more careful in their use of it. Even more clearly, prices play a role in making sure only interested clients sign up for swim lessons or CPR instruction. Nor are there large externalities associated with the use of either of these services. Collection of fees is relatively straightforward. Finally, since the blood payments go through hospitals and not directly from individuals and since the health classes provided by the Red Cross are clearly nonessential, ideological objections to fee setting are also modest. On all counts, both blood provision and health classes are appropriately supported by fee-for-service activity. Note, we are not suggesting here that the Red Cross activities in these areas cannot be subsidized by other funds, simply that supporting at least part of the activity through fees seems to be a sensible strategy.

Disaster relief is quite another story. First of all, a substantial portion of the Red Cross' relief efforts are public goods; roads are cleared of debris after a hurricane, for example. Externalities are also substantial in disaster relief. A community as a whole is hurt when there are large numbers of homeless after a flood or homes remain covered with debris. Finally, from an ideological perspective it would be very difficult to charge people who have just been burned out of their homes for shelter and soup from the Red Cross. For this product, then, fees are clearly not advisable.

In sum, there are a number of factors that a nonprofit should consider in deciding whether or not to charge fees for a particular activity or goods. These factors are summarized in Figure 7.3. We turn now to a further

Use Fees When We Need:	Avoid Fees When We Have:
User motivation	Public goods
Manager motivation	Externalities
Competition among programs	Ideological barriers
	High costs of collection

Figure 7.3. Factors That Encourage or Discourage the Use of Fees in Nonprofits.

question: If an organization does decide to charge for an activity, what should guide the decision about how high a price to charge?

Pricing in the Nonprofit Sector: How Much Do We Charge?

Prime School is a moderately sized private school, serving children from kindergarten to ninth grade located in the Northeastern United States. We have described Prime in several earlier chapters, and we continue using it as an example here.

Prime runs a summer program each year. The program is run by the school as a resource-attracting activity, and it charges fees as a way to generate those resources. The summer program is a simple case that illustrates the components of pricing in the nonprofit.

Many nonprofits set the fees they charge on the basis of the costs of producing those goods or services. In so doing, the nonprofit will typically add a fixed percentage to the costs of the good or service, in a process known as *markup pricing*. Markup pricing is an example of a cost-oriented price system.

In applying cost-oriented pricing, the nonprofit begins by identifying the *variable* and *fixed costs* associated with the service. A cost is fixed from the viewpoint of a particular program if changes in scale of that program have no effect on those costs. Variable costs, on the other hand, vary with the scale of the program. For example, Prime's summer camp has a number of fixed program costs including incremental insurance to cover summer attendance, director's salary, recreational equipment, and so on. These costs could be avoided if the summer program were eliminated, but they do not vary with the scale of the program. The program also has some variable costs—supplies, food, counselor salaries—that increase with the number of campers.

Suppose the fixed costs of the camp for the summer are $40,000. The camp runs a set of independent classes, each of which has a capacity of twenty children and a variable cost of $800/week, principally in salaries. Camp runs for six weeks, and the maximum physical capacity of the school is twenty classes, or 400 children per week, or 2,400 per summer. The elements of a cost-oriented pricing schedule for this example are given in Table 7.1.

Table 7.1. Cost Directed Pricing, Camp Example

1. Variable costs per child per week:		$800/20 = $40
2. Fixed cost per child per week:		
2.1 camp runs at capacity		$40,000/2400 = 16.67
2.1 camp runs at .75 capacity		$40,000/1800 = 22.22
2.1 camp runs at .5 capacity		$40,000/1200 = 33.33
Prices:	full capacity	$56.67
	3/4 capacity	$62.22
	1/2 capacity	$73.33

Associated with each child is a variable cost of $40. We assume in this example that if classes are under enrolled, fewer counselors will be hired and fewer classes mounted. Thus, the counselor costs are treated as truly variable. The second line of the table treats the fixed costs, and here the enrollment levels are key. As the enrollment level falls, with a fixed cost of $40,000, the charge per child rises.

In this simple example, we see that Prime must charge between $56.67 and $73.33 per camper per week to *break-even* on its summer program. The formula for calculating the break even price or volume is:

$$\text{Break-even volume} = \frac{\text{fixed costs}}{\text{price-variable cost}}$$

By using this formula, the nonprofit can calculate either the volume of sales it needs to break even, given a price, or the price it needs to charge, given a volume assumption.

In fact, applying a cost-oriented pricing strategy in this case may be more complicated. In particular, the camp has fixed program costs and it also uses facilities of the school-at-large, and thus depends on the fixed costs of the overall school—buildings, grounds, vans, and so on. Thus, some of the school's fixed cost are *joint costs*. So far in the calculation, we have treated these costs as zero and there is considerable logic in doing so, in the program budgeting, since eliminating the camp would have no effect on these costs. On the other hand, since the camp uses the school facilities, there is also a sense in which prices should, on fairness grounds, reflect those costs. Moreover, to the extent that Prime initiated the summer camp as a resource-attracting activity, funding part of the fixed costs from the camp makes economic sense.

For costs that are truly joint, as in the example here, allocation principles are almost always somewhat arbitrary. In many cases, particularly in sectors that depend on government funding, allocation of joint fixed costs is governed by set rules. For example, considerable university research is funded by the federal government. Rules for covering indirect or joint costs (buildings, library, student services, and so on) are closely governed by the Office of Management and Budget. Similarly, foundations may impose set allocation rules on agencies that enter into fee decisions. Where no rules exist, nonprofits often allocate joint costs based on simple operating measures. Thus, hospitals often allocate joint housekeeping costs based on square feet occupied by cost centers.[27] Prime might decide to allocate joint fixed costs based on the operating time of the camp versus the school as a whole (six weeks versus forty weeks).

An alternative approach to allocating shared costs is to use information about the demand side of the market to determine how joint costs will be allocated to the various activities of the nonprofit. We turn now to look at the use of demand-side information in the pricing decision. As Prime raises its summer program tuition to cover some of the shared costs, more revenue will be generated per camper. On the other hand, there may be fewer campers. The critical question for demand-side pricing analysis is how much demand falls with a price rise. The answer to this can be found in the shape of the demand curve or the *elasticity of demand*. The elasticity of demand is defined as the percentage change in quantity demanded over the percentage change in price. An elasticity of greater than one indicates that the market responds fairly strongly to price changes. Under these circumstances, price increases will reduce the total revenues of the firm. In other cases, where elasticities are less than one, the market is less responsive to a price change and increases in prices raise total revenues.

One of the central determinants of demand elasticity is the availability of substitutes. If there are other equally good camping facilities around, then Prime will find itself with relatively elastic demand and price increases will cause considerable loss of market. In fact, in a perfectly competitive market, Prime will find that if it wishes to attract any customers at all, it will need to charge no more than the rest of its competitors. Even if there are no other camps in the vicinity, and Prime has some market power, it may still be influenced by the availability of other recreational opportunities. In general, the fewer the substitutes, the more inelastic the demand will be and the higher the price that can be charged without substantial loss of customers. Of course, the elasticity of demand will not typically be constant over various price changes. In particular, as the price increases, it is typical to expect the demand to become more elastic. It is thus important for nonprofits who experiment with price increases or decreases to recognize that the responsiveness of the market may also change as the range of the prices changes.

In general, economic considerations suggest that a larger share of joint costs be allocated to programs with relatively inelastic demand.

As the price of camp increases and the number of campers attending falls, the program costs of Prime will also change as the average fixed costs per camper rises. In order to calculate the profit-maximizing fee to charge, Prime must look simultaneously at its costs and its demand response. Figure 7.4 is an example based on the program cost data already developed. At a price of $175, Prime attracts very few campers, given the competition. As prices fall, the number of campers attracted increases until, at a price of $100, the camp is full. Columns 1 and 2 thus show the "demand schedule" for camp classes. Column 3, shows the total revenue from each of the possible price/quantity combinations, and the marginal revenue per camper per week is shown in column 4. *Marginal Revenue* is the increase in total revenue associated with one additional camper. The marginal revenue from moving from 50 to 200 campers is $142; adding another 100 campers has a marginal revenue of $75 per camper, and so on. Marginal revenue typically declines as quantity rises. The final step in the exhibit is to add the cost side, which has been taken from Table 7.1. The profit-maximizing strategy is to reduce price and build volume until marginal revenue equals marginal costs. In this example, Prime would maximize its earnings from

PRICE/CAMPER/ WEEK	QUANTITY OF CAMPERS	TOTAL REVENUES PER WEEK	MARGINAL REVENUES PER CAMPER	MARGINAL COSTS PER CAMPER
$175	50	$8750		
$150	200	$30,000	$142	$73.33
$125	300	$37,500	$75	$62.22
$100	400	$40,000	$25	$56.67

Figure 7.4. Calculation of Profit Maximization of Prime Camp.

the summer camp by setting a price at just under $125 and running the camp at approximately three quarters capacity. At this scale, the camp would be earning somewhat over $225,000 in revenue ($37,500 per week × 6 weeks) with a total cost of $112,000, thus contributing $113,000 to covering the fixed costs of the school as a whole.

From the perspective of maximizing profits, it pays an organization to expand its goods and services so long as the marginal revenue from that expansion exceeds its marginal costs.

In this example, Prime is treating its camping program strictly as an income-earning operation and making profits from it. In other circumstances, the nonprofit may, for ideological reasons, not wish to extract maximum surplus from the users of even its resource-attracting ventures. Some of these cases were described earlier. Even in these cases, however, it is useful for the organization to know how its costs and demand are influenced by changes in its fee levels and capacity.

Conclusion

This chapter has covered considerable ground. It began with a discussion of the product choice of the nonprofit and outlined some of the reasons the nonprofit may wish to expand its goods and services, including expansions to the for-profit venture. We have explored some of the tax and management issues associated with such expansions. Finally, the question of pricing in the nonprofit was discussed. When do we want to use prices and how should we set them? We turn in the next chapter to an analysis of an alternative way nonprofit can generate revenues through fundraising.

8

Fundraising for Nonprofits

Charitable Contributions: Magnitude and Sources

Table 8.1 is a time-series, from 1960 to 1990, of aggregate giving patterns in the United States. As the table indicates, in nominal terms charitable giving has increased substantially in the last twenty years from $11 billion in 1960 to $122.6 billion in 1990. When we correct for inflation, as in Figure 8.1, private contributions still exhibit growth over time as national income has risen. Indeed, growth in national income explains virtually all the year-to-year variation in real private charitable contributions.[1]

There has also been considerable stability in the source of contributions over time in the United States, as shown in Table 8.1. In the last thirty years, individual gifts have comprised between 80 and 90% of total contributions in every year. In the United States, foundation and corporate giving are much less substantial. It is interesting to note that this pattern differs across countries. In Japan, for example, which has a less-developed tradition of private charitable giving than does the United States, corporate gifts play a more significant role.[2] In Australia, corporate contributions constitute one third of charitable giving.[3] In Canada and the United Kingdom, government payments substitute for private charitable gifts in many sectors so that, as Figure 8.2 indicates, the private propensity to donate is relatively small.[4]

While private contributions, as a broad category, have grown faster than the rate of inflation in the recent past, the picture is less sanguine for some markets within the nonprofit sector. Figure 8.3 shows the distribution of gifts by type of charity in 1989. Almost two thirds of total contributions in the United States go to religious organizations, and the shares going to various nonprofits have been changing over time. In 1991, for example, whereas total giving was up 1.4% in constant dollars, contributions to human services and health both declined dramatically. International agen-

Table 8.1. Total Giving: Private Contributions to All Sectors of the Economy by Source, 1960–1990 (in Billions of Dollars)

Year	Total*		Gifts by living persons		Personal bequests		Gifts by foundations		Gifts by corporations	
	Amount	Percent	Amount	Percent	Amount	Percent	Amount	Percent	Amount	Percent
1990	$122.6	100.0	$101.8	83.0	$7.8	6.4	$7.1	5.8	$5.9	4.8
1989	115.9	100.0	96.8	83.5	7.0	6.0	6.6	5.7	5.6	4.8
1988	104.6	100.0	86.5	82.7	6.6	6.3	6.2	5.9	5.4	5.2
1987	93.4	100.0	75.9	81.3	6.6	7.1	5.9	6.3	5.0	5.4
1986	90.9	100.0	74.6	82.1	5.7	6.3	5.4	5.9	5.2a	5.7
1985	80.1	100.0	65.9	82.3	4.8	6.0	4.9	6.1	4.5	5.6
1984	70.7	100.0	58.6	82.9	4.0	5.7	3.9	5.6	4.1	5.8
1983	64.7	100.0	53.5	82.7	3.9	6.0	3.6	5.6	3.6	5.6
1982	59.8	100.0	48.5	81.1	5.2	8.7	3.2	5.4	2.9	4.8
1981	55.6	100.0	46.4	83.5	3.6	6.5	3.1	5.6	2.5	4.5
1980	48.7	100.0	40.7	83.6	2.9	6.0	2.8	5.7	2.4	4.8
1979	43.4	100.0	36.6	84.3	2.2	5.1	2.2	5.1	2.3	5.3
1978	39.0	100.0	32.1	82.3	2.6	6.7	2.2	5.6	2.1	5.4
1977	35.5	100.0	29.6	83.4	2.1	5.9	2.0	5.6	1.8	5.1

Year										
1976	32.0	100.0	26.3	82.2	2.3	7.2	1.9	5.9	1.5	4.7
1975	28.6	100.0	23.5	82.2	2.2	7.7	1.7	5.8	1.2	4.2
1974	27.0	100.0	21.6	80.1	2.1	7.8	2.1	7.8	1.2	4.4
1973	25.7	100.0	20.5	79.8	2.0	7.8	2.0	7.8	1.2	4.7
1972	24.5	100.0	19.4	79.2	2.1	8.6	2.0	8.2	1.0	4.1
1971	23.5	100.0	17.6	74.9	3.0	12.8	2.0	8.3	0.9	3.7
1970	21.0	100.0	16.2	77.1	2.1	10.0	1.9	9.0	0.8	3.8
1969	20.7	100.0	15.9	76.8	2.0	9.7	1.8	8.7	1.0	4.8
1968	19.0	100.0	14.8	78.1	1.6	8.4	1.6	8.4	1.0	5.3
1967	17.0	100.0	13.4	78.8	1.4	8.2	1.4	8.2	0.8	4.7
1966	15.8	100.0	12.4	78.5	1.3	8.2	1.3	7.9	0.8	5.1
1965	14.8	100.0	11.8	79.7	1.0	6.8	1.1	7.4	0.8	5.4
1964	13.7	100.0	11.2	81.7	1.0	6.9	0.8	5.8	0.7	5.1
1963	13.2	100.0	10.9	82.6	0.9	6.8	0.8	6.1	0.7	5.3
1962	11.9	100.0	9.9	83.2	0.7	5.9	0.7	5.9	0.6	5.0
1961	11.6	100.0	9.5	81.9	1.0	8.6	0.7	6.0	0.4	3.4
1960	11.0	100.0	9.2	83.6	0.7	6.4	0.7	6.4	0.5	4.5

Sources: See Table 2.1. *Source:* V. Hogkinson et al., *Nonprofit Almanac*, 1992, p. 60.

*Totals may not add to 100 because of rounding. *Includes a significant portion of grants made in 1987, but reported on 1986 corporate returns for tax purposes.

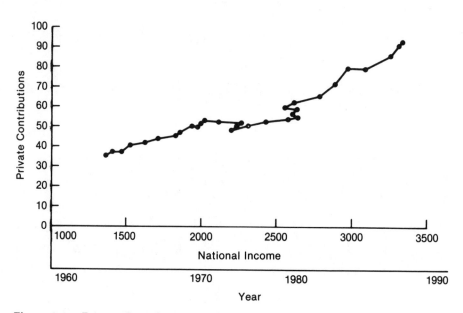

Figure 8.1. Private Contribution vs. National Income (in Billions of Dollars; Data from 1960 to 1990, in real terms.)

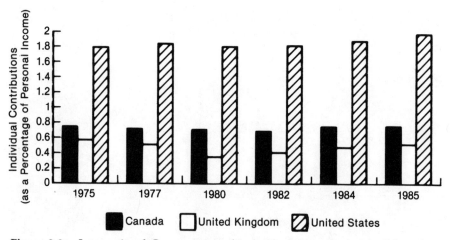

Figure 8.2. International Comparisons of Individual Contributions—Selected Years: Canada, United Kingdom, and the United States. *Source:* V. Hodgkinson, et al., *Nonprofit Almanac,* 1992–1993, San Francisco: Jossey-Bass, p. 82.

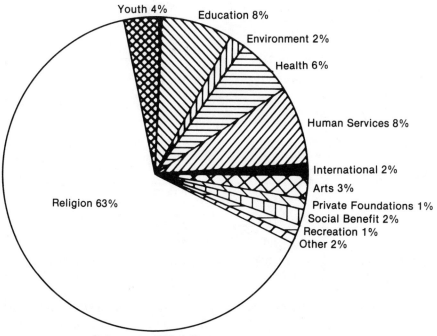

Data are in 1989 dollars.

Figure 8.3. Average Contribution per Household by Type of Charity in 1989. *Source:* V. Hodgkinson, et al., *Nonprofit Almanac*, 1992–1993, San Francisco: Jossey-Bass, p. 64.

cies, environmental organizations, and arts organizations, on the other hand, all gained substantially.[5] Thus, the apparent stability of the category as a whole masks considerable volatility within the particular markets in which most nonprofits operate.

The Optimal Level of Fundraising Effort

As the data suggest, contributions from individuals, foundations and corporations, are an important revenue source in many nonprofit sectors. Generating these contributions typically requires some expenditures on fundraising. A critical issue both for private nonprofits and the public agencies that regulate them is how much money should be spent on fundraising efforts.

We can begin our analysis of fundraising by looking at a production function for charitable dollars, using an approach developed by Boyle and Jacobs.[6] A production function is a mapping of the maximum output of a particular good that can be obtained from a prescribed set of inputs. In this

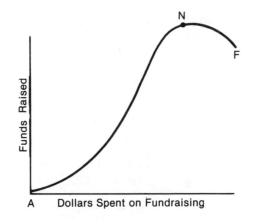

Figure 8.4. A Production Function for Fundraising.

case, the output is funds raised, while the input is fundraising effort measured in dollars. A production function is typically constructed assuming some particular technology, and assuming that the chosen technology is used as efficiently as possible. So, the production function maps the maximum funds that can be raised with a well-run campaign as a function of the effort devoted to that campaign.

Figure 8.4 shows a typical production function for fundraising. Point *N* represents the level of effort that gives the maximum value of gross funds raised. Since fundraising efforts often pay off only in the future, these funds should be expressed in present value terms. The graph shows that as the effort spent on fundraising is increased, the total funds raised also increase up to point *N*. At *N*, donations actually decline with increased number of appeals.

Some insight into the question of how much to spend on fundraising can be achieved by adding a line to the graph as in Figure 8.5. At every place along this 45-degree line, fundraising costs are exactly equal to funds raised. Suppose the goal is to maximize the funds raised, *net of fundraising expenses*. In this way, we have as much as possible left after fundraising costs to spend on programs. In the diagram, this point is represented by the point at which the difference between line *AD* and curve *AF* is largest, or point *M* on the graph.

At *M*, a line drawn tangent to curve *AF* will be parallel to line *AD*. But a line tangent to the production function is simply the Marginal Revenue of Fundraising; it shows how much revenues raised increase with a small increase in effort. The value of the *AD* line at that point is the Marginal Cost of Fundraising, measured at a given effort level. In other words, the optimal stopping point is one at which the marginal revenue from fundraising is equal to its marginal costs. This is, however, exactly the same principle used in trying to find the profit maximizing point in the for-profit world! The first test of fundraising is to look at the next dollar being spent

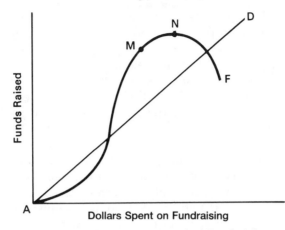

Figure 8.5. The Efficient Level of Fundraising.

on fundraising and ask whether it brings in more or less than an incremental dollar. If it brings in more than an incremental dollar it is worthwhile; otherwise, it is not.

> **Fundraising efforts should be subjected to marginal analysis. If incremental fundraising efforts yield higher revenues than incremental costs, fundraising should be expanded.**

Compare this advice with more typical procedures used in nonprofits. The Leonardo Museum is a small craft museum in the Northeast. In its early life, it struggled along without a paid development staff, relying instead on volunteers and a small effort by the director. Historically, the museum raised approximately $50,000 per year in donations. Several years ago, the museum hired a development director. In the two years since her arrival, the museum's donations have increased to $75,000 and her projections suggest that this new level can be sustained over time with her continued efforts. The question for the board is whether hiring a development director was a good idea.

Assume the director's salary is $30,000 per year. One way to do the evaluation is to look at the net funds raised, here $45,000 per year. On these grounds, the development officer appears to be successful. Another possibility is to measure the ratio of fundraising costs to program expenses and compare that to some national average, to see if fundraising costs are "reasonable." The Philanthropic Advisory Service, part of the Better Business Bureau, calls for a ratio of fundraising costs to program expenses of less than 50%, while the National Charitable Information Bureau, another watchdog agencies, suggests 60% as a limit. On this basis, the $30,000 development salary appears modest. A third way to do the evaluation, in the spirit of the discussion in this chapter, is to look at the marginal contribution of the director. The change in costs from hiring the director is $30,000 per year. The increase in revenue is $25,000. Clearly, from a marginal perspective, hiring a development director was not a profitable strategy.

Save the Children provides another good example of the importance of focusing on marginal returns from fundraising. Approximately 85% of the funds donated to Save the Children go to programmatic needs, and this is the number that the organization typically cites. On the other hand, a considerable fraction of the donations received by Save the Children is in the form of commodity assistance. By their very nature, these donations go 100% to programs. By including these donations in the pool, the figure representing the average funds going to programs has been artificially inflated. Of the private donations, considerably less than 85% go to programs. In fact, it has been estimated that for organizations like Save the Children that run sponsorship programs, the incremental costs of getting a new sponsor is more than fifty cents for each dollar raised.

In evaluating fundraising efforts, nonprofits have historically paid considerable attention to the value of fundraising costs on *average* and very little attention to the *marginal returns*. The two watchdog agencies referred to earlier concentrate on average fundraising costs, as does the United Way. The I.R.S. requires that fundraising costs be "commensurate" with programmatic expenses, and thus it, too, looks at average costs.[7] Most nonprofit organizations, in describing their fundraising efforts, also focus on average figures.

If looking at marginal returns would be advantageous, why is it that nonprofits focus so heavily on average fundraising costs in their strategy and their literature? The answer comes from the nature of nonprofit organizations. Donors to nonprofits find it difficult to measure organizational performance, and must instead rely on imperfect signals that the organization is not wasting their money. Data on average fundraising costs serve as such a signal, albeit a rather imperfect one.[8] Indeed, there is some evidence that donors are discouraged from giving by evidence of high average fundraising percentages.[9] As Steinberg suggests in his parallel discussion of fundraising from a donor's perspective, in a world of perfect information, the donors *should be* indifferent to the average use of funds.[10] Rather, the question that donors should consider is: If I give you a dollar, how much of it will go to programs and how much to fundraising costs? But in the real world of nonprofits, information on marginal returns is very difficult to obtain, and information on average costs may be all that is available. Thus, for nonprofits providing hard-to-measure services the economist's advice to focus on marginal returns may need to be tempered by the realities of the imperfect donor marketplace.

Determinants of Giving: The Individual Level

One of the best surveys of the determinants of donor behavior was done by Jencks.[11] Jencks' review develops a series of stylized facts about the demographic profile of givers in the United States. First, while the amount of money donated to charities increases with family income, the *percentage* of income given actually shows a U-shaped relationship with income. For moderate income families, the percentage of income given to charities falls as income rises. As we move to the very wealthiest individuals, however, philanthropy again begins to increase as a share of income. Second, in the list of stylized facts, older people tend to give away more money than younger, even holding income constant. Feldstein and Clotfelter, in a classic study in this area, found that a one-year increase in the age of the head of household increased household giving by 1%.[12] Later studies have indicated an even stronger age effect.[13] Third, having children increases one's propensity to give, even holding income constant. There is modest evidence that women give more than men, and that Protestants give more than Catholics.[14] The evidence on race is mixed. A small survey run by the Federal Reserve Board concluded that, with income and tax status controlled, whites gave 28% more than nonwhites in 1963.[15] Work by Carson, however, suggests that at low income levels, blacks contributed more to charities than did whites, while at higher incomes, the differences disappeared.[16] Carson's study does suggest, however, that black contributions are more likely than white contributions to go to religious organizations. Education also increases giving, again holding income constant.[17] Finally, there is some evidence that people in moderate-sized cities give more than do their neighbors in larger cities.[18]

> **Charitable giving increases with income, education, age, and number of children. Women also have a higher propensity to give as do people in moderate-sized cities.**

These results come largely from an analysis of surveys and tax returns, all of which concern charitable contributions in general. There appear to be substantial differences, however, not only in what people with different characteristics give in the aggregate, but in the composition of those donations. For example, of the total gifts given to charities, approximately two thirds goes to religious organizations. For the most part, these funds are given by members of particular congregations to support the services provided to themselves and other members of their congregations. Poor congregations thus beget poor churches, and the knowledge that on average people contribute substantially to churches is not of much help to these poor churches. For organizations whose members are traditionally nongivers in terms of their demographic profiles, the fundraising effort is likely to be an arduous one.

Jencks has argued that philanthropy takes two, very different forms in the United States: "paying your dues" and "giving away your surplus."[19] Giving to churches in the way just described is a typical example of "paying your dues." Members of churches give their fair share, and do so to those organizations which they believe have a claim on them. The only way to get access to these funds is to convince people you have a claim on them. The United Jewish Appeal, for example, has helped to foster a claim by Israel on American Jews. Jencks argues that United Way is another organization that depends on "paying your dues" kinds of contributions by tying its fundraising into the corporate community. The various child-related activities funded by tapping parents (i.e., Little League, Girl Scouts, local schools) are other clear examples of organizations clustered around dues-paying forms of giving.

For fundraising initiatives based on a "fair share" model, the form of the campaign may be very important. Recent work in economics suggests that free rider problems are minimized and charitable projects most easily accomplished when there is some credible way that donors can insure that their colleagues will also contribute their fair share. For example, campaigns in which contributions are finalized only if and when a fixed level of total contributions is reached are quite successful in experimental settings in reducing free ridership.[20]

"Giving away your surplus" is a very different kind of activity and this pool of funds is a much more fungible one. Much of the giving of wealthier individuals falls into this category, and tapping this pool requires not so much staking a claim but rather capturing peoples' imaginations and perhaps their consciences. Giving to the arts, higher education, hospitals, and social service organizations often comes under this category. This fundraising is very different from the kind of fundraising seen in the local Little League or in the church.

We can see some of these differences in the character of fundraising campaigns by comparing the fundraising campaigns of the typical United Way and Save the Children, one of the largest relief and development organizations. The Yale United Way Campaign begins with a letter from the President of Yale and then continues with profiles from four Yale people, describing the work of several of the United Way fund recipients. The focus of the presidential letter is clearly of the "dues paying" mode. As is typical of United Way campaign literature, the focus is on contributions as part of an assertion of community and belonging. The payment schedule, typically tied to salary, is another manifestation of the paying your fair share theme. This approach is quite different from ones used by Save the Children. This organization is clearly trying to tap into the "giving away the surplus" needs of donors. Here the message is "for a small amount of your money, you can help a child." The thrusts of the two messages are quite different and reflect a different perception by the two organizations about what drives their typical donors.

Thus fundraising begins with the recognition that different kinds of individuals give very different amounts and that their motives for giving may be quite different. The first task for an individual organization in the fundraising area is to identify those individuals and groups to whom the particular message of the organization has the most intrinsic appeal and to begin to understand those individuals. One way to learn this information is to survey current donors; another useful piece of information is the donor list of close competitors. Many organizations share or sell mailing lists, which contain valuable information about the donor base. Large donors are typically publicized. Using this information, the organization can ask: Who are my target donors and what drives them to give? Is the form and content of my fundraising efforts consistent with what I know about these target donors and their motives? Are my traditional bases for support growing or shrinking? If they are shrinking, is there a way I can broaden my appeal or will I need to turn to other sources of funds or shrink the organization? All of these questions stem naturally from an analysis of the demographics of the donor population.

Charitable giving varies by the demographics of potential donors. In addition, there are several factors that affect giving overall. As indicated earlier, growth in national income induces growth in contributions. Figure 8.1 suggests that growth in charitable contributions slowed in the recessionary periods of 1974 to 1975 and 1980 to 1982. There does not, however, appear to have been as large an effect in the more recent recessionary periods.[21]

There is also evidence that the tax structure matters considerably. As indicated earlier, in the United States gifts to 501c(3) organizations—the public charities consisting of churches, schools, hospitals, arts organizations, and social welfare organizations—are tax deductible. This tax provision was adopted in 1917, four years after the enactment of the income tax law itself, and allows individuals to deduct contributions to eligible institutions from their taxable income. Thus, if the marginal tax rate is 28% and a donor gives $1 to charity, the true "cost" is only $.72, since had the donor kept the dollar, twenty-eight cents of it would have gone to pay additional taxes. Therefore, all else equal, the higher the marginal tax rate, the lower the true cost of charitable contributions. In much the same way, contributions from corporations are also deductible up to a limit in calculating the corporate income tax.

The "price" of giving to charities falls as the marginal tax rate rises.

The principal complication to the story just told comes from the issue of eligibility. In the 1940s, the standard deduction was introduced to the tax code. For many people, this simplification eliminated the charitable deduction. In 1986, the charitable deduction was eliminated for non-itemizers, thus limiting further the number of people eligible for charitable deductions.

What effect would one expect a change in the marginal tax to have on giving? Suppose the highest tax rate falls, as it did under President Reagan. There are two effects from this. First of all, as the tax rate falls, the after-tax income from which individuals can make contributions rises. This should increase the rate of giving. On the other hand, there is also a price effect. As the top tax rate is reduced, the price of giving goes up and this should reduce the amount of giving. The net effect is ambiguous, although in other markets price effects typically dominate.

Over the years, since the deductibility provision has been passed, there have been a number of relatively large changes in the marginal tax rate. The Tax Reform Acts in 1981 and 1986 provided the most dramatic recent changes, cutting the marginal tax rate for the wealthiest individuals from 50 to 28%. In 1993, President Clinton raised the marginal tax rate again. Using historical changes, as well as tax differences in international comparisons, economists have attempted to estimate the effect of tax rates on rates of giving. The consensus from these studies is that reductions in the marginal tax rate reduce giving and that the absolute value of the price elasticity for giving is just over 1.[22] That is, if tax rates decline and cause a rise in the price of giving of 10%, giving would be expected to drop, all else equal, by 10%. It also appears that the elasticity rises with income (i.e., high income individuals are more responsive to tax changes than low-income people).

The effect of general changes in the tax code governing charitable deductions are even more pronounced than are changes in tax rates. In 1986, the tax code rules on treatment of donations on appreciated property were changed to radically reduce the tax value of such profits. In the late 1980s, the Guggenheim Museum in New York saw its property donations drop over 80%. It is no accident that when the I.R.S. opened a window in 1991 to allow donations at appreciated value that the substantial art collections of Annenberg and Paley were donated. Efforts to monitor and influence tax changes of this magnitude are clearly worthwhile for large nonprofits.

Corporate Giving: Trends and Determinants

In 1991, corporations gave just over $6 billion to U.S. charities,[23] approximately 5% of the total charitable gifts given. The United Negro College Fund receives approximately 25% of its contributions from corporations. Junior Achievement, a nonprofit closely allied with business, receives almost all of its contributions from the corporate sector. Other nonprofits, churches, for example, receive almost no corporate gifts. Corporations often donate personnel, products, and facilities as well as cash. Kraft General Foods, for example, donates about $10 million in foodstuffs to food banks.[24] United Way depends critically on the help of corporate volunteers as well as access to payroll deductions.

Why do corporations give to charities? For the most part, the motives for corporate giving are in the paying your dues category rather than in the giving away the surplus style. Particularly in the 1990's, as corporate profits fell, pressure grew to use philanthropy to serve strategic objectives of the corporation.[25] Large corporate gifts are most commonly given to organizations that have some natural claim on the corporation. Thus, Weyerhauser, a forest products company, gives primarily to environmental causes. Dalton, a book chain, heavily supports literacy campaigns. Equitable Life Insurance Company sponsors health research. Local banks and local utilities invest primarily in local charities and nonprofits that influence the local economy on which they are dependent.[26]

Logsdon et al. have identified three variations of strategically oriented corporate philanthropy.[27] First, corporations may use philanthropy to expand their markets either geographically or to a new customer segment. Donations of computer hardware or software are good examples here. The Logsdon survey suggests that this form of strategic philanthropy is practiced primarily by high-technology firms. A second form of strategic philanthropy involves employee development. Corporations fund child-care programs and health services used by employees. Manufacturing firms, in particular, have adopted this orientation. Finally, some corporations link their philanthropy to their outside stakeholders and focus on improving their image. Contributions to public television are a good example here. Service sector firms, and highly regulated firms, commonly adopt this orientation.

Enlightened self interest has perhaps reached its peak with the *cause related marketing* in which companies agree to donate funds to particular charities in response to consumer use of their products.[28] Thus, American Express tied its gifts to restore the Statue of Liberty to use of its credit cards, and Johnson and Johnson contributed to shelters for victim of domestic violence in proportion to coupon redemption of its products. For the non-profit organization, the message of the current era is to find the corporations who are your natural constituents, and design a fundraising campaign to make your claim clear.

Cooperation Versus Competition in Fundraising

For many organizations, fundraising competition has increased in the last few years. Save the Children's revenues from child sponsorship programs have fallen not because of an overall decline in donors to this kind of cause, but because its market share fell from 14% of the market in 1986 to 9% in 1989. At the same time, World Vision has increased its share from 20 to 30%. The role of competition in fundraising currently cannot be overemphasized.

What stance should nonprofits take toward competition in their markets? In the for-profit sector, with modest exceptions, public policy encourages competition, recognizing that it brings with it improved performance. For-profit firms, while they recognize that coordination might well bring pay-offs in the form of higher profits, also typically recognize the economic and legal difficulties of coordination. For nonprofits, however, the situation is somewhat different. First, coordination may be in society's interests in the nonprofit sector in that it reduces wasteful duplication. Second, as we have indicated throughout this book, the nonprofit world, with its strong ideological focus and tight networks, may provide a more forgiving environment for cooperation than we typically see in the for-profit world.

The United Way is the quintessential vehicle for cooperation in fundraising by nonprofits. In lieu of separate, competing fundraising campaigns by a multitude of local groups, the United Way runs a single campaign, and divides up the proceeds. The result is lower fundraising costs, precisely because fundraising efforts can be directed at encouraging giving, and not influencing the direction of the gifts.[29] Gains from cooperation are particularly strong when agencies serve very similar needs. In fact the most common cooperative arrangements do involve alliances among similar agencies: The United Way allies local groups; the United Negro College Fund is an alliance of traditionally black colleges; the Combined Health Appeal groups together health research organizations in fundraising. As the number of nonprofits increase, we are likely to see more organizations doing similar things, and instances of cooperation are likely also to increase. Agencies serving similar needs will also often share the same networks and similar values, both of which also help ease the path to cooperation.

In many ways, U.S. law also discourages competition among nonprofits, particularly in the fundraising area. In the face of increased competition, many nonprofits have turned to professional, for-profit fundraisers. Further competition has increased the share of receipts these nonprofits have had to pay fundraisers.[30] In response to this competition, a number of states have attempted to impose limits on fees paid to professional fundraisers.[31] In one case, the United Cancer Council, which paid 93% of its gross income to a profit-making fundraiser, IRS threatened to revoke the Council's charity status.[32] Laws governing fundraising clearly have the effect of reducing competition. Their goal, for the most part, is to reduce the tendency of competition to use up funds otherwise available for programs.

Cooperation, however, is not without its problems. Again, the United Way serves as a good exemplar. The United Way provides an efficient fundraising vehicle for the local agencies it serves, but what of the agencies left out? Much of the authority to decide which organizations are worthy causes and which are not, authority originally vested in the individual donor, shifts to the bureaucracy of the United Way. This clearly raises concerns over equity and legitimacy. Even among constituent organizations, a united fund bureaucracy exerts substantial power. The ability of a united fund to distribute its funds after organizations receive funds from other sources allows it to make compensatory contributions with a marginal value considerably beyond actual dollars given.[33] Moreover, the excesses of competition may play themselves out not in the direct donor contact, but in the market for inclusion in to the United Way. In language familiar to those who work in the regulatory area, we may well see local agencies spending resources in "rent-seeking" behavior designed to give them access to the United Way machine. In this case, inefficiency is only displaced, not averted.

Conclusion

For many nonprofits, fundraising is the most troublesome aspect of management. Competition in the area has increased substantially in the last decade in part as fundraisers struggle to deal with the depressing effects of tax code changes on charitable giving. Few directors of nonprofits, and even fewer board members, enjoy fundraising with its image of an outstretched hand, hat turned up. Moreover, fundraising often brings to the fore struggles over the mission and future direction of the organization. Odendahl, for example, argues that even though private giving is only the fourth or fifth most important source of funds for most colleges, the wishes of private donors exert a disproportionate effect on the shaping of their programs.[34] Pfeffer and Salancik similarly cite universities as classic battlegrounds for control by donors, granting agencies, alumnae, and staff.[35] Similar concerns about the role of donors in changing the mission have been voiced by Salamon looking at the broader body of nonprofits: funding sources "frequently have their own priorities and concerns that may or may not accord with the priorities of voluntary agencies."[36]

Many managers bemoan the role of donors in shaping their programmatic agendas, yet the influence of donors on nonprofits may be quite valuable. As indicated earlier in this text, donors play a vital role in helping to monitor the performance of the nonprofit, a role accentuated by the absence of either an equities market or quantifiable performance measures. In many ways, the donor plays the enforcement role typically played by the price system in the private market, and this role is a very important role. Donors provide one of the important checks and balances in the nonprofit network.

Donors are also one of the forces that help keep nonprofits vital, by encouraging evolution. As we suggested earlier, one of the principal sources of change for a nonprofit is change in the resources available to it. Such change can be for the better or worse. In analyzing the public television show, *Dance in America,* Powell and Friedkin suggested that the loss of resources by a variety of funders and resulting concentration of donors created a situation in which "the staff lost its room to maneuver and the funders gained much greater say in program content."[37] Artists have argued that the National Endowment for the Arts, a government funding agency, has at times used its grant-making power to influence the progress of the visual arts in America. Wilson argues that the Julius Rosenwald Foundation, started by the founder of Sears and Roebuck, used its charitable grants to force universities to hire black faculty member in the 1940s.[38] Again, in each of these cases, donor pressure helped to induce organizational change.

9

Managerial Control

A well-designed financial reporting system is key for both planning and control in nonprofit organizations. Yet, as Anthony and Young suggest, in many nonprofits financial controls are woefully inadequate.[1] Moreover, the financial information used by staff and given to trustees is often unnecessarily confusing.[2] This chapter focuses on fundamental principles of the financial reporting and control process as a way of showing how a well-designed, well-constructed budgeting process can help nonprofits grow and develop.

Why Do We Have Financial Reports?

Financial reports, including budgets, are intended to provide information to one or more of the constituents of the organization. First, consider the publicly traded organization. For these corporations, the Security Exchange Commission requires regular income statements and balance sheets to provide information to investors, both current and potential. These statements show both the current flow of resources in and out of the organization (the income statement) and the stock position of the firm (the balance sheet). The form of such statements is regulated, based on generally accepted accounting principles. The data provided are typically historical (i.e., we have a record of what happened in the past, not a future plan for spending). Notice, the constituent for this set of financial information is typically an outsider to the firm.

The typical firm also generates a series of budget documents. A budget is a plan, cast in quantitative terms—typically monetary terms—of what the organization or a part of the organization expects to accomplish in some particular future period. Unlike the typical income statement, a budget is a projection of the future. Thus, the budget can be thought of as a tool of managerial accounting, since its prime function is not to inform outsiders but to help inside management decide what to do in the future and to evaluate how well they have been doing. Such budgets are typically partial (i.e., they are often designed to cover only one part of the organization or another). Since the budget is intended to help guide internal managers, the form of budget is typically tailored to the managerial needs of the organization and its market.

The nonprofit world similarly uses two kinds of reports. In order to fulfill its obligations both to donors and to the governmental authorities, nonprofits must generate a set of financial reports comparable to the income statement and balance sheet of the for-profit. Financial reports are also used for planning and control and thus serve an internal function for the nonprofit. These financial reports are governed by a set of standards developed by the Financial Accounting Standards Board (FASB), the same organization governing for-profit corporations. In general, the accounting principles used in the two sectors are quite similar and becoming more so over time.

Nonprofit organizations require both financial reports for outside constituents and budgets for the use of management.

While nonprofits should follow many of the same accounting principles as for-profits, they are distinguished by their use of *fund accounting*. A fund is a self-balancing set of accounts. The typical nonprofit consists of a set of funds categorized in several different ways. Each of these funds has its own revenues, expenses, assets, liability, and equity. The *current* or *general fund* contains information similar to that reported in the operating statement of a business. The typical current fund may have unrestricted funds and restricted funds, whose use is designated by a donor, for example. It carries the revenues generated by the year's operation, including earned income and donations designated for use in operations, and accounts for the operating costs of the organization. The nonprofit also has a *contributed capital fund* usually consisting of an endowment fund and a plant fund. The contributed capital fund shows the amounts added to plant and endowment from earnings and contributions. The land, buildings, and equipment used by the nonprofit are carried in the plant account, and are typically based on the original cost of these assets. The *endowment fund* includes those gifts that, under terms of their donation, must be maintained intact in perpetuity.[3] For these gifts, earnings may eventually be used to fund current operations, but the body or corpus of the gift is not available for current operations and hence must stay in its own fund, the *endowment fund*. Each of these funds has a set of assets and liabilities, indicating its cumulative position, and a set of current revenues and expenses to the fund. For each fund, the difference in current revenue and current expenses is known as the *Excess* or *Deficiency* of the fund. Finally, each fund has a balance, known as the *fund balance,* and this balance changes each year in response to the activities within the fund and transfers among funds.

It is important to remember that money is not fungible across funds. In many cases, requirements of donors legally prevent organizations from moving endowment funds (e.g., to the operating fund). Transfers from the operating fund—perhaps in response to operating surpluses—to the plant fund or endowment fund, are typically voted by the board. Thus, the nonprofit funds are quite different from the divisional accounts produced in the for-profit sector, among which money can freely flow from a legal perspective.

Funds in the nonprofit are self-contained, self-balancing accounts.

An example of the financial report of the Boys and Girls Clubs is given in Figure 9.1. In the case of the Boys and Girls Clubs, the unrestricted current account, for example, has a fund balance of $11,420,103. This figure represents a cumulated result of activities for a number of years. It is part of the balance sheet of the club. Below the balance sheet, we see the Statement on Support, Revenue, and Expenses. This is the income statement of the Boys and Girls Club. In this account, most of the activity is in the current fund. For any given year, the difference between revenues and expenses, the income of the fund, is known as the *change in fund balances*. For the Boys and Girls Clubs the current fund has an excess of $199,774, generated by the year's operations.

Funds have traditionally been formed on the basis of their use (i.e., current fund, plant fund). FASB, however, has proposed a change in nonprofit accounting that would class assets by the nature of the restriction imposed on them. Thus, all revenues would be either unrestricted, temporarily restricted, or permanently restricted. Many nonprofits, particularly large ones, are moving toward this modified basis of classifying funds, in part because it is expected to make financial statements easier to understand and use.

Fund accounting developed because of the dependence of the typical nonprofit on charitable gifts. Fundraising, because it is often accompanied by restrictions by donors on the use of their funds, led to fund accounting, which embodies the restrictions of those donors. In contrast, for the for-profit organization, the entity is the corporation as a whole, since it is the entity as a whole in which people invest. Thus, the financial statements in the for-profit reflect the results of the organization's activities as a whole, while the nonprofit statements are partitioned by funds. Unfortunately, the use of fund accounting often obfuscates the financial picture of an organization, particularly to outsiders more familiar with the language of corporate accounting. For this reason, many experts have argued in favor of moving away from some of the complexities of fund accounting. Indeed, Anthony has argued that "nonprofit accounting should be entirely consistent with business accounting, except for the special treatment required for contributed capital."[4]

Even now, however, despite the difference in the unit of account there are considerable similarities in the financial reports of the for-profit and the nonprofit. In both cases, the reports are intended for an outside audience. In both, the perspective is historical—what happened last year or the year

Balance Sheet

December 31, 1990 (with comparative totals for 1989)

	Current Funds Unrestricted	Current Funds Restricted	Land, Buildings and Equipment Fund	Endowment Funds	Total 1990	Total 1989
Assets:						
Cash and cash equivalents	$ 1,346,684	255,731	13,821	27,440	1,643,676	713,539
Investments (note 2)	7,578,432	1,964,386	34,735	8,887,200	18,464,753	19,908,052
Pledges receivable (note 3)	3,741,753	–	–	–	3,741,753	2,340,980
Membership dues and other receivables, net	521,446	364,204	132,000	–	1,017,650	957,932
Accrued interest and dividends	89,381	52,419	174	–	141,974	160,655
Inventory of supplies—at cost	149,715	38,789	–	–	188,504	114,472
Prepaid expenses and travel advances	180,767	–	150	–	180,917	216,989
Land, buildings and equipment, net (note 4)	–	–	4,986,430	–	4,986,430	4,614,683
Interfund receivables (payables)	367,889	(57,465)	(310,424)	–	–	–
Total assets	$13,976,067	2,618,064	4,856,886	8,914,640	30,365,657	29,027,302
Liabilities and Fund Balances:						
Liabilities:						
Accounts payable and accrued expenses	$ 716,289	73,479	1,583	–	791,351	986,149
Deferred support	1,839,675	37,827	–	–	1,877,502	439,974
Total liabilities	2,555,964	111,306	1,583	–	2,668,853	1,426,123
Fund balances:						
Unrestricted—Board designated	11,420,103	–	–	–	11,420,103	11,839,295
Restricted	–	2,506,758	–	–	2,506,758	2,549,106
Land, buildings and equipment:						
Expended	–	–	4,748,538	–	4,748,538	4,364,682
Unexpended—restricted	–	–	106,765	–	106,765	92,194
Endowment, including accumulated net realized gains of approximately $3,271,000 in 1990 and $2,989,000 in 1989	–	–	–	8,914,640	8,914,640	8,755,902
Total fund balances	11,420,103	2,506,758	4,855,303	8,914,640	27,696,804	27,601,179
Total liabilities and fund balances	$13,976,067	$2,618,064	4,856,886	8,914,640	30,365,657	29,027,302

See accompanying notes to financial statements.

Statement of Support, Revenue and Expenses, and Changes in Fund Balances

Year ended December 31, 1990 (with comparative totals for 1989)

	Current Funds Unrestricted Undesignated	Current Funds Unrestricted Board Designated	Total	Restricted	Land, Buildings and Equipment Fund	Endowment Funds	Total 1990	Total 1989
Public support and revenue:								
Public support:								
Contributions	$ 7,590,705	–	7,590,705	348,822	–	–	7,939,527	6,920,837
Government grants and contracts	243,267	–	243,267	370,315	–	–	613,582	761,624
Bequests	430,000	109,320	539,320	–	–	–	539,320	2,059,502
Income from funds held in trust by others (note 7)	–	–	–	896,000	–	–	896,000	810,000
United Way	15,263	–	15,263	–	–	–	15,263	17,367
Fund raising events (net of direct costs of $434,000 in 1990 and $294,000 in 1989)	996,673	–	996,673	–	–	–	996,673	668,268
Sweepstakes	112,357	259,999	372,356	–	–	–	372,356	377,645
Total public support	9,388,265	369,319	9,757,584	1,615,137	–	–	11,372,721	11,615,243
Revenue:								
Member organization dues	1,581,109	–	1,581,109	–	–	–	1,581,109	1,582,699
Investment income, net of advisory fees	604,017	8,876	612,893	547,846	2,287	–	1,163,026	1,127,791
Net realized gain (loss) on investment transactions	(11,918)	740,340	728,422	29,560	–	281,765	1,039,747	903,184
Miscellaneous	206,794	21,651	228,445	214,143	2,924	118	445,630	348,693
Total revenue	2,380,002	770,867	3,150,869	791,549	5,211	281,883	4,229,512	3,962,367
Total public support and revenue	11,768,267	1,140,186	12,908,453	2,406,686	5,211	281,883	15,602,233	15,577,610
Expenses:								
Program services:								
Services to member clubs and extension of clubs	6,359,698	3,457	6,363,155	1,349,964	120,744	–	7,833,863	7,057,628
Training of leadership, development and maintenance of programs for youth	2,406,122	11,833	2,417,955	1,085,804	170,463	–	3,674,222	3,342,174
Total program services	8,765,820	15,290	8,781,110	2,435,768	291,207	–	11,508,085	10,399,802
Supporting services:								
Management and general	1,254,538	865,756	2,120,294	–	28,411	–	2,148,705	1,653,938
Fund raising	1,548,135	266,170	1,814,305	–	35,513	–	1,849,818	1,964,687
Total supporting services	2,802,673	1,131,926	3,934,599	–	63,924	–	3,998,523	3,618,625
Settlement award (note 8)	–	–	–	–	–	–	–	740,000
Total expenses	11,568,493	1,147,216	12,715,709	2,435,768	355,131	–	15,506,608	14,758,427
Excess (deficiency) of public support and revenue over expenses	199,774	(7,030)	192,744	(29,082)	(349,920)	281,883		
Transfers (note 6)	(199,774)	(412,162)	(611,936)	(13,266)	748,347	(123,145)		
Fund balances at December 31, 1989	–	11,839,295	11,839,295	2,549,106	4,456,876	8,755,902		
Fund balances at December 31, 1990	$ –	11,420,103	11,420,103	2,506,758	4,855,303	8,914,640		

See accompanying notes to financial statements.

Figure 9.1. Financial Reports of the Boys and Girls Club of America. *Source:* Boys and Girls Club, *Annual Report*, 1991.

before, not what is expected to happen next month. In both cases, there is an integration between what happens in the income statement and the balance sheet.

In addition to the formal reports, nonprofits also typically have a series of budgets. The audience for these budgets are the managers and board of the nonprofit. Here there is considerable variation in budget format, perhaps more so than in the for-profit sector. Unfortunately, it is in the use of budgets that the gap between nonprofit performance and for-profit performance is often most pronounced. Nonprofits are much less likely to use budgets as living, working documents, helping to guide decision making than are for-profit organizations.[5] In part, this may reflect the particular characteristics of the nonprofit. It is clear that, for most nonprofits, performance is not strictly measurable based on quantitative indices. Many nonprofits are limited in terms of strategies by their missions. Governance of nonprofits differs from that of the for-profit. All of these features make managerial control more difficult in the nonprofit organization. They may also make nonprofit managers shy away from budgets as a control device; however, such shying away is a mistake, for even in situations in which budgets tell only part of the story, it is a chapter that is vital in terms of helping nonprofits thrive. Thus, in this chapter, we focus heavily on understanding the nonprofit budget process.

The Budget Process

The proposition that a budget should be a management planning document, leads one to four principles of budgeting that should hold in all nonprofits. First, budgets should be developed based on the *accrual principle*. Second, with some exceptions that we will discuss, nonprofits should aim to create a *balanced budget,* in which revenues and expenditures balance on an annual basis. Third, budgets should be developed on a *program basis*. Finally, responsibility for formulating the budget should be pushed to as *low a level of management* as possible, subject to some guidelines by senior management.

Perhaps the most fundamental idea in modern accounting is the concept of accrual accounting. In accounting for expenses, the cost of resources used to generate output is used, rather than cash paid out. Similarly, revenues are recognized as they are earned. The use of accrual accounting allows an organization to match revenues earned with the costs of generating those revenues. Thus, accrual accounting is vital if a budget is to be an operating document.

A few examples will help to clarify the differences between accrual accounting and cash accounting and illustrate its importance. Prime School works on a fiscal calendar ending June 30 each year. Budgets are thus constructed on a July 1 to June 30 basis. Tuition payments for the next year, however, are due on June 10. Under principles of accrual accounting, those tuition revenues would appear in the budget of the next year because they will be earned in that next year, even though they are being paid in this year. Similarly, in early July, the business office may well pay some bills for supplies used in the earlier year. These bills should have appeared in the prior year's budget because they represent resources used in that prior year. For this reason, last year's budget is often not "closed" until several months into the current year, so outstanding bills can be reconciled.

Why is accrual accounting important? Without accrual accounting, a nonprofit has no way of telling whether it is covering the costs of running its business! It lacks the fundamental financial information needed to decide whether to expand or contract its program offerings, raise its user fees, mount new fundraising efforts, or cost control programs. Accrual accounting allows us to create time-delineated boundaries on the finances of an organization, to create a meaningful snapshot of those finances.

Accrual accounting allows an organization to match revenues with expenses used to generate those revenues.

The second principle of budgeting involves the optimal balance between revenues and expenses. For-profits, of course, try to maximize the difference between revenues and expenses (their profits). Nonprofits have a different task to perform. Many nonprofit organizations, seeking to maximize service levels they provide, begin their budget process with an estimate of the resources they will have available.[6] Spending is then planned to match these resources, while providing the level of service consistent with revenue predictions. In general, Anthony and Young argue that, given their service orientation, nonprofits should manage their budgets such that current expenses are equal to current revenues. In other words, nonprofits should manage for a *balanced budget*. Indeed, this was the goal implicit in the earlier discussion of the Prime School budget. The advantages of a balanced budget have largely to do with conditions of equity across users of the nonprofit over time. In particular, in the absence of a balanced budget, future generations will either benefit from the largesse of current clients or be taxed to pay for present profligacy.

There are some complications in the balanced budget rule and some exceptions. A number of nonprofits do not take depreciation as an expense, despite FASB rules. To the extent that real economic depreciation of buildings and equipment is occurring, a budget that ignores this depreciation will penalize future generations of users, who will have to pay for replacing those building assets. So, one complication to the balanced budget rule is that it should be implemented in the context of an organization that recognizes the real economic deterioration of its assets, and appropriately charges for that depreciation in its accounts. Surpluses from the operating budget can then be accumulated in the plant fund to replace plant and equipment.

The balanced budget rule must also be modified somewhat in the case of organizations which face large year-to-year fluctuations in their budgets.[7] In general, organizations would wish to budget for the average year, rather than swing wildly up and down as their fortunes ebb and flow. This averaging policy, however, is a complicated one. In 1985 Catholic Relief Services (CRS) received an enormous increase in donations in response to the Ethiopian relief problems. CRS recognized that the donation increase was a one-time phenomenon, and believed it would be more efficient to spread the new funds over several years. On the other hand, donors who thought they were responding to an immediate problem were outraged that the funds were not immediately spent. Again, there is a complicated set of issues involving the interests of donors, clients, and managers. In fact, Tuckman and Chang argue that two of the criteria which should be used to determine if a nonprofit is accumulating excessive equity is whether it has earned surpluses over four consecutive years and whether they are disproportionate to growth in programs.[8]

Nonprofit organizations should avoid large persistent surpluses or deficits.

In fact, recent studies suggest that the majority of large nonprofits earn surpluses regularly and thus see the real value of their equity grow over time.[9] Figure 9.2 provides some evidence on the extent of surpluses in a range of nonprofit fields. Tuckman and Chang have argued that nonprofit

Organization Type	Sample Size	Percentage With Positive Surplus	Average Dollar Value of Surplus
Churches	61	67	$1,054,173
Educational institutions	1239	91	$6,686,171
Health care institutions	2143	88	$3,266,982
Charitable institutions	663	74	$1,051,222
Supporting organizations	1673	81	$2,317,016
Omitted organizations	389	69	$2,827,412
Entire sample	6168	85	$3,441,389

Categories are defined in text. Averages include nonprofits with negative surpluses. The church category is included for comparative purposes, but see the text for caveats regarding its representativeness. Note, too, that the IRS sample has been shown to be biased in favor of the larger nonprofits [Hodgkinson and Weitzman, 1989].

Source: Tuckman, Howard and Cyril F. Chang, "Nonprofit Equity: A Behavioral Model and its Policy Implications," Journal of Policy Analysis and Management, Vol. 11, No. 1, p.78. (1992).

Figure 9.2. Surpluses of 501c(3) Charitable Nonprofits and of the Combined Sample, 1985 Taxable Year. *Source:* Tuckman, Howard and Cyril F. Chang, "Nonprofit Equity: A Behavioral Model and its Policy Implications," *Journal of Policy Analysis and Management*, vol. 11, No. 1, p. 78. (1992).

managers deliberately seek to increase the real value of the equity in their organizations to increase their own discretionary power.[10] By building equity, managers shield themselves from market pressures. At the same time, when this occurs, the current clients of the organization receive less service than is optimal.

Treatment of earnings from the endowment poses special problems in terms of balanced budget questions. Income from an endowment, whether realized or not, represents a real flow of resources that should generally be included in the budget as a program resource. Many nonprofits have adopted a total return/spending rate approach to their endowments. The spending rate, or amount recognized as revenue in the current year from the endowment is a fixed percentage (often 5%) of the average endowment principal, where that principal is measured as a 3–5-year average.[11] By using a 3–5-year average, the organization shields itself somewhat from large market fluctuations in the value of the endowment. Differences between the actual return on the endowment and spending from that endowment are used to maintain purchasing power of the endowment, given inflation over time.

The third principle of budgeting is that, wherever possible, the budget should be developed on a *program basis,* rather than a line-by-line basis. The importance of program budgeting in the public and nonprofit sectors was highlighted by work that emerged in the 1960s from the Department of Defense, in a concept called PPBS—the Planning, Programming, and Budgeting System. While PPBS has been at best imperfectly implemented as a formal system, and is not without its critics, the idea behind PPBS is quite sound. All budgets should begin with a planning system. Because planning is done at the program level, the budgets that support those plans must also be done at the program level. These program budgets, of course, can later be aggregated up to form functional line by line budgets. For organizations to really formulate strategy and understand what is driving their businesses, however, program budgets are an essential starting point.

Program budgets allow managers to plan and evaluate their programs.

Figure 9.3 presents examples of a line-item budget that is used by the small social service agency, the Waverly Community House, discussed in Chapter 5. This budget provides a good illustration of some of the deficiencies of line-by-line budgets. This agency runs programs in four areas—a children's program, an adult program, a program for the retarded, and an emergency food program—but the budget is constructed on a functional basis, without regard for any matching of costs and revenues by program area. We can see from this budget that the main revenue source for the Waverly Community House is the United Way. These revenues are not matched to programs. On the other hand, this organization also receives substantial contributions from user fees and grants that are tied to particular programs. In fact, more than 80% of the grants are generated in the

Revenues:	Estimated:
Contributions	10,000
Grants	204,459
Program Fees	54,200
Room rentals	19,289
Interest	500
United Way	155,706
Total revenue	444,154

Expenses:	
Salaries	337,416
Professional fees	2,820
Office and recreation supplies	25,300
Buildings and grounds	40,830
Transportation	31,788
Miscellaneous	6,000
Total expenses	444,154

Figure 9.3. Waverly Community House Line Budget.

programs for the mentally retarded, and the bulk of the program fees come from the children's program. The earned income, however, is attributed to the organization as a whole, not the individual program. Moreover, while the line-by-line budget indicates that salaries are the main expense category, we have no idea how those salaries are divided among the various programs. This budget cannot give us an answer to the question of how various programs are doing financially. Without this information, it is difficult to make a sound judgment about program expansion or contraction.

Why is it that nonprofits often avoid program budgets? In part, it may be because nonprofit managers until recently often did not have the management training needed to develop and use a budgeting system.[12] Program budgets are somewhat more complicated to construct than are line-by-line budgets. Herzlinger has argued that a lack of technical skills, coupled with an aversion to quantitative measurement, has led nonprofit managers to abdicate the budget process to the accountants, keeping the budget process from the management process.[13] There are, however, more important reasons as well that managers eschew program budgeting. A program budget invites controversial discussion about what programs should be expanded or contracted in ways that line-by-line budgets, precisely because they often obscure program level activities, do not. Program budgets reveal the extent of cross-subsidization across programs and this can create organizational tensions. Nevertheless, without program budgets, organizations will find it very difficult to make the kinds of management planning and control decisions essential for a successful nonprofit organization.

Program budgets often bring to light controversies across program areas.

The last principle for budget control flows directly from the program budget emphasis. Preparation of the budget should be pushed to the *lowest level possible* in the organization. Managers in charge of operations should also have budget responsibility. Of course, budget preparation by operational managers cannot go on in a vacuum. Senior management will normally provide program managers with budget guidelines: What kind of growth does senior management expect in input prices? What trends do they see in broad-based revenue sources? What program changes do they anticipate that will have organization-wide effects? Senior management also normally provides guidelines on the preparation of the budget itself. What kind of cost allocation rules will be followed? What are the categories? What format will be used? These guidelines are intended to provide some consistency across programs and allow senior management to make some comparisons. Beyond these guidelines, however, budget preparation should be *participatory* so that the people who are going to have to live with the budget are the ones who make it up in the first place. This process insures both better information in budget design and more compliance with the budget, once instituted.

Budgets should be built up from information provided by program managers.

The Problems of Inadequate Budget Control: Using Variance Analysis

Figure 9.4 presents two years of data on the budget of Prime School, the medium-sized private school discussed in earlier chapters. In this case, the budget presented is for the school as a whole. As with most nonprofit budgets, the revenue and expense categories used in the budget shown are tailored to the particular organization. Thus, tuition is a prime revenue category, while instructional expense (i.e., teachers' salaries and books), administration, scholarships, and operations are major cost categories. This school, like many others, does not take depreciation; instead, it makes some provision for future building maintenance and repair through its Prism account. (Provision for Plant Replacement).[14] The budget itself is done on an *accrual basis*, and Prime aims to run a balanced budget. Finally, this budget is organized more-or-less on a line-by-line basis, by functional category of revenues and expenses.

The primary feature of the two budgets presented that should strike the reader is that in both years reported, the school ran an unanticipated deficit. How should the managers or trustees of Prime interpret these deficits? Are they due to declining enrollments? Increased teacher costs? Lower fundraising? The managerial control technique of *Variance Analysis* is very helpful in sorting out the causes of deviations from budgets.

	1988–89		1989–90	
Revenues	**Actual**	**Budget**	**Actual**	**Budget**
Tuituin & Fees	$3,112,500	$3,037,500	$3,344,000	$3,240,000
Other Programs	175,000	150,000	189,000	155,000
Other Income	48,400	50,000	45,600	50,000
Total	**$3,335,900**	**$3,237,500**	**$3,578,600**	**$3,445,000**
Expenditures				
Instructional Expenditures	$1,624,000	$1,588,375	$1,745,130	$1,687,600
Other Programs	120,000	100,000	120,000	100,000
Student Activities	11,500	10,000	11,100	10,000
Operations and Maintenance	210,000	205,000	245,000	220,000
General Administrative	605,800	520,000	629,600	550,000
Employee Benefits	410,690	387,210	453,400	396,900
Development	48,000	40,000	61,000	50,000
Student Aid	310,000	300,000	350,000	342,000
Debt Service	30,000	30,000	28,000	28,000
Total	**$3,369,990**	**$3,180,585**	**$3,643,230**	**$3,384,500**
PRISM expenses	40,000	40,000	50,000	50,000
Total expenditures	$3,409,990	$3,220,585	$3,693,230	$3,434,500
Excess (Deficit) of Revenues over Expenses	($74,090)	$16,915	($114,630)	$10,500

Figure 9.4. Prime School Budget.

Variance analysis is a technique for understanding the sources of deviations from budget.

A *variance* is the difference between planned performance and actual performance. Column 1 of Figure 9.5 gives the variances for Prime school for 1990. It comes from subtracting actual performance from budget, line by line. Even this first step provides a rough-cut idea of where some of the problems may lie. For example, in the analysis here, there are very large expenditures variances in the administrative line and the benefits line, while tuition payments created large variances on the revenue side. To what can these be attributed?

In general, variances between actual and planned performance can be attributed to four factors: volume of business, mix of business, price, and efficiency.

Begin with the volume variance. If the actual amount of services provided by the organization differs from that in the budget, there will be differences in both the revenue and expenditure side of the budget. In Prime School, for example, the budget is voted on by the Board in January so that tuition levels can be set in time to make offers to prospective and returning children. This budget is thus predicated on some *forecasts* of prospective students. In the same way, a hospital budget is predicated on forecasts of patient volumes, the budget of the Cleveland Symphony Orchestra assumes some level of subscribers, and so on. Any mistakes that the managers and board make in these forecasts will have repercussions in several places in the budget. As a whole, they comprise the volume variance.

Volume variance is the difference between budget and actual revenues and expenses due to misforecast service levels.

Column 2 of Figure 9.5 shows the volume variance. In this case, the management underestimated the number of students who would attend the school. The revenue variance in this case is positive. In fact, while the board estimated it would have 405 students at $8,000 per student, it actually had enrollments of 418. Tuition revenues were thus $104,000 higher than they were budgeted to be as a consequence of the low forecasts for enrollment. Volumes for other programs run by the school—the summer camps and after-school program—were also underestimated. The higher than expected enrollment also had implications on the cost side. In this example, the school hired several new aides to help deal with the additional student flow. This increased both instructional expenses and benefits. There was also some modest increase in instructional supplies, which tend to vary with enrollments. The equivalent of one additional full scholarship was added to maintain the targeted scholarship proportions. For the most part, the rest of the cost categories in this school example do not vary with enrollment fluctuations of the type described here. The last row of column 2 sums up the effects of volume on the revenue and cost side. If the management of Prime had correctly forecast volumes, and done nothing

	Variance	Volume Variance	Price Variance	Efficiency Variance
Revenues				
Tuition	$104,000	$104,000	$0	$0
Other Programs	34,000	34,000	0	0
Other Income	(4,400)	0	(4,400)	0
Total	**$133,600**	**$138,000**	**($4,400)**	**0**
Expenditures				
Instructional Expenditures	$57,530	$40,000	$17,530	0
Other Programs	20,000	10,000	5,000	5,000
Student Activities	1,100	200	0	900
Operations and Maintenance	25,000	0	10,000	15,000
General Administrative	79,600	0	0	79,600
Benefits	56,500	8,000	48,500	0
Development	11,000	0	0	11,000
Student Aid	8,000	8,000	0	0
Debt Service	0	0	0	0
Total	**$258,730**	**$66,200**	**$81,030**	**$111,500**
PRISM	0	0	0	0
Total Variance	**($125,130)**	**+$71,800**	**($85,430)**	**($111,500)**

Figure 9.5. Variance Analysis: Prime School.

else different, the deficit would have been even larger than it was; indeed, it would be $71,800 larger. The mistakes made on the volume side in this case helped the school and should have led to large surpluses. Whatever management control problem there is at Prime appears even larger once we see the volume variance.

The second contributor to variance is the mix of services supplied. In the case of Prime, the enrollment consists of students in various grades, and tuition varies among the grades. In the Cleveland Orchestra case, tickets vary by price. Thus, even if the volume of services remains the same, the mix of services may contribute to a budget change. In practice, accounting for mix variances is often fairly complicated relative to its pay-off, and few nonprofits do much of this.[15] In this case, we will assume that the enrollment boom affected grades equally.

A second source of variance from budget is a change in the mix of business.

The third factor affecting the budget is variance in the price at which services are sold or inputs are bought. In the school example, had the management decided it needed to reduce tuition levels below that voted on by the board, this would have clearly had an effect on revenues, and should be accounted for by a price variance effect. In fact, such change is highly unlikely in the school example, and did not occur here. For other nonprofit organizations (e.g., hospitals) price variances are common, particularly as regulatory rules affecting reimbursements occur. For a symphony orchestra, experimentation with ticket prices will also be common. For all organizations, including the school described here, changes in interest rates will affect earnings from endowment and should be captured in a price variance. Changes in the prices of inputs will also be quite likely. For example, the budget of the school assumes teachers may be hired at particular salaries. The School Head may well find that some incremental salary increases are needed. These increases would fall under the category of price variance. Increases in health costs, utilities, and the like are captured in the price variance.

Price variance is the difference from budget associated with misforecasts of prices of inputs or outputs.

The price variance for Prime School is given in column 3 of the exhibit. We can see that price changes do help explain part of the unexpected budget deficit. Interest rates were lower than expected in 1990 and so earnings from other income were down. Teachers' salaries were slightly higher than expected and fringe costs—largely due to health insurance costs—were also considerably higher than forecasted. On net, $85,430 of the total budget variance comes from unexpected price changes. An obvious concern for the future is whether these costs will continue to rise at unusually high rates.

The fourth category of variance is the *efficiency variance*. The efficiency variance is a residual category, the difference between the results, and the budget not accounted for by the other three categories. This category is typically most under the control of management and most susceptible to change in the short term. In the case of Prime, most of the variance falls in the category of efficiency. In particular, all of the increases in administrative costs are categorized as efficiency-related. This should provide a clear signal to the management and to the board that a control problem exists and considerable attention should be paid to how to improve the situation in the future. When we look at how the Prime School budget was developed in the first place, we will learn more about just how this variance arose.

To understand more about the source of the variances at Prime, it is useful to review the budget process used. The board approves a budget in the January before the fiscal year begins in July. The budget itself is drawn up by the business manager, in consultation with the head of school, and the treasurer, a board member. Once the budget is set and tuition and salaries approved, the budget is then put aside until the next September when school is in full swing.

The first problem in the budget process should already be clear. The process itself is very top-down. The primary budget developer is not a program person at all, but the business manager. Given this, it is quite understandable that the budget itself is done on a line-by-line basis, because business managers are keyed to functional areas and not program areas. Divisional heads, even lower- and upper-school administrators, play no part in the budget process. Indeed, the school head is consulted only in a stop-gap way. If revenues are expected to be less than expenses, given moderate tuition increases, the head is asked to figure out where cuts should be made. As a consequence none of the program people, including the head, have "bought in" to the budget in a strong way. Under these conditions, it is difficult to encourage people to work hard to make sure the budget does indeed balance.

Difficulties also crop up for Prime School in the way the budget is used, once it is approved. Beginning in September, the board reviews the budget at regular intervals. The form they have historically used to examine the budget is one in common use in nonprofits, particularly the small ones. In particular, board members receive a sheet each month with the budget as voted and then, in an adjacent column, a budget labeled "Year to Date," in which are recorded the resources earned and those used up until that period. But using this format, it is typically very late in the year before the board realizes that the organization is going over budget. Many budget items do not occur on a regular basis, and so at any one point in time it is very difficult to extrapolate from the month to date figures to an annual figure. Of course, as the year progresses, a careful look at the year-to-date budget may well reveal some problems; for example, by March, some lines may already be overspent. But the system provides very few early warnings. In fact, in the case of Prime School, the board did not know it was running a deficit until spring, by which time it had already generated and voted on a new budget. The new budget, which took off from the prior year's budget as so many do, embodied many of the misforecasts of the earlier budget. Since the board had no idea its earlier budget had failed, it took no corrective action. Under these circumstances it is no surprise that problems should persist for several years. Failure to create a budget process that responds to the organization builds in rigidities and gives mistakes unnaturally long lives.

What alternative process might Prime School have used? As we have seen in the variance analysis, some of the mistakes in the early budget were well known by September. Enrollments were forecast to be too low, but this—with all of its revenue and expense implications—was known by midsummer. The unexpected increase in health costs and teachers' salaries were also known by summer. As soon as these structural defects with the budget become known, a revised budget should be prepared, reflecting the changes since the original budget was voted. This budget should reflect management's best judgment about where the organization will be the next June, if they follow the pricing and spending principles outlined by the Board in the context of the new structural conditions. The function of this revised budget is to provide an early warning system for both management and the board. With such early warning systems, the organization is often in a position to make some adjustments in either its revenue or costs. At the least, the organization can adjust in the next budget year.

Conclusions

This chapter has covered considerable ground. We have described the uses of a financial reporting and budgeting system in nonprofits and the way in which the systems are responsive to the varying constituencies of the organization. We have concentrated on developing a few simple principles of budgeting. In all of the discussion, however, we have focused on one central theme: The budgeting system and the financial reporting system are as fundamental to planning and control in a nonprofit as they are in a for-profit organization.

10

Program Evaluation

The nonprofit organization begins with a mission. We have spent considerable time in this book in discussing the way in which that mission is formulated and implemented, on the role of values, economics, organizational design, and accounting. The last task of a management system is to evaluate its programs to determine if those programs are being delivered effectively and serving the overall mission of the organization. This topic is the focus of this chapter.

Performance evaluation is a difficult task in any organization. Even with clear profit criteria and well-developed financial reporting systems, it is often hard to gauge performance on a program-by-program basis. Many organizations, both for-profit and nonprofit, treat units within the organization as profit-centers in evaluations.[1] Many costs, however, are shared across programs, making it difficult to allocate costs to come up with measures of profitability by program. Many programs are interdependent on the demand side as well. The success of a hospital's cardiac unit may depend in part on its reputation for care in other areas. A school's summer camp recruits students from the academic program. Separating out programs to gauge their individual contributions to the organization is a complex task.

It is also difficult to identify causes of program failure, even in for-profit firms with easily measured output. In 1991, General Motors had a very bad year, based on either conventional accounting measures or stock price changes. Was this poor performance the result of the U.S. recession? A result of slow-moving management? Or, a reflection of the loss of the United States' comparative advantage in making automobiles? There are clearly very different prescriptions associated with each of these diagnoses of G.M.'s recent poor performance. United Way's 1993 stagnation in contributions could be attributed to the scandal associated with its former head, the economic recession in the United States, or increased competition from other funds. Here, too, the solution depends critically on the diagnosis. A well-designed performance evaluation system should at least begin to help an organization make the right diagnosis.

For the nonprofit firm program evaluation has further complications. Profits are often difficult to measure and, even when measured, often provide an inadequate index of performance. The value of the output of the organization—since it is often not purchased on the marketplace—is ambiguous. Clients may value the service quite differently from either donors, the public, or the staff. In part because the nonprofit serves these varied constituents, the process of program evaluation will be inherently a political process. In this setting, program evaluation is inherently conflictual and subunits within the organization likely to advocate quite different measures of effectiveness.[2] Moreover, even when performance can be measured, the centrality of the mission of the nonprofit often prevents that organization from making the kinds of adjustments suggested by the program evaluation. Nevertheless, program evaluation plays a vital role in the nonprofit sector, in helping it to innovate and to adjust to changes in its environment. For the for-profit firm, the market will discipline organizations that run inefficient or valueless programs in relatively short order; in the nonprofit sector, the absence of a consumer focus and the amorphous quality of the product will often blunt the market discipline. As a result, internal evaluations will play an even more valuable role in program decisions.

> **Nonprofit program evaluation is complicated by the organization's multiple goals, multiple constituencies, and market insulation.**

Effectiveness Versus Efficiency: A Few Definitions

There are two tasks in evaluating the programs of an organization. One task involves an *operations analysis,* or management audit.[3] In this task, programs are taken as given and the analysis asks how efficiently the task is accomplished. For example, an operations audit of the job placement department at the Yale Management School asks questions like: How many interviews did you arrange per dollar spent?; How many students were counseled?; What is the placement rate?; and so on. In an operations analysis at a hospital, the number of operating procedures of a particular sort done per resources used would be collected. Indeed, the kind of data that are used to implement the Diagnostic Related Groups (DRG) reimbursement procedures used in the health care area would also be used in an operations analysis of that hospital. At the Boys and Girls Club, we might ask the number of recreation hours provided per dollar spent. The focus of an operations analysis is on the process or operations of management; the objectives of the unit being evaluated are taken as given.

> **Operations analysis takes objectives as given and focuses on the efficiency of accomplishing articulated goals.**

In addition to doing an operations analysis, most nonprofit organizations do periodic *program evaluations.* Program evaluations focus on the

results of operations, rather than on the process; they ask whether the objectives of the programs are appropriate and how well the organization is accomplishing those objectives. For example, the nonprofit hospital, in doing a program evaluation, might ask questions about the mix of patients it serves, the level of service given, and the mix of programs that it offers. The Boys and Girls Club might ask questions about how programs help children gain self-esteem and skills, rather than focusing on numbers of recreation hours provided.

Organizations should distinguish between operational analysis and performance evaluation.

In practice, the distinctions between operations analysis and program evaluation are not always so easily made. Because operations analysis uses more easily measured criteria, it is often used as a substitute for program evaluation. Drucker describes the problems created by this kind of confusion in his description of evaluation at a mental hospital:

> It may sound plausible to measure the effectiveness of a mental hospital by how well its beds are utilized. Yet a study of the mental hospitals of the Veteran's Administration brought out that this yardstick leads to mental patients being kept in the hospitals—which therapeutically is about the worst thing that can be done to them.[4]

In this case, a measure of operational efficiency—bed occupancy—has been substituted for more difficult-to-measure effectiveness criteria. When goals are vague, or long-term, the tendency to substitute operational measures for deeper evaluation is especially strong.[5]

For Whom Are We Evaluating Programs?

In the discussion thus far, program evaluation has been defined in terms of accomplishing the goals of an organization. Of course, it is clear that in nonprofit organizations, just as in for-profit organizations, the goals of the organization may not be so clear cut. Consider the typical urban museum. It has multiple constituencies: museum visitors, art donors, professional artists and critics, and even public-funding agencies. The urban public is typically quite interested in "blockbuster" exhibitions. Art critics and professionals prefer the select, esoteric show. Donors want their work displayed prominently and continually. Museums, however, lack space and customers want variety. When Thomas Krens, the director of New York's Guggenheim Museum, began a policy of expanding the space of the Guggenheim to show a larger portion of its collection, coupled with a de-acquisition program, there was considerable debate about the value of this program. Unlike the case of the publicly traded firm, where the stock market serves as the final arbiter of managerial decisions, judgments in the nonprofit world come slower and with less force. March and Olsen recognize the problem of vague, contradictory, multiple goals in the state university system by their description of the system as "organized anarchy."[6]

Program evaluation is complicated by the multiple constituencies of the typical nonprofit.

How is performance evaluation affected by the existence of multiple constituencies of the nonprofit? Recent political models of organizations suggest that performance criteria are chosen in part because those standards advance the interests of those in power in the organization.[7] Pfeffer, too, has argued that there are clear differences in the kinds of performance standards favored by the various stakeholders in an organization. Clients of the nonprofits are typically most interested in outcome measures; managers favor structural, operations measures; donors are typically most interested in financial measures of performance.

Perrow provides a fascinating case study of the importance of the dominance of different groups in setting performance standards in a hospital, looking at a broad span of its organizational history.[8] Perrow's central theme is that organizations tend to be controlled by those individuals or groups who perform the most difficult tasks in the organization. One of the ways this control is manifest is through the kinds of goals the organization sets for itself and the ways in which it measures success. Valley Hospital, a pseudonym, is a general hospital in the western United States studied by Perrow. It was organized in 1885 as a voluntary hospital under Jewish auspices. During the first several decades of its life, the hospital was dominated by its trustees; the clear performance standard during this period was contribution to community welfare, through provision of medical care, particularly for the poor. Beginning in the late 1920s, the medical staff came to dominate the hospital, as medical technology increased the importance of their skills. As a consequence of the change in control, the performance standards set for the hospital also changed to focus on medical research. By the mid-1940s, the hospital had changed again to come under the control of administrators. During this regime, the hospital saw a focus on efficiency, on measures of operational success. Finally, in the last period, the hospital emerged as an institution with multiple leaders, representing each of the major constituency groups. Along with the multiple leadership has come a hiatus in the planning efforts, a de-emphasis on performance evaluation, since, as Perrow points out, "planning could expose conflicting interests."[9]

A similar story about the role of conflicting interests in the health care area is told by Kanter and Summers.[10] In their study of Healthco, a multiunit health care organization that operates over fifty hospitals and nursing homes, Kanter and Summers found clear conflicts in the performance standards favored by trustees, doctors, and administrators. In their evaluation of Healthco, Kanter and Summers argue:

> Effectiveness becomes a key issue since it is also difficult to decide which areas in the organization are central to the mission and which require evaluation to determine strategic concerns, let alone which process of measurement is appropriate. (161)

We see in this discussion the renewed themes of "Who owns the mission?" that were discussed in Chapter 2. For Valley Hospital, Healthco and many

other organizations like them, working out a process by which program evaluation and planning can occur in the face of the conflicting interests of their constituents, is one of the challenges of management. Moreover, unless such conflicts are brought out in the open with evaluation and planning efforts, it will be very difficult for nonprofit organizations to adapt to their changing environments.

The Mechanics of Program Evaluation

Who does the evaluation? Program evaluation, inasmuch as it makes concrete the goals an organization sets for itself, is inherently a political process. How should this process be managed?

Anthony and Young, looking at the process from the perspective of management control, argue: "Human nature is such that it is unreasonable to expect an operating manager to conduct a review of his or her own activities."[11] Organizational theorists like Staw echo a similar theme as they describe "escalation" situations in which managers throw good money after bad in part because they are unable to evaluate dispassionately their own earlier efforts.[12] Organizations with strong ideologies and vague or hard-to-measure goals are particularly susceptible to escalation problems. These are, however, precisely the characteristics we associate with nonprofit organizations!

The role of outsiders is accentuated in nonprofit evaluations.

In most cases, then, program evaluations should be conducted by a person or group not associated with the unit being evaluated. Of course, input by current operating managers is vital in this process. In a well-functioning operation, evaluations are done in the context of goals set by the operating managers of programs in conjunction with senior management. Overall organizational evaluation should be done with reference to goals agreed on by the management and the trustees of the organization. Program managers should compile the required data need for evaluations, and they should lay out their views of the program goals and performance. The responsibility, however, for design of the evaluation process should be outside the hands of those managers.

For nonprofits, overall evaluation of the organization is often done with the help of outside accrediting institutions. The Joint Commission on Hospital Accreditation periodically evaluates hospitals and issues certificates without which hospitals cannot operate. For independent schools, the various state associations of independent schools run five or ten year evaluations that cover all aspects of school life. Many federally funded programs in the social service area require periodic review by outside agencies. Outside evaluations perform a function both for inside managers and for the outside constituents of the nonprofit. For inside managers, these evaluations are an opportunity to learn about what other similar nonprofit organizations are doing; they are also a prime vehicle for the diffusion of organi-

zational innovation in this sector. In addition, in the nonprofit sector, independent evaluations perform a control function carried out in the for-profit world by the consumer and the stock market. For the nonprofit, outside evaluations help protect both clients and donors, and for these constituencies the independence of the outside evaluators is critical.

Outside evaluations are especially helpful in nonprofits.

On what basis is the evaluation conducted? In looking at either the organization as a whole or a particular program within the organization, there are two broad types of methods that can be used: *statistical comparisons* and *subjective evaluation*. For most organizations, a mixture of techniques are used. It is important to keep in mind when designing the evaluation method both the multiple uses to which such evaluations are put— inside versus outside perspective—and the way in which such evaluations influence the various interests associated with the nonprofit organization.

Most evaluations done at either the program level or the organizational level begin with the collection of some *statistics*. Data are collected on the financial and program outcomes of the organization. In a hospital, we might ask: Is the hospital breaking even? How many patients are being served? How many beds are occupied? What are the ratios of medical personnel to patients? What is the ratio of pay to free patients? How much does the hospital raise in research grants?

Collecting the data, however, is only a first step in doing a statistical evaluation of an organization or one of its programs. We need some *yardstick* to use to help us interpret the statistics we have collected. Typical yardsticks include other similarly placed organizations or programs and comparisons of oneself over time. As we will see in the example which follows, neither yardstick is a perfect one.

Program evaluations use yardsticks to measure relative performance.

In many states, adoption and foster care placement are contracted out by states to various nonprofit agencies. In recent years, most states have emphasized the importance of placing children in adoptive homes if possible. Thus, in evaluating whether or not nonprofits are doing a good job in this arena, it might be reasonable to look at the adoption rate of the various agencies. For what adoption rate should the state aim? For legal reasons having to do with their family situations some children are not adoptable. Others may be very difficult to place in adoptive homes. What standard of placement should the state use as a criteria for success?

One possibility in this situation is to compare nonprofit organizations against each other as a way of measuring performance. Indeed, one of the advantages of the large number of different organizations competing within various nonprofit sectors is that this variety can be used to help judge performance. Comparisons are only possible, however, if the competing organizations face comparable initial conditions. In the example of the child care organizations, it might well be the case that these agencies re-

ceive a different mix of children to start with. Thus, one would expect different adoption rates at the various agencies even if they were otherwise identical. Agencies that have an older mix of children, or more children with handicaps, would be expected to generate fewer adoptions than agencies with a more easily placed group of children. To make useful comparisons across agencies, we need to be able to control for these demographic differences in the agency inputs.

Another example of the comparability problem comes from the medical care area. Under current federal law, hospitals are reimbursed for their Medicare and Medicaid patients under a formula based on the expected costs of caring for patients suffering from particular disorders. This method, the DRG system, is an attempt to impose some efficiency on the medical care system by reimbursing hospitals not on the basis of their own costs of treatment but on the basis of costs of treatment of the most efficient hospital in their geographic area. Applying such a system can be thought of as tantamount to imposing a performance evaluation scheme using hospitals as yardsticks for one another. The difference is that this evaluation scheme has revenues attached to it. But some of the same problems we saw in the child care situation also crop up in the implementation of DRGs. Repairing an appendectomy in an indigent woman of seventy requires considerably more resources than curing a similar problem in a well-to-do twenty year old. Moreover, hospitals have very different economic and demographic profiles of patients, depending in part on where they are located, as well as on their overall mission. A useful performance evaluation system should take these differences in initial conditions into account before proceeding with the comparison.

The use of other organizations as yardsticks requires similar initial conditions for the competing organizations.

In both of the examples just given, the evaluation of the organization was done by a funding unit. For cross-organizational comparisons, outside evaluators who are either funders or accrediting agents are invaluable, because they typically bring information about the practice and performance of other similar organizations with them.

An alternative yardstick to use in applying statistical measures to an organizational or program evaluation is to look across time at the organization or program being evaluated. Here, too, there are comparability questions. The National Resources Defense Council (NRDC) is a large, environmental litigation nonprofit organization. In the last few years, its membership has grown dramatically, as has its revenues. Thus, on some measure, its program has become more successful over time. At least a part of the reason for this growth, however, reflects an exogenous increased interest in environmental problems by the public. Indeed, most of the U.S. environmental groups have grown over the period. To evaluate the NRDC, we would need to account for these exogenous effects as well.

For most nonprofit organizations, with their ill-defined output and financial performance measures, a statistical evaluation of either the organization or programs within the organization tells only part of the story. Nevertheless, some measures of objective, output based information are extraordinarily helpful in managing nonprofits. Kanter and Summers in their description of the planning problems at Healthco tie this back into their description of the politics of nonprofit life:

> The existence of ambiguous operating objectives creates opportunities for internal politics and goal displacement, for loose coupling between official and stated mission and operative goals. Because objectives are stated vaguely and planning concentrates on resource acquisition, managers inside the organization gain considerable leeway in their activities, opening up the possibility for political maneuvering for ignoring the needs of clients while trying to please powerful donors.[13]

In the previously given examples, it was possible to articulate at least some of the goals of the program in quantifiable form and to find some yardstick against which to measure performance. The nature of nonprofit production, however, suggests that it will be the rare nonprofit that can be evaluated strictly on quantifiable measures. Therefore, for virtually all evaluations, some subjective element will be required. One of the central questions in a program evaluation is: How well does the program serve the overall mission of the organization? The answer to this question will inevitably be partially subjective. An evaluation of a hospital must somehow take into account the quality of the care given, and the nature of the teaching and research done. An evaluation of a child care agency must contain some subjective judgment about how well the overall interests of the children are being served. Here the importance of outsiders cannot be over emphasized. When performance measures are amorphous, it becomes increasingly important for nonprofits to use outsiders to lend credibility to their operations from the perspective of both donors and clients. Moreover, as we suggested earlier, with amorphous goals, it is more likely that management will pursue programs that have high strategic value for them, but little value for anyone else. For the same reasons, the evaluation team should have well-recognized expertise, for it is their credentials and not their data that will have to convince both current management and outsiders of the truth of their evaluations.

Concluding Thoughts on Performance Evaluations

In an ideal world, conducting an evaluation of a program or an organization should be relatively straightforward. Before the program begins, management sets out clear goals for the program. Everyone agrees on those goals and shares them. The goals themselves are easily quantifiable, and, as the program progresses, data are kept on the performance of the program. Evaluations are done dispassionately, by knowledgeable people with no stake in the program, using data from comparable programs at other organizations.

In fact, in the nonprofit sector, there are deviations from this ideal in almost all dimensions. While programs often do begin with an articulation of goals, the goals themselves are typically rather diffuse, not easily quantified, and not always shared by all of the constituents of the nonprofit. Data systems, in the typical nonprofit, often fail to provide management with meaningful information that could be used in performance reviews.[14] Comparable programs are hard to identify and, even if identified, often fail to have adequate data themselves. Many of these problems come directly from the nature of the nonprofit business. Goals are by their nature less easily quantified in this sector. We cannot rely on the market to provide us with values for the goods and services the sector produces. Ownership in the organization is more widely shared among donors, clients, and management. Comparable organizations are difficult to find. Despite these problems, evaluation is central to the continued ability of nonprofits to innovate, adapt, and use their scarce resources well in serving their missions.

11

The Potential for Change

The last ten chapters of this book have discussed a wide range of issues affecting nonprofit organizations: setting a mission, determining the industry structure, managing human resources, fundraising, and financial management. In this last chapter we turn to the issue of organizational change: How adaptive are nonprofit organizations? What are the pressures for change for nonprofits? What determines how successful change will be?

The Adaptability of the Nonprofit

Over time, there have been considerable changes in the economic landscape, changes in the kinds of goods and services produced, how they are produced, and where they are produced. In the nonprofit sector, as well, there have been substantial changes. In the last thirty years, the share of resources going to the arts and the environment in the United States has increased substantially, while those going to human services have declined.[1] Similar changes have been documented among Norwegian nonprofits where organizations devoted to the arts and language have increased in prominence at the expense of missionary, teetotalling, and humanitarian organizations.[2] The nonprofit sector, like the for-profit sector, has become more international. In addition, the use of more businesslike management techniques in the sector has increased.[3]

How much of the change we observe in the structure of economic activity comes from adaptation by older organizations, and how much results from the death of older organizations and the birth of new, different firms? In recent years, there has been considerable research on this question, stimulated in large measure by new work in population ecology. This work has particular relevance for the study of nonprofits.

Population ecologists argue that most organizations are relatively passive, with only modest capacity for change. Thus, change occurs principally as a result of one form of organization replacing another, rather than through radical restructuring of existing organizations.[4] Inertia within organizations comes from physical characteristics of the organization—fixed capital equipment, for example—and from organizational characteristics— the structure of the hierarchy, compensation rules, and the like. Rules of thumb, which economize on decision-making time under normal operations, further contribute to rigidity.[5] External forces—the existence of regulatory, supervisory units, for example—may contribute as well to structural inertia. Under these conditions, when the environment changes—customer needs or donor preferences change, for example—individual organizations that are no longer suited to that new environment die and other organizations, more well-matched to the new environment, grow up.

Of course, the role of population change versus individual organizational change varies across areas. Hannen and Freeman, however, identify four conditions that increase the inertia in an organization, conditions that are often present in the nonprofit world.[6] One of the major sources of inertia is the pressure for accountability. These pressures are especially acute when organizations produce symbolic or hard-to-evaluate services or goods, when risk exists, when the relationship between the organization and either its staff or clients is long-lived, and when the organization is political. These characteristics, however, often adhere in the nonprofit world. Under these conditions, organizations will cling to routines, even when they lose their survival value. The professionalism of the sector may also reduce adaptability to change as the canons of the profession create, in Dimaggio and Powell's terms, an "iron cage" from which it is difficult to escape.[7]

There is some evidence that organizational turnover is relatively high in the nonprofit sector, supporting the view that most change comes from the population, not from the individual organism. In Table 11.1, I have calculated the rate of founding and extinctions among U.S. nonprofits, over the two-year period, 1987–1989, in a variety of areas, based on I.R.S. data.[8]

Table 11.1.   Openings and Closings of Nonprofit Organizations, 1987–1989

Organization	Growth in Number of Organizations	Percentage of 1987 Organizations Closed by 1989	Percentage of 1989 Organizations Less Than 2 Years Old
Human Services	27.2	7.7	26.7
International and Foreign Affairs	58.2	9.6	41.9
Civil Rights	19.9	13.1	27.6
Community Improvement	27.3	10.0	30.1
Foundations	8.3	11.1	17.9
Science	19.4	11.0	25.4
Religious	24.9	6.2	24.9
Environmental	32.8	10.5	32.6
Educational	18.5	9.1	23.3
Arts	16.9	9.7	22.8

Table 11.2. Founding and Extinction Rates of
Voluntary Organizations, 1980–1988, Norway

Organization Type	Percentage	Percentage
Economic	15.2	4.2
Political	9.9	12.3
Sports	16.0	10.5
Language	34.9	17.2
Teetotal	6.9	20.8
Missionary	6.2	11.7
Youth/children	17.9	17.9
Song/music/theater	29.6	26.2
Humanitarian/social	10.8	10.2
Culture/leisure	43.7	11.8
Total	18.3	13.8
Women	4.1	14.9
Youth/children	20.1	20.2
Christian	9.4	15.4

Source: Per Selle, Bjorne Oymyr, *Nonprofit and Voluntary Sector Quarterly,* Summer 1992, p. 154

Note: Four municipalities are excluded.

Among civil rights organizations, for example, 13.1% of the organizations alive in 1987 had ceased to exist by 1989; of the civil rights organizations alive in 1989, 27.6% were founded in the prior two years. Indeed, in most of the sectors one-quarter or more of the 1989 organizations were founded since 1987 and 8–10% of the organizations alive in 1987 had died two years later. These data are roughly comparable to those collected for Norwegian nonprofits, given in Table 11.2. Also in this sample, both founding and extinction rates are quite high.

Data that reveal high organizational turnover, like that in Tables 11.1 and 11.2, are often used to support the premise of population ecologists that most change occurs through the birth and death of organizations. The data also suggest, however, the turbulent pressures for change in the sector. Nonprofit organizations—particularly small ones—are typically run with very little organizational or financial slack. These organizations are very vulnerable to even relatively small changes in their environments. For many nonprofits, environmental changes are growing more profound. For these organizations, change—however difficult it may be—may well be critical to survival. The next section of this chapter explores the sources of pressure for change among nonprofits.

Sources of Change

The literature identifies three major sources of change for organizations: internal pressures, resource pressures, and mimetic forces. All three appear to play a role in the nonprofit sector.

As organizations grow, tensions often arise that can induce change. Churchill and Lewis[9] argue that most firms pass through five stages of growth, stages that are distinguished by different roles for the founder-entrepreneur, for the formal reporting and evaluation system, and for the management style of the organization. Growth in size and maturity acting together, even in the absence of either external change or internal initiative, induce change in an organization.

One example of internally generated change in the for-profit world is described by Chandler.[10] Chandler traces the evolution of the multidivisional organizational structure as a response to the growth of the diversified corporation. Size and internal complexity required a structural change in the way business was conducted and led firms to abandon functional structures in favor of more adaptive multidivisional firms. In Chandler's historical description, the major source of change was adaptation by existing firms, rather than by population change, and the source of that change was the internal pressure of growth.

We see similar internal pressures in the nonprofit world. The early life of many nonprofit organizations is dominated by the mission. At this point, nonprofits typically worry little about waste or inefficiency; instead, they concentrate on the "demand" side of the business, selling the mission to clients and donors. As the organization matures, and particularly if it grows, bureaucratization follows and cost considerations often become more salient. In part because cost considerations grow in importance, the role of professional staff typically increases as well, as does the political power of this group. Perrow's fascinating classic study of the evolution of a Western nonprofit hospital is an excellent example of the changes in the internal political landscape as a nonprofit grows.[11] Valley hospital's early life was dominated by trustees; as it matured, first the medical staff and then the professional staff came to dominate the decision-making process.

A second example of the power of internally generated forces is Jenkins' study of organizational change in the National Council of Churches (NCC) in the 1960s.[12] During the 1960s the NCC became increasingly active, in particular in its support of the Farm Workers Union. Jenkins argues that the radicalization of the agency resulted from internal forces—changes in training of the clergy, growth in the size of the organization, and consequent power of the staff. In this case, too, internal pressure changed the organization itself.

Organizational growth creates pressures for change.

There are other, potentially more important sources of change as well. Internal change comes in part because of the exigencies of the external world. In particular, organizations change in part because it is no longer profitable to continue doing business the same way. Organizational theorists have labeled this the *resource dependence theory*,[13] and there have been a number of studies of nonprofit organizations indicating the power of external resources to force change.[14] For nonprofits that often have limited

reserve funds, current conditions in the environment that affect either the ability to sell goods and services or the ability to raise funds can create enormous changes. Resource scarcity can cause changes in the board of trustees, programmatic changes, and large-scale staff changes. In this area, the responsiveness of an organization may depend less on whether it is a nonprofit or a for-profit than on its size and its financial reserves. Small, lean organizations in any sector must be able to adapt or they will not survive.

For the nonprofit organization, the major external sources of change are three: economic, social, including demographics and political. An excellent example of the role of external economic changes in stimulating organizational change comes from the adoption of "donor choice" by many United Ways across the United States. United Ways have traditionally operated as monopoly workplace solicitors, focused on the manufacturing sector. In 1990 in Connecticut, for example, 85% of United Way giving came from the manufacturing sector, despite the fact that manufacturing accounted for only 52% of the state payroll. The importance of manufacturing in the U.S. economy, however, has been declining over time. Moreover, competition in workplace solicitation has also increased over time. In 1983 nontraditional local funds raised only $2 million in payroll deductions; by 1990 this figure had increased fivefold.[15] This dual pressure, from a decline in its focus sector and increased competition, led many United Ways in the early 1990s to give donors for the first time a choice about which organizations their dollars would support. Here outside pressure induced radical change.

An interesting example of the importance of external demographic changes in stimulating innovation is provided by the adoption of a classical jazz program by Lincoln Center in New York City. Lincoln Center, Inc., represents ten constituent organizations, including the Metropolitan Opera, the New York Philharmonic, the New York City Ballet, and Lincoln Center Theater. These organizations are among the most well-known cultural organizations in the United States, and like most organizations in this area, depend heavily on earned income, through ticket sales, for revenues. For Lincoln Center, approximately one third of revenues come from ticket sales. Many of these ticket sales are to local audiences; in the case of Lincoln Center, approximately one half of the audience comes from New York City. The match between Lincoln Center's programs and New York's demographic profile, however, has been deteriorating. Two thirds of the Lincoln Center population comes from those aged forty-five and up. Only 45 percent of the New York population is in this age group, and the fraction of people in this group is shrinking as older people leave the city. Moreover, Lincoln Center's population is predominantly white, while New York City has become increasingly multiethnic. One response Lincoln Center has taken to this environmental change has been to add classical jazz to its repertoire, a program more in line with New York City's demographic profile. Here, again, we see an old organization adapting to change.

Environmental pressures often induce organizational change.

Of course, environmental changes also create opportunities for new nonprofit organizations to emerge. Habitat for Humanity, for example, is a small nonprofit established in 1976 that builds, rehabilitates and repairs homes for people in need, using volunteer labor and funds. In some ways, this organization is taking over the kinds of building efforts once run through the large federal Housing and Urban Development bureaucracy. In this instance, changes in the public sector created an opportunity for a new nonprofit. Growth in public interest in environmental issues has led to both change and expansion in existing environmental nonprofits and growth of new nonprofits.

Dimaggio and Powell have argued that much change can also be explained as a result of imitation pressures, or what they call *institutional isomorphism*.[16] In many sectors, fieldwide norms develop governing the way organizations should be structured and the way business should be carried on. To retain legitimacy, with clients, donors and regulatory agencies, conformity with those norms is important. In the educational field, many changes like increases in the multicultural curriculum, whole-language reading programs, and the use of manipulatives in mathematics appear to be driven by professional norms, rather than either life-cycle changes or resource pressures.

Institutional norms create pressures for conformity within sectors.

The heightened professionalism of the nonprofit sector, and the importance of reputation in the field, both increase the pressures for conformity.

Experiencing Change

Thus far, we have seen that nonprofits face considerable pressure to change and may be simultaneously more resistant to those pressures. In this section, we examine the evidence on when organizational change is most likely.

Zald's study of the Young Men's Christian Association (YMCA) in the United States is a classic study of a successful organizational change.[17] The YMCA began as an evangelical organization, to provide Christian fellowship to young men. As early as the late 1800s, however, the New York association adopted a model of general service to young men and by 1889 the national committee had abandoned evangelism as a goal. This change came in part from resource pressures. The original church funding of the YMCA was fragile and moves to replace that funding with income-earning opportunities like hostels demanded a wider potential client base. The emphasis on democratic decision making at the Ys and the federated structure were also instrumental in creating change.

The role of the federated or franchise structure in promoting organizational change is especially interesting.[18] Many nonprofits operate as semi-

autonomous units with a national headquarters. This structure, which I have called the "nonprofit franchise," allows nonprofits to share in the benefits of a national reputation while exploiting the advantages of local control. Through local control, nonprofits will find it easier to attract local volunteers and, in many cases, local capital. This local autonomy also provides national laboratories for experimentation. At the same time, the protection of the national unit may shield nonprofits from changes too far from the original mission. When a local United Way introduces donor choice, for example, it is serving as an experimental laboratory for United Ways across the country. In the Zald study, the New York YMCA was a laboratory for the rest of the system as it rejected evangelism. Franchise systems are particularly suitable vehicles for organizational change.

Local autonomy within a national system encourages successful organizational change.

A second study of the structure of organizational change comes from the health care area. Recent federal legislation has removed many of the key advantages of nonprofit status for health maintenance organizations (HMOs). With these changes, for-profit HMOs typically outperform the nonprofits.[19] Under these conditions, one might well expect some conversion of nonprofits to for-profit status. Ginsberg and Bucholotz find that the speed of response to this change by nonprofits is highly variable.[20] Older nonprofits and nonprofits in tightly coupled groups convert more slowly than do younger, more autonomous organizations. For these organizations, there is typically more organizational and economic capital invested in the older form. Nonprofits located in states with high concentrations of for-profit HMOs are also more likely to change, supporting the institutional isomorphism model. It is interesting that the size of the HMO has no effect on its propensity to convert.

The propensity to change decreases with age, and membership in a tight network. Exposure to other organizations increases the propensity to change.

Concluding Thoughts

Nonprofit management is in a particularly exciting time. Managers are faced every day with challenges involving whether to compete or cooperate with other organizations in their markets, how to motivate and control a highly professional, ideological workforce, and how to adapt to changing environments without abandoning the organization's history. In facing these challenges, nonprofits are increasingly turning to models from the for-profit and public sector, but the task of adapting those lessons to the nonprofit sector is just beginning.

APPENDIX

Guide to the Cases

The cases contained in this book cover a variety of nonprofit organizations. The cases are, for the most part, comprehensive and can be used to illustrate a range of management issues. In this guide, however, I have noted particularly close chapter–case connections. Teaching notes are available from the author for all of the cases.

People for the American Way

People for the American Way is a political educational and lobbying organization founded in 1980. Since its founding, the organization has grappled with a changing environment, and a changing focus. The case illustrates some of the issues involved with nonprofit start-ups, evolution in organizations and the mission. It is thus very useful in a nonprofit management class and fits especially well with Chapters 1 and 2. The case can also be used later in the course to deal with fundraising issues in conjunction with Chapter 8.

United Hmong Association

This case involves small-scale development in the context of Hmong refugees. The case is focused around three alternative proposals to improve the economic situation of the Hmong, in Providence, Rhode Island. There is sufficient information in the case to allow students to do a structural analysis of the three proposals. The Hmong case works quite well in conjunction with Chapters 3 and 7, and allows students to examine economic viability and fit with mission from a program perspective.

Public Broadcasting System

PBS is a nonprofit cooperative consisting of public television stations across the nation. This case centers on the role of PBS in an environment made increasingly competitive by the growth of cable. The case asks students to ponder the role of PBS in the new environment. How competitive should PBS be vis-à-vis the commercial networks? Are cooperative ventures a good idea? Is PBS obsolete? The case also examines the relationship between national PBS headquarters and its member stations. This case works quite well with either Chapter 4, 7, or 11.

American Red Cross

The American Red Cross is a large, well-established national nonprofit, with local operations throughout the country. It is heavily dependent on volunteers, and this case focuses on the problems of attracting and motivating those volunteers. It thus works particularly well used in parallel with Chapters 5 and 6. The case takes a close look at one local Red Cross Chapter, located in an urban Northeastern city.

Good Faith Fund

The Good Faith Fund is a small organization in rural Arkansas that uses lending to try to stimulate local entrepreneurs and aid in grass-roots economic development. The case can be used in many areas, as an illustration of the concerns in a start-up, the development of a mission, or human resource management.

Classical Jazz at Lincoln Center

Lincoln Center houses some of the finest performing arts companies in the world. In 1990, the organization explored the possibility of adding a new independent arts organization to their group, classical jazz. This case considers the economics and politics of this decision. It fits in extremely well in conjunction with Chapter 7 of this book, and can also be used earlier to illustrate mission change in Chapter 2.

The Future of Donor Choice at United Way

One of the central issues in nonprofit management in the 1990s is the role of competition versus cooperation. The United Way case focuses on the balance in the context of fundraising, and thus works well when used with Chapter 8. It looks closely at a recent innovation in United Way, donor choice, as a competitive response to other organizations moving into workplace solicitation. The instructor should be prepared to probe alternative solutions to the "problem" of competition as well as to think about the merits of competition in this section.

Guggenheim Museum

Thomas Krens, the director of the Guggenheim Museum, is one of the most controversial museum heads in the United States. This case looks at his vision for the museum, an aggressive expansionary plan. Detailed data on the accounting statements of the Guggenheim and its competitors, as well as information on financing are provided. This case can be used either to examine competition (in Chapter 4) or to understand accounting information in line with Chapter 9.

Leeway, Inc.

Leeway, Inc., is a proposed hospital for AIDS patients. The case takes the reader from the early ideas for the hospital through the development of a business plan. It emphasizes the role of change in the nonprofit and the importance of flexibility. The case works well either as a last case, in conjunction with Chapter 11, or as an early case, with Chapter 2, 5, or 6.

Nonprofit Cases

Case	Most Relevant Chapters
People for the American Way	1, 2, 8
United Hmong Association	3, 7
Public Broadcasting Systems	4, 7
American Red Cross	5, 6
Good Faith Fund	2, 5, 6, 11
Classical Jazz at Lincoln Center	2, 7
United Way	8
Guggenheim Museum	4, 9
Leeway, Inc.	2, 5, 6, 11

CASE A

People for the American Way

Art Kropp, president, stared blankly at the wall in his office, pondering the grim results of People for the American Way's (PEOPLE FOR) latest focus group study.[1] The organization had conducted many focus groups over the years, but the responses had never been so negative. Reluctantly, Art picked up the report and reread the consultant's conclusion:

> The clearest—and most problematic—findings relate to the organizational profile of People for the American Way when compared to those of ACLU, Common Cause, and other organizations. PEOPLE FOR faces a trio of very tough issues—low name recognition, a diffuse sense of PEOPLE FOR's mission, even among those who have heard of the group, and outright hostility on the part of many potential donors to the organization's name.

How different things seemed from when Art first joined the organization back in 1984 as director of membership. At that time, PEOPLE FOR had gained national recognition by challenging the political agendas of religious right and fundamentalist extremists. Through advertisements, editorials, and lobbying, PEOPLE FOR presented itself as the "majoritarian" voice of tolerance and pluralism, inviting the public into a debate that the organization considered to be increasingly dominated by powerful and well-funded extremists.

The public reacted positively and between 1984 and 1986—PEOPLE FOR attracted some 175,000 additional members and more than doubled its annual budget to $9.2 million. Now, just four years later, the public seemed confused about PEOPLE FOR's purpose and unconcerned with its "urgent" issues. Art attributed this confusion in part to external factors:

> PEOPLE FOR is perceived as the organization of the 1980s . . . there to respond to Ronald Reagan's conservative agenda and to the religious right. Now, the "kinder and gentler" Bush administration appears less threatening to our members . . . other issues like the environment, education, and abortion are dominating political agendas, replacing issues concerning democratic values. And the fall of Jim Bakker, Jimmy Swaggart, and company has made our role less clear.

Between 1987 and 1989, PEOPLE FOR became involved in a wider array of issues, intensified lobbying and communication efforts, and relied more heavily on marketing research—focus groups, telephone surveys, polling—and consultants as a means of boosting membership interest in the organization. The results of these efforts, however, were disappointing, as the latest focus group study revealed. By January 1990, the estimated budget dropped to $7.3 million and the number of active members declined by 33%. Internal pressure was building for PEOPLE FOR to make some changes, but just what those changes should be and

[1]Sherry Mandelbaum and Mary Freeborn Standley prepared this case under the direction of Professor Sharon Oster as the basis for class discussion rather than to illustrate either effective or ineffective handling of a management situation.

how the organization should meet them was a source of contention within PEOPLE FOR. A consultant had already been commissioned to re-evaluate PEOPLE FOR's mission. Art knew PEOPLE FOR had an identity problem but was unsure whether the problem lay with the mission, with the organization's strategy, or with external, uncontrollable factors. Whatever the problem, it was time to figure out what issues the organization would pursue and how the organization was to survive in the 1990s.

Background

People for the American Way was founded in 1980 by television producer/writer Norman Lear and a group of national religious, educational, labor, and business leaders who felt that a growing number of political and religious extremists were threatening the very essence of American democracy: tolerance, diversity and the free exchange of ideas. Lear and his supporters believed that many of these "extremists," such as televangelists Jerry Falwell, Jimmy Swaggart, Pat Robertson, and Nation of Islam leader Louis Farrakhan, were defining the "American Way" through their religious framework, labeling those who maintained different religious and political beliefs as ungodly, immoral, or unAmerican. Furthermore, these figures had gained support from a national television audience and received millions of dollars through over-the-air fundraising efforts, wielding them considerable power in the political arena. Lear feared that the increasing political tone of the religious rights' agenda would be well received by Ronald Reagan and his conservative administration. So he founded an organization to protect Americans' individual freedoms and named it People for the American Way as a reminder that the "American way" includes the "traditions of liberty, justice, tolerance, and pluralism." (see Fig. A.1 for Statement of Purpose). During the first five years, the organization implemented its mission by focusing on the power of the Far Right in three primary areas: the separation between church and state, the education system, and the judiciary.

Church and State

PEOPLE FOR sought to uphold the separation of church and state by calling attention to Far Right leaders and political extremists who publicized "Christian" positions on a number of political issues and who denounced people who held positions different from their own as "immoral," "unbiblical," and "unChristian." PEOPLE FOR described this intolerance in the political process as "Moral McCarthyism," and attempted to expose its existence by publicizing instances of "religious bigotry," including:

- The increasing use of religious tests for public office.
- The existence of the voting scorecard published by the Christian Voice that rated candidate's positions on "key moral and family issues."
- A legislative amendment that mandated school prayer in public schools.

PEOPLE FOR initiated a public education campaign to "defend religious liberty" and to stir up support for creating guidelines for the "appropriate" mix of religion and politics. In addition, the organization became a watchdog, taping televangelist shows, subscribing to their literature, and monitoring their public and political

Figure A.1   Statement of Purpose

In times of hardship, in times of crises, societies throughout history have experienced wrenching dislocations in their fundamental values and beliefs. The decades of the 1980s and 1990s will be troubled times—some predict the most turbulent since the 1930s—and we are alarmed that some current voices of stridency and division may replace those of reason and unity. If these voices continue unchallenged, the results will be predictable; an increase in tension among races, classes and religions, a rise in "demonology" and hostility, a breakdown in community and social spirit, a deterioration of free and open dialogue, and the temptation to grasp at simplistic solutions for complex problems.

PEOPLE FOR THE AMERICAN WAY was established to address these matters. Our purpose is to meet the challenges of discord and fragmentation with an affirmation of "the American Way." By this we mean pluralism, individuality, freedom of thought, expression, and religion, a sense of community, and tolerance and compassion for others. We stand for values and principles, not for single issues, chosen candidates, or partisan causes.

PEOPLE FOR THE AMERICAN WAY will reach out to all Americans and affirm that in our society, the individual still matters; that there is reason to believe in the future—not to despair of it—and we must strengthen the common cords that connect us as humans and as citizens.

The long agenda of PEOPLE FOR THE AMERICAN WAY is broad. It includes reducing social tension and polarization, encouraging community participation, fostering understanding among different segments of our society, and increasing the level and quality of public dialogue.

Yet, we cannot address everything at once. So, we are confronting first what we believe to be the greatest immediate threat to our pluralistic society: the growing power of the Religious New Right.

This new movement—as documented by the statements of some leaders of the Religious New Right—would impose on the public debate a rigid and absolutist set of positions on what is and is not "Christian," implying that there is only one Christian position on any given political issue. We support the right of the religious community to speak out on social and political issues. However, religious leaders overwhelmingly contend—and we also believe—that "it is arrogant and destructive to assert that one set of political questions is Christian, and endorsed by God, and that all others are un-Christian."[1]

As an education institution, we shall communicate with the American people through printed materials, radio, television, public lectures, and discussions. We will gather information, analyze it, and distribute our findings to the public in a manner that provides for full and fair exposition of the issues.

Our highest purpose is to nurture a national climate that encourages and enhances the human spirit rather than one that divides people into hostile camps. By educating the American people and raising their level of understanding about the basic tenets by which our society is sustained, PEOPLE FOR THE AMERICAN WAY will fulfill its mission.

---

[1] Statement of the Washington Inter-religious Staff Council.

appearances. As a result, the organization developed an extensive library that contained examples of religious right bigotry.

Freedom to Learn

In keeping with their dedication to upholding individual liberties, PEOPLE FOR challenged the Far Right's attempts to censor educational materials in public school classrooms across the country. Considering such attacks on education as "limiting the open exchange of ideas," PEOPLE FOR became actively involved in publicizing attempts to ban such works as *The Adventures of Huckleberry Finn*, *To Kill a Mockingbird*, and *Of Mice and Men*. The organization chronicled attempts at censorship through its annual national report, entitled "Attacks on the Freedom to Learn," and developed a handbook to help communities organize against book-banning campaigns. PEOPLE FOR also became immersed in the battle against fundamentalist Christian attempts to have creation theory written in biology textbooks. The organization pressured the largest textbook publishers to address the absence of "controversial" subjects in public school textbooks across the country, such as the role of religion in American history and the discussion of evolution science in biology textbooks. PEOPLE FOR chalked up significant victories in promoting quality education and intellectual freedom in schools. In 1987, PEOPLE FOR's legal department was instrumental in winning two Supreme court cases that thwarted censorship attempts in public school systems and effectively neutralized the fundamentalists' threat.

Independent Judiciary

PEOPLE FOR sought to protect equal justice under the law by promoting an independent judiciary. PEOPLE FOR believed that judicial appointments made by the Reagan administration were based on ideology instead of competency and therefore undermined the independence of the federal judiciary. PEOPLE FOR lobbied heavily on Capitol Hill, arguing that judicial nominees should be evaluated according to their qualifications, not their religious and political beliefs. Through its efforts, PEOPLE FOR:

- Exposed the use of ideological "litmus" testing of potential nominees.
- Helped defeat the nomination of Daniel Sessions and came within one vote of defeating Daniel Manion.
- Led the campaign to defeat Judge Robert Bork's nomination to the Supreme Court. This campaign alone brought in 30,000 new members to PEOPLE FOR.

Tactics in the 1980s

By 1987, the organization had racked up substantial victories on Capitol Hill, in the courts, and in local communities across the country. The organization boasted 264,000 members and a $9.7 million budget (see Figs. A.2, A.3, and A.3a for budget and membership growth). The staff ballooned to almost ninety employees and moved to larger, more plush offices. In addition to its national office in Washington, D.C., PEOPLE FOR had opened three state "satellite" offices in New York, North

Figure A.2. PEOPLE FOR Membership and Donations

	1980	1981	1982	1983	1984	1985	1986	1987	1988	1989	Estim. 1990
Total # Members	10,000	18,000	28,000	65,000	87,000	133,000	214,000	264,000	275,000	289,000	na
Donations (in dollars)											
Membership		1,709,989	1,842,692	1,252,341	2,043,001	3,059,404	5,154,758	4,593,887	3,872,516	4,228,482	3,376,787
Special donors		926,715	880,556	650,031	1,059,263	904,733	1,679,468	2,804,362	1,055,882	1,075,293	1,456,500
Foundations		697,699	864,575	556,500	659,169	676,710	1,114,763	1,083,383	746,025	351,200	1,350,000
Special Events		0	0	0	532,659	620,893	870,734	620,210	527,993	863,561	769,500
Total		3,334,403	3,587,823	2,458,872	4,294,092	5,261,740	8,819,723	9,101,842	6,202,416	6,518,536	6,952,787

Carolina, and California to wage battles over a number of education and religious issues popping up in those states.[2]

PEOPLE FOR's success resulted directly from its ability to identify urgent issues and popularize them through public media campaigns. Since its inception, PEOPLE FOR had relied heavily on developing high-quality media campaigns to educate the public. Between 1980 and 1987, the organization produced approximately eighteen television advertisements and public service announcements, three films/videotape documentaries, twenty-five print ad campaigns, and twelve radio spots. In addition, PEOPLE FOR wrote and distributed press releases, opinion editorials, and editorial information to newspapers and press people across the nation. The organization used its acumen with the media not only to increase public awareness of its issues but also to solicit new members. Concomitantly, PEOPLE FOR established an aggressive direct mail program aimed at targeting new members and multiyear donations.

PEOPLE FOR's tremendous success in certain issues elevated its status within Washington, D.C., as well. For instance, to defeat the nomination of Judge Robert Bork to the Supreme Court, PEOPLE FOR led a coalition of organizations, developed a substantial lobbying network, and staged dramatic and effective publicity campaigns. PEOPLE FOR had earned the reputation as "the organization that gets things done."

Despite such success, Art Kropp and other members of the senior staff started to question how the organization might exist in a less-conservative political climate. The upcoming 1988 presidential election would influence which issues the public deemed "urgent" and could affect significantly PEOPLE FOR's future. However, the organization was still reeling from its victory in defeating Robert Bork's nomination to the Supreme Court and, as a result, attempts to refocus PEOPLE FOR's strategy—and even its mission—never came to fruition.

In the absence of any refocusing, in 1988, PEOPLE FOR widened its issue pool to spur interest from membership and to attract new donations. New issues included "access to information" (minimizing secrecy in government and promoting the public's right to access information), voter registration, civil rights, "hate" crimes, abortion, and a proposal to require all education be done in English. PEOPLE FOR also increased its involvement in "front-page," timely, but not necessarily enduring, issues, such as Jessie Helms' movement to prevent federal funding of "obscenity" in art. As a result, PEOPLE FOR's media attention came more and more from short-term, one-time-hit issues. As the membership ranks and total donations declined, PEOPLE FOR became increasingly confused over where to concentrate its efforts.

Organizational Structure

Almost everyone agreed that PEOPLE FOR's staff was its greatest asset. Over its ten-year life, PEOPLE FOR had attracted and maintained an experienced and dedicated staff, especially at the director level, where turnover had been particularly low. Having grown to ninety people at its height, the organization now divided itself into ten departments. The senior staff included directors from each department, some of whom were also vice presidents, and President Art Kropp. The

---

[2]The location and number of state offices was dependent upon funding and need. For example, the Texas office was established to monitor textbook publishers who primarily resided in that state; recently, that office was relocated to California where publishing battles had intensified.

Figure A.3.   Statement of Revenues, Expenses and Fund Balance 1982–1990

	1982	1983	1984
Revenues:			
Membership Contributions	1,842,692	1,252,341	2,043,001
Special Donors	880,556	650,031	1,059,263
Foundation grants	864,575	556,500	659,169
Special grants	0	0	532,659
Association grants	0	0	0
Interest income	11,382	4,908	20,807
Sale of books and materials	7,947	14,654	17,510
State income	0	0	0
Other (1)	98,536	(38,336)	41,186
Total Revenues	3,705,688	2,440,098	4,373,595
Less Adjustments	0	0	0
Net Revenues	3,705,688	2,440,098	4,373,595
Expenses:			
Membership and public information	89,574	139,716	830,228
Public policy	423,241	592,294	577,363
Program management and development	186,399	171,292	222,947
Communications	2,005,725	245,590	909,001
Issues development	0	0	1,167,918
Fundraising	523,762	636,362	339,258
Finance and administration	530,411	387,512	397,312
Legal Defence	0	0	0
State operations	0	0	0
Total Expenses	3,759,112	2,163,766	4,444,027
Excess (deficit of revenue of expense)	(53,424)	276,332	(70,432)

(1) 1982: includes $79,528 in royalties from I LOVE LIBERTY film; 1986: includes $61,742 of In-Kind contributions; 1987: includes $189,978 of In-Kind and Advertising; 1989: includes $49,388 of In-Kind $251 in royalties.

senior staff met weekly to discuss programs plans; general staff meetings occurred twice a month. Changes in program or strategy were discussed among the senior staff; however, Art had the final decision-making power. Major institutional changes were brought before the board for approval during any one of the three scheduled board meetings in the year. Art maintained excellent communication with board members, contacting them regularly for input on various issues.

PEOPLE FOR measured its programmatic success by its ability to (1) attract media attention, (2) raise money, and (3) change public policy. Each department contributed its share to the "success triangle," but achieving high scores in all three areas was difficult to do, especially when resources were limited.

1985	1986	1987	1988	1989	1990 (projected)
3,059,404	5,154,758	4,593,887	3,872,516	3,932,895	na
904,773	1,679,468	2,804,362	1,055,882	1,305,193	na
676,710	1,114,763	1,083,383	746,025	528,800	na
620,893	870,734	620,210	527,993	863,911	na
162,000	148,050	127,200	75,250	167,500	na
34,379	48,232	101,576	117,739	127,759	na
11,982	17,143	12,521	14,968	13,602	na
0	0	21,023	22,324	43,127	na
18,035	113,830	334,133	420,437	246,786	na
5,488,176	9,146,978	9,698,295	6,853,134	7,229,573	7,298,007
0	0	0	0	0	0
5,488,176	9,146,978	9,698,295	6,853,134	7,229,573	7,298,007
2,302,574	3,611,362	4,030,744	1,847,596	2,256,523	na
713,077	884,016	489,162	435,591	554,942	na
464,265	670,821	953,149	448,710	305,317	na
428,241	744,740	542,646	510,006	373,540	na
295,438	611,406	504,934	523,999	567,583	na
365,521	1,117,551	1,021,939	1,335,464	1,792,386	na
533,038	772,913	1,177,624	974,906	916,915	na
0	0	223,027	227,453	183,179	na
0	0	623,529	749,095	598,387	na
5,102,154	8,412,809	9,566,754	7,052,820	7,548,772	7,300,786
386,022	734,169	131,541	(199,686)	(319,199)	(2,779)

Communications

The communications department functioned as the voice to the public, publicizing
PEOPLE FOR's efforts through the media. Over the years, PEOPLE FOR had become well known for its ability to use the media effectively. Through a constant
barrage of press releases, op-eds, issue papers, editorial meetings, and broadcast
and print advertisements, the communications department helped put PEOPLE
FOR's issues on front pages around the country. Yet, the communications department was having a harder time selling its stories to the news media. Even PEOPLE
FOR's involvement in newer issues like abortion, voter registration, and civil rights
received little attention. More recently, the department had been sending out as
many as three press releases to the media per day. Like the fundraising departments, the communications department believed PEOPLE FOR needed to rethink

Figure A.3a. Statement of Allocation of Functional Expenses

	1982	1983	1984
Employees' salaries and benefits	856,932	822,813	912,679
Travel	73,668	51,997	92,535
Staff education & training (1)	0	0	0
Consulting fees	270,875	288,438	334,412
Legal/accounting fees	79,325	27,564	39,129
Data processing	0	96,491	115,614
Media production/advertising	451,640	35,826	1,167,046
Printing and production	894,829	206,798	603,155
Postage and mailing	487,301	235,085	415,870
List rental	193,847	9,752	93,043
Equipment rental and maintenance	50,911	40,951	26,336
Office supplies and expenses	67,239	48,446	45,419
Meetings and special events	0	61,500	114,266
Office rental	95,734	90,526	80,491
Telephone	60,384	53,866	165,066
Corporate insurance	9,176	20,928	16,353
Depreciation and Amortization	148,746	55,891	199,562
Miscellaneous	18,505	16,894	23,051
Interest	0	0	0
Fundraising (2)	0	0	0
Total Expenses	3,759,112	2,163,766	4,444,027

(1) Staff education and training became a separate line item in 1987.

(2) Fundraising expense is among other expenses.

its mission in order to clarify the underlying responsibility of the organization. An updated mission would enable the department to target publicity more effectively and, in the long term, revitalize the public's understanding of PEOPLE FOR's purpose.

Fundraising

People for the American Way's fundraising efforts were carried out by both the membership and development departments.

Development The development department oversaw all fundraising from high-profile donors and foundations. The high-dollar donors received special literature, attended special event parties, and were cultivated increasingly on a personal basis. Table A.1 shows the donor categories used by People for the American Way.

In 1989, these donors contributed almost $2 million via mail and special event parties. Yet, in the previous year, the department had become concerned that the organization's largest contributors had reduced the size of their annual contributions (see Figs. A.4 and A.5). The department hired consultants to study all aspects of the development program, including promotional materials, program plans, and financial projections, to see how it could be improved. Among the conclusions they offered, the consultants suggested that PEOPLE FOR

1985	1986	1987	1988	1989	1990E
1,304,963	2,156,147	2,723,438	2,490,369	na	na
105,638	156,385	201,968	142,265	na	na
0	0	7,722	1,161	na	na
425,239	527,372	539,709	534,078	na	na
29,606	247,632	148,682	91,584	na	na
198,574	216,445	209,919	219,161	na	
178,533	654,011	900,450	124,737	na	na
939,454	1,590,422	1,633,421	906,171	na	na
953,534	1,305,236	1,441,082	959,381	na	na
328,623	399,154	180,034	93,297	na	na
45,472	61,409	71,882	95,048	na	na
99,277	163,278	237,421	108,974	na	na
221,019	367,380	382,130	272,621	na	na
92,404	144,194	373,133	463,944	na	na
92,056	193,092	243,295	219,831	na	na
17,409	24,228	56,991	68,203	na	na
26,454	49,014	122,591	182,772	na	na
41,973	156,868	92,886	79,223	na	na
1,926	542	0	0	na	na
0	0	0	0	na	na
5,102,154	8,412,809	9,566,754	7,052,820	7,548,772	7,300,786

take steps to clarify the organization's image, by initiating a process that will result in the production of a clear statement of its purpose and program priorities—which can then be reflected in organizational materials and in the fundraising program. While there have been some efforts to do that already, none has yet succeeded in doing so effectively. Perhaps that is because there is a lack of agreement within the organization about the role it now should be playing and because new program areas have been adopted without an explicit understanding of how they relate to and serve as extensions of the organization's central purpose.

Foundation support had changed over the years both in the size of grants given and in the type of foundation making grants. In 1987, PEOPLE FOR attracted support for the first time from the Ford, Rockefeller, and Carnegie foundations, in addition to fifty smaller funds that had supported PEOPLE FOR in previous years. This change in the composition of foundation support presented significant prob-

Table A.1. Special Donor Categories

Committee Name	Amount of Contribution
Citizens	$ 1,000–$4,999
Sponsors	5,000– 9,999
Patrons	10,000–24,999
Founders	25,000 +

Donations by Category
(in dollars)

	Actual 1986	Actual 1987	Actual 1988	Actual 1989
Citizens	467,306	103,773	258,097	357,666
Sponsors	313,497	261,729	277,074	271,209
Patrons	342,031	363,430	266,362	377,421
Founders	1,175,801	293,897	207,500	346,370
Other	0	584,284	230,524	561,835
TOTAL (Actual)	2,298,635	1,607,113	1,239,557	1,914,501
TOTAL (Projected)	2,549,433	1,839,000	2,191,383	1,914,501

Renewals by Category

	Actual 1986	Actual 1987	Actual 1988	Actual 1989
Citizens	57.0%	47.6%	70.0%	82.8%
Sponsors	70.0%	56.3%	93.6%	93.8%
Patrons	75.0%	63.4%	95.9%	92.2%
Founders	89.0%	72.2%	82.6%	82.4%

Figure A.4. Special Donor History.

Year	Total Active Members	Membership Donations	# of Special Donors	Special Donors' Donations
1989	92,763	$3,935,794	462	$1,764,206
1988	98,893	$3,750,123	484	$1,549,877
1987	139,370	$4,977,194	665	$2,022,806
1986	127,772	$4,394,468	320	$1,405,532
1985	83,203	$2,427,490	241	$872,510

Figure A.5. "People For" Comparative Analysis of Active Member Base Composition.

lems to PEOPLE FOR. The smaller foundations were starting to wonder if PEOPLE FOR had outgrown them while the larger ones were resistant to continue funding PEOPLE FOR if its issues were too political and controversial. To maintain the flow of foundation funds, PEOPLE FOR had begun focusing on new issues, such as voter registration, to attract grants.

Membership The Membership department raised money and recruited new members through direct mail and telemarketing campaigns. The department's aggressive direct mail program consisted of annual renewal letters, "special appeals"—letters mailed to current members requesting support for specific issues—and prospecting letters that were sent to attract new members into the organization. Table A.2 summarizes the data on membership mailings over time.

The membership department monitored membership behavior by dividing them into response groups according to issue, donating behavior (i.e., number of yearly contributions), and size of donation. A sophisticated computer analysis was devised that tracked how different types of members donated and how their behavior changed over time. This analysis also served to keep the organization informed about its most important group of members, the "active members"—members who donated each year, specifically within the previous twelve months.

In 1987, PEOPLE FOR's leading role in opposing Judge Robert Bork's nomination to the Supreme Court brought some 30,000 new members into the organization (refer to Table A.3a and Table A.3b). As PEOPLE FOR developed positions in a wider array of issues, the membership department continued its aggressive direct mail program, using innovative package designs to attract new members and to increase contributions. Acquiring new members was particularly important to stave off attrition in the active membership pool.

Moving into the 1990s, the membership department was looking to use more sophisticated marketing techniques like telemarketing, "900" numbers, and, more specifically, targeted mail appeals to improve recruiting results.

Both the membership and development departments felt that through its expo-

Table A.2. Number of Membership Mailings

	1984	1985	1986	1987	1988	1989
Renewals	8	8	9	13	16	14
Special appeals	6	6	6	7	7	8
Prospecting	5	6	6	14	10	23

Table A.3a.   Total Active Membership

Year	Members	Active Income[a] ($ Million)	Average Gift
1985	83,203	3.3	$40.67
1986	127,772	5.8	45.61
1987	139,370	7.0	49.91
1988	98,893	5.3	54.05
1989	92,763	5.7	61.80

[a] Includes income from Special Donors. See Fig. A.5 for breakdown.

nential growth in the 1980s, PEOPLE FOR had lost sense of its purpose and needed to clarify its mission. As the membership director stated:

> We don't have the umbrella that other organizations like the Wilderness Society or the Sierra Club do. The public knows what those organizations represent, what their purpose is. We don't have that anymore and that's a problem.

Lobbying

Lobbying and organizing activities on national and local levels were conducted by the public policy and field departments, respectively. The success of both departments was critical to PEOPLE FOR's fundraising and communication functions as it provided them with the issues around which funds were raised and publicity generated.

Public Policy The public policy department attempted to affect policy change on a national political level. Through its extensive network of public interest group contacts, legislative leaders, and public agencies, PEOPLE FOR's public policy department worked to ensure that "extremist" ideology did not confound the political process. The department spearheaded monitoring of the judicial nomination process, provided expertise on the religious right to various coalitions (e.g., education organizations), and lobbied for specific causes like the Civil Rights Restoration Act.

Over the last few years, the public policy department had become increasingly proactive in the legislative process over and above its traditional monitoring function. As Director and Executive Vice President Melanne Verveer explained:

> PEOPLE FOR has become more involved in deeper levels of the democratic process . . . we now concentrate on "inside lobbying" more than general public education, applying our expertise in the initial stages of legislation rather than reacting to what's already happened.

The department's deeper legislative focus often involved a slow and careful approach to developing issues. The department sometimes worked with a coalition

Table A.3b.   Bork Membership Performance (1989)

Member Type	Percentage Renewed	Avg. Gift
Non-Bork Single Members	39.19	$23.55
Bork Single Members	12.56	$20.89

of organizations to affect legislation; or, Melanne worked directly with key politicians, using PEOPLE FOR's expertise to develop legislation. Such work required diplomatic lobbying skills and even confidentiality in order to ensure success. As a result, the issues developed by the public policy department took longer to cultivate and were more difficult to "sell" from a fundraising and publicity perspective. Still, the public policy department's effective lobbying and success in judicial issues (especially the Bork campaign) had secured PEOPLE FOR's position as a popular and credible political force in Washington, D.C.

Field Department The field department had changed drastically over the last two years. Originally, the department split the country among four coordinators, each of whom was responsible for coordinating grassroots efforts and tracking developing issues in their respective regions. In 1989, Art hired a new director who reorganized the department according to issues, not geographic regions. The new director envisioned the department as a proactive organizing tool whose function was to coordinate PEOPLE FOR's involvement in issues on a state and local legislative level. To accomplish this, the department was assembling a broader state legislative network and relying more heavily on members and volunteers to target grassroots activities.

The field department employed this new strategy for three reasons: (1) PEOPLE FOR believed the religious right's movement had not ceased; rather, its focus had shifted to the local level, where these issues emerged in state and local elections around the country; (2) since PEOPLE FOR's issues were selling less well on a national level, the organization could use the field department's grass-roots strength to develop a presence on highly visible local issues in key states where targeted membership groups would be more likely to get involved and donate. Since PEOPLE FOR's members were predominantly concentrated in the Northeast, Florida, and the West Coast, this strategy was particularly appealing; and (3) the organization's experience in both grass-roots activities and direct mail had shown that people were more likely to get involved or contribute when the issues were closer to home.

Strategic Alternatives

Heading into the 1990s, the fundamental question the organization confronted was, "How do we deal with change?" Founding board members believed the world was no more tolerant a place than it had been during the Reagan years and therefore dissolution of the organization was not viewed as an alternative. To confront this period of change, then, the organization was considering several strategic alternatives.

One alternative was to rewrite the mission statement to help PEOPLE FOR redefine its ideology for the 1990s. The need to do so was identified by consultants hired by PEOPLE FOR to review the development program. In their study, the consultants asked board members and senior staff an open-ended question about PEOPLE FOR's purpose. The consultants concluded:

> To [our] surprise, the question revealed a disturbing lack of consensus and some inconsistency of views about the mission of the organization. Some saw it as organization whose purpose should be confined to protecting and defending the First Amendment. Others saw the organization's original mission—to fight the Radical Right—as an ongoing priority requiring a shift in focus from the national to the local level, where

they increasingly would be focusing their attention and where an effective counter-force would be needed. Still others saw the organization's primary purpose in more amorphous terms, describing it as needing "to ensure mutual respect in diverse communities," or to selectively defend "constitutional liberties," or to promote democratic values. This lack of agreement about so fundamental an issue as the organization's purpose has the potential to evolve over time into a very serious problem.

The purpose of refining the mission, as presented to the board in January 1990, was to help the organization develop a framework for a program plan to guide the organization's future activities. This included "helping the organization to define its main goals and the main techniques—such as legislation, litigation, public education, or community organizing—it will use to reach its objectives."

Some people in the organization agreed that the mission process would help PEOPLE FOR redefine its image and focus its press efforts and resources more effectively. Conversely, others felt that PEOPLE FOR's membership enrollment would continue to suffer until the organization found an issue that excited the liberal community. As one senior staff person stated, "Public interest politics does not live in a vacuum. It depends on demand from the outside. The public needs to see a threat before it will react."

Alternatively, PEOPLE FOR could leave its current mission statement intact, and instead make structural changes in marketing the organization to address the changed environment. A critical component of this more market-driven approach was the shift away from weaker national issues to more pressing local ones. The field department's increased focus on the state and local legislative process reflected this shift of concentration on to local issues. Moreover, as of 1989, New York, California, and Florida contained the dominant proportion of PEOPLE FOR's members, with 43,000, 55,000, and 18,000 members, respectively. Evidence suggested that these three states would continue to be hotbeds of issues related to intolerance and the religious right. For example, California was preparing to adopt a new science and biology textbook series that prompted fierce debates over the treatment of creationism and evolution in those textbooks; also, organized right-wing groups had "declared war" on a language arts reading series adopted by California in 1989. By employing a more local approach, PEOPLE FOR could target mailings to in-state residents and allocate lobbying and press resources more efficiently.

Some people in the organization worried that focusing on local issues would not necessarily pull PEOPLE FOR out of its slump, and might even alter the public's perception of the organization in the long run. As one director said, "Should PEOPLE FOR shift its energies to local battles because local battles exist today but national battles do not?"

Finally, rather than altering the mission or focusing operations on local issues, PEOPLE FOR could scale back the organization and focus on its original objective: ensuring that political and religious extremists did not interfere with citizen's individual liberties. This strategy would involve cutting back the staff and increasing PEOPLE FOR's role as a watchdog rather than a leader of change. As one senior staff member described it:

> Cutting back would allow PEOPLE FOR to accommodate downsizing in down periods. There doesn't always have to be an issue . . . it shouldn't be the tail wagging the dog. Look at NOW . . . or Common Cause, organizations that cut back when their issues were less popular. But now they are experiencing tremendous growth just like we did in the earlier part of the 1980s. That's the natural process for organizations like PEOPLE FOR.

Yet others in PEOPLE FOR had serious reservations about cutting back to a "core" organization and wondered how a scaled-back organization would look. After experiencing such cutbacks, could PEOPLE FOR generate the resources and the staff necessary to be effective when the time came?

Art faced a difficult decision. PEOPLE FOR had grown accustomed to plentiful budgets and growing membership ranks. Clearly, each alternative had its merits. Changing the mission or implementing a new marketing strategy could help reposition PEOPLE FOR in this changing environment. Yet, pursuing a mechanistic approach in response to change seemed counter to PEOPLE FOR's vision-driven roots. After all, as Art himself had said, "PEOPLE FOR was founded not to be an organization, but to be a message."

CASE B

The United Hmong Association

Tong Thao spends much of his time at work thinking. As a drill press operator he is able to do his work properly while concentrating on thoughts far removed from his factory job. Today, as usual, Tong was thinking about his other job, that as President of the United Hmong Association (UHA).

This weekend, the board of directors of the Association was going to decide on several proposals designed to increase the self-sufficiency of the Hmong community in South Providence. Tong was extremely concerned about the upcoming decisions because they represented the Association's first major step into the business world, and each proposal seemed to move in a different direction. A misstep could lose the UHA's fragile community support and Tong's reputation along with it.

The first proposal was presented by the Rhode Island Vocational, Educational, and Technical School (RIVETS). They proposed a partnership between themselves and the UHA in which RIVETS would train Hmong entrepreneurs in small business management. With this training, Hmong refugees would be able to start and develop their own businesses.

The second proposal was from Teng Vang, Kao Vang, and Blong Vang, three leaders of one of the larger clans in the community. They proposed a start-up retail business that would sell fresh poultry. This enterprise would fill an immediate community need and serve as a model for further business development. Technical assistance for the initial planning and start-up phase would be provided by the Community Consulting Center, a local consulting firm that specialized in minority business enterprises.

The third proposal, from the University of Rhode Island Agricultural Extension Service, proposed the development of a comprehensive and integrated agricultural project. The project would include a full program of training and initial assistance in the early years of the project. Eventually, Hmong would be able to instruct new trainees themselves and the program would be self-sustaining.

The three proposals to the UHA are included as Figures B.1–B.3 at the end of this case study. All the proposals sounded good to Tong. He hated to turn down any offers of assistance. On the other hand, they all required money and time; unfortunately, the Association had only limited amounts of both. The UHA, however, did have access to some federal grant money from the Office of Refugee Resettlement for economic development projects. Applications for grants were due the following week.

This case was written in 1983 by Dean Takahashi under the supervision of Professor Sharon M. Oster at the Yale School of Organization and Management. The case is intended as a basis for class discussion. Names and proposals within are fictionalized.

Background

Laos

The Hmong (pronounced "mung") of Laos were originally from the Hunan region of southern China. In the eighteenth century, they were forced southward and westward by the Han Chinese. During this migration, the Hmong avoided others and moved along the mountain highlands. Eventually, the Hmong established themselves in the plateau area of northern Laos known as the Plaines des Jarres (Plain of Jars).

In Laos, the Hmong continued to dwell high on the flanks of mountains, isolated from other groups. They practiced swidden (burn and slash) agriculture, growing dry rice and vegetables. They raised livestock such as chickens, pigs, buffaloes, and horses. The Hmong also cultivated opium poppies that they used primarily as a cash crop. Every few years as the soil became depleted, the village cleared and burned new fields; frequently, this involved moving the entire village. Before they moved, families would first send out trusted leaders to scout out and pick the new village site.

The Hmong economy was simple. The primary economic activity was subsistence farming; excess crops and livestock were sold or bartered, often with silver or opium as the medium for exchange. Some of the Hmong were skilled silversmiths and blacksmiths. Many of the women were extremely adept at needlework, although these skills were used for costume design, not economic trade.

Politically, socially, and economically, the Hmong operated on a strong family and clan system. The basic societal unit was an extended family or household that was headed by an elder male. Although the patriarch would not act without consulting with the men under his authority, once a decision was reached, his word was final. All members of a family carried the clan name of the leader. All marriages were exogamous and seen as ties between clans. Consequently, divorces were discouraged since they tended to disrupt clan relations. Polygamy was common, especially between a man and his brother's widow.

Villages were sometimes composed of one clan, but they were often comprised of several. When a village had more than one clan, community decisions were usually made by a council of elders, which was frequently led by the household head of the largest clan. As with a family, this leader would not act without first consulting with the other leaders, and they were free to leave if they felt oppressed or abused. Disputes were negatively valued and handled at the lowest levels of authority possible.

Hmong families were usually large. Couples courted during the new year's celebration, and often married at thirteen or fourteen years old. Usually, the groom paid the bride's family an agreed-upon "bride price." Since children, particularly sons, were highly treasured, parents were encouraged to have many children. When both parents were working away from home, they frequently left their children under the care of the husband's mother.

Spiritually, the Hmong were animists. They believed in many spirits and relied on shamanlike religious practitioners to interpret dreams and cure the sick. Although Christian missionaries devised a system of transliteration using the Arabic alphabet in the 1950s, the Hmong traditionally had no written language. Information was transmitted orally, frequently in the form of long folktales. More recently, however, some Hmong have learned to read and write Lao so they could better interact with the surrounding Laotian society.

War

Hmong isolation from outside forces was violently disrupted in the 1960s by the Indochinese War. Because of their strategic location, the Hmong soon became heavily involved in civil war. Some of the Hmong combined forces with the Communists, but the majority sided with the French and later with the Americans. As the conflict deepened and spread, the whole Hmong way of life was altered by the war. Many of their villages were destroyed and the Hmong became refugees in their own country. The men were recruited for the army, and whole villages were supported by air-dropped supplies provided by the CIA and USAID. The Hmong were considered by many to be one of the most effective fighting forces in the war. They were heavily involved in guerilla combat around the Ho Chi Minh Trail, and they were frequently sent out to rescue downed American pilots. It is estimated that more than 10% of the Hmong lost their lives in combat.

When the United States withdrew from the war in 1975 and the Lao Royal Government fell to the Pathet Lao, the Hmong who had sided with the Americans were persecuted by the Communists. Forced to flee, the Hmong made long, dangerous treks through the jungle to reach the Thai border. Many of those who survived the journey reached the border only to drown or get shot while trying to cross the Mekong River.

Resettlement

In total, approximately 125,000 Hmong fled to Thailand from Laos. Upon reaching asylum in Thailand, the Hmong were placed in six United Nations High Commission for Refugees (UNHCR) camps, the largest of which, Ban Vinai, held some 30,000 of the refugees. In the camp the refugees were screened for placement in the United States by staff from the Joint Voluntary Committee (JVC). The JVC collected and assembled refugee "bio-data" that was passed on to the Immigration and Naturalization Service (INS). The INS officer reviewed the applications, established priorities, and approved admissions for those that met all the necessary criteria. This review process frequently disqualified Hmong who practiced polygamy, or who were diseased or severely handicapped. When the INS approved an application, the JVC contacted the American Council of Voluntary Agencies (ACVA), which assured sponsorship of the refugee in America.

Because of their priority status, the first Hmong to be resettled in the United States were officers in the CIA-backed "Secret Army." They began arriving in 1975 with assignment to one of the dozen different volags (voluntary agencies) that comprised the ACVA. Placed where these agencies were best able to find sponsors and provide the necessary resettlement services, the Hmong were dispersed across the country. This dispersion was congruent with Federal policy that attempted to minimize the economic and political impact on resettlement communities. Because the volag's prior experiences focused on resettling Europeans, most of their programs centered on receiving and placing refugees in urban areas. As a consequence, most of the first Hmong to come to America were resettled in cities such as St. Paul, Seattle, Portland, Missoula, Santa Ana, and Providence.

Most of the Hmong were resettled in the United States. A large number also went to France, Canada, Australia, French Guinea, and China. In addition, there are approximately 55,000 Hmong refugees still residing in the camps in Thailand.

Subsequent to the haphazard initial placements, later refugee migrations were frequently directed toward reunification with family or close friends. Since the early refugees tended to be community leaders as well as military officers, they were able to call followers to their resettlement communities. This affected both newcomers direct from camps as well as refugees already placed in other U.S. communities. Free to move once they were initially placed (frequent moves being consistent with tradition) many Hmong searched out and subsequently rejoined former relations in what is termed *secondary migration*.

The Volags

ACVA often assign Hmong refugees to a volag, on the basis of the volag's ability to facilitate reunification. While the refugee is still in the Thailand camps the volag lines up a family, church group, or sponsor. If none can be found, the volag itself will often act as sponsor. The volunteering sponsor is expected to greet the refugees on arrival, show them around, see that their immediate needs are met, and be an accessible source of help and advice.

In addition to matching a refugee with a sponsor, the volags are responsible for "core services," which include counseling, liaison with public agencies, and referral for orientation, housing, health needs, and employment. These responsibilities are broadly and loosely defined in the volag's cooperative agreement with the State Department. For the provision of these services, the volag receives a subsidy grant of between $300 and $500 per refugee.

Under their agreement with the State Department the volags are responsible only for referrals to other social services. Most volags, however, also provide many of these services with funding from the Office of Refugee Resettlement (ORR) in the Department of Health and Human Services (HSS). In particular, many volags provide housing assistance, medical screening and monitoring, and, perhaps most importantly, employment services. Employment assistance often includes English as a Second Language (ESL) training, job counseling, and placement and referrals to conventional government-sponsored employment programs.

A volag's ability to provide resettlement services varies according to its size, approach, funding, and expertise. Many offices lack personnel with appropriate cultural or linguistic expertise. Small volags often lack the staff and programs to provide a comprehensive package of services. Large volags frequently try to treat all refugees the same within existing, standardized programs. While some volags do an excellent job in resettling refugees, the government's loosely defined expectations and standards allow others to perform very poorly.

The Government

Prior to the passage of the Refugee Act in 1980, the government's policy toward refugee resettlement was conducted on an ad hoc basis. Refugees were admitted to the U.S. under standard immigration quotas. When necessary, these quotas could be temporarily raised to respond to a particular international crisis. Federal funding for refugees was channeled through three major programs: (1) Department of State reception and placement grants to voluntary resettlement agencies; (2) Cash assistance, medical assistance, and social services for refugees administered by states through Title XX programs; and (3) specific refugee-related projects to provide employment services, ESL training, and mental health services through direct fed-eral grants. There was little coordination or integrated planning among these three programs.

With the passage of the Refugee Act in 1980, primary responsibility for coor-dinating resettlement was placed in the hands of the states. Each state was to appoint a refugee coordinator and develop a state plan to coordinate the activities of both public and private agencies. Since states were free to place the Office of the Coordinator where they wished, the placement and visibility of the coordinator varies from state to state. Usually, however, the office is positioned in the welfare or social service department. In a few states, the coordinator works out of the labor and employment department.

The Refugee Act of 1980 also created the U.S. ORR as part of the U.S. Depart-ment of HHS. This federal office coordinates and funds the state offices, and it makes grants to nationwide refugee projects.

While the placement and reception programs and the special refugee projects are vital to refugee resettlement, the program with the greatest impact on the lives of refugees are the public assistance programs. Because arriving refugees have extraordinary need for public assistance, and because there are important equity implications for states accepting refugees, the federal government fully funds initial public assistance to refugees. These assistance programs are administered through the states' conventional welfare programs. Although there are special eligibility exemptions, the refugees generally must meet standard requirements to receive welfare assistance. The two cash assistance programs that most affect refugees are Aid to Families with Dependent Children (AFDC), and Supplemental Security In-come (SSI) for the aged, blind, and disabled. Medical assistance is delivered through Medicaid, and dietary assistance through Food Stamps. Until 1982, special federal funding for these programs covered refugees for 36 months; coverage now lasts for 18 months. After this year and a half, conventional joint funding by the state and federal government covers program costs. These financial and social costs of having welfare-dependent refugees are leading many of the states toward em-phasizing projects that encourage and develop greater refugee self-sufficiency through employment and economic development.

Mutual Assistance Associations

The primary institutional means of developing greater self-sufficiency among the refugees have been the MAAs. These nonprofit ethnic associations were set up with encouragement from the government to help refugees work together as a community. MAAs play an especially important role in the community's interaction with American organizations and governments. Another important role of MAAs is to help refugees retain a sense of cultural stability and support.

States are now increasingly looking to MAAs as the best vehicle for delivery of social services to the Hmong. Direct funding of MAA programs fosters greater cooperation among refugees as well as greater and more direct interaction between the Hmong and the government. MAAs that have received their tax-exempt status are now receiving ORR funds to provide career counseling, job placement, job development, vocational training, language training, day care, referral services, translation and interpretation services, transportation services, and legal services.

While helpful and consistent with Hmong culture, the MAAs are not a tradition-al form of organization for the Hmong. MAAs are an adopted institution that the

Hmong have used for dealing with Americans. The board and directors of most Hmong MAAs are refugees with English skills. They are not always the real community leaders.

The Hmong Community of Providence

In the spring of 1976, several Hmong officers and their families were brought to the United States and resettled in Providence. Three volags—the International Institute, Catholic Social Services, and Church World Service—provided most of the initial services. Individual families and church groups sponsored the new arrivals. In addition to being military leaders, some of the first refugees in Providence were also family leaders. They sent word back to the refugee camps in Thailand and told relatives and close friends to come join them. Providence rapidly developed into a major Hmong community. Some Hmong who had been resettled in other parts of America came to Providence on a secondary migration.

Virtually all the Hmong who came to Rhode Island settled in a depressed neighborhood of South Providence. There they found large, three-story Victorian houses with plenty of room for their large extended families. Although frequently substandard, the houses were readily available and their rents relatively inexpensive.

Moving to Providence, the Hmong placed themselves in a major commercial, financial, and industrial center of the Northeast, and one of the oldest cities in America. Providence's fine port and ideal mill sites helped it become an important manufacturing center in the late nineteenth century. The city reached its peak in the 1940s when its population exceeded 150,000. Like many other northeastern cities, however, Providence has lost significant portions of its population and its manufacturing base over the past 40 years.

The addition of the Hmong community has added another dimension to the ethnic diversity of the city's population, now approximately 150,000. Thirty percent of Providence's residents are of Italian descent, 12% Irish, 11% Black, 8% Portuguese, 7% English, and 6% Hispanic. The immediate neighborhoods surrounding the Hmong in South Providence are mixed black, white, Hispanic, and Cambodian.

The Providence economy has also diversified since the 1940s. Services in retail and wholesale commerce, the government, and financial sectors have become increasingly significant sources of growth and employment. Nonetheless, Providence remains a manufacturing center with principal products of jewelry, silverware, and other light-manufactured goods. Because Providence relies heavily on manufacturing, economic downturns hit its residents particularly hard. In 1982, the city's 11% unemployment level was well above the national average. This unemployment existed despite Providence's relatively low manufacturing wage rates, which average $6.50/hour, compared with the national average of $8.50/hour.

Resettlement in Providence

Prior to resettlement, the only contact the Hmong had had with Western society was through the military. Upon coming to America they faced a completely foreign and unfamiliar environment with its large urban areas, complex government bureaucracy, and the fast-paced business economy. This confusing and bewildering situation was only made worse by the lack of English skills of the refugees.

The International Institute offered a short basic survival orientation and several language classes in an effort to help ease the resettlement process. While some of the Hmong were able to pick up English skills fairly easily, most had great difficulty in learning to speak, read, and write English. The lack of teachers with appropriate linguistic skills and cultural knowledge made the problem worse.

Finding employment was very difficult for the Hmong who were unable to speak English. Even those Hmong who learned English found getting and keeping a job hard. The classes taught little of the practical language needed on the job. Neither the orientation nor the classes taught the Hmong what it means to work in America. Unlike European refugees, the Hmong were unfamiliar with industrial society and culture, and they needed to learn the norms and customs of their new work environment. For instance, in Laos it was customary for a Hmong to send his brother in his place when he himself was unable to go to work.

Despite the obstacles, most of the first Hmong who came to Providence were able to find employment. The economy was healthy and jobs were available. Furthermore, many of the first arrivals had received education and training as preparation for military service. Some of the refugees had experience as mechanics, air controllers, radio operators, and other military support services.

The Hmong, in general, were good workers. The refugees typically found positions such as factory workers or as manual laborers, which required little English. Frequently, these positions had no health benefits and little job security or opportunity for advancement. Hmong with good English skills were commonly employed by volag and social service providers as outreach workers and translators.

In 1980, when the second wave of refugees came to Providence, conditions had turned for the worse. There were fewer jobs available and more Hmong in need of them. Helping refugees had become less of a fashionable novelty, and there were fewer sponsors to help with job placement. This wave of Hmong tended to be villagers who had less education, training, and employable skills than did their predecessors. Moreover, they had been relatively inactive and dependent for several years in the Thai refugee camps. Many of the Hmong refugees had come to believe that they were entitled to payments from the U.S. government. This belief evolved from rumors in the Thai camps about the CIA's obligations and from observing other Hmong receive welfare payments. Many Hmong were particularly upset when they were told to get a menial job with little opportunity for advancement while others received welfare and went to English and vocational classes. The Rhode Island Office of the Refugee Coordinator estimates that currently well over half of the refugees in the state are receiving public assistance.

Traditionally proud and self-sufficient, many of the Hmong are disturbed by their community's reliance on public assistance. They fear continued and self-perpetuating welfare dependency. Public officials also want to avoid having the Hmong fall into the "welfare trap," but because of political equity issues, they feel unable to give special assistance to the Hmong. Welfare issues are further complicated by the refugees' willingness to move. Communities with good refugee programs can be overwhelmed by secondary migration. The limited funds available for refugee programs are often mismatched to refugee populations because of difficulties in directing funds toward transient populations.

The Hmong community in Providence has been deeply affected by secondary migration, both in and out. As of today, roughly 40% of the Hmong in the Rhode Island have come from other states. Two years ago almost half of the refugee population, disillusioned with the cold urban environment, left Rhode Island for

North Carolina and California in search of better living conditions, particularly warmer weather and farming opportunities. Unfortunately, the rural areas with farmland had neither the social service capability to serve, nor the economic base to employ large influxes of refugees. Despite the apparent problems inherent in secondary migration, many families still seriously consider the possibility of moving to better their situations.

Although many of the older Hmong have had tremendous difficulty in adjusting to life in America, the young children have been able to adapt much more quickly and easily. Through frequent contact with Americans in school the Hmong children have learned both English and other basic subject matter. They have also picked up many American cultural norms. Like many other young immigrants, the Hmong children wish to assimilate, yet they find many American customs (i.e., dating) at odds with their traditions. They also find their elders' apparent misconceptions frustrating and embarrassing. These conflicts put great pressure on the traditional Hmong reverence and respect for one's elders. The pressures to adopt American ways often prevail.

The effects of this contest between the old and new ways are felt most severely by the older Hmong. As traditional leaders they deeply feel the responsibility to give guidance and direction to their families and community especially in this time of great uncertainty. Yet with neither English skills nor knowledge of their new environment, the elders often feel incompetent and inadequate. Once proud, independent, and resourceful, many of the older Hmong are scared, lonely, and unable to find employment with which to support their families.

The adjustment to life in America has also disrupted traditional gender roles. Many Hmong women are forced to find employment out of economic necessity. Hmong women often find it easier to find work than do Hmong men. This reversal of the breadwinner role is particularly disturbing in the patriarchical Hmong society. The contrast in cultural norms also causes conflict over the leadership role of women. Life in America puts tremendous pressures on the traditionally quiet and acquiescent Hmong women to form and voice their own ideas, even in public. This, too, creates tension in the community.

The shocks of these cultural changes and the consequent sense of lost identity are aggravated by the refugees' difficulties in understanding and dealing with various organizations and individuals. After being taken advantage of a few times, the Hmong have become very wary of Americans. Many refugees feel that even some of those who profess their desire to help are actually exploiting the Hmong. Yet the Hmong are very reluctant to turn down any offers of assistance. The Hmong are also extremely troubled by crime. Many will submit to, and take no action against criminals because the refugees do not fully understand the law and its enforcement. Afraid and cautious, the Hmong painstakingly avoid dangerous situations.

The refugees respond to these problems in America by looking to their close relatives and friends for help. Successful Hmong will frequently support both their immediate family, and various friends and relatives. Such assistance may include help with finances, housing, food, and, perhaps most importantly, advice and guidance. This system of support within small units of close relatives and friends is typical of Hmong tradition.

Many of the problems the Hmong face as refugees require responses of a less traditional nature. Whereas a few Hmong families once comprised a whole village, today the entire Hmong population is but a small community in Providence. Issues confront not individual families, but the whole refugee community. Interaction with non-Hmong, particularly the government, requires that the refugees act and speak together as one. Recognizing this need, state and federal officials have encouraged and fostered the development of refugee MAAs. With help from the state coordinator's office and a local resource development group, the Providence Hmong formed the United Hmong Association (UHA) in 1979.

The United Hmong Association

The UHA played a quiet role during its first few years. Its purpose within the community was social and fraternal. It worked on issues and events such as bride prices and the New Year's Festival. It served as the ears and mouth of the leading elders in dealing with the outside community. Based on the hopes and expectations of repatriation, the Association did not focus on the long term. It had no paid staff and only a minimal budget. It left the provision of social services to the state and to volags.

Over time, many of the Hmong grew to recognize the permanence of their situation, and they realized that their future lay in the United States, not Laos. Some of the refugees grew more competent and confident in their dealings with Americans. Leaders saw that community needs were not being met and they themselves could provide services better than the volags. They saw the UHA taking on a more direct and active role in the community. The growth of this sentiment led to the narrowly decided election of a new and generally younger board. Tong Thao was elected as the new president of the UHA.

With encouragement and support from the state coordinator's office, the UHA took on new, expanded roles. It applied for and received funding from the government to provide a community garden, emergency translation, day care, English classes, and a community census. The Association hired three staff members with its budget of $85,000.

Several older and influential leaders disagreed with this new, more active approach. Unhappy with the lost election, they left the UHA, taking with them aligned families and clans. As a result, the Association currently represents only some of the clans and roughly half of the 240 families in the community.

Thus far, the new UHA programs have been fairly successful. The emergency translation service has been operating largely on the efforts of a few bilingual volunteers who can be called on to help when needed. Day care is not yet in operation, but the program coordinator is close to finishing her training, and prospects for a successful program are good. The community garden has probably been the biggest success. The Association has tilled, fertilized, and marketed crops grown from ten acres of farmland leased from the state. In this project, the UHA took advantage of the existing clan structure and left the task of assigning families to plots to the clan leaders. Virtually all the families in the community participated, growing thousands of dollars worth of produce.

Although the success of these programs is apparent, the overall effectiveness of the UHA is less clear. The emergency translation and orientation services were already existing through volags and informally before they were institutionalized into UHA programs. Similarly, the day care and the garden projects were developed outside and then incorporated into the MAA for reasons of funding and legitimacy. Many of the Hmong doubt the Association's effectiveness in developing truly innovative and significant programs. This skepticism is the principal reason half the community does not belong to the Association.

Tong's Dilemma

Tong pondered this situation as he broke for lunch. He was painfully aware of the community needs still unfulfilled. Because of rumors that his company might soon lay off 30% of its workers, Tong was particularly concerned about business and employment opportunities. There were too few jobs with any real future, and virtually none for the older refugees who were unable to speak English. Perhaps these proposed economic development projects could really work. If they did, they would bring confidence to the Hmong community and credibility to the UHA. With greater hope, the Hmong would look to the future with greater vision and courage. On the other hand, failure would only reinforce the community's apathy and fears. Tong wondered how he and the board could decide on which, if any, of the proposals to try.

The time was certainly ripe for business development. The need was great. There were refugees and volunteers who were interested, and the government as well as foundations were willing to fund such projects. Other Hmong MAAs and communities had begun business enterprises with apparent success. On the other hand, in Providence, the three privately initiated attempts to develop businesses had met with mixed results.

The first enterprise started by the refugees was the Hmong Textile Cooperative. The Co-op sells intricate Hmong needlework, called Pa ndau, in a small storefront in downtown Providence. The Co-op was started in 1981 with help from American volunteers who had sponsored refugees and seen their beautiful needlework. These volunteers have remained active, donating many hours to staffing the store, helping with marketing, and keeping the books. Currently, the store sells about $40,000 of Pa ndau a year. Membership in the Co-op at one time exceeded 100 but now includes roughly sixty active members. The Pa ndau business provides a sense of cultural continuity, and it allows women to earn money while at home. Unfortunately, the return on the labor devoted to this effort is very low; one study estimated an hourly wage of $1.50.

The now defunct community burial society was also created in 1981. The society was initiated by Hmong to help pay for burials. In Laos, close relatives and friends of the deceased would help provide for burial ceremonies. In Laos, this contribution was relatively inexpensive, requiring more time than money. Here in America, however, burials are expensive and often a family and close relatives are unable to pay for one by themselves. The clans created the burial society in an effort to pool and spread the costs. From the beginning, the society was plagued by confusion over government regulations and its own operating rules. The effort finally disintegrated when one clan withdrew after most of its older members who were likely to die, died. The clan saw little reason to continue paying in, and other clans got upset at subsidizing the one clan's burials.

The third Hmong business is the Indochinese Food Store. Initiated and financed by two closely allied clans, the store sells both Asian and American grocery items. The food store supplies the community with ethnic foods they were previously unable to get conveniently. Most items, however, are more expensive than in nearby supermarkets. The store is staffed by two paid and numerous volunteer Hmong. Despite troubles with suppliers, taxes, and crime, the store manages to stay open. One of the keys to its success has been the loyalty of its Hmong patrons.

Recently, the idea of starting up businesses picked up considerable momentum in the Hmong community. In addition to the poultry shop and farm, numerous other possible enterprises have been suggested. Various Hmong have expressed interest in starting businesses such as gas stations, loan businesses, painting, security guard services, and restaurants. However, few Hmong will commit themselves to a business since they do not know what is involved in starting or running it. Tong himself wondered what it would be like.

Figure B.1.   Proposal #1: Refugee Management Development Project

Statement of Purpose

The purpose of the project outlined in this proposal is to develop business and management skills of refugees to facilitate the formation and expansion of viable, refugee-owed businesses. The proposed training and support program will equip refugee entrepreneurs with the skills and knowledge necessary to start and develop their own businesses. Successful businesses will contribute to refugee adjustment and self-sufficiency in a number of ways. Refugee small businesses will provide much-needed jobs, supply the Hmong with needed goods and services, increase refugee commitment to the resettlement community, and reestablish the refugee's sense of self-worth.

The Proposed Project

The Refugee Management Development Project (RMDP) is a proposed partnership between the United Hmong Association (UHA) and the Rhode Island Vocational Education and Training School (RIVETS). RMDP will make available a wide array of technical assistance services in business development and management to Mutual Assistance Associations (MAAs) and refugee entrepreneurs. These services will be geared to the needs of small community and family based businesses and the needs of individual participants.

Coordinated and delivered by RIVETS, the RMDP project will provide twenty-five Hmong refugees small-business management training and support that will include:

- management training seminars
- "going into business" orientation workshops
- a clearing house of technical information
- referral to appropriate management resources
- development of model business plans

After participating in the proposed project, Hmong who have had little experience with business will be prepared to start and manage enterprises of their own initiation and control.

Project Approach

In considering approaches to business development and management technical assistance, the RMDP emphasizes training the refugees rather than providing technical skills itself. This strategy meets the refugee need to not only understand management concepts but also to be able to carry out management functions. Too often economic development efforts provide management services that carry out management functions for the refugee such as accounting, marketing, financial plans, and so on. The refugee entrepreneurs may never acquire adequate management skills themselves. Since the Hmong place strong emphasis on the link between doing and understanding, the ability to perform management functions is crucial to understanding and directing the business.

Course material will be on both group and individual levels. Translation will be available and used as needed to ensure clear understanding of business concepts.

To the greatest degree possible, conceptual material will be related to the actual businesses the individual Hmong entrepreneurs are familiar with through their work or are interested in starting. The course outline is as follows:

Curriculum for Small Business Management Training Seminars

Unit	1	Advantages and disadvantages of small businesses
Unit	2	Choosing businesses
Unit	3	Market feasibility studies
Unit	4	Skills assessment
Unit	5	Keeping business records
Unit	6	Financial planning and control
Unit	7	Cash flows
Unit	8	Break-even analysis and maximizing profits
Unit	9	Financing a small business
Unit	10	Taxes and small businesses
Unit	11	Forms of business organization
Unit	12	Personnel and employee relations
Unit	13	Purchasing and supplier relations
Unit	14	Marketing and sales
Unit	15	Advertising and promotion
Unit	16	Insurance and crime prevention
Unit	17	Inventories, equipment and machinery
Unit	18	Contracts and leases
Unit	19	Customer service and relations
Unit	20	Business growth and transition

Business Start-Up Workshops

The business start-up workshops are designed to bring together the refugees' training and desires. Begun after the training seminars, the workshops will be focused on structuring the concerns and answering the questions of the Hmong who will be working on their own specific business ideas. Hmong will be taught the detailed and concrete steps necessary to start up a business. Subject to participant approval, topics covered in the course will include:

• setting up bookkeeping records
• raising and handling money
• writing bylaws and articles of incorporation
• licenses and regulations
• paying taxes and government fees
• choosing a location
• standard operating procedures
• suppliers and distributors
• inventory methods
• advertising
• where to go for help

The culmination of the workshop program will be the development of actual business plans. After consultation with business experts, and referrals to appropriate government agencies, financial institutions, and volunteer advisors, the Hmong will be able to start operations within a short period of time.

The Refugee Management Development Project will be available to all interested Hmong at no cost. Training and workshop sessions will be held twice a week for two to three hours in the evening. The training seminars will be taught during the first eight months of the year. The business start-up workshops will be conducted during the following four months. At the completion of the first cycle, a new class can enter the management program for the next year. A budget for the proposal is given in Table B.1.

Table B.1. Program Budget (For 1 Year): Refugee Management Development Project

Salaries		
Primary instructor/coordinator	$28,000	
Hmong liaison/assistant	16,000	
Secretary/office administrator	12,000	
Total Salaries		$56,000
Benefits and payroll taxes		14,000
Contracted services		
Management training consultant	$3,000	
Business development consultant	3,000	
Attorney[1]	5,000	
Accountant (CPA)[1]	8,000	
Total contracted services		$19,000
Other expenses		
Travel 2,500 miles × $.20/mile	500	
Telephone	1,000	
Printing and copying	500	
Office supplies and equipment	1,300	
Office rental[2]	1,200	
Classroom rental[2]	600	
Total other expenses		$ 5,100
Total Expenses		$94,100
less contributions[1,2]		(8,300)
less cash donations[3]		(5,000)
Total Grant Request		$80,800

1. Earnest Thompson, esq., and Mary Morelli, CPA, have both volunteered to contribute half of their fees to RMDP.

2. The Southwood Community Center has agreed to conribute ofice and classroom space to RMDP.

3. The Roger Williams Foundation has pledged $5,000 for a management-training program.

Figure B.2 Proposal #2: Establishment of a Hmong Poultry Shop

Objective of Study

The objectives of this study were to determine the feasibility of opening a Hmong-owned and operated poultry shop in Providence, Rhode Island, and to provide the basic elements of a business plan for such a shop.

Background Information

This study has been done at the initiation of Teng Vang, Pao Vang, and Blong Vang. Interested in opening a poultry shop, they approached the Providence University Cooperative Education Center and proposed a feasibility study of the shop as a possible project. The proposal was accepted by the Center and chosen as a semester project by Pam Hoffman and Thomas Magney, two graduate business students interested in minority business development.

The Vangs wished to study the poultry shop project for several reasons. First, the Hmong have a strong culinary preference for freshly slaughtered chicken. Many travel several miles to buy poultry from two small Italian shops located in the Federal Hill section of Providence. Second, the Hmong and other Indochinese people living in Providence have had great difficulty obtaining chickens that are prepared correctly for their important religious rituals. Third, the Hmong recognized that they had acquired some experience raising and butchering chickens in Laos. Finally, the Vangs saw the shop as a means of creating jobs and recirculating money within their own community.

The Poultry Industry

In 1980 there were five large poultry slaughter houses in New England, but due to high heating and labor costs, only one remains operational today. Most of the poultry sold in New England has not been freshly slaughtered; rather it was shipped north from the Mid-Atlantic states where it was processed and packed in ice. According to Mark Smith, Cooperative Extension Specialist in Poultry at the Rhode Island State University, no large company has entered the business in years. He cites competition and the cost of compliance with regulatory standards as the principal deterrents to new entry.

The slaughtering of poultry is regulated by the U.S. Department of Agriculture (USDA) when more than 20,000 chickens are processed annually or when any quantity of slaughtered chickens is shipped across state lines for sale. In both cases, a federal inspector must oversee the slaughter. The USDA requires the separation of live poultry storage and processing, and stipulates a variety of requirements during slaughter. It is difficult to process both poultry and other meats with the same facilities. Poultry-slaughtering operations that are exempt from federal regulations are under the jurisdiction of the Food Protection Division of the Health Department of Rhode Island. In general, the state's regulatory requirements are less stringent than those of the USDA.

Slaughtering chickens within a retail establishment for direct sale to the public is a very small and long-standing industry. The businesses tend to be family owned and located in an urban market. Because their operations often predate regulatory legislation, these small shops are usually exempt from state and federal codes for meat handling, processing, and inspection. Known as "New York dressed" (kosher) or "Buddhist" (head and feet attached) chicken, products from these small shops are rarely shipped interstate; such shipping requires a special permit. Because there have been no recent small entrants as precedents, there is also uncertainty over the exact regulatory requirements that would govern the proposed poultry shop. However, both Mark Smith and the local USDA poultry agent expect that the proposed shop would be eligible for exemptions that would relax regulatory requirements. Furthermore, they both maintain that even the full requirements would not be overly burdensome to the proposed operation.

Target Market

The proposed poultry shop will meet the demand for fresh poultry products among the Indochinese refugee population of Providence, Rhode Island. The store will be located in South Providence, the area of the city where most of Providence's estimated 6,000 Indochinese residents live. South Providence is made up of older, lower income neighborhoods and has large populations of black, Hispanic, and white residents in addition to the Indochinese. Most of the dwellings in South Providence are large, older, single-family homes, many of which have now been subdivided to house more than one family.

Indochinese people are heavy consumers of poultry. In an informal survey of twenty-three Indochinese households—twenty Hmong, two Cambodian, and one Lao—it was found that chicken is eaten more than any other meat. On a per capita basis, the average refugee eats 1.9 pounds of chicken per week, as opposed to 1.4 pounds of pork, .9 pounds of beef, and .3 pounds of fish. (The average American eats 1.0 pound of chicken per week, 1.3 pounds of pork, and 2.1 pounds of beef.)

The Indochinese in general, and the Hmong in particular, are selective buyers of chicken. They have a strong preference for freshly slaughtered birds over those commonly available in most supermarkets, which have often been dead for 24–72 hours. The survey results indicate that roughly two thirds of the Indochinese travel 1–3 miles out of their neighborhood to get fresh meat.

In addition to the Indochinese, other local residents, especially blacks, Hispanics, and Italians are potential markets for the poultry shop.

Products

The major product of the shop will be freshly slaughtered poultry, with both whole birds and parts being offered. The store will offer both young broilers and older fowl, which are retired egg layers or "spent hens." Fowl are smaller, and their flesh is harder and whiter in color than those of broilers.

Most American consumers prefer broilers to fowl, and hence one does not find fowl in most stores. The Hmong, however, prefer fowl to broilers because they taste more like the chickens they used to raise and eat in Laos. Fowl is also significantly cheaper than broilers. The household survey revealed that, on average, the Indochinese eat spent hens at a rate of 2:1 over broilers.

In addition to poultry, roughly one third of the store's sales will likely be eggs, milk, rice, and assorted fresh fruits and vegetables. These latter goods are consumed by the Indochinese; they make shopping more convenient, and they add to profit margins. The shop will also offer specialty preparation of chickens for

Hmong and other Indochinese religious rituals requiring the sacrifice of a chicken. At present, no Providence area poultry shop prepares chickens properly for religious purposes.

Competitive Environment

The store will face competition from two sources: other small poultry shops, of which there are two in Providence, and large supermarkets. The two existing poultry shops, Hillside Poultry and Mario's, are both older family run businesses located in a primarily Italian neighborhood several miles away. These shops are similar to the proposed Hmong shop, except that they do not handle produce or do religious preparations.

Supermarkets which sell non–fresh poultry may provide the toughest competition to the Hmong poultry shop. Several large and modern supermarkets are located in South Providence, and most of the Indochinese now shop for most of their groceries in these stores. Through great economies of scale, supermarkets can offer ice-packed or packaged broilers at a price at least $.10 per pound cheaper than existing poultry shops. Should Indochinese taste preferences shift from freshly slaughtered poultry toward less fresh forms, it could significantly hurt the business of a poultry store (Table B.2).

Promotional Strategy

The poultry shop will be entering an entrenched and competitive business environment and therefore must develop strategies to attract and retain customers. During the start-up phase, the store will implement a major campaign designed to introduce the store to the Hmong and Indochinese community. In addition to freshness and low price, another logical focus might be cultural factors. An attempt will be made to induce a feeling of community pride, that this is a store designed to serve the special needs of Indochinese people. Such a perception could significantly aid the store in establishing strong customer relationships.

Among the means available for advertising the store, leaflets, posters, promotions in the local newspaper, and word of mouth will likely be most effective because they are relatively inexpensive and can be focused most closely on the target market segments. A grand opening party will also help create community good-will toward the store.

Table B.2.   Selected Retail Poultry Prices in Providence

	Mario's Poultry	Hillside Poultry	Star Market (Large Supermarkets)
Whole Broilers	.85/lb.	.77/lb	.49/lb. (Ace brand) .59/lb. (Best brand)
Breast Halves	$1.20	NA*	.59/lb. (Ace brand) .79/lb. (Best brand)
Whole Fowl (soup chicken)	NA*	.65/lb	NA*

*NA refers to prices not available in the specific stores. In the case of Star Market, whole fowl were not available.

Operations

The poultry shop will consist of two operations: a retail outlet and a poultry processing plant. The store will be open forty hours a week, five days a week, Tuesday through Saturday.

The poultry shop will consist of three rooms. The first will serve as a loading and holding area for live birds. The second will be for killing, scalding, defeathering, and eviscerating the chickens. The third room will be storefront retail area. In total, the area required for the shop and processing area will be roughly 700 square feet. In South Providence suitable retail space with basic utilities included costs approximately $1 per square foot per month. To be made ready for processing, the facilities must be renovated. The expected cost for these leasehold improvements is $5,000.

Equipment will be required for all operational phases of the poultry shop. A truck and cages will be needed for picking-up and holding the chickens. Scalding tanks, batch pickers, stainless steel tables and sinks, and assorted racks, knives and other instruments will be used for processing. Basic processing capacity will exceed 100 birds an hour. Refrigerators, cash registers and shelving will be needed for retailing. Much of this equipment is available used at a sizeable discount. Consequently, the expected cost of all the equipment is projected to be $20,000.

Personnel

The poultry shop will need a manager and several workers who will be responsible for the daily operation of the plant and store. The manager's duties will be to direct the business affairs of the store. This would include supervising the workers' tasks, coordinating with the poultry suppliers, monitoring the financial condition of the store, and filling in where necessary. The manager's salary (not including payroll taxes) will be based on the current rate in the industry, around $14,000–15,000 per year.

The shop staff will be responsible for running the store and for processing the chickens. They should be able to slaughter, wash, segment, and pack the chickens at a rate of thirty birds per hour each. When they are working at this task, they will also be responsible for keeping a clean and sanitary work area, feeding, and picking up the chickens. The hourly wage for the staff including payroll taxes is estimated at $5.00 per hour.

Once a week, one of the workers will make the 150-mile circuit to various farms to pick up chickens. The truck will be able to carry up to 1,800 chickens per load. Weighing three pounds apiece, the chickens cost roughly $.15/lb. for spent hens and $.30/lb. for broilers. The birds eat about $.02 worth of feed each day they are kept at the store, however, they are not fed the twelve hours immediately preceding their slaughter. As a result of bleeding, defeathering, and evisceration, the chickens lose 25% of their body weight during processing.

Training and Development

The poultry shop will be a great economic development opportunity for the Hmong as a community owned and operated business. There are a variety of skills that will be required of the employees of the business, including managerial expertise (such as accounting, budgeting, sales, marketing, inventory management) and butchering skills for processing poultry. Both skills are already possessed to a limited degree by other Hmong in the Providence community and certainly by other Hmong in the United States.

A variety of sources of professional help will be required by the Hmong on a consulting basis during the start-up phase of the business, and later as problems or questions arise. The Cooperative Extension Specialist in Poultry at the Rhode Island State University, and knowledgeable suppliers are examples of such resources that are free. Others, such as accountants and lawyers will likely charge a reduced fee. The Hmong will manage and staff the shop and employ help on an as needed basis. Two thousand dollars should cover yearly fees and costs of attorneys, accountants, and insurance.

Figure B.3. Proposal #3: Refugee Employment through Agriculture Project (REAP).

There are approximately 6,000 Indochinese refugees in the Providence, Rhode Island, area. Many of these refugees, particularly the Hmong, are having severe economic and cultural difficulties. Their simple agrarian backgrounds are not suited for most work opportunities in America. Unable to find appropriate employment, the refugees are forced to rely on public assistance. The result has been demoralizing to the refugees. This project proposes to utilize the refugees' long tradition of agricultural production by providing the opportunity for the refugees to develop employment on their own farms. Project REAP proposes to bring together the refugees, high-quality farmland, the necessary capital investment, and complete training in both agricultural techniques and in marketing and management for small farmers. The result will be a comprehensive, self-supporting program of appropriate employment and training.

In recent years there have been several attempts to develop small, Hmong-operated farms. These projects have been helpful, but because of their small scale, their success has been limited. The REAP project continues to meet Hmong's desires to farm, but does so in a more comprehensive manner that will ensure long-term success. By developing many individual small farms on a large scale, REAP will better provide the necessary training, economies to scale through cooperation, and a coordinated distribution and marketing program. Sustained over four years, REAP will allow for complete training and smooth transition to totally Hmong controlled agricultural enterprises. There will be immeasurable benefits in terms of jobs created, food produced, and spirits mended.

Project REAP will take full advantage of the Rhode Island State University Cooperative Extension Service personnel. The involvement of their agricultural expertise is a key strength to this project. The 800 acres of prime farmland already committed to be donated are also crucial to REAP. Similarly, the integration of the REAP program with the CETA employment training program will join together two government agencies in a more effective manner than either alone.

A budget for this proposal is given in Table B.3.

Time Table

Project REAP will be carried out in three phases:

Phase I: Research, Development, and Planning (1 year)
Staff and participants will be recruited and selected

Farmland will be marked off and soil samples tested

Table B.3. Operating Budget

Item	Year 1	Year 2	Year 3	Year 4
Salaries	$350,000	$380,000	$415,000	$450,000
Programs	300,000	350,000	400,000	450,000
Total	$650,000	$730,000	$815,000	$900,000

Income from harvest will go to program participants.

Participants will be paid additionally by CETA special employee development program.

800 acres of prime farmland has been donated to the REAP project for ten years.

Research will determine the best vegetable and specialty crops to grow and the proper soil preparation for such produce

Livestock program will be developed

Farm management training curriculum and syllabus will be established

Marketing research and market development will begin

Feasibility of ancillary projects such as housing, greenhouses, nurseries, large-scale washing, packing and cold storage, and food processing will be studied and determined

Phase II. Technical Assistance, Training, and Production (2 years)
Staff will teach refugees modern farming techniques

Crops and livestock will be raised and marketed

Staff will teach refugees small farm management

Markets will be developed and expanded

Ancillary projects planned

Phase III: Growth and Transition (1 year +)
Farming operations continue

Experienced refugees will begin teaching new participants

New projects implemented

Staff phases out; refugees take over

Staffing Requirements

Project Director: Head supervisor of entire project. Must be experienced in personnel management and project administration. Ph.D. in agricultural discipline.

Farm Economist: Responsible for farm management planning and training. Ph.D. or MS with experience in farm management and with demonstrated teaching skills.

Horticulturalist: Responsible for soil preparation, crop selection, and farm technique training. Ph.D. or MS with teaching experience. Knowledge of greenhouse techniques preferred.

Animal Scientist: Responsible for livestock and husbandry program and training. Ph.D. or MS with experience in poultry and swine production.

Food Scientist: Responsible for crop harvesting, preparation, and packing. Responsible for training harvest and post harvest techniques. Ph.D. or MS with work experience. Communication skills required.

Food Marketing Specialist: Responsible for developing markets for project products. Work experience in food distribution required. Excellent communications skills necessary.

Administrative Assistant: Responsible for bookkeeping and office management. Demonstrated ability to work well with people; must be organized.

Hmong Assistants (7): Liaison between above staff and participants. Must be fluent in English, and committed to farming. Leadership abilities important.

CASE C

PBS Strategy Case

Introduction: PBS at a Crossroads

In 1988, with the increasing variety and availability of television programming through cable television, satellite telecommunications, and VCRs, the Public Broadcasting Service's (PBS) position as the leading provider of alternative, high-quality programming was being challenged. Some even argued that if cable was now providing alternative viewing choices previously offered by public television, then perhaps public television had outlived its purpose. After years of growth, public television's audience was shrinking. At the same time, reliance on corporate funding was escalating, giving rise to concerns over public television's ability to keep programming fresh and "on-the-edge." As president of PBS, Bruce Christensen was considering what, if anything, PBS should do in the next several years about the way it selects, provides, and promotes programs for American public television stations. In a 1988 address to the nation's public television stations he asserted that "public television must contemplate drastic change."

Public television, traditionally decentralized and slow to change, was operating in the midst of a telecommunications revolution during the mid- and late 1980s. The rapid pace of technological development and the growth of cable services, independent stations, and superstations throughout the 1980s created a very dynamic and competitive environment. As Mr. Christensen stated in July 1988, "over the past few years, change in the world of television has been abrupt and unsettling . . . it's enough to make you count the years to retirement." While Americans were becoming more dependent on television for information and entertainment, new technological advances created more choices for television viewers. Cable was perceived to be the greatest threat for PBS. Peter Downey, senior vice president for program support group, described cable as a "railroad train racing in our direction." With the greater array of options, viewing habits changed dramatically and audiences became fragmented.

PBS needed to adapt in order to survive and thrive within this new competitive environment. Clearly, Mr. Christensen needed to consider significant changes in PBS's structure and operations. He also realized that the changing competitive environment could create substantial opportunities for public television (PTV) as well. Because PTV's very existence was being called into question, Mr. Christensen saw that cable's challenge might be the necessary catalyst for invigorating change in public television.

This case was prepared by Paul Connolly, Bruce Ellman, and David Kluchman in cooperation with the Public Broadcasting Service under the supervision of Professor Sharon Oster at the Yale School of Organization and Management. It is meant to serve as a basis for class discussion rather than as an example of effective or ineffective management.

PBS and Public Television

History and Overview

The current public broadcasting system evolved from what was called "education-al" television in the 1950s. The nation's first noncommercial television station, KUHT, was based at the University of Houston and began broadcasting in 1953. By 1960, forty-nine noncommercial stations were established and the number grew to seventy-five by 1962. The vast majority of these stations were operated by educational institutions. Relying on limited local funding, these stations were dedicated to the needs of the local communities they served.

The Public Broadcasting Act of 1967 provided a national commitment to encourage the development of "programming which will be responsive to the interests of people both in particular localities and throughout the United States, and which will constitute an expression of diversity and excellence." The Corporation for Public Broadcasting (CPB) was incorporated in 1968 to administer the federal appropriations, and to provide support to the public radio and television stations and national program producers. CPB was also to act as a buffer between the federal government and producers in order to keep editorial decisions separate from funding decisions.

In 1969, PBS was born as a private, nonprofit corporation whose members are the nation's PTV stations. PBS is a membership organization that is owned and controlled by its member stations, which are accountable to their local communities. Because PTV stations are local, community-based organizations, they are fiercely autonomous and wary of centralized power. Consequently, significant power is retained by member stations, and decision-making processes are democratic in nature.

PBS's mission is to serve these member stations. Some 300 staff members administer program acquisition and scheduling, education services, advertising and promotion, audience research, broadcast and technical operations, development and revenue-producing activities, and engineering and technological development. For these services, member stations pay PBS a fee that is related to their financial resources (see Figure C.1 for a PBS Organization Chart).

PBS is different in many ways from both the American commercial networks and foreign "public" television. While the three main commercial American networks pay their affiliates to broadcast the programs they produce, the member stations pay PBS for the central services it renders. PBS itself does not produce programming. Furthermore, unlike the public service broadcasters in many other countries, PBS is not under direct governmental control. (Figure C.2 depicts the relationship among PBS, CPB, and member stations.)

Because PBS is controlled by its member stations, the services it provides must reflect the diversity of these stations. In 1988, there were 170 noncommercial, educational licensees operating 327 member stations. Of these licensees, 49% were community organizations, such as the Greater Washington Educational Telecommunications Association, Inc. (WETA) in Washington D.C.; 31% were colleges or universities, such as Pennsylvania State University; 14% were state authorities, such as South Carolina Educational Television; and 6% were local educational or municipal authorities, such as WNYC in New York City. These stations often have different programming objectives. Furthermore, within this group certain larger

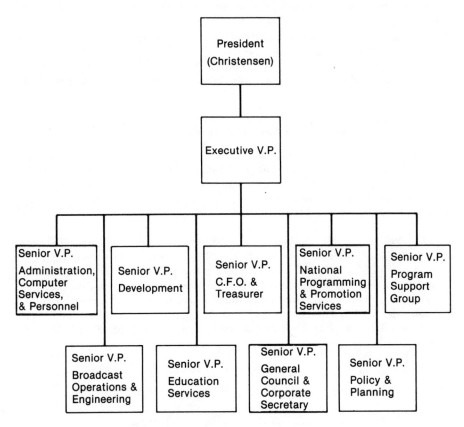

Figure C.1. PBS Organization Chart.

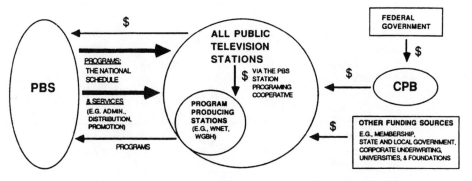

Figure C.2. The Public Television Network. *Source: PBS*

licensees such as the New York area's WNET or Boston's WGBH wield significant influence, often to the dismay of many smaller member stations.

PBS is governed by a thirty-five-member board of directors consisting of eighteen lay representatives from member stations' governing boards, 13 professional representatives from station management, three general directors and the PBS president.

Public Television Financial Structure and Position

In FY 1987, total revenue for the entire PTV system was $1.03 billion. This money was primarily raised by the individual stations. The largest portions of this $1 billion were from subscribers (22%), state governments (19%), the federal government (18%) and private businesses (16%). The complete revenue break-down by source is presented in Table C.1.

PBS The $97 million PBS budget for FY 1989 (July 1, 1988–June 30, 1989) was funded primarily by member stations (87%); 11% came from self-supporting activities, such as PBS VIDEO; and 2% came directly from CPB in the form of grants for audience research and programming support. More than three quarters (78%) of PBS's FY 1989 budget was allocated to program acquisition ($63 million or 64%), including the Station Program Cooperative described later, and distribution services ($14 million or 14%), such as the operation of the satellite interconnection system.

Member Stations In the mid- and late 1980s, the PTV system lacked funds and, on an aggregated station basis, operated with deficits. Aggregated income of PTV li-

Table C.1.   Public Television Income—FY 1987

Source	Dollars (millions)	Percentage of Total
Federal Government	186.4	18.1
CPB (TV only)	147.6	14.3
Education and Commerce Dept. (NEA, etc.)	38.8	3.8
Nonfederal	843.7	81.9
Subscribers	222.0	21.5
State Governments	196.9	19.1
Businesses	160.4	15.6
State Colleges	68.1	6.6
Foundations	41.7	4.1
Local Governments	33.5	3.3
Private Colleges	23.0	2.2
Auctions	22.5	2.2
Other Public Colleges	9.3	0.9
All Others	66.3	6.4
Total	1,030.1	100.0

Source: CPB

Figure C.3. Income of PTV Licensees FY 1982–FY 1986 ($ in millions)

	FY 82	FY 83	FY 84	FY 85	FY 86
In-kind & Indirect (all sources)	81.0	94.7	105.9	117.0	119.3
Cash Income					
Federal Government					
Federal Government	17.3	18.5	18.2	20.5	16.6
CPB	93.2	85.8	90.6	101.3	104.1
State & Local Govt					
Local Government	27.3	29.8	26.4	29.6	29.3
State Government	133.2	130.4	143.2	154.0	164.9
State & Other Tax Supp Coll	34.7	37.4	35.2	38.3	40.9
Private					
Private Colleges	6.3	7.1	7.2	9.9	9.0
Foundations	16.6	19.4	20.6	34.9	27.2
Businesses	57.5	68.2	88.3	110.5	100.8
Subscribers	120.1	146.6	158.0	184.2	199.7
Auction	19.7	20.2	21.7	22.4	21.9
All Other Private	40.4	40.9	48.7	53.6	59.0
Gross Income	647.3	699.0	764.1	877.0	892.7
(Less In-kind & Indirect)	−81.0	−94.7	−105.9	−117.0	−119.3
Net Cash Income	566.2	604.3	658.3	760.0	773.4

Figures may not add due to rounding.

Source: CPB; 11/87

censees in FY 1986 totalled $893 million (see Figure C.3), while aggregated expenditures reached $959 million (see Figure C.4).

The financial structure of PTV is extremely complex as it includes funds flowing among CPB, PBS, individual stations, independent producers, and regional networks. Figure C.2 depicts the relationships among the major players. Figure C.5 displays in detail how the money flows among the different entities to fund the creation and distribution of original broadcast programming, PTV's primary product.

Public Television Programming

Public television stations offer a wide array of programming to audiences across the nation, providing high-quality, noncommercial, and innovative programs of educational, public affairs, or cultural value. Most programs seen nationally on PTV are distributed to member stations by PBS through the National Program Service, which adopted the following mission in 1988:

> The mission of the PBS National Program Service is to provide to a general audience a unique program service distinguished by integrity, excellence, innovation, diversity, and educational value. Its exclusive purposes are to add to the quality of life of viewers and to help them cope with a complex world, and to assist PBS member stations

Figure C.4. Expenditures of PTV Licensees FY 1982–FY 1986 ($ in millions)

	FY 82	FY 83	FY 84	FY 85	FY 86
Capital Expenditures	62.6	75.0	72.0	94.8	87.4
Operating Expenditures					
Programming & Production	287.7	307.2	347.4	408.7	412.1
Broadcasting	124.1	140.5	146.5	154.0	162.3
Program Information	35.6	39.3	41.5	47.4	50.2
Fundraising	62.6	72.6	81.3	95.4	104.8
Management & General	103.0	112.6	115.5	131.4	142.3
Gross Expenditures	675.6	747.3	804.2	931.6	959.1
(Less Capital Expenditures)	−62.6	−75.0	−72.0	−94.8	−87.4
Net Operating Expenditures	612.9	672.2	732.2	836.8	871.7

Figures may not add due to rounding.

Source: CPB, 11/87

in being recognized and valued as an indispensable community service, providing formal and informal educational opportunities to the largest number of television viewers.

Local stations supplement material from the National Program Service with local productions, such as news shows, and acquisitions, such as *Benny Hill.*

The 1,645 hours of original broadcast programs (those programs new to national public television, excluding rebroadcasts of programs premiering in prior years) distributed by PBS in FY 1988 broke down in detail as in Table C.2. These programs were drawn from many sources including PTV stations, independent producers, foreign production entities, and other television systems and program distributors throughout the world. PBS itself does *not* produce programming. Rather, it facilitates national distribution of programs, performs technical evaluation of programs, ensures that programs meet certain editorial standards, develops a national scheduling strategy, and provides very limited production funds. PBS reserves the final decision to distribute a program, regardless of its source. Thus, its responsibility includes selecting particular programs and organizing those selections into a coherent national schedule.

Of the 1,645 hours of original broadcast programs in FY 1988, 48% were acquired from PTV stations such as New York's WNET and Boston's WGBH. These larger-producing stations develop original programming ideas, raise funds (from both within and outside the PTV system), and oversee production of such series as *NOVA* and *Adam Smith's Money World.* Most of the remaining hours of original broadcast programs were purchased from American independent producers (40%) and foreign acquisitions/coproductions (12%), where primary editorial control is not held by PBS or the local station.

PBS Program Funding and Approval

The Station Program Cooperative In terms of programming hours, the Station Program Cooperative (SPC) was the single most important source of supply for the

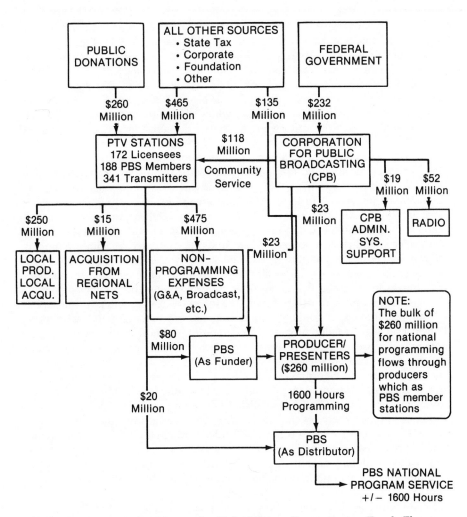

Figure C.5. Public Television in the United States Programming Funds Flow (1989 Estimates). *Source:* PBS internal documents.

Table C.2. Programming by Category

Programming Category (with example)	Hours	Percentage of Total Hours
Public Affairs (*Frontline*)	723	44.0
Cultural Programs (*Great Performances*)	378	23.0
Children's Programs (*Sesame Street*)	178	10.8
Science and Nature (*NOVA*)	127	7.8
How-To Programs (*This Old House*)	127	7.8
Instructional (English as a Second Language)	109	6.6
Sports (Tennis)	3	.1

Source: PBS

National Program Service in 1988. Approximately 1,000 hours of the 1,645 original programming hours were selected and financed by the SPC. Reflecting the democratic values of the PBS system, the SPC provided a market mechanism for the nation's PTV stations to choose collectively and fund national programming distributed by PBS. Through this mechanism administered by PBS, programming decisions for many major series, such as *Sesame Street, Wall $treet Week, Nature,* and *American Playhouse* were made by station voting. Throughout the 1980s, each year about twenty-six to thirty series were purchased through the SPC and distributed nationally.

The SPC operated in the following manner. Every year, both independent producers and stations submitted proposals to the SPC. In most cases, partial funding had been obtained from other sources (such as private corporations, foundations, CPB, or other limited PBS funding pools) and the producer sought financing for the shortfall. The smaller the deficit, the easier it was to sell the program. Once a year, local station programmers had an opportunity to meet with producers, discuss their projects, and choose programming through a computerized bidding process. The eventual cost of a program to any one station was determined by the size of that station's federal grant, as well as by the number of other stations making a commitment to purchase the same program. The greater the number of stations who made a commitment to a program, the lower the cost was to any one station.

Although the SPC, through granting programming autonomy to local stations, allowed licensees to tailor programming according to local tastes and needs, the cooperative approach made it difficult to introduce new programs and remove outdated ones. New submissions were rarely able to be viewed at SPC, as production funds were still being raised. Member stations needed to rely solely on the written proposal for brand new programs. For returning series, this did not present a problem. For example, in the 1988 SPC, fifty-one proposals were submitted to the market including twenty-seven of the twenty-eight series purchased in the year's prior SPC. Only one new PTV series was funded through the 1988 SPC. Interstation political pressures were often present. Producing stations had substantial purchasing power and could wield significant influence in the market. Many criticized SPC for inhibiting programming innovation and extending the lives of less deserving programs.

In addition, the SPC did not allow for quick decision making. In its former days as the only outlet for certain types of programming, the PBS system was not severely hampered by the slow moving market mechanism of program selection and funding. By 1988, the environment had clearly become more competitive.

Other Funding Sources Nearly 70% of the $210.2 million spent on programs for original broadcast in FY 1987 was funded by three sources: corporations (30%); the licensees, which included the SPC (14.5%); and CPB (25.7%). The complete breakdown is presented in Table C.3. Some PBS watchdogs were concerned that corporate underwriting comprised such a large share of program funding. They found corporate underwriters to be conservative by nature and reluctant to fund controversial "on-the-edge" programming. Given the problems with SPC and the proliferation of alternative viewing options, some asked whether PTV was still bold and innovative.

A Public Television Series and Its Funding The *NOVA* science documentary series illustrates the funding and production of a PTV series distributed by PBS in 1988.

Figure C.6. Cume and Average Prime Time Ratings Based
on All TV Households

Service	Weekly Cume %			Average Audience %		
	1985–1986	1986–1987	1987–1988	1985–1986	1986–1987	1987–1988
HUT	—	—	—	60.3%	59.7%	58.2%
PBS	31.7%	33.1%	31.4%	2.6	2.7	2.4
ABC	77.9	77.6	75.8	13.8	12.8	12.2
CBS	79.3	78.8	75.3	14.4	13.8	12.0
NBC	82.0	82.1	79.2	16.3	16.3	14.7
Total networks	93.3	93.1	93.0	44.7	43.0	38.9
Independents	53.0	54.6	59.7	7.2	7.7	8.3
HBO	13.8	14.3	14.6	1.8	1.9	2.0
Total Pay	20.6	20.6	21.4	3.3	3.3	3.6
WTBS	13.3	14.3	16.9	1.0	1.1	1.4
Total Superstns	28.6	28.2	32.6	3.0	2.8	3.4
A&E	1.8	3.2	4.6	0.1	0.1	0.2
CNN	6.7	7.5	8.3	0.4	0.5	0.5
Discovery	NA	1.1	5.0	NA	0.1	0.3
USA Network	8.8	10.7	12.2	0.5	0.7	0.8
Total Cable Originated	31.5	35.7	40.8	3.8	4.7	5.9

One PBS executive characterized the "PBS style" as exhibited by a hypothetical rain-forest documentary where "lugubrious voices drone on while a leaf drips water for an hour." The PTV audience had maintained a consistent demographic profile for many years. Overall, the PTV audience in 1987–1988 was quite reflective of the general U.S. population in terms of such household characteristics as race, education, and income level. Figure C.9 presents PTV audience demographics data for the 1987–1988 season.

PBS Promotion

PBS's main promotional efforts consisted of on-air publicity, editorial reviews, and paid advertising. Due to the traditionally small budgets for paid advertising (approximately $3–8 million per year between 1983 and 1988), PTV relied mostly on free publicity from television program critics in newspapers and magazines. On an institutional level, PBS's slogan, "TV Worth Watching," and logo had very high recognition levels. However, it was hard for PBS to promote a single identifiable image, as many cable services did, given its diverse programming. National advertising for programming was also difficult because PBS had few regular series and little thematic scheduling and local stations aired programs at different times. With these scheduling problems, it was difficult to get reviewed by television critics or buy advertising on a national basis. Consequently, there was a low level of aware-

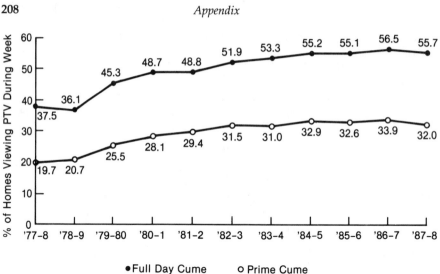

Figure C.7. Average One-Week Cume Audiences, 1977–1988.

ness of PTV scheduling and weak viewing habits for PBS. A very common reason for not watching a PBS show was: "I didn't know it was on."

The Changing Competitive Environment

Networks

Overview of Networks Historically, the television industry in the United States was dominated by the three major national networks: NBC, CBS, and ABC. These three commercial networks own and operate their own stations in many of the bigger urban areas and substantially control most of their affiliates. Commercial networks provide mass appeal entertainment that aims to attract a large viewership so as to maximize advertising revenues.

NBC began broadcasting as the first national network in 1939 and the industry grew rapidly after World War II. By 1959, 50 million television receivers were used throughout the United States. During the 1960s and 1970s, the networks enjoyed successful programs, augmenting viewership, and heightening advertising revenues. However, by the 1980s the networks began to face new competition from cable services and independent stations. In addition, in 1986 the Fox network was launched as a fourth network, and it successfully achieved a profit in 1987.

Networks' Performance During the 1987–1988 season the commercial networks' audience erosion continued and network prime-time ratings plummeted to all-time lows. Their collective prime-time share for the season was 38.9%, a steep decline from the previous season's 43.0% share. Between 1983 and 1988, average weekly viewing of the networks dropped 12 share percentage points.

According to the qualitative ratings, the networks' programs did not have a high degree of "appeal" or "impact" for viewers. This is not surprising, considering that most Americans watch television for "escape" and leisure, rather than education or emotional involvement. Viewers consider network television to be more relaxing than either cable or PTV.

Figure C.8. Qualitative Program Ratings Ranked on Program Appeal (Viewers with Cable)

Network	N	Program Appeal	Program Impact	Planned Ahead	Touched Feelings	Learned Something	Would Watch Again
PBS Programs	523	81	68	68	64	73	88
CBN Network	176	79	67	68	68	66	88
Discovery Channel	144	77	66	26	59	73	84
Cable News Network	462	76	59	62	48	69	86
Nashville Network	254	76	60	72	59	60	87
ESPN	213	75	50	64	49	50	86
NBC Network	4,646	75	51	72	57	45	83
WTBS-TV	430	75	47	62	50	44	87
ABC Network	2,611	75	55	68	58	52	84
CBS Network	3,509	74	53	72	57	49	83
WGN-TV	299	74	54	59	57	50	81
Arts & Entertainment Network	71	73	58	49	59	58	78
Syndicated Programs	2,672	73	51	80	46	56	86
MTV Networks	41	72	30	20	33	26	82
Lifetime Network	109	71	56	44	56	55	78
Showtime	93	68	50	47	55	46	72
USA Network	226	68	43	49	47	39	76
Nickelodeon	82	67	39	24	48	29	77
Home Box Office	459	66	43	41	49	38	68
FOX Network	164	61	37	49	41	33	69

Figure C.9. PTV Audience Demographics Twelve Weeks: October 1987–September 1988

	U.S. TVHH (000)	%	PTV Audience Full Day	PTV Audience Prime	Indexed to U.S. Full Day	Indexed to U.S. Prime	Penetration Full Day	Penetration Prime	Avg Min per Viewing HH Full Day	Avg Min per Viewing HH Prime
All TV households	88,600	100.0	100.0	100.0			55.7	32.0	173	94
Persons 2+	229,120	100.0	100.0	10.0			39.0	20.5	128	83
Head of household demos										
Race										
Black	9,560	10.8	9.0	7.4	83	69	46.1	21.6	160	80
Non-Black	79,040	89.2	91.0	92.6	102	104	56.6	32.6	174	95
Education										
LT 4 yrs. HS	21,860	24.7	22.5	22.0	91	89	50.1	27.7	156	85
4 Yrs. High School	31,790	35.9	35.1	32.7	98	91	53.6	28.2	146	82
1–3 Yrs. College	16,010	18.1	18.3	8.1	101	100	55.6	31.0	177	91
4+ Yrs. College	18,940	21.4	24.2	27.1	113	127	62.0	39.3	210	112
Occupation										
Prof/Owner/Mgr	20,180	22.8	24.2	25.5	106	112	58.7	35.0	189	96
Clerical & Sales	13,480	15.2	14.8	14.1	97	93	53.7	29.1	157	83
Skilled & Semi-Sk	28,770	32.5	30.9	25.8	95	80	52.8	25.0	153	77
Not in Labor Force	26,170	29.5	30.2	34.6	102	117	56.5	36.6	184	110
Income										
Less than $10,000	15,320	17.3	14.5	12.9	84	75	46.4	23.5	144	81
$10,000–$19,999	18,160	20.5	18.7	19.0	91	93	50.5	29.0	177	102
$20,000–$29,999	16,070	18.1	17.2	16.7	95	92	52.5	29.0	156	92
$30,000–$39,999	13,410	15.1	16.3	16.0	108	106	59.5	33.1	180	88
$40,000+	25,640	28.9	33.4	35.4	115	122	63.3	38.0	188	99

County size										
A	36,930	41.7	44.2	45.4	106	109	59.2	34.5	180	96
B	26,660	30.1	29.1	29.3	97	97	53.8	30.8	173	99
C and D	25,010	28.2	26.7	25.3	95	90	52.8	28.4	163	85
Cable										
Noncable	43,400	49.0	48.6	51.5	96	102	55.0	33.2	205	108
Pay Cable	25,040	28.3	27.9	24.5	103	90	55.1	27.6	140	74
Basic Cable	20,160	22.8	23.5	24.0	105	108	57.5	33.3	152	89
Persons viewing										
Kids 2–5	14,170	6.2	8.5	3.5	137	56	52.8	10.2	192	48
Kids 6–11	20,190	8.8	8.4	4.7	95	53	36.7	10.6	63	36
Teens 12–17	19,880	8.7	5.4	3.8	62	44	23.8	8.9	75	52
Women 18–34	33,970	14.8	11.2	9.9	76	67	29.0	13.3	115	63
Women 35–49	24,180	10.6	10.1	10.4	95	98	36.4	19.4	113	78
Women 50–64	17,000	7.4	9.1	11.3	123	153	46.9	30.1	140	92
Women 65+	16,750	7.3	9.5	12.4	130	169	49.4	33.3	162	106
Men 18–34	33,560	14.6	12.0	11.2	82	77	31.5	15.2	87	61
Men 35–49	23,110	10.1	10.6	12.8	105	127	40.1	25.1	105	73
Men 50–64	15,130	6.6	8.4	10.8	127	163	48.5	32.1	137	99
Men 65+	11,180	4.9	6.8	9.6	140	197	53.4	38.9	169	115

Percentages may not sum to 100% due to rounding.

*Penetration is the weekly cume for each specific demographic group.

"Indexed to U.S." represents the demo's PTV proportion relative to the household/person universe. An index of 100 means the group was in the same proportion of the PTV audience as their makeup in the total population. An index above 100 means the group was ever-represented while a score below 100 indicates their numbers fall short of their population share.

Future Outlook for Networks In 1988, the networks' profits were shrinking and advertising revenues were flat. Furthermore, program costs were increasing and there was even speculation that total revenues would not be sufficient to sustain all three networks.

Although the networks were losing market share, they still remained the dominant force in television. They continued to have the largest viewing audiences and were most producers' top choice for first-run series. Despite their recent production cost-cutting, some television analysts believed that the networks would renew their commitment to quality in order to appeal to younger, more affluent viewers. The networks increased and improved their promotional efforts. In response to competition they made heavy investments in advertising and increased their on-air promotions.

Independents and Superstations

The growth of independent stations and superstations created additional competition for the networks and PBS. While in 1981 there were 135 independent stations without network affiliations, there were over 300 by 1988. These independent stations primarily aired syndicated reruns and movies. During the 1980s, their combined ratings rose steadily, but at a slightly slower rate than the growth in the number of stations. In 1988, their average audience rating was 8.3%.

By 1988, about six of the larger independent stations had become "superstations" by retransmitting their programs via satellite to local cable operators, regionally and nationally. A wider audience base allowed superstations to charge much higher advertising rates than local independent stations. WTBS was the first and largest superstation. Operated by Turner Broadcasting System since 1976, WTBS boasted 45.6 million subscribers and $250 million in advertising revenues by 1988. WTBS's programming was designed for family viewing and included classic movies, sporting events, and entertainment specials.

Cable

History and Overview of Cable Industry In the 1980s, cable was by far the most salient new competitor in the television industry. Cable services were developed in 1948 in order to provide program reception to viewers in remote areas who were unable to receive broadcast signals.[3] The 1970s saw a large push toward cable wiring of urban areas. This spurred the development of "for cable" networks. The big breakthrough came in 1975 when Home Box Office (HBO) began distributing movies via satellite as a pay cable service.

In 1982 cable crossed the 33% penetration level, a critical point at which it became a viable advertising medium. It began dramatic growth funded by a dual revenue stream—subscription fees and advertising. Technological developments soon made it possible to deliver up to fifty channels on a single piece of cable, thus opening the door to a whole array of cable-originated services. As cable developed

---

[3]Television signals are transported on electromagnetic waves that need a medium through which to travel. Cable networks transmit programs to cable operators via domestic satellite. The cable industry employs antennas on high ground to receive signals from these satellites, as well as local broadcasters and microwaves, and transmits them to local cable systems. The television signals are then delivered through a network of coaxial feeder cables to neighborhoods. From this feeder cable, a "drop" cable is connected directly to individual subscriber homes. (*Source:* National Cable Television Association.)

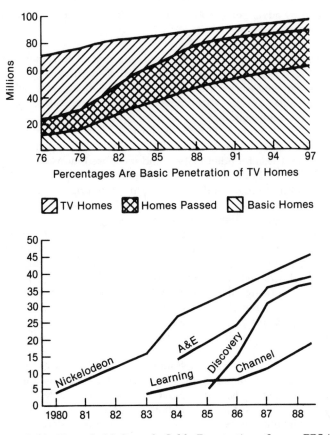

Figure C.10. Cable Household Growth Cable Penetration. *Source:* PBS internal documents.

in the early 1980s, highly publicized failures, such as The Entertainment Channel and CBS Cable, made some doubt the potential for cable's success. Yet, the industry as a whole broke even in 1984, and as penetration levels further increased, cable's strength and longevity were ensured. By 1988, there were 12,000 cable system operators nationwide.[4] Figure C.10 shows actual and expected cable household growth as well as cable channel penetration levels.)

The structure of the cable industry became increasingly complex and vertically integrated as it grew and matured. Multiple System Operators (MSOs), large companies that owned and operated more than one local cable system, became gatekeepers of cable programming since they chose which cable services to deliver. Many cable networks were owned by various media groups. For example, Viacom International owns Nickelodeon, and both NBC and Tele-Communications Inc., a major MSO, partially own Bravo. Cable services consisted of "basic cable," which

---

[4] A cable system is a communication system licensed by a local government that delivers multiple channels of programming to subscribers in a community via coaxial cables. A cable operator is a firm that holds the franchise to operate the local cable system. The cable operator assembles the packages of programs, pays a fee to program providers for the rights to show their programs, markets the programs, and provides maintenance and customer service. (*Source:* National Cable Television Association.)

was supported by advertising, and such "pay cable" services as HBO and Disney, which do not show commercials.

Cable Programming Realizing that households subscribed to cable because of the diversity it offered, cable operators supported and encouraged "niche" programming that was targeted to specific audiences. Several major cable networks developed PBS "look-alike" services that offered science, nature, children's, educational, and public affairs programming.

Arts and Entertainment, Discovery, Nickelodeon, The Learning Channel, C-Span, and Cable News Network were PBS's chief cable competitors in 1988. Arts and Entertainment was founded in 1984 and its subscriptions have grown from 4 million to more than 42 million homes. A&E offered performing arts, drama, documentary, and cultural programming and produced no original programming. Discovery began in 1985 with 5 million subscribers; with 42 million subscribers in 1988, Discovery grew faster in 1988 than any other cable service. Discovery showed nature, science, and world exploration documentaries, and it relied heavily on program acquisition and coproduction. Nickelodeon was founded in 1980 and had 48 million subscribers by 1988. Nickelodeon offered entertainment, quiz, comedy, and adventure shows, aimed mostly at children. The Learning Channel, another one of the fastest growing cable services, was founded in 1986 and delivered educational programming to remote areas. C-Span offered live coverage of Congressional hearings. Finally, Cable News Network (CNN), which was founded in 1980, showed all-news programming, with completely original productions.

Cable Performance and Audience By 1988 more than 90% of households were passed by cable, giving over 88 million homes access to cable programming; 50% of them subscribed to cable services. Throughout the mid-1980s, cable channel audience ratings grew, taking viewers away from both the networks and PBS. As the amount of time spent watching television remained flat, it became apparent that cable was a substitute for whatever people previously watched. Basic cable subscribers tend to be younger and more urban than the network audience and general population. Pay cable homes are younger and higher income families who watch TV more than the average viewer.

Overall, cable channels have higher impact and appreciation ratings than the networks, but lower qualitative ratings than PBS. Yet the Discovery Channel came quite near to PBS's impact and appreciation measurements. Likewise, CNN scored only slightly lower than PBS on program appeal.

Cable Promotion The cable services allocated a high proportion of their revenues to be spent on marketing and promotion. Advertising was particularly effective for many cable channels since they had "single theme" programming for which the content could be easily conveyed. Some cable channels compared themselves to PTV in their advertising. For example, Bravo described itself in a promotional flyer as a "cable TV network with only the highest quality programming for the selective viewer, with no commercials and no endless pleas for donations."

By 1988, listing information for cable was also widely available. In 1980, cable program information comprised 16% of *TV Guide's* listing space. By 1988 it was 53%. Moreover, new viewer guides were being published especially for cable subscribers.

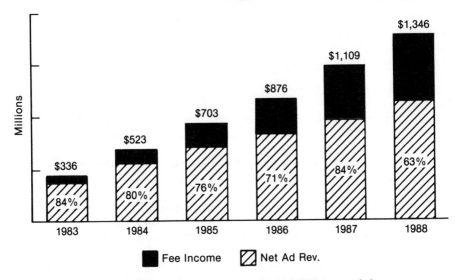

Figure C.11. Cable Network Revenues. *Source:* PBS internal documents.

Future Outlook for Cable In 1988, cable was in a very strong position, with high profits and margins, and expected continued growth. Cable services benefitted from two revenue streams: subscription fees and advertising. (Figure C.11 shows the growth of cable revenues between 1983 and 1988). The cable industry's profits in 1988 were $372 million, compared to a $54 million loss in 1983. According to the Cable Advertising Bureau, at least twelve of the fifteen largest basic cable services were profitable in 1988. Basic cable networks grossed about $1.3 billion in revenues in 1988.

After the capital-intensive early 1980s, cable began spending more on programming in the late 1980s. In 1988, seven of the leading cable networks (ESPN, CNN, USA, Nashville, Lifetime, Nickelodeon, A&E, and Discovery) spent $433 million on programming. In comparison, PTV spent $412 million in direct program and production expenses in FY 1986. Some industry analysts believed that, in order to increase audience size, certain cable channels would broaden their programming to become more mass-market oriented, thereby decreasing program quality.

Despite an optimistic economic outlook, the cable industry still had vulnerabilities. Many cable services had weak capital structures given the high levels of debt used to fund their growth. Also, many subscribers complained about poor customer service and low technical quality. In order to respond to the weaknesses and pursue nonsubscribing passed homes, cable operators were attempting to raise perceived value by improving service and further increasing diversity.

Other Technological Developments

VCRs and Remote Controls Video cassette recorders (VCRs) and remote controls have significantly changed viewer behavior. From 1985 to 1988, VCR penetration rose from 19% to 60%. VCRs were used primarily to watch rental movies and to tape TV shows; 71% of taped shows came from commercial TV, 15% from PTV, and

14% from cable. Industry experts believed that increased recording might make program scheduling less important. However, many people used VCRs solely for playback of rental cassettes. In addition, the heavy penetration of remote controls also changed viewing habits by promoting channel switching and "grazing."

Future Technological Developments In 1988, other revolutionary advances were on the horizon, including Direct Broadcast Satellite (DBS) and fiberoptic systems. These technological developments could dramatically alter the telecommunications industry, creating new distribution methods that could make both broadcasting and cable outmoded systems. Vastly increasing the number and capability of channels in the home, these alternatives to cable could eliminate local broadcast stations' role as the primary providers of programs to viewers by directly supplying continuous programming.

Similar to cable systems that deliver programs through coaxial cables, fiberoptic systems would transmit images over ultrapure hair-thin strands of glass. This new system could possibly be available by the end of the 1990s, yet many obstacles remained to be overcome. This interactive system would enable viewers to order what they want when they want and could provide a virtually unlimited number of television channels and supply of programs. Fiberoptics systems could be operated by multiple system operators or by telephone companies as both enjoy entrees into the home via coaxial cables and telephone lines, respectively. At present, telephone companies are prohibited from offering this type of service; however, the regulatory environment may change.

DBS, likely to compete with cable by 1995, involved the evolution of smaller and smaller satellite dishes that would be easier to install and less expensive than the large dishes. The DBS system would be a more efficient distribution system than cable since there would be no need for multiple system operators. Like many technological developments, DBS and fiberoptics could either help or hinder PTV.

Conclusion: PBS's Need to Decide on a Strategy

While still noncommercial, PTV was no longer the sole provider of "alternative" television with the growing strength of cable. Many said that PBS was not designed to be competitive, having developed a complacent attitude from more than two decades in a monopolist position. Inefficiencies were evident in the lengthy response time for project funding and the complex approval process. Moreover, it was not easy to claim that PTV was bold, innovative, and stretching boundaries as new cable services proliferated.

Bruce Christensen realized that PBS should examine its position and change in order to succeed within the new competitive environment. By late 1988, the issue had come to a head and he needed to consider his advisors' strategic recommendations and act decisively.

Several key advisors recommended meeting cable head on. Some had even suggested setting up a PBS cable network, and creating "niche" PBS channels. Others speculated on the possibility of surrendering some programming areas to cable, such as British period drama. The program funding and selection system had to be addressed to enhance efficiency without abandoning the democratic values and attention to local interests which were embodied in the SPC. Christensen wondered that some of his advisors might be overreacting to the cable threat.

Perhaps, he pondered, an effective strategy would be to stay the course and not institute major changes.

Bruce Christensen needed to devise a competitive strategy for PBS. He knew that he had to carefully consider PBS's organizational structure, program content, program selection process, and marketing efforts in order to design an effective strategy. In addition, he had to keep in mind PTV's public service mission as a noncommercial provider of programming. Regardless of the strategy chosen, the plan would have to be approved by the diverse and autonomous member stations.

CASE D

American Red Cross—South Central Connecticut Chapter

The telephone rang impatiently and two people hovered anxiously in the doorway of her office. Nancy Silverman, director of volunteer services, was frantically assembling a packet of information that she needed for a meeting of the Golf Tournament Committee, the group responsible for planning and executing the largest single fundraising event in the history of the South Central Connecticut Chapter (SCCC)[1] of the American Red Cross. "I can't go to the meeting tonight," she explained into the telephone. "I have to be in New York for the kick-off of National's young adult recruitment campaign. Can you go in my place? We need to get some specifics from this committee. It's an eight-day event and they keep telling me they'll need lots of volunteers, but I've gotten nowhere trying to find out how many people they need, or what skills they require. This committee seems to think I can produce volunteers at a moment's notice. They don't understand that I have to *recruit* these people."

Silverman's invitation to the kick-off celebration for the advertising campaign was the result of her successful nomination of Hugh Kline, Jr., as one of the American Red Cross's "rising stars: volunteer leaders for the next century." Kline's involvement with the Red Cross grew out of a family tradition: He began to volunteer when he was only ten. Now, eleven years later, he represents the class of young people that the Red Cross hopes to attract to its volunteer ranks in the next decade.

Silverman turned to the doorway where Sally Cohen, coordinator of blood drive volunteers, stood shaking her head. "I have no one left to call," Cohen said. "Between Thursday and Friday we have seven blood drives. I just don't have any people left to call." She only needed three volunteers, but the three positions were Health History Interviewers (HHIs), which were always the hardest to fill. Cohen encountered the Chapter's shortage of available HHI volunteers every time Blood Services scheduled several concurrent blood drives.

Next Silverman turned to another co-worker, John Perry, the director of emergency services. "You wanted to see me?" he asked. "Yes," she replied. "You had a meeting with the Disaster Services Administrative Committee last night, didn't you? Please turn in an attendance list so I can make sure their volunteer hours are being recorded. Also, ask them to keep a log of the time they spend gathering information for the Disaster Plan. That all counts toward volunteer hours."

Although the Chapter's volunteer rolls boast thousands of names, the numbers do not tell the whole story. The long list of volunteers masks the increasingly challenging task of attracting enough volunteers with the specific skills required by the various volunteer positions. Equally disquieting are national forecasts for a

---

[1]Terry Cowdrey and Rachel Miller prepared this case under the direction of Professor Sharon Oster. It is intended to be used as a basis for class discussion and not to illustrate either effective or ineffective management.

reduction in the segments of the population from which the Red Cross has traditionally drawn its volunteers. Silverman recognized the value of planning for this
eventuality, but limited resources and conflicting priorities often seemed to con-
spire against her best intentions.

History of the American Red Cross

In 1881, Clara Barton and a group of supporters formed the American Association
of the Red Cross, the American affiliate of the International Red Cross. In 1893 the
organization was reincorporated as the American National Red Cross. In 1900 and
again in 1905, Congress granted Congressional Charters to the Red Cross, designating it as the agency responsible for providing services to disaster victims and to
members of the U.S. armed forces. For the first twenty years of its existence the
organization devoted itself to disaster relief. In 1906, President Theodore Roosevelt
appointed the Red Cross as the agency officially responsible for assisting the victims of the San Francisco earthquake, describing the Red Cross as "The only organization chartered and authorized by Congress to act at times of great national calam-
ity." In the next decade, the Red Cross added first aid, industrial safety, and water
safety education programs to its services.

When war broke out in Europe in 1914 there were 107 chapters of the Red Cross.
By the end of the war there were 3,864 chapters and one in every five Americans
was a Red Cross member. During World War II, the Red Cross provided humanitarian assistance to separated families and displaced refugees; between 1942 and
1944 the number of volunteers more than doubled, reaching a record 7.5 million in
1944. In addition, Americans responded to Red Cross appeals to patriotism through
their generous financial support of the agency's efforts.

Today, the fifty-member National Board of Governors, of which the president of
the United States appoints eight including the chair, sets policy for the national
organization. Since 1947 local chapters have elected thirty of the fifty governors,
effectively placing the future of the Red Cross in the hands of local volunteers. The
National Board fills its remaining seats by electing governors on an at-large basis.
Every year the Red Cross collects about 6 million units of blood and assists at the
scene of more than 40,000 disasters. The agency issues 6 million certificates each
year to graduates of cardiopulmonary resuscitation (CPR), first aid, and water
safety courses.

Currently, the Red Cross provides these services through 2,900 local chapters.
Every community in the United States and its territories falls within the geographic
jurisdiction of a Red Cross chapter. National Headquarters dictates the agency's
mission and operating guidelines, while providing materials, supplies, and professional development opportunities to the Chapters. In addition, in times of disaster,
National provides both financial and staff support if the relief effort becomes too
large for the Chapter to handle (normally defined as an effort costing more than
$50,000). In exchange, the Chapters must adhere to strict standards in their person-
nel policies and organizational structure, the services they offer, and their use of the
Red Cross name and emblem. Most importantly, the Chapters must pay a portion
of their annual revenues to National as their "Fair Share" dues. Through 1990 the
Fair Share requirement was calculated as a percentage of revenues raised through
United Way contributions, membership collections, and special events. Beginning
in 1991, a flat Fair Share amount was assigned to each Chapter based on its demographic characteristics.

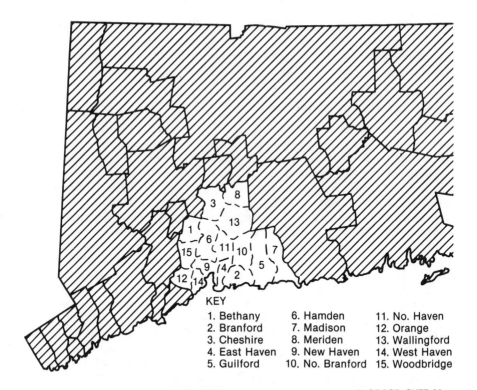

KEY

1. Bethany	6. Hamden	11. No. Haven
2. Branford	7. Madison	12. Orange
3. Cheshire	8. Meriden	13. Wallingford
4. East Haven	9. New Haven	14. West Haven
5. Guilford	10. No. Branford	15. Woodbridge

COMMUNITY	POPULATION			% OF POP. OVER 65		
	1980	1990 (est.)	2000 (est.)	1980	1990 (est.)	2000 (est.)
Bethany	4,330	16,200	17,550	27.7%	9.3%	11.0%
Branford	23,363	27,050	30,050	11.5%	14.2%	14.5%
Cheshire	21,788	25,000	28,350	10.1%	13.0%	13.2%
East Haven	25,028	26,850	27,700	11.2%	14.2%	15.3%
Guilford	17,375	19,900	21,650	8.0%	9.8%	10.9%
Hamden	51,071	51,000	50,600	17.0%	19.6%	17.9%
Madison	14,031	15,250	16,450	10.2%	12.7%	15.1%
Meriden	57,118	57,950	57,550	12.7%	14.8%	14.6%
Milford	50,898	50,950	50,200	9.9%	13.8%	14.7%
New Haven	126,109	140,300	155,400	36.9%	11.2%	9.9%
North Branford	11,554	12,750	13,800	6.7%	9.7%	11.7%
North Haven	22,080	22,600	22,950	11.5%	17.2%	18.9%
Orange	13,237	13,100	12,700	11.0%	15.6%	17.4%
Wallingford	37,274	41,750	45,250	11.3%	14.5%	14.1%
West Haven	53,184	56,200	58,350	12.9%	14.3%	13.6%
Woodbridge	7,761	7,950	8,300	10.1%	13.0%	14.9%

Figure D.1. (A) Map of the South Central Connecticut Chapter of the American Red Cross. (B) Characteristics of Communities in SCCC Jurisdiction. *Source:* U.S. Bureau of the Census, *Census of Population.* Washington, D.C.

The South Central Connecticut Chapter

The South Central Connecticut Chapter was formed in 1906. Connecticut has twenty-six chapters that range from single-town, strictly volunteer chapters to massive affiliates such as the Greater Hartford Chapter, which covers about a third of the state. The SCCC has jurisdiction over fifteen communities in the greater New Haven area, serving a total population of almost 575,000 (see Figure D.1A and 1B for a map of the SCCC's geographic domain and selected population statistics, respectively). Chapter headquarters are located in New Haven and the branch office is in Wallingford. The staff is composed of twenty-five full-time paid members: Seventeen administrators and eight clerical and maintenance staff. The seven service directors and the Wallingford branch manager report to the executive director (Figure D.2 depicts the Chapter's organizational structure). The offices are open Monday through Friday, from 8:30 A.M. to 4:30 P.M., and an answering service enables staff to respond to emergency calls twenty-four hours a day. In addition, many of the health services classes and committee meetings are held in the office during the evening and on Saturdays.

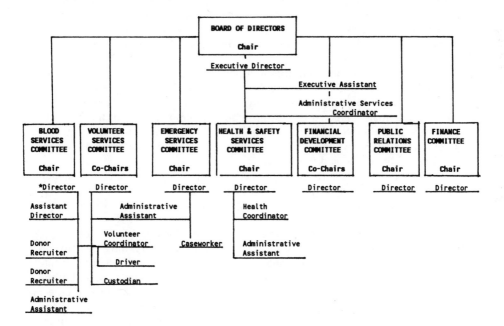

All **bold** positions are filled by volunteers.

*This position is filled by a member of the Farmington Blood Center staff who only spends two days each week at the South Central Connecticut Chapter.

In addition, the Branch Office in Wallingford houses the Branch Manager, Health Service Coordinator, Blood Service Coordinator, Community Service Coordinator and Administrative Assistant: all paid positions. The work of the Branch is directed by the all-volunteer Advisory Board.

Figure D.2. Organizational Chart South Central Connecticut Chapter of the American Red Cross. *Source:* American Red Cross, internal documents.

The Chapter currently provides three functional services and four support services: blood services, health and safety services, and emergency services; and volunteers, public relations, financial development, and administration, respectively. A full-time paid director and a part-time volunteer chair, who also sits on the board of directors, share equally in the responsibility for each service area. Each management team oversees the operations of a service area in consultation with an all-volunteer committee.

Volunteer Involvement

The mission of the American Red Cross, as stated in the preface to *Volunteer 2000*,[2] is "to improve the quality of human life; to enhance self-reliance and concern for others; and to help people avoid, prepare for, and cope with emergencies." The agency achieves this through services that are governed and directed by volunteers and that are consistent with its congressional charter and the principles of the International Red Cross (see Figure D.3). The "primacy and empowerment" of volunteers are at the heart of Red Cross policy, constituting one of its five core institutional values (Figure D.4).

Volunteer 2000 defines a volunteer as "an individual who, beyond the confines of paid employment and normal responsibilities, contributes time and service to assist the American Red Cross in the accomplishment of its mission." Donors of money and blood are excluded from the volunteer count unless they also donate time in a service capacity.

Until the early twentieth century the American Red Cross had no paid employees. Paid staff were hired only when they were needed to do work for which volunteers could not be found—namely, when positions required professional medical credentials. National leadership remained almost totally in the hands of volunteers until after World War II. The position of chairperson and president were combined until 1950, when for the first time the organization designated a volunteer chairperson and a paid president.

In 1989 the Red Cross reported the participation of approximately 1.4 million volunteers throughout the United States. The ratio of volunteers to paid staff was 70:1. Volunteers literally serve in every capacity, including governance, advisory, management, and service.

Many of the smaller chapters continue to be staffed exclusively by volunteers; others pay only clerical staff while the leadership and workforce remain all-volunteer. The Red Cross today employs paid staff to complement, not substitute for, volunteers. Paid staff generally work more hours than volunteers do, but the ultimate responsibility for the operation of the organization lies with its volunteer leadership. It is Red Cross policy that no major initiative may go forward at any level of the organization without appropriate volunteer input and without an assessment of its implication for volunteers. This includes reorganizations, new program development, partnerships or agreements with outside parties, policy studies, and modifications of established policies or procedures.

The motivations of Red Cross volunteers range from an interest in "doing good"

[2]*Volunteer 2000* is a study of volunteerism in the American Red Cross commissioned by Richard F. Schubert, the former President of the Red Cross, and Charlotte Lunsford, National Chairman of Volunteers. It was prepared by the Department of Corporate Planning and Evaluation at National Headquarters, and published in December 1988. Project managers and authors were Frank Larkin and Maria Smith. There are references to its findings and recommendations throughout this case.

Figure D.3. The Fundamental Principles of the International Red Cross Movement

HUMANITY

The International Red Cross Movement, born of a desire to bring assistance without discrimination to the wounded on the battlefield, endeavours, in its international and national capacity, to prevent and alleviate human suffering wherever it may be found. Its purpose is to protect life and health and to ensure respect for the human being. It promotes mutual understanding, friendship, cooperation, and lasting peace among all peoples.

IMPARTIALITY

It makes no discrimination as to nationality, race, religious beliefs, class or political opinions. It endeavours to relieve the suffering of individuals, being guided solely by their needs, and to give priority to the most urgent cases of distress.

NEUTRALITY

In order to continue to enjoy the confidence of all, the movement may not take sides in hostilities or engage at any time in controversies of a political, racial, religious or ideological nature.

INDEPENDENCE

The movement is independent. The national societies, while auxiliaries in the humanitarian services of their governments and subject to the laws of their respective countries, must always maintain their autonomy so that they may be able at all times to act in accordance with the principles of the movement.

VOLUNTARY SERVICE

It is a voluntary relief movement not prompted in any manner by desire for gain.

UNITY

There can be only one Red Cross society in any one country. It must be open to all. It must carry on its humanitarian work throughout its territory.

UNIVERSALITY

The International Red Cross movement, in which all societies have equal status and share equal responsibilities and duties in helping each other, is worldwide.

---

and "helping others" to the desire for social interaction, personal or professional growth, experience, achievement, and prestige. Others come to the agency to carry on family traditions of volunteering with the Red Cross; still others are motivated because they received Red Cross services or instruction. Volunteers tend to work for the organization for at least as long as paid staff.

Attracting volunteers is an ongoing and time-consuming process. SCCC volunteer recruiters design and distribute recruitment announcements through newspaper advertisements, posters for churches, schools, and stores, and fliers for blood drives. Silverman works with local high schools and colleges in an effort to attract young volunteers. At the South Central chapter, management of volunteers is officially centralized in the office of Volunteer Services; in reality, however, departments are often possessive of their volunteers and prefer to coordinate their own workforces.

Figure D.4.   Values of the American Red Cross

HUMANITARIANISM

We are committed to people and their well-being and dedicated to caring for those who suffer.

IMPARTIALITY

We provide our services equitably and impartially to those in need regardless of their citizenship, race, religion, age, sex, or political afiliation.

SERVICE EXCELLENCE

As stewards of the human and financial resources contributed by the American people, we strive toward the highest quality of service and management.

VOLUNTEERISM

We are a community based, voluntary organization governed, supported and principally staffed by volunteers who work with paid staff in all programs and services.

INTERNATIONALISM

Recognizing that human suffering knows no borders, we are a national society that is part of the worldwide Red Cross movement through our cooperation with the International Committee of the Red Cross and membership in the League of Red Cross and Red Crescent Societies.

Blood Services

The American Red Cross supplies about half of the blood in the United States. In Connecticut, because of the prohibition of commercial blood banks, the only blood available comes from volunteer donors through the Red Cross. The Red Cross collects blood through its chapters, and charges hospitals for the cost of collection through a statewide blood center located in Farmington (it is Red Cross policy not to "sell" blood; each pint is considered a gift from its donor). Collection fees are set by the blood center in accordance with the prevailing market price for blood. In addition to the Connecticut blood center, the "market" for blood includes blood from out-of-state Red Cross and commercial blood banks. The Red Cross's commitment to public service also precludes steep increases in blood collection fees even where competition is scant.

Throughout the country, about half a million volunteers participate in the Red Cross blood service program, compared to 9000 paid staff. The SCCC houses six paid blood services staff: the director, two donor recruiters, a volunteer coordinator, and an administrative assistant. In addition, a Red Cross regional supervisor comes twice weekly from the state Blood Center in Farmington, forty miles from New Haven. With a skeletal paid staff, the SCCC blood services unit relies on some 2,000 volunteers to staff blood drives.

The blood services staff is technically employed by the Farmington Blood Center, although Farmington reimburses the SCCC for the blood this staff collects within the Chapter's jurisdiction. Prior to 1988, the Blood Services staff was on the SCCC payroll, and the Chapter received both a per-pint reimbursement and an administrative grant to help cover the costs of collection. The Chapter relinquished control of the blood program in 1988 when it became clear that the Blood Center grant did not cover the SCCC's collection costs. In addition to the per-pint reimbursement, the Blood Center currently provides salaries for the blood services administrative staff, rent for the office space that the staff occupies, supplies for donor recruitment, paid, unionized medical personnel responsible for the actual blood collection, and a good-faith effort to collect the number of pints of blood on which the Chapter bases its projected revenues.

In exchange, the Chapter agrees to provide volunteers, who prepare for blood drives by recruiting donors and making logistical arrangements with blood drive hosts, and who work at the drives as donor room aides, health history interviewers, canteen supervisors, and registrars. The Chapter also provides clerical support and rents office space to the Blood Services staff. Personnel decisions are made jointly by the Chapter and the Blood Center, as are the initial projections of pints to be collected. Annual collection forecasts are based on population statistics, while individual drive collection targets are based on the past performance of the drive sites. In its 1985 strategic plan, the Chapter predicted an 8% increase in blood collections each year for the next five years. Because of chronic shortfalls, however, the Chapter subsequently lowered its annual goals to reflect its collection capacity more realistically, resulting in a 1990 goal that is only 66% of the original 1985 projection. In 1988 and 1989, the agency failed to meet even its revised collection objectives.

Health and Safety Services

One of the SCCC's most visible services is health and safety instruction. The Chapter offers courses in first aid, CPR, water safety, and babysitting, among others. Classes that are open to the public are typically taught at chapter headquarters or the branch office in Wallingford. Occasionally, outlying communities host classes. Corporate clients contract with SCCC for course instruction at their own facilities. Corporate courses are taught by instructors who are paid on a per-diem basis; the corresponding cost is included in the charge to the client. Noncorporate, "community" courses have traditionally been taught by volunteer instructors, but in 1988, due to a shortage of available qualified volunteers, the department has begun to pay some instructors. The agency is not able to charge students a higher fee when the course is taught by a paid instructor because registration and payment occur before the department has assigned an instructor to the course. In addition, the health services staff is reluctant to raise its course fees, which they believe are already higher than comparable courses at competing organizations. Volunteer instructors are still scheduled whenever possible, but as a last resort the Chapter is willing to pay an instructor to prevent having to cancel the course. Even with the option of offering a per-diem rate, however, last minute instructor cancellations sometimes force paid staff to teach daytime courses themselves.

Emergency Services

The largest component of emergency services in terms of time, money, and volunteers involves providing disaster preparedness and relief as mandated by Congress. The responsibilities conferred upon the Red Cross in the 1905 Congressional Charter were restated in the Federal Disaster Relief Act of 1974, and are recognized in the formal agreements with state and local governments. Although the Red Cross has the authority to determine the scope and direction of the emergency relief it provides, it is not permitted to surrender its Congressional mandate. Accordingly, emergency services are the very minimum a chapter provides.

The Red Cross provides emergency care for victims of disasters of all scales; in fact, most beneficiaries have suffered from house fires. Assistance may be in the form of food, clothing, shelter, first aid, or supplementary medical care. The Red Cross also refers disaster victims to local social services and public assistance agencies, and handles inquiries about disaster victims from relatives outside the disaster area. Volunteers work with emergency services as members of Disaster Action Teams (DATs), which respond around the clock to small-scale disasters. DATs are primarily responsible for securing temporary shelter and other basic needs. During large-scale disasters, volunteers work as shelter managers, damage assessors, disaster nurses, and mass care providers. As with the other services, volunteers also hold leadership positions in the emergency services department.

The other component of emergency services is service to military families (SMF). The Red Cross facilitates emergency communication between local families and their relatives who are on active military duty abroad.

Financial Information

The ultimate responsibility for financial oversight of the Red Cross and its chapters rests with the board of governors and chapter boards, which are all-volunteer entities. Approximately 1,600 chapters raise funds in conjunction with the United Way. The SCCC works with all of the United Way offices that represent the communities within the Chapter's boundaries.

Additional Red Cross revenue sources include membership donations and other gifts, foundation and government grants, interest, special events and fees from courses. The Red Cross receives no federal appropriations, despite its unusual obligation to the federal government.

The need for a comprehensive fundraising program at the SCCC is relatively new; prior to 1987, the Chapter received almost all of its funding from the United Way. In 1989–1990, the SCCC raised approximately 74% of its unrestricted funds through United Way donations. However, after paying its Fair Share requirement, United Way contributions provided only 34.6% of the Chapter's revenues. Traditionally, and as recently as the early 1980s, the United Way provided more than 80% of revenues. Health services course fees are expected to provide an additional 18%, and 34% comes from other sources, including revenue from the projected number of pints to be collected, leaving a balance to be raised by the Chapter. Figure D.5 displays the SCCC's revenue and expenditure projections for 1990.

Volunteer Profile

Through its paid and volunteer staff, the SCCC is responsible for recruiting the volunteers necessary to achieve its programmatic and fiscal objectives. SCCC is required to meet performance standards set by the national Red Cross office, the Eastern Operations office, and the Farmington Blood Center. These standards are expressed in terms of the number of blood drives to be held, pints of blood to be collected, CPR courses to be taught, dollars to be raised, and so forth.

Counting SCCC Volunteers In 1989, nearly 4,800 volunteers participated in SCCC activities, managing and carrying out all of the Chapter's events. This group, how-

Figure D.5. Fiscal Year Revenue Projections 1989–1990

United Way	
Greater New Haven	291,111.00
Wallingford-Meriden	110,000.00
Branford	13,400.00
Guilford	5,250.00
Lower Naugatuck Valley	2,440.00
Subtotal	422,201.00
Membership enrollment campaigns	
New Haven	82,763.00
Wallingford-Meriden	20,000.00
Subtotal	102,763.00
Special events	
New Haven	40,000.00
Wallingford-Meriden	8,000.00
Subtotal	48,000.00
Subtotal	572,964.00
Less: National Fair Share at 32.09%	(183,864.00)
Chapter Share	389,100.00
Grants	
United Way Blood Grant	127,000.00
CRCBS Grant—New Haven	
22000 units × 1.50 each	33,000.00
CRCBS Grant—Wallingford	
6000 units × 1.50 each	9,000.00
Transportation—Wallingford	10,000.00
Food Pantry—Wallingford	450.00
Subtotal	179,450.00
Contributions	11,000.00
Contributions—Restricted	10,500.00
Investment income	37,000.00
Rent	
Junior League (485.00 per month)	5,820.00
VAC (640.00 per month)	7,680.00
Hemophilia (297.00 per month)	3,564.00
CRCBS (583.34 per month)	7,000.00
Leitner (50.00 per month)	600.00
Wallingford-Meriden	10,936.00
Subtotal	35,600.00
Program fees	
New Haven	108,000.00
Wallingford-Meriden	42,000.00
Subtotal	150,000.00
Sale of fixed assets	
New Haven	4,500.00
Grand total of all revenue elements	817,150.00
Grand total of all expenditures	807,150.00

ever, represents a broad spectrum of time commitments. Roughly two thirds restrict their volunteer activity to sporadic "special events," which might not involve more than one commitment of several hours per year. The balance of the volunteers, some 1,560 individuals in 1989, constitutes the core of the SCCC's active workforce, working, on average, at least once a month.

The Office of Volunteer Services maintains extensive records on the participation of its volunteers. Management has only recently acquired the capability to record this information on a computerized database. For now, volunteer records are kept on large index cards filed in a room full of metal cabinets.

Counting Red Cross volunteers has always been a challenge, and inconsistencies persist from chapter to chapter. Some chapters specify a minimum number of hours a volunteer must work before being counted. Some chapters count paid staff as volunteers if they volunteer in another service area or perform responsibilities outside the scope of their paid job. The general trend is to adopt a liberal definition of volunteer activity for the purpose of volunteer counts. High volunteer counts are useful in marketing the organization's image in fundraising, specifically for enhancing United Way funding bids.

For all the tedium of a manual record keeping system, the office maintains up-to-date records on volunteer activity, recording the number of hours every volunteer works as well as limited demographic data on each. There are separate files for "active volunteers," defined as those who have worked at least once during the current fiscal year. This definition is misleadingly generous, as it includes both those volunteers who have worked once in the last year and those whose activity is essentially full-time. Moreover, the active file is heavily skewed in favor of the most recent recruits, whose participation is often by definition limited to this fiscal year. Table D.1 indicates the number of volunteers by year, from 1985 to 1989, and the number of volunteer hours worked.

The SCCC further records volunteer activity by community and programmatic area. Organizing the volunteer rolls geographically enables the agency to identify unusually strong or weak rates of participation, and to formulate its recruitment strategy accordingly. For example, the SCCC routinely has trouble staffing New Haven blood drives because some volunteers from the suburban towns have expressed fear of the city's comparatively high crime rate. Moreover, Silverman believes that people prefer the convenience of volunteering in their own communities, and there is often local pride associated with a large "active" file for an individual community.

Similarly, reporting volunteer activity by service area allows the SCCC to identify functional areas for which attracting or retaining volunteers is problematic. The numbers themselves do not necessarily reveal specific difficulties, rather, they serve to alert the volunteer services staff to possible recruitment or retention trouble. For instance, the fact that many more volunteers work in blood services than

Table D.1.   Number of Volunteers and Hours Worked, 1985–1989

	1989	1988*	1987	1986	1985
Numer of Volunteers	4,745	3,980	3,177	3,947	3,796
Number of Volunteer Occasions	7,780	8,201	8,120	8,843	8,310
Number of Volunteer Hours	94,280	75,373	82,960	94,069	89,181

*On July 1, 1988, the Wallingford/Meriden Red Cross chapter merged with South Central.

fundraising may be more indicative of the agency's programmatic emphasis than of any particular difficulty in recruiting fundraising volunteers.

Furthermore, what appears to be a healthy rate of participation in one service area may obscure the trouble SCCC has in recruiting volunteers for specific functions within that programmatic area. One prominent example of this is in blood services, where the large number of volunteers masks the agency's critical shortage of HHIs. Because they screen blood donors for health problems that could jeopardize their own health and the blood supply, federal law requires that HHIs be medical professionals (including physicians, nurses, physician's assistants, nursing or medical students, and so forth).

Demographic characteristics The SCCC's volunteer files reveal a paucity of demographic information. However, the Volunteer Services staff believes that SCCC volunteers generally mirror *Volunteer 2000's* profile of Red Cross volunteers nationally. Figure D.6 provides a concise characterization of Red Cross volunteers.

Table D.2 details the length of service of SCCC volunteers. Nationally, according to the *Volunteer 2000* study, approximately one third of the volunteers have been with the Red Cross for five years or less, one third between six and fifteen years, and one third for sixteen or more years. A majority of Red Cross staff, both volunteer and paid, reports current volunteer involvement in other agencies, with church or religious organizations topping the list, followed by school and youth groups.

Morale

In recent years, some volunteers have complained that the paid staff inappropriately dominates operations, and fails to take them seriously. Others are weary of urgent requests for volunteers, asserting that full-time employees should anticipate their staffing needs farther in advance.

The paid directors, for their part, are frustrated by last-minute cancellations of line volunteers and the irregular presence of volunteer leadership, which often delays decision making. They also protest that leadership volunteers sometimes propose ambitious projects without fully appreciating the difficulties of implementation. As one paid director commented, "I'm tired of my livelihood depending on someone else's hobby."

Turnover among paid staff is high. In January 1990, three of the seven service directors had been with the Chapter for less than six months. Two other directors and the Executive Director had been at South Central for just over a year. In 1989–1990, twelve of the twenty-one paid staff at the New Haven office left their positions; the single position of health coordinator was held by three people.

Looking Ahead

According to *Volunteer 2000,* the majority of chapters across the country reported that volunteer participation had increased or remained the same during the period 1984–1989. Ten percent of chapters reported an overall decline in volunteer participation. Silverman believes, however, that these largely reassuring figures do not guarantee a solid base of new or active volunteers in the next decade. In particular, she anticipates that the chapter will continue to struggle to fill specialized volunteer positions and those related to large fundraising events. Moreover, she is concerned about the general availability of volunteers, and the SCCC's ability to compete with

Figure D.6.   American Red Cross Volunteer Profile 1988

National		Local	
Sex			
Women	70%	Women	76%
Men	30%	Men	24%
Age			
18–24 years	1.6%	N/A (Assumed to be	
25–34	11.4%	comparable)	
35–44	14.1%		
45–54	17.1%		
55–64	22.6%		
65–74	25.4%		
75+	6.5%		
Race			
White	92.0%	Available for leadership	
Other	8.0%	volunteers only; line	
		volunteers assumed to	
		have less minority	
		representation:	
		White	92.7%
		Black	4.9%
		Hispanic	2.4%
Marital Status			
Single	32.7%	N/A (Assumed to be	
Married	66.7%	comparable)	
(This ratio differs across service areas; for example, among Blood Service volunteers, only 7.9% are single, while 88.2% are married.)			
Employment Status			
Employed full-time	28.7%	N/A (Assumed to be	
Employed part-time	9.0%	comparable)	
Retired	37.4%		
Unemployed (seek employment)	1.8%		
No employed	20.6%		

other service agencies for them. As part of an overall recruitment strategy, the Volunteer Services Office was considering a number of innovations.

Wages In recent years the SCCC has experienced serious difficulties in finding volunteer HHIs, a phenomenon echoed by Red Cross chapters in other parts of the country. From their analysis of the nationwide HHI shortage, Red Cross executives forecast continued—even accelerated—impediments to recruiting HHIs. Because

Table D.2.   Length of Volunteer Service
at SCCC

Year began volunteer service	Percentage of volunteers as of March 1990
1988–90	38.2
1985–87	21.5
1980–84	21.2
1975–79	13.5
Pre-1975	5.6
Total	100.0

of the shortage of qualified volunteers, some chapters have turned to offering wages to HHIs. If it cannot recruit enough volunteer HHIs, the SCCC may have to amend its agreement with the Blood Center. Under a new agreement, the Blood Center would provide more nurses at the Chapter's blood drives who would rotate between the interviewing and blood drawing tasks. However, Silverman fears that the Blood Center would pass on its greater personnel costs in the form of a lower per-pint reimbursement.

Similarly, some SCCC administrators would like to adopt the per-diem payment of health and safety instructors as an official Chapter policy, but other staff disagree. Michelle Donlin, director of health services, argues:

> Even though hiring instructors might make our job easier, I just don't want to give up on volunteers. Volunteers are what the Red Cross is about. I think it's our responsibility to organize and run this office in a way which makes people want to volunteer for us.

Donlin cites instructors' charges that course instruction is too time-consuming, with actual class times of six to eight hours. They complain that national headquarters frequently modifies course content and then requires instructors to be recertified by completing refresher courses—at their own expense. Other teaching opportunities in the community are often more flexible or better compensated.

Other Benefits In response to volunteer concerns, Silverman has proposed a contract with a local day-care center that would provide for a certain number of reserved day care slots for the children of SCCC volunteers. In exchange, the Red Cross would offer instruction in infant/child CPR for day-care workers, in which the state requires certification. Another child-care option under consideration is the provision of on-site care at the Chapter headquarters operated by local student interns.

Other volunteers need transportation between chapter headquarters, blood drive sites, and their homes. The SCCC currently has one paid driver. Occasionally, volunteers supplement him, but in general they prefer to restrict their driving to their home communities. It is not uncommon for a blood drive to be delayed because of problems in transporting volunteers.

Targeting a New Volunteer Pool At the national level, the Red Cross has embarked on a campaign to recruit young adult professionals; Silverman is enthusiastic about adopting National's campaign locally. She needs young adults to fill the more strenuous volunteer positions for the upcoming golf tournament fundraiser, and she hopes to entice some of them to continue their Red Cross involvement.

As she settled into the two-hour train ride to New York, Silverman contemplated the ideas her volunteer counterparts and other staff had suggested recently. She resolved that at the next meeting of the Volunteer Services Committee she would present a formal plan for recruiting and retaining volunteers.

CASE E

The Good Faith Fund—Managing a Grass-Roots Organization in Rural Arkansas

Located in Pine Bluff, Arkansas, the Good Faith Fund (GFF) is an innovative attempt to alleviate rural poverty. The GFF uses a peer group support technique to lend for the purpose of starting or expanding a self-employment enterprise. In place of the collateral or credit evaluation that is required in traditional lending transactions, GFF borrowers form small groups with two to four other individuals. A combination of support and peer pressure from the group is intended to ensure repayment of loans.

Arkansas, with a per capita income of $12,219, is the third poorest state in the country. Southeastern Arkansas, where the GFF operates, has the state's poorest counties. Unemployment in this region in December 1990 was 8.6%, compared to the state average of 7.1% and the national average of 5.9%.

The Good Faith Fund was established in 1988 with a staff of three: two loan representatives and Jenine Vale, the twenty-nine year old program director. By January 1991, the Fund had grown to include an office manager and seven new loan representatives who had just completed a five-month training program.

It was the spring of 1991 and Jenine was writing her quarterly report. She was less concerned with GFF's loan portfolio's performance than with the progress the Fund had made towards its goal. GFF, a community development loan fund, lent money to local entrepreneurs using a peer-lending model. To accomplish its goals, forming local lending groups was vital. Jenine thought the prior day's monthly staff meeting was symptomatic of the Fund's underlying organizational difficulties.

As the eight loan representatives gave their latest reports, Jenine became aware of the disparate levels of progress in the four field offices. "It seems as if you're having problems forming groups. I haven't received field reports from either of you for the past month. How many presentations have you organized in the Dermott and Eudora areas?" Jenine asked Larry Hoffman and Cynthia Dunning, the two loan representatives covering that region.

"Jenine, you know how we feel about those field reports. Since we arrived in the community, on average, we've held three presentations and attended four community meetings a week. And we've followed up," replied Cynthia.

"We do have a growing list of potential members, but it takes a while for things to happen. Especially something as new as the Good Faith Fund. There's a special tempo to Chicot and Desha counties. Things are slower," continued Larry.

"We've been trying to get our name out by getting to know the local community

Prepared by Alexander Brown, Jackie Khor and David Stern under the supervision of Professor Sharon Oster as the basis for class discussion rather than to portray either effective or ineffective management. Some names, dates, and places have been changed.

leaders. As you know, the Dermott and Eudora communities are more racially segregated than say . . . Lake Village, and the community leaders are not so willing to devote effort towards helping the poor in their towns, which makes it hard for us to find out more about the community," added Cynthia.

"All right, but one quarter of the year has gone by and you don't seem to be making much progress towards forming your six groups," Jenine said, reminding the loan representatives of the year's target of three new groups per loan representative that had been agreed upon between them and Jenine earlier that year.

"Well, maybe that target isn't realistic given the situation in our communities," Larry commented.

Jenine responded. "We can certainly work towards making more realistic targets, but I can't tell if these targets need revision if I don't have a sense of what you're dealing with or doing in these towns."

"Our past delinquency rate shows that group formation is a delicate process that takes time. Pushing any harder could have an adverse effect. What's the point of making people join a group unless they're ready? As we've seen, when we rush things, they just default." Cynthia said.

Sandra Morgan, the veteran loan representative interjected, "Community organizing takes time and patience. We're not here just to form groups or make loans. Forming groups and making loans are not ends in themselves. They're just the tools we're using to accomplish our mission."

Southern Development Bancorporation

The parent organization of the Good Faith Fund is a for-profit bank holding company, Southern Development Bancorporation ("Southern"). The GFF is Southern's microenterprise-creation program in southeastern Arkansas. Southern is unerringly committed to the borrowing group approach as a way to address poverty alleviation in southeastern Arkansas. Southern's programs emphasize the delivery of credit, capital, and marketing/management assistance to encourage the creation of small business enterprises (Figure E.1).

Modeled after Chicago's Shorebank Corporation, Southern was founded in 1988 through the efforts of Shorebank, with funds provided by the Winthrop Rockefeller Foundation, to apply innovative development techniques toward promoting economic growth among low- and moderate-income residents of rural Arkansas. *Inc.* magazine has described Southern as one of the "most radical experiments in the history of rural economic development."

In 1987, Southern conducted a demographic survey of Arkansas to determine the "Preferred Development Regions" for its affiliates. The criteria used to select the Good Faith Fund's target area included the following parameters:

Minimum population: 80,000–130,000;

Maximum driving time for any loan area: "diameter" of 1½ hours;

Sizeable low to moderate income population;

At least one area with a large Black population;

Contiguous to region targeted by other Southern programs (such as the Arkansas Enterprise Group);

Strong local support;

Good probability of success.

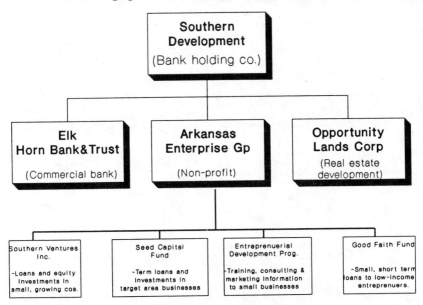

Figure E.1. Southern Development Bancorporation.

The eight counties designated as the GFF area are among the poorest in the state. They exhibited the following demographic characteristics given in Table E.1.

Internal Organization and Operations of The Good Faith Fund

As the organization chart in Figure E.2 indicates, the Fund's staff of ten is composed of eight loan representatives, an office manager, and Jenine, the program director.

Table E.1. Characteristic of GFFs Target Sites

County	Population[1]	Percentage Black[1]	Per Capita Income (1986)[1] ($)	Population Density[2]	Unemployment Rate (1990)[3] (%)
Ashley	26,200	27.3	10,544	28.1	6.1
Bradley	13,200	29.1	9,999	20.2	9.0
Chicot	17,200	52.9	7,064	26.5	11.0
Cleveland	8,300	15.2	10,214	13.9	6.9
Desha	19,400	42.7	8,424	26.0	9.6
Drew	18,000	27.3	9,066	21.7	8.5
Jefferson	90,000	40.6	10,529	102.0	8.8
Lincoln	13,200	35.9	7,299	23.5	8.2
Target Area	**205,500**	**37.0**	**9,660**	**58.2**	**8.6**
ARKANSAS	2,372,000	16.3	11,042	46.0	7.1

1. Arkansas Statistical Abstract, 1989.

2. City/County Data Book, 1988 (measured in people per square mile).

3. Labor Market Information, Arkansas Employment Security Division.

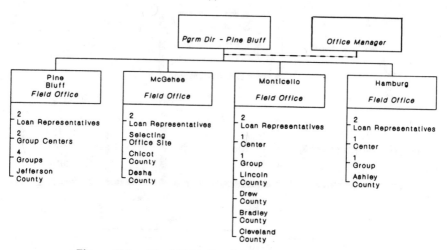

Figure E.2.   Good Faith Fund Organization Structure.

The head office is in Pine Bluff, the largest city in the Good Faith Fund target area. Three field offices were established in late 1990 and early 1991 in towns to the south of Pine Bluff. Driving time from Pine Bluff to McGehee and Monticello is about an hour and a half, and about two hours to Hamburg.

All the Fund's staff are women except for one white male loan representative. There are two blacks and one Hispanic; the remainder of the staff is white. All the loan representatives have attended college and they range in age from twenty-two to the mid-thirties. Four of the women had been in the Peace Corps prior to joining the Fund. Many of the loan representatives are either from Arkansas or other Southern states.

The Good Faith Fund's Approach to Lending

In the words of a GFF member, the Good Faith Fund is "an organization that will help you if you help yourself." It is a membership organization of low-income individuals who are either already self-employed or interested in becoming self-employed. Instead of providing collateral or a credit history, members join borrowing groups that use peer pressure and support to make and enforce credit decisions on borrowers. No group member can receive additional loans unless all the group's members are current in their repayments. The borrowing group is also intended to be self-regulating and self-enforcing so that it replaces some of the monitoring functions of loan representatives.

The borrowing group approach to small enterprise development stands between traditional small business assistance programs and cooperative programs. Small business assistance programs generally provide technical assistance and credit to entrepreneurs. Cooperative programs are based on the premise that a group can most successfully operate a business collectively.

The borrowing group model was first developed and implemented in 1976 by the Grameen Bank, a microenterprise lending institution founded in Bangladesh by Dr. Muhammad Yunus. (A detailed description of the Grameen Bank's lending system appears in the Appendix.)

Group Formation and the Lending Process

Although borrowing group members select themselves, the Fund acts as a resource for potential members to locate other interested individuals within the same community. Groups are formed through the initiatives of individual prospective members. They are self-selected to ensure that borrowers choose other responsible members who they feel are committed to each other.

During the orientation period for new groups, the loan representative teaches members about borrowing requirements and cash flow management, and acquaints group members with each other's different business ideas. The orientation period also provides an opportunity for group members to screen out unreliable or uncommitted members. The experience in Bangladesh and other U.S. programs indicates that groups composed of neighbors or workmates who have frequent contact tend to be more successful. Member selection is an ongoing process so that groups can remove unreliable members at the end of each loan. A chart tracing the development of the group appears in Figure E.3.

Each group is required to maintain a savings account to which all members contribute an agreed upon amount on a biweekly basis. An average contribution is $5.00 per group member per meeting. The savings account is the property of the borrowing group and is designed to be an additional source of loan funds for a group's members. The group savings account is also used as a guarantee fund to apply toward any delinquent loans.

All loans are scrutinized at two levels: first in the borrowing group and then in the loan review committee chaired by Jenine and attended by three other staff members and the loan representative presenting the proposal. Loan review committee meetings have only recently been implemented. The meetings are intended to give the Fund a bigger role in the loan approval process. Jenine hopes that a "bit of hierarchy" will formalize the process so that borrowers will be more responsible for their loans. As the organization grows, these meetings will also add institutional memory.

Group members are required to attend center meetings twice a month. Center meetings consist of up to three borrowing groups within one community. At these meetings, loan repayments and proposals are made and members can exchange information and ideas. The meetings are chaired by an elected chairperson and the groups' loan representatives act merely as facilitators.

Functions of the Borrowing Group

The borrowing group replaces the need for collateral because of the support and monitoring functions it is intended to provide. A borrowing group's functions are:

1. Act as a screening mechanism to select trustworthy borrowers.
2. Serve as a loan committee to oversee its members' credit applications. It reviews members' loan proposals and acts as the first and most important level for loan approvals.
3. Assume the responsibility for its loan decisions. Members are encouraged to monitor each other's repayments and use of loans. In the event that one member defaults on their obligations the entire group is theoretically liable for the debt. In practice, however, the Fund has not been enforcing this rule.

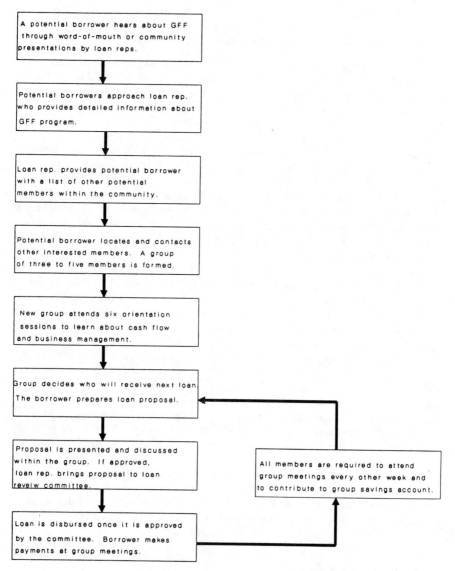

Figure E.3.   The Group Formation and Lending Process.

4. Provide a forum for business support and learning from each member's experiences.

5. Serve as the principal point of contact with the Fund's loan representative.

Good Faith Fund Loans

Loans are given exclusively for starting or expanding a self-employment enterprise. Most loans are used for equipment, working capital, or special inventory purchases. They are repaid in biweekly installments. Arkansas usury laws limit the

Table E.2. Sample Projects Financed
Through Peer Group Microlending

Lending Institution	
Grameen	*Good Faith Fund*
Rickshaw	Beautician
Cow Fattening	Janitorial Service
Timber Trading	Lawn Service
Grocery Stall	Plumbing Fixures
Tailor	Mobile Bar-B-Que
Rickshaw Mechanic	Day-Care
Milk Cow	Upholstery
Goat Fattening	Welding
Poultry Raising	Property Mgmt.
Cattle Trading	Laundry
Rice Trading	Seamstress
Old Cloth Selling	Photography

interest rate on loans to a maximum of 12%. A schedule of equal installment amounts is calculated at the time the loan is made. Table E.2 presents a list of some of the projects that have been financed in Bangladesh and Arkansas. From 1988 through the end of 1990, the Fund made forty-five loans to thirty-two individual borrowers. Figures E.4 to E.8 show the forms the GFF use to help small businesses organize their finances in preparation for GFF loans.

For most of 1990, the organization had focused on recruiting and training the new loan representatives. Consequently, its loan portfolio suffered. Virtually no new loans were made. The lack of new loans and of management attention on monitoring repayments resulted in delinquency rates of up to 86% by October 1990. In the previous year the majority of previously made "good" loans had been paid-off. Only troubled loans, which had not been paid-off, remained on the books, making it appear that the Fund was making huge numbers of bad loans.

The Fund's basic loan product has a one-year term and twenty-five equal bi-weekly payments. Table E.3 presents a schedule of other loan terms. A farm loan product is also being designed to accommodate the special cash flow requirements of the area's small farmers, produce growers and market gardeners.

The Functions of the Loan Representative

Loan representatives are responsible for forming and maintaining borrowing groups. Over 70% of a loan representative's day to day activity centers around locating potential new members and disseminating information about the GFF. In addition, they attend regularly scheduled borrowing group meetings. At these meetings, their role is not so much to manage the meetings as to facilitate the process and to act as a resource for group members. The loan representatives have limited experience in providing technical assistance to small business owners: only one loan representative has managed a self-employment enterprise.

Loan representatives take a two-pronged approach to entering a community: (1) developing a network of support among community leaders in local government,

CASH is KING...
Sales and profits don't guarantee success! Run out of cash and you are out of business.

CASH FLOW PROJECTION & ANALYSIS

Name of business:		Month of:		Month of:		Month of:	
		Projected	Real	Projected	Real	Projected	Real
CASH IN	Starting Cash Balance (carry over from previous month)						
List all the items that bring cash in to your business. 							
	Total Cash Available						
CASH OUT							
List all the items that use up money from your business. 							
	Total Cash Out (Expenses)						
	Ending Cash Balance = Cash Available — Cash Out						

The Good Faith Fund

Figure E.4. Good Faith Fund: Cash Flow Procedure.

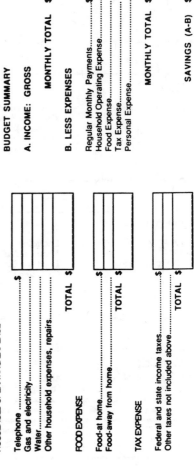

THE GOOD FAITH FUND
COST-OF-LIVING BUDGET
(Based on average month - does not cover purchase
if any new items except emergency replacements)

DETAILED BUDGET
REGULAR MONTHLY PAYMENTS

House payments (principal, interest,
taxes, and insurance) or rent............ $
Car payments (including insurance)............
Appliance-TV payments............
Home improvement loan payments............
Personal loan, credit card payments............
Health plan payments............
Life insurance premiums............
Other insurance premiums ....
Savings and investments............

TOTAL $

HOUSEHOLD OPERATING EXPENSE

Telephone .... $
Gas and electricity............
Water............
Other household expenses, repairs............

TOTAL $

FOOD EXPENSE

Food-at home............ $
Food-away from home............

TOTAL $

TAX EXPENSE

Federal and state income taxes............ $
Other taxes not included above............

TOTAL $

PERSONAL EXPENSE

Clothing, cleaning, laundry............ $
Drugs............
Doctors and dentists............
Education............
Dues............
Gifts and contributions............
Travel............
Newspapers, magazines, books............
Auto upkeep and gas............
Spending money and allowances............

TOTAL $

BUDGET SUMMARY

A. INCOME: GROSS

MONTHLY TOTAL $

B. LESS EXPENSES

Regular Monthly Payments............ $
Household Operating Expense............
Food Expense............
Tax Expense............
Personal Expense............

MONTHLY TOTAL $

SAVINGS (A-B) $

Figure E.5. Sample Budget Form.

THE LOAN PROPOSAL MACHINE

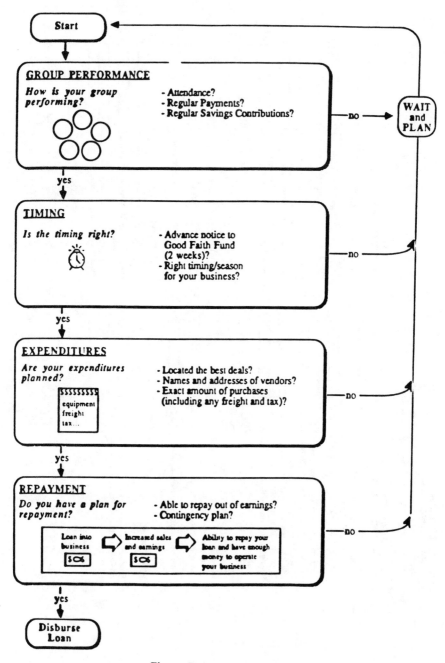

Figure E.6. Loan Process.

The Good Faith Fund

A self-employment loan fund

1210 Cherry, Suite 9
Pine Bluff, AR 71601
501-535-6233

Hamburg's Branch Office
101 North Cherry
Hamburg, AR 71646
501-853-9114

The Good Faith Fund offers a 3-month, 6-month, and 1-year term loan. Each loan type is repaid in bi-weekly instalments at market interest rates.

For example, if your 1-year loan is made at the rate of 12%, your payments would be as follows:

Amt. of Loan	Biweekly Payment	Finance Charge	Total of Payments
$ 500	$ 21.22	$ 30.55	$ 530.55
750	31.83	45.83	795.83
1,000	42.44	61.10	1,061.10
1,250	53.06	76.38	1,326.38
1,600	67.91	97.77	1,697.77
1,700	72.16	103.88	1,803.88
1,800	76.40	109.99	1,909.99
1,900	80.64	116.10	2,016.10
2,000	84.89	122.21	2,122.21
2,100	89.13	128.32	2,228.32
2,200	93.38	134.43	2,334.43
2,300	97.62	140.54	2,440.54
2,400	101.87	146.65	2,546.65
2,500	106.11	152.76	2,652.76

Businesses that The Good Faith Fund will not finance include clubs or taverns or businesses in which financial transactions, credit, or investment are the principle focus such as life insurance, mortgage financing, check cashing, or pawn shops.

For more information, please call our main office at
501-535-6233
or
our branch office at
501-853-9114.

A program of
Southern Development Bancorporation

Make your own job!

Figure E.7. Promotional Material.

The Good Faith Fund,

headquartered in Pine Bluff, Arkansas, is a revolving loan fund that provides very small, short-term loans to local residents interested in self-employment.

Through a peer-group support technique, Good Faith Fund (GFF) loans are made exclusively for the purpose of starting or expanding a self-employment enterprise.

Loans are made to match the needs of your project or activity. You can scale up your loan amount after each loan is successfully repaid.

As a member of the GFF, you will:

- *Meet other entrepreneurs;*
- *Save money as you make money;*
- *Learn important strategies for success;*
- *Receive supportive financing to get started and stay in business.*

Good Faith Fund borrowers:

- Belong to a group of 4 to 6 people all of whom are currently self-employed or interested in becoming self-employed. The members of a group should be from the same community or operate businesses within the same community and should select themselves. No more than one immediate family member or business partner can participate within a community.

- Participate in six orientation sessions over at least a 3 to 4 week time period. The goal of the orientation sessions is to become your own loan committee: to understand all of the rules and regulations of the loan fund, to learn about the other borrowers and their businesses, and to discuss some basic business planning and management techniques.

- Meet every two weeks with their group and other groups in their town. At these meetings, members discuss and screen their business ideas and expansion ideas, make loan proposals, receive their loan proceeds or make payments on their loans, contribute to their group savings accounts, and update each other on business progress.

- Contribute to a group savings fund every two weeks whether they are currently borrowing or not. The amount of the individual savings contribution is decided upon by the group, but must be an amount that every member can afford. These funds have been used for emergency loans to group members.

The Good Faith Fund operates as follows:

- At the last orientation session, the members will decide who the first members will be to take out a loan.

- Borrowers will make their first biweekly loan repayment two weeks after the loan is disbursed. 3-month, 6-month, and 1-year loans are available.

- Members will be eligible for loans only if all borrowers within the group are actively participating in the group and are current on their payments.

- Every two months, up to two loans may be disbursed to other members, providing all borrowers are current on their payments and everyone in the group is attending meetings and making savings contributions.

- The interest rate on Good Faith Fund loans will be a fixed market rate.

Figure E.8. Informational Brochure.

Table E.3. The Good Faith Fund Loan Limits

Incidence of Borrowing by Individual	Repayment Period			
	3 months	6 months	12 months	18 months
1st time	$300	$600	$1,200	—
2nd time	$500	$900	$1,800	—
3rd time	$700	$1,200	$2,400	$3,400
4th time	$900	$1,500	$3,000	$4,200
5th time	$1,100	$1,800	$3,600	$5,000

Source: The Good Faith Fund 1991 Program Plan.

industry, and elsewhere, and (2) identifying and reaching out to the low-income target population of the community. The loan representatives have identified the following targets for their marketing efforts in new (and existing) communities:

Marketing targets	*Audiences for Marketing Support*
Women and minorities	Banks
Low-income people	Educational institutions
Unemployed people	Community leaders (formal and informal)
Self-employed people operating very small businesses	Business people
People with hobbies they can turn into businesses	Community organizations
People who need resources to convert a skill into a business	Government agencies concerned with human services and/or community development

Loan representatives conduct door-to-door surveys of low-income areas of the community as the first stage of identifying and reaching the target population. These surveys provide loan representatives with information on the target population's economic status, employment situation, degree of community involvement, and demographics. The surveys also enable the Fund to develop a network of potential borrowers among the low-income community. One loan representative stated, "No matter how scientific we try to be, the surveys are much better for getting a general feeling of the town and for building contacts than for obtaining hard data."

Marketing

Print and radio advertising are sometimes used, but most marketing is done by loan representatives through personal contact. Loan representatives have found that the most effective way of communicating any idea in small rural towns is through word of mouth.

Community meetings provide excellent marketing opportunities for loan representatives to inform town residents about the Fund and to demonstrate their own commitment to their towns. Loan representatives all live in their target communities. Once groups have formed in a territory, the loan representatives divide their time between helping and monitoring existing groups and trying to form new ones.

In addition to the main activity of forming borrowing groups, each loan representative is responsible for one outside project that is intended to contribute indirectly to the Fund's primary mission. These projects are identified by Jenine and assigned to each loan representative, depending on the latter's interest and expertise. The outside projects include:

- development of overall GFF marketing strategy;
- formation of an agricultural loan product to encourage microscale farming, including an effective technical support program;
- increasing GFF's involvement and expertise in family home day-care enterprises;
- expanding the number of GFF customers who are participants in the Department of Human Services (DHS) through greater involvement with DHS programs, and
- increasing the number of home-based crafts producers among GFF's membership.

Although loan representatives believe the projects will enhance the Fund's ability to reach more potential clients, they also feel "there are sometimes blocks of time where you don't feel you are doing the real business of the Fund—forming groups—at all."

Reporting Systems

The loan representatives report directly to Jenine through monthly staff meetings and hourly activity reports that each loan representative submits to Jenine at the end of every month. There is also contact with Pine Bluff via telephone or modem about four out of the five working days. Monthly reports have engendered some controversy among the staff. The loan representatives understand the necessity for accountability, but some feel that giving hourly reports diverts an excessive amount of time from their main function of group formation. Some loan representatives fall weeks behind in submitting their reports.

In general, the loan representatives feel that they are given a high degree of autonomy on a day-to-day basis, but they feel more constrained by Jenine in ways to establish groups and to approach their individual projects. Some loan representatives say they would like more autonomy in formulating ways to approach their assigned communities because they are better acquainted than Jenine with the particular characteristics of these locales.

Tables E.4 and E.5 contain information on GFF's recent lending history. As part of the effort to raise loan volume, specific quantitative goals for each loan represen-

Table E.4.   The Good Faith Fund Historical Loan Development

Period	No. of Groups	No. of Members	No. of Borrowers	No. of Loans Made	Total $ Loans Made
12/31/88	2			10	21,286
12/31/89	4	36	23	25	79,419
12/31/90	9	36	9	10	23,156
Total			32	45	123,860

Table E.5. Overview of GFF Activity, 7/88–4/90

Date	Number of Loans Disbursed	Number of Loans Repaid	Number of Loans Charged-Off	Number of Loans Outstanding	Number of Members	Number of Groups
7/88	2	—	—	2	5	1
8/88	4	—	—	6	15	3
9/88	—	—	—	6	15	3
10/88	—	—	—	6	15	3
11/88	—	—	—	6	15	3
12/88	3	—	—	9	20	4
1/89	—	—	—	9	20	4
2/89	3	—	—	12	25	5
3/89	3	—	—	15	30	6
4/89	1	—	—	16	30	6
5/89	1	—	3	14	25	3
6/89	7	—	—	21	36	8
7/89	6	2	—	25	41	9
8/89	2	—	—	27	46	10
9/89	—	—	2	25	45	9
10/89	2	—	—	27	50	10
11/89	—	—	3	24	50	10
12/89	1	2	2	21	36	8
1/90	1	—	—	22	36	8
2/90	1	—	—	23	36	8
3/90	—	—	—	23	36	8
4/90	1	—	—	24	36	8
5/90	2	—	—	26	36	8
Cum. Totals	40	4	10			

tative have been set. These goals were formulated by the loan representatives and Jenine. Each person is expected to form at least three borrowing groups by the end of 1991, the first full year for the seven new loan representatives. No tangible reward or punishment has been attached to this goal. The loan representatives' fixed annual salary is unaffected. Beyond their salary, loan representatives receive a bonus of $10 for each loan disbursed by their groups and also for each new group that is formed.

Tables E.6 and E.7 contain information on the overall financial condition of GFF.

Conclusion

As Jenine was writing the quarterly report, she realized that much had been accomplished over the past three months. Two new groups had been formed and two more were on the verge of forming. The fund had reached several new communities and loan performance was improving. However, the organization's growth presented several new issues. Jenine knew she needed an effective system to

Table E.6. The God Faith Fund Statement of Revenue,
Expenditures & Changes in Equity (Fiscal Year Ending)

	12/31/89	12/31/90
Revenue		
Grant Income	$160,145	$248,319
Interest Income	47,370	52,054
Misc. Income	400	1,771
Total Revenue	$207,915	$302,144
Expenditure		
Salaries	$118,224	$163,449
Fringe Benefits	17,743	21,355
Consulting Expense	6,594	25,223
Mktng & Communication	0	17,001
Travel & Entertainment	12,389	13,889
Accounting & Legal	0	7,500
Bad Debt & Interest Exp	0	24,695
Depreciation Expense	0	11,887
Other Operating	52,965	17,145
Total Expenditure	$207,915	$302,144
Excess/(Deficit)		
Revenue over Expense	$0	$0

manage a geographically dispersed staff. The loan representatives were all genuinely committed to the Fund's mission, but Jenine felt she needed a more formalized structure to motivate and monitor them. All the loan representatives were relatively new to the GFF and the expanded geographic scope made it difficult to retain the informal supervisory systems that had previously been in place. What, then, was the best way to structure the organization and reporting systems to effectively administer the loan representatives without overmanaging them?

How could Jenine best evaluate the performance of the loan representative, and in a more general sense, the performance of the Fund? Should tangible goals be set for either the loan representative or the fund, and if so what should they be?

Appendix A: The Grameen Bank

The Good Faith Fund's approach to poverty alleviation is modeled on an extremely successful approach to poverty banking pioneered in Bangladesh by the Grameen Bank. Grameen was the originator of the "circle" approach to credit extension that uses social collateral to replace physical or financial collateral. The great success that Grameen has experienced with this technique has inspired many replications of its efforts in the United States and around the world. The GFF was one of the first programs to adopt this model in the United States.

Bangladesh is a country roughly the size of Wisconsin with a population of over 114,000,000 people. It has a population density of 2,122 per square mile. The economic and social organization of Bangladesh centers around the rural village,

Table E.7. The Good Faith Fund Historical Balance Sheets

	12/31/89	*12/31/90*
Assets		
Current Assets		
Cash & Liquid Assets	$673,770	$615,537
Accounts Receivable	383	278
Interest Receivable	2,253	8,096
Loans Outstanding	40,302	11,153
Reserve for Bad Debts	(3,019)	0
Prepaid Expenses	54	55
Employee Advances	325	0
	$714,068	$635,119
Fixed Assets	$24,294	$38,479
Interfund Transfers	(45,173)	167,201
Total Assets	$693,189	$840,799
Liabilities & Fund Balance		
Liabilities		
Accounts payable	$5,072	$2,912
Accrued Expenses	2,750	1,695
Deferred Revenue	58,333	162,268
Total Liabilities	$66,155	$166,875
Fund Balance	$627,033	$673,924
Total Liabilities & Fund Balance	$693,189	$840,799

which is where Grameen concentrates much of its efforts. The population is generally poorly educated, frequently illiterate, and has few land rights.

The focal point of Grameen's initial efforts in a new area is the branch manager (BM). These people are generally culled from the college educated population of Bangladesh and they represent the bank's interests to a specific geographic area. Initially, the BMs have a number of responsibilities in their district. Facilitating group formation and recognition is a crucial aspect of the job. Generally, once a few groups have formed in an area new borrowers begin to approach the BM on their own initiative. They have frequently already formed groups, an aspect of the program that they have heard from friends. The BM must begin to acquaint the new groups with the rules and policies of Grameen as well as insuring that they learn these guidelines. Once the branch becomes established in an area more bank workers will be added to take on the day-to-day tasks and the BM will begin to function in more of an oversight capacity. It is not uncommon for a branch to have eight staff members and 1,500 circles formed after five years. A BM's territory may cover many villages within an area.

The bank workers have day-to-day contact with the borrowing groups in their centers. Bank workers visit two loan centers each day. A loan center consists of about five groups (thirty individuals) and meets regularly in a special one room

Table EA.1. Grameen Bank Performance Figures, January 1991[1]

			U.S. $ (Millions)
Number of Branches	808	Total Amount Disbursed	302.55
Number of Villages	19,984	Amount Disbursed this Month	8.18
Number of Centers	34,730	Cumulative Amount of Savings	
Number of Members	884,135	in Group Funds	20.81
Female	806,283		
Male	77,852		
Number of Houses Built with Grameen Funds	92,268		

Source: Grameen Dialogue, March 1991.

house which the members have donated or constructed. At these meetings the bank worker accepts loan and savings payments as well as discussing new projects and problems with the borrowers. At the bank worker's discretion, additional advice and assistance may be offered to troubled groups. Table EA.1 summarizes Grameen Bank's 1991 operations.

Grameen emphasizes employee autonomy at each level of the organization. Each employee's territory is his or her own province and the ability of other people to interfere in this area is extremely limited. For example, Dr. Yunus, the Bank's founder, can only visit the centers at the invitation of the staff member in charge. An American who recently returned from observing Grameen's operations commented, "Grameen does not like to step on the toes of its people."

CASE F

Classical Jazz at Lincoln Center

Lincoln Center, Inc.'s (LCI), Classical Jazz series was the subject of much discussion in the fall of 1990. Trustees and staff debated the merits of turning the four-year-old jazz program into an independent performing arts organization, like the Metropolitan Opera or the New York City Ballet. Those in favor of making jazz a separate entity argued that the art form was extremely important and deserved such recognition. Supporters also argued that the new independent program would further aid in attracting a larger and more diverse audience to Lincoln Center and ease the financial burden placed on LCI by the program (Figure F.1 and F.2). As a separate entity, the jazz program might attain the visibility and prestige necessary to embark on a successful fundraising campaign.

Several trustees were opposed to the formation of the independent jazz entity because they did not believe that jazz was worthy of the same recognition that was accorded opera or ballet. In addition, some members of LCI's staff felt that spinning off the Classical Jazz program would leave LCI a less-dynamic organization, thereby harming morale and fundraising efforts.

As the board debated the issue, questions arose as to the programming and scheduling of performances of the independent jazz entity. Would the independent organization offer performances on consecutive nights in August, as had LCI's original program, or would performances be featured throughout the year? Would the new entity offer only "classical" jazz, or would newer types of jazz be performed? How would jazz complement the existing independent organizations at Lincoln Center? Thus, the board and staff of LCI were grappling with the programmatic structure of Classical Jazz, as well as the question of whether or not to make jazz a separate organization within the Lincoln Center complex.

Background

LCI was founded in 1955 to raise funds for and construct the world's first performing arts center. Its original ongoing role was to maintain the public spaces, manage the concert facilities, and present programs to fill artistic gaps left by the other constituents. Over the years, this last role has become dominant. The complex originally housed the Metropolitan Opera, the New York Philharmonic Orchestra, the New York City Ballet, the Juilliard School of Music, and a branch of the New York City Public Library. Over the years, the number of financially independent "constituent" organizations has grown to eleven, making Lincoln Center the largest center for the performing arts in the world (Figures F.3 and F.4). The organization's first programs, Great Performers and Mostly Mozart, were designed to fill the halls on "off" nights and to fill programmatic gaps left by the activities of the constituents. As a result, LCI might attract a broader audience to Lincoln Center. LCI now

Prepared by Mary Ida Compton and Elena Kugler under the supervision of Professor Sharon Oster.

Figure F.1.   Participation Rates for Various Arts Activities by Demographic
Characteristics 1985

| | *Percentage Attending/Participating at Least Once in Last 12 Months* | | | | | |
	Jazz	Classical Music	Opera	Musical	Plays	Ballet
Grand Mean	10	13	3	17	12	4
Age						
18–24	14	11	2	15	11	4
25–34	15	12	2	16	12	5
35–44	10	16	4	21	14	6
45–54	8	15	4	20	13	3
55–64	5	11	3	18	10	4
65–74	3	13	3	13	10	4
75–96	1	10	1	8	7	2
Race						
White	9	14	3	18	12	5
Black	13	6	1	9	6	2
Other	8	15	4	13	8	5
Income						
Under $5,000	8	9	2	10	8	3
$5,000–$9,999	7	7	1	8	4	2
$10,000–$14,999	6	8	1	11	8	3
$15,000–$24,999	8	11	2	12	9	4
$25,000–$49,999	11	15	3	22	14	5
$50,000 and over	19	30	8	37	28	11
Not ascertained	9	12	2	17	11	3
Marital Status						
Married	8	12	2	17	11	4
Widowed	3	10	2	12	9	4
Divorced	12	14	3	16	14	4
Separated	13	11	3	14	11	5
Never married	17	16	3	19	14	6

Source: John P. Robinson, Carol Keegan, Marcia Karth and Timothy A. Triplett,
"Public Participation in the Arts: Final Report on the 1985 Survey, Volume 1,
Overall Project Report." Prepared for the National Endowment for the Arts,
December 1986, p. 101.

presents over 250 performances a year that range from traditional classical music
programs to avant garde performance art events by artists such as Karen Finley.

LCI is a constituent organization of the Lincoln Center complex. Constituent
organizations are stand-alone entities that share the cost of maintaining the Lincoln
Center facilities. Each constituent has its own board, does most of its own fundrais-

Figure F.2. Overlapping Audience for Arts Activities 1982

	Jazz	Classical Music	Opera	Musical	Plays	Ballet	Art Museums
	Percentage Who Also Attended at Least Once in Last 12 Months						
Among those who attended:							
Jazz	NA	34	9	41	31	14	51
Classical music	25	NA	15	54	41	19	62
Opera	27	63	NA	64	51	32	69
Musicals	21	38	10	NA	39	14	52
Plays	25	44	13	62	NA	18	60
Ballet	32	58	23	64	50	NA	68
Art museums	22	37	10	44	33	13	NA
Reading	13	20	5	27	18	7	33

Source: John P. Robinson, et al, survey Research Center, University of Maryland. "Public Participation in the Arts: Final Report on the 1982 Survey," prepared for Grant 12-4050-003, National Endowment for the Arts, Research Division, October 1985, Table 3-5, p. 208.

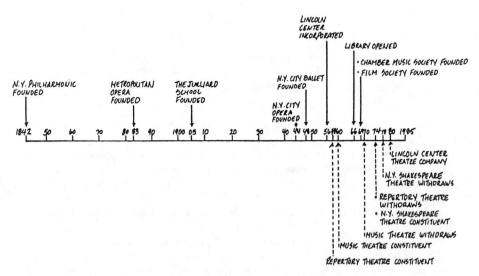

Figure F.3. History of Constituents of Lincoln Center.

Figure F.4. Lincoln Center, Inc. Activities

Role	Major Activities
Owner	—Building maintenance and renovation —General services, garage operations —Negotiations with service providers —Booking of Avery Fisher Hall and Alice Tully Hall —Visitor and patron services
Coordinator	—Consolidated Corporate Fund Drive —Administrative services to selected constituents —Contracting: Stagebill, Restaurant Associates —Government Relations
Educator	—Lincoln Center Institute —Avery Fisher Fellowships —Internship program
Presentor	—Live from Lincoln Center —Great Performers —Mostly Mozart —Serious Fun! —Classical Jazz —Midsummer Night Swing —Outreach programs (e.g., Community Holiday Festival, Lincoln Center Out-of-doors) —Special programs (e.g., Festival of India, Film Retrospective) In support of the above: —Fundraising —Relationships with external constituencies —Marketing

Source: Adapted from "Positioning Lincoln Center to Meet the Challenges of the Future," Report submitted to the Committee for the Future of Lincoln Center, March 1986.

ing, and makes its own programming decisions with regard to performers and artistic pieces. (Figure F.5 shows the organizational structure of Lincoln Center.) Constituents are required to sign a contract that includes a "primacy clause." This provision insures that no constituent will violate the artistic specialty, or primacy, of another constituent. The contract limits competition among the constituents and contributes to a diversity of offerings at Lincoln Center.

Education is considered central to the mission of Lincoln Center. The primary vehicle for education is the Lincoln Center Institute, a department of LCI, which offers programs for teachers. Constituent organizations are also responsible for educational programs, by furthering the education of new artists and audiences in their respective fields. Juilliard, for example, provides training for young musicians

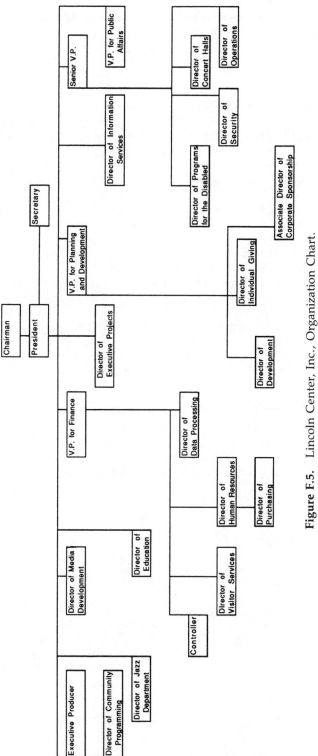

Figure F.5. Lincoln Center, Inc., Organization Chart.

and singers. The New York Philharmonic conducts open rehearsals, and the Metropolitan Opera Guild offers free lectures to the public.

Programming

LCI's programming serves three main functions. First, programs must complement the offerings of the constituents and thus guarantee a wide range of artistic expression of the highest quality at the Lincoln Center complex. Second, LCI's programs should provide opportunities for emerging artists and outlets for new art works. Finally, LCI's programs are designed to attract new and diverse audiences to insure the future health of the organization. Existing LCI performing arts programs are summarized in Table F.1.

New programs, which must be approved by the board, must satisfy the three functions described earlier. However, new program proposals frequently force staff and trustees to rethink the mission of LCI. The organization's mission has clearly expanded to include artistic programming, but the extent and content of the programming function is frequently evaluated (Figure F.6).

Program implementation is not consistent across all programs. LCI's oldest and most traditional programs—Mostly Mozart and Great Performers—are administered in LCI's own programming department. Newer series, such as Serious Fun! and Classical Jazz, are programmed by outside consultants who are knowledgeable in the field. Public relations and marketing for several programs are also contracted out. The capacity of LCI to perform these programmatic and administrative functions has been strained by the addition of new programs in recent years.

Transition to Constituent

Other LCI programs have been "spun off" into independent constituent organizations over the years. In 1969, both Chamber Music and an LCI film program were elevated to the level of constituent. The transition from LCI program to constituent has never been smooth. For example, Board members were reluctant to make the

Table F.1. LCI Performing Arts Programs

Name	Description	Number of Performances	Ticket Prices ($)	Percentage of Capacity
Classical Jazz	jazz	6	12–35	90
Community Holiday Festival	seasonal themes	16	free	—
Great Performers	orchestral	65	20–25	93
Lincoln Center Out-of-Doors	various styles	100	free	—
Midsummer Night Swing	dance music	16	4–5	65
Mostly Mozart	orchestral	42	12–35	91
Serious Fun!	multimedia performance art	16	20–25	72

Figure F.6. Selected Lincoln Center, Inc. Mission Statements

A. Lincoln Center presents the highest quality performing arts to the widest possible audience.

B. Lincoln Center is a unique and creative partnership of performing arts and educational institutions dedicated to fostering the finest expressions of music, dance, drama and film. Through live performances, television and radio broadcasts, educational programs and the development of new artistic talent, Lincoln Center provides an international showcase for all the performing arts and encourages the widest possible public enjoyment and understanding of those arts.

Lincoln Center of the Performing Arts, Inc. is the unifying member of the Lincoln Center family of 11 constituent organizations which include: the Metropolitan Opera, New York Philharmonic, New York City Ballet, New York City Opera, the Juilliard School, the Chamber Music Society of Lincoln Center, the Library and Museum of the Performing Arts, the School of American Ballet and Lincoln Center for the Performing Arts, Inc.

C. "Lincoln Center stands for artistic excellence throughout the world and that is the ultimate goal of all our efforts . . . For those who have enlisted under the banner of Lincoln Center as an entity, the challenge is to make the whole even greater than the sum of its parts." (Chairman's Report, 1984)

D. Lincoln Center for the Performing Arts is one of the country's leading performing arts organizations, presenting and producing more than 250 performances annually through such series as *Mostly Mozart, Great Performers, Classical Jazz, Serious Fun!, Lincoln Center Out-of-Doors* and "Live from Lincoln Center." In addition to preserving the great artistic traditions of the past. Lincoln Center is deeply committed to developing new works, supporting today's creative performers and building the audiences of tomorrow. Besides its role as a presenter, Lincoln Center for the Performing Arts is also the "umbrella" organization for the entire Lincoln Center complex and provides overall support for its family of performing arts institutions.

Source: Internal Lincoln Center documents.

film program a constituent because many felt that film was not an art form worthy of such recognition. Similarly, trustees felt that chamber music was not in line with the artistic traditions of the other constituents. However, in the case of Chamber Music, the spin off was critical in order to relieve LCI from the large deficit generated by the program.

Both Chamber Music and the Film Society struggled financially in the first several years of their existence as independent organizations within the Lincoln Center complex. The Film Society, for example, had a fund deficit of $85,543 for FY 1970, the first full year of the organization's existence. In FY 1971, the deficit was reversed and the balance sheet showed a small fund balance of $13,969 (Figure F.7). Both the Film Society and Chamber Music were able to increase contributions

Figure F.7. Part 1 The Film Society of Lincoln Center, Inc.
December 31, 1970

Balance Sheet
Assets

Cash	$ 560.00	
Accounts receivable	16,400.00	
Deferred program costs	2,114.30	
	$ 19,074.30	

Liabilities and Fund Balance (Deficit)

Accounts payable and accrued expenses	10,235.89	
Payable to Lincoln Center for the Performing Arts, Inc.	66,281.82	
Contributions for use in subsequent year	27,500.00	
Deferred program income	600.00	
Fund balance (deficit)	(85,543.41)	
	$ 19,074.30	

Statement of Income and Expenditures
Income

Contributions		$219,700.00
Program fees and admissions:		
New York Film Festival	$114,201.00	
Spring Film Festival	17,096.00	
Film-in-Education Program	10,700.00	
National Student Film Festival	4,748.00	146,745.00
Film benefit, net of related expenses of $18,080.28		12,969.72
Other		97.17
Total income		379,511.89

Expenditures:		
Programs:		
New York Film Festival	262,170.38	
Spring Film Festival	42,444.04	
Film-in-Education Program	9,382.59	
National Student Film Festival	10,121.70	
Movies-in-the-Park	59,115.53	
Swedish Film Week	64.47	
	383,298.71	
Administrative — wages and benefits	79,470.25	
Lincoln Center supporting service costs	37,000.00	
Total expenditures		499,768.96
Excess of expenditures over income		120,257.07

Fund balance (deficit):		
Beginning of year	34,713.66	
End of year	$ (85,543.41)	

Source: Lincoln Center Annual Reports, 1971, 1972.

Part 2 The Film Society of Lincoln Center, Inc.
December 31, 1971

Balance Sheet

Assets

Cash		$ 35,345
Investments, at cost (which approximates market)		49,321
Accounts receivable	$ 33,329	
Less allowance for doubtful accounts	2,938	
Net receivables		30,391
Deferred program costs		3,446
Total assets		$118,503

Liabilities and Fund Balances

Liabilities:

Accounts payable and accrued expenses		25,898
Payable to Lincoln Center for the Performing Arts, Inc.		75,561
Deferred program income		3,075

Fund balances (deficit):

Unrestricted		(49,202)
Restricted		63,171
Total fund balances		13,969
Total liabilities and fund balances		$118,503

	Total	Unrestricted	Restricted

Statement of Revenues, Expenditures and Unrestricted Fund Balance

	Total	Unrestricted	Restricted
Revenues:			
Contributions	$386,772	144,228	242,544
Program fees and admissions:			
New York film festival	46,530	46,530	—
Movies for kids	12,829	12,829	—
Film in education	14,300	14,300	—
Upstate education expansion	350	350	—
CBS documentary	13,650	13,650	—
Preview club—net	2,020	2,020	—
	89,679	89,679	—
Net loss on investment transactions	(3,724)	(3,724)	—
Total revenues	472,727	230,183	242,544
Expenditures:			
Programs:			
New Yew film festival	181,302	92,637	88,665
Movies for kids	90,943	13,224	77,719
Film in education	21,392	18,892	2,500

(continued)

Figure F.7. Part 2 The Film Society of Lincoln Center, Inc.

December 31, 1971 (*Continued*)

	Total	Unrestricted	Restricted
Upstate education expansion	11,110	3,550	7,560
Movies in the park	72,638	6,538	66,100
CBS documentary	7,151	7,151	—
	384,536	141,992	242,544
Supporting services:			
Administration	46,350	46,350	—
Fund raising	5,500	5,500	—
Total expenditures	436,386	193,842	242,544
Excess of revenues over			
expenditures	36,341	36,341	—
Fund balance (deficit):			
Beginning of year	(85,543)	(85,543)	
End of year	$ (49,202)	(49,202)	

Note: The Society has pledges receivable of approximately $36,500 at December 31, 1971.

Part 3 The Chamber Music Society of Lincoln Center, Inc.
June 30, 1970

Balance Sheet
Assets
Current funds:
Unrestricted:

Cash	$22,535.44
Accounts receivable	9,430.97
Deferred program costs	23,750.00
	55,716.41
Restricted—cash	12,165.00
Total current funds	$67,881.41

Endowment and similar funds:
Investments, at cost (quoted market value

$251,912.50)	250,670.00
Cash	654.50
Total endowment and similar funds	$251,324.50

Liabilities and Fund Balances
Current funds:
Unrestricted:

Accounts payable	23,816.14
Fund balance (Exhibit B)	31,900.27
	55,716.41
Restricted fund balance (Exhibit C)	12,165.00
Total current funds	$67,881.41
Endowment and similar funds—balance (Exhibit C)	$251,324.50

	Total	Unrestricted	Restricts
Statement of Revenues, Expenditures, Appropriation and Unrestricted Fund Balance			
Revenues:			
Contributions	$352,329.31	349,494.31	2,835.00
Box office admissions	96,534.25	96,534.25	—
Investment income (net of loss on invest-			
ment transactions of $4,597.76)	9,105.34	9,105.34	—
Total revenues	457,968.90	455,133.90	2,835.00
Expenditures:			
Programs:			
Salaries and employee benefits	38,356.15	38,356.15	—
Artists' fees and expenses	91,060.70	91,060.70	—
Advertising and promotion	39,466.33	39,466.33	—
Consulting fees	8,083.32	8,083.32	—
Hall rentals	28,670.31	28,670.31	—
Miscellaneous	7,937.16	5,102.16	2,835.00
	213,573.97	210,738.97	2,835.00
Supporting services:			
Lincoln Center supporting service costs	24,999.98	24,999.98	—
Administrative—general office expenses	7,030.90	7,030.90	—
	32,030.88	32,030.88	—
Total expenditures	245,604.85	242,769.85	—
Excess of revenues over expenditures before			
appropriation	212,364.05	212,364.05	—
Appropriation to endowment and similar			
funds	233,824.50	233,824.50	
Excess of expenditures and appropriation			
over revenues	21,460.45	21,460.45	
Fund balance:			
Beginning of year	53,360.72	53,360.72	
End of year	$31,900.27	31,900.27	

Note: Commitments for compositions, hall rentals, public relations, and artists' contracts amounted to approximately $100,525.00 at June 30, 1970.

Part 4 The Chamber Music Society of Lincoln Center, Inc.
June 30, 1971

Assets
Current Funds:
  Unrestricted:
    Cash $18,883.60
    Accounts receivable   22,392.83
    Deferred program costs   7,071.25
    Marketable securities (quoted market value
      $8,000.00)   7,949.01
                                                           56,296.69

(continued)

Figure F.7 Part 4 The Chamber Music Society of Lincoln Center, Inc.

June 30, 1971 (*Continued*)

Restricted—marketable securities (quoted market value $3,700.00)	3,611.93
	$59,908.62
Endowment and similar funds:	
Investments, at cost (quoted market value $513,750.00)	$513,674.50
Liabilities and Fund Balances	
Current Funds:	
Unrestricted:	
Accounts payable	32,937.47
Fund balance (Exhibit B)	23,359.22
	56,296.69
Restricted fund balance (Exhibit C)	3,611.93
Total current funds	$59,908.62
Endowment and similar funds—balance (Exhibit C)	$513,674.50

	Total	Unrestricted	Restricted
Statement of Revenues, Expenditures, Appropriation and Unrestricted Fund Balance			
Revenues:			
Contributions	$155,038.30	145,485.23	9,553.07
Box office admissions	111,771.50	111,771.50	
Investment income (includes gain on investment transactions of $4,006.80)	36,666.01	36,666.01	—
Total Revenues	303,475.81	293,922.74	9,553.07
Expenditures:			
Programs:			
Salaries & employee benefits	76,505.79	76,505.79	—
Artists' fees & expenses	103,939.19	103,939.19	—
Advertising & promotion	41,020.00	41,020.00	—
Consulting fees	8,199.92	8,199.92	—
Hall rentals	40,253.50	37,316.50	2,937.00
Miscellaneous	10,095.47	3,479.40	6,616.07
	280,013.87	270,460.80	9,553.07
Supporting services:			
Lincoln Center supporting costs	16,000.00	16,000.00	—

	Total	Unrestricted	Restricted
Administrative—general office expenses	16,002.99	16,002.99	—
	32,002.99	32,002.99	—
Total expenditures	312,016.86	302,463.79	—
Excess of expenditures over revenues	8,541.05	8,541.05	—
Fund balance:			
Beginning of year	31,900.27	31,900.27	
End of year	$23,359.22	23,359.22	

Note: Commitments for compositions, hall rentals, public relations, and artists' contracts amounted to approximately $120,000. at June 30, 1971.

during the first few years of their existence as constituents. The success of these constituents benefitted the entire Lincoln Center complex.

Demographic Trends

LCI attempts to attract a diversified audience in order to fulfill the organization's mission and increase its funding base. The success of Lincoln Center in attracting a diverse audience may be estimated by examining the organization's current audience with respect to the demographic profile of the region. Such a comparison will also provide information about the future success of Lincoln Center. If, for example, the organization's audience is significantly different from the emerging demographic profile of the region, Lincoln Center will probably have trouble attracting support in coming years.

LCI Audience

Lincoln Center conducted a major audience survey of Mostly Mozart and the New York City Opera audiences in 1985[1] that suggested that almost 70% of these audiences were over forty-five years of age. A similar survey prepared in 1982 found that only 55% of the audiences at Mostly Mozart concerts were over forty-five years of age. Over half of LCI's audience comes from outside New York City. The average audience member attended more performances at Lincoln Center in 1985 than he or she did five years earlier. Ticket sales over the same period have remained relatively flat, suggesting that the audience base may actually be shrinking. A 1985–1986 survey of Lincoln Center audiences revealed that 91% of the audience had completed college and 57% had graduate degrees (Figures F.8 and F.9).

[1]Lincoln Center administrators suggest that there is no reason to believe this profile has changed substantially since 1985.

Manhattan and New York City

The total populations of Manhattan and New York City (Manhattan and the boroughs) have declined by 9% and 5%, respectively, from 1970 to 1980, and have both increased by only 4% from 1980 to 1990. Census data suggests that the percentage of whites is declining rapidly while blacks and Hispanics represent an increasingly large proportion of the city's population. The average age of the population has declined in recent years. The percentage of people in the twenty-five to forty-four year old range is increasing, while the percentage over forty-five is decreasing. The average level of education is increasing, as evidenced by the growing percentage of people with greater than twelve or sixteen years of schooling (Figure F.10).

Condition of the Performing Arts Industry

Interest in and support for the performing arts appears to have declined slightly since the 1980's. A study of the performing arts industry commissioned by the National Endowment for the Arts in 1987 reveals decreases in audience participation rates for live performances across a variety of performing arts. A similar decline is also apparent in the participation in the arts via media (Figures F.11 and F.12). Plausible explanations for this decline include decreased leisure time and the emergence of home videos. These problems are compounded by the fact that young audiences today have not been brought up on classical music as were older generations.

Interestingly, the declining audience base is accompanied by an increase in the percent of "Total Recreation Expenditures" spent on "legitimate theater, opera and entertainment of non-profit institutions" (excluding sports). This fact suggest that fewer people are spending more on performing arts events. A 1987 study prepared for the National Endowment for the Arts revealed that time was the most significant barrier to increased attendance at performing arts events. Other frequently cited "barriers" included cost, access, and personal factors.

Competition among performing arts centers in New York is limited. According to Lincoln Center administrators, brand loyalty among major performance spaces is virtually nonexistent. Fans of a given artist or piece will probably attend a performance at any of New York's performance spaces, such as Carnegie Hall, Lincoln Center's Alice Tully Hall, or others. (However, someone wishing to see a performance without preference for a particular artist would recognize Lincoln Center as a producer of high-quality programs.) Ticket prices are fairly constant for a given art form, although a 1965 study by Baumel and Bowen indicated that consumers of performing arts are not very price sensitive. Competition in programming is limited because there are many popular artists and many nights on which to book these artists.

Fundraising is one area where competition does exist. Declining corporate sponsorship and uncertainty regarding government and foundation funding has strained performing arts organizations and caused them to aggressively pursue individual donors (Figure F.13). The effects of competition have been compounded by an increasing number of nonprofit organizations soliciting donations.

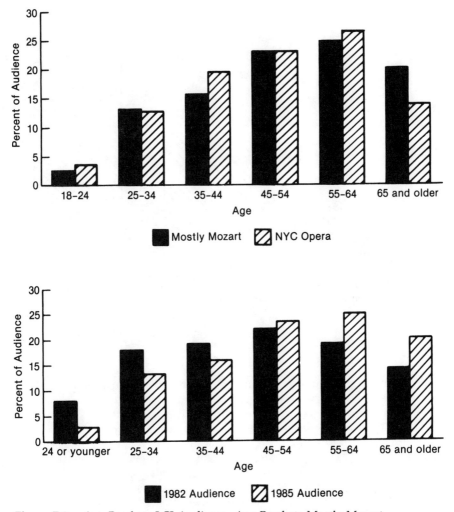

Figure F.8.   Age Brackets LCI Audience. Age Brackets Mostly Mozart
Audiences. *Source:* 1982 and 1985 Survey cited in report for the Committee for
the Future of Lincoln Center.

Classical Jazz

Classical Jazz[2] was developed in an attempt to develop programming that would fill
the halls during the summer months and attract a more diverse audience to LCI.
The staff of LCI enlisted the help of Wynton Marsalis to persuade the board to

[2]The following discussion describes the creation of the Classical Jazz *program* in 1987. The question of
constituency had not yet been considered.

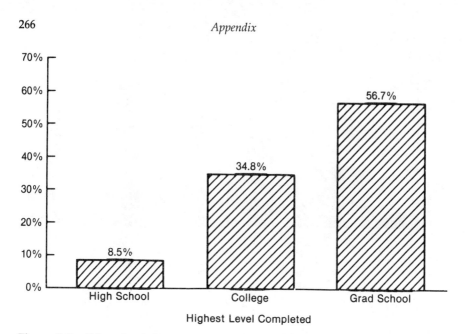

Figure F.9.   Education LCI Audiences. *Source:* LC Audience Survey, 1985–1986.

institute the jazz program. Under Marsalis' guidance, the Board created a committee to formally evaluate the viability of a jazz program at LCI.

The jazz committee was composed of board members and outsiders familiar with jazz. The board members selected to be on the committee included those most adamantly opposed to a jazz program; if the detractors could be persuaded, the new program would certainly have the full support of the board. The committee listened to jazz recordings and visited jazz clubs; eventually, all members came to support the proposed program. One of the committee members went so far as to say that she was now convinced that jazz was *the* most important American art form.

The committee returned to the board with glowing reports of jazz. The remainder of the board accepted the proposal and thus was born the Classical Jazz program at LCI. Classical Jazz, inaugurated in 1987, consisted of six evening performances during one week in August. The performers are well-known artists and the music is defined as traditional jazz. A 1990 roster included programs such as "Good Vibes with Benny Carter" and the "Ellington Express," performed by artists like Marsalis and Ron Carter.

In order to evaluate the success of the new program, LCI conducted audience surveys in 1987 and 1989. The results of the surveys suggest that Classical Jazz was fulfilling its function of attracting a younger, more diverse audience to Lincoln Center (Figure F.14). Both board and staff were inspired by these results, but they continue to be interested in the program structure that will maximize the benefits of the program.

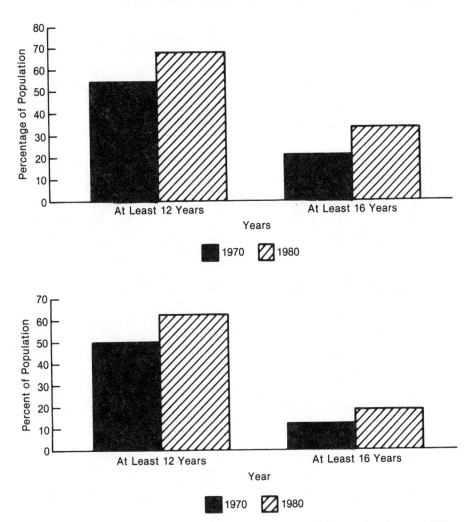

Figure F.10. Education Manhattan. Education NYC and Boroughs. *Source:* 1979 and 1986 Stats and Metro Area Data Books published by the U.S. Bureau of the Census.

Figure F.11. Rates of Public Participation in the Arts 1982 to 1985

At Least Once in Last 12 Months[a]	Estimated Participation Rates (%)		Evaluation of Rate Change
	1982 (N=9,263)	1985 (N=13,675)	
Attended			
Jazz performance	10	10	No change
Classical music	14	13	Decrease[b]
Opera performances	4	3	Decrease[b]
Musical plays or operetta	19	17	Decrease[b]
Plays (non-musical)	12	12	No change
Ballet performances	5	4	Not significant
Motion pictures (went out to)	60	59	Not significant
Visited			
Art museums or galleries	23	22	Not significant
Parks, monuments, buildings or neighborhoods for historic or design value	34	36	Not significant
Arts or crafts fairs or festivals	35	40	Increase[b]

[a] Arts participation by adults (18 years of age or older) in 12 months preceding interview.

[b] Statistically significant at the 95 percent confidence level.

Source: National Endowment for the Arts, Research Division, "Public Participation in the Arts: 1982 and 1985 Compared," Washington, D.C., Note 27, December 1987.

Figure F.12. Rates of Public Participation in the Arts via Media 1982 to 1985

Watching at Least Once in Last 12 Months[a]	Estimated Participation Rates (%)		Evaluation of Rate Change
	1982 (N=1,385)	1985 (N=1,385)	
Jazz			
TV	20	17	Decrease[b]
Radio	21	18	Decrease[b]
Recordings	24	21	Decrease[b]
Classical Music			
TV	27	24	Decrease[b]
Radio	25	21	Decrease[b]
Recordings	25	21	Decrease[b]
Opera			
TV	13	12	Not Significant
Radio	8	7	Not Significant
Recordings	9	7	Not Significant
Musical Theater or Operatta			
TV	20	18	Not Significant
Radio	6	5	Not Significant
Recordings	9	8	Not Significant
Plays (nonmusical)			
TV	27	21	Decrease[b]
Radio	4	4	No Change
Ballet			
TV	19	15	Decrease[b]

[a]Arts participation by adults (18 years of age or older) in 12 months preceding interview.

[b]Statistically significant at the 95 percent confidence level.

Source: National Endowment for the Arts, Research Division, "Public Participation in the Arts: 1982 and 1985 Compared," Washington, D.C., Note 27, December 1987.

Figure F.13. Lincoln Center, Inc.—Total Funds Raised for the 12 Months Ended June 30

	1989	1988	1987	1986	1985	1984	1983	1982
Corporations								
—Restricted	2,223,801	2,872,247	2,563,082	2,594,146	2,078,124	1,732,501	1,548,423	1,500,648
—Unrestricted	653,078	613,024	590,603	588,936	512,128	523,719	487,334	492,380
—Total	2,876,879	3,485,271	3,153,685	3,183,082	2,590,252	2,256,220	2,035,757	1,993,028
Percentage change from previous year	-17.5	10.5	-0.9	22.9	14.8	10.8	2.1	
Foundations								
—Restricted	1,838,834	1,487,343	1,636,998	1,108,895	1,363,486	1,222,833	495,591	492,736
—Unrestricted	201,300	185,300	196,299	193,500	146,250	131,459	39,100	17,350
—Total	2,040,134	1,672,643	1,833,297	1,302,395	1,509,736	1,354,292	534,691	510,086
Percentage change from previous year	22.0	-8.8	40.8	-13.7	11.5	153.3	4.8	
Individuals								
—Restricted	430,044	258,890	178,432	195,138	151,761	152,124	76,391	22,169
—Unrestricted	481,788	515,647	535,021	449,827	452,979	398,409	494,460	514,073
—Total	911,832	774,537	713,453	644,965	604,740	550,533	570,851	536,242
Percentage change from previous year	17.7	8.6	10.6	6.7	9.8	-3.6	6.5	
Government								
—NEA	438,500	393,500	409,100	354,188	348,700	407,900	421,200	371,460
—NYSCA	295,800	280,300	275,300	263,500	245,500	199,000	233,000	258,000
—Misc	421,400	393,250	365,250	365,000	315,063	212,544	122,148	77,754
—Total	1,155,700	1,067,050	1,049,650	982,688	909,263	819,444	776,348	707,214
Percentage change from previous year	8.3	1.7	6.8	8.1	11.0	5.6	9.8	
Misc—Total	258,572	75,884	248,797	3,616	0	0	190,863	173,645
TOTAL	7,243,117	7,075,385	6,998,882	6,116,746	5,613,991	4,980,489	4,108,510	3,920,215
Percentage change from previous year	2.4	1.1	14.4	9.0	12.7	21.2	4.8	

Source: Development Department Overview, Report Prepared by William Keller and Robert Greenberg, August 12, 1989.

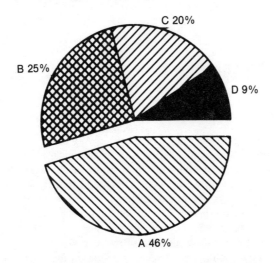

C 20%

B 25%

D 9%

A 46%

A: Percent of audience that has attended both f
   ticketed (fee) performances at Lincoln Center
B: Percent of audience that has attended a tick
   performance, but not a free performance at
   Lincoln Center
C: Percent of audience that has never attended
   performances at Lincoln Center
D: Percent of audience that has attended a free
   performance, but not a ticketed performance
   Lincoln Center

Figure F.14. Classical Jazz Audience Prior Exposure to Lincoln Center. *Source:* 1987 Classical Jazz Audience Survey.

CASE G

The Future of Donor Choice at the United Way

The phones were ringing off the hook at the United Way of Southern Connecticut. It was March 1993 and callers were responding to an article in the morning paper regarding the local Boy Scout chapter's opposition to admitting homosexuals as scouts, employees, and volunteers. The article stated that the United Way, which had funded the local Boy Scout council consistently for the past fifty years, was re-examining its support of the Scouts due to the agency's position on homosexuals. By mid-afternoon phone calls were about evenly distributed, both for and against the United Way's continued funding of the Boy Scouts.

As he fielded the last call of the day, Doug Higginbottom, executive director of the United Way of Southern Connecticut, realized that regardless of the stance the United Way took regarding the Boy Scouts, it would alienate a large number of contributors. This was a highly controversial issue in which emotions ran high and reconciliation was extremely difficult.

When people give to the United Way their contributions support all of the agencies under the United Way's umbrella. Since the Boy Scouts fall under this umbrella, donors are giving part of their contribution to the Scouts. Higginbottom was afraid that those who opposed the Boy Scout's ban on gays would withdraw their contributions altogether.

Background and History

The United Way is one of the oldest and largest charitable health and human service organizations in the United States. The United Way of Southern Connecticut is one of 2,200 local United Way organizations located in communities throughout the United States. Each organization is autonomous, and decision making is based at the local level. The basic functions of each United Way include fundraising and fund distribution, both of which are conducted within the local community in which the United Way is based.

The national organization, United Way of America, does not dictate policy to the locals but is instead a support arm for local organizations. United Way of America provides training, consulting, national advertising, and research services to local United Ways. In exchange for these services, participating locals pay 1% of their annual fundraising revenues to United Way of America.

The United Way movement began more than 100 years ago in response to companies that found it cumbersome to respond to the solicitation requests of a growing number of charitable organizations. The United Way emerged as the con-duit through which funds could be channeled to all local health and human service agencies. This consolidated effort reduced the administrative burden on compa-

Please note that this case is not a depiction of any particular United Way organization but is based upon various United Ways in the state of Connecticut.
This case was written by Meher Vakharia under the direction of Professor Sharon Oster.

Figure G.1. United Way of Southern Connecticut's Nine Town Area

Population of Southern Connecticut region = 350,000
Towns: Bethany
            East Haven
            Hamden
            New Haven
            North Branford
            North Haven
            Orange
            West Haven
            Woodbridge

nies. Recipient agencies also benefited by not having to devote a large percentage of their resources to fund raising.

Fundraising

The United Way of Southern Connecticut raises funds from a nine town geographic area in the southern portion of the state (see Figure G.1). Like other United Ways, the vast majority of funds are raised at the work place. Work place donations consist of both corporate gifts and individual employee gifts (see Figure G.2). The bulk of work place solicitation is conducted by volunteers called loaned executives (LEs). The larger companies in the local area "loan" personnel to the United Way during the fund raising season, which typically runs from September through December. The company continues to pay the employee's salary, and United Way receives a full-time volunteer.

LEs spend an intensive week of classroom training at the United Way before beginning their volunteer assignments. Once they are trained, LEs solicit company CEOs for corporate gifts, and also conduct employee solicitations. A "textbook" employee campaign consists of verbal presentations to small groups of employees at the work place. Presentations typically include showing the annual United Way film, in which a well-known celebrity narrates stories of actual individuals who received help through United Way agencies. At the conclusion of the presentation, brochures and pledge cards are distributed and employees are encouraged to fill out their pledge cards before leaving.

Figure G.2. United Way Fund Raising History

	Total Donations ($)	Workplace Donations ($)	Nonworkplace Donations ($)
1988	4,050,000	3,240,000	810,000
1989	4,171,500	3,328,200	843,300
1990	4,254,930	3,616,691	638,239
1991	4,255,856	3,489,980	765,876
1992	4,568,648	3,769,135	799,513

When contributors make a donation, they give a single gift to the United Way. It is then up to the United Way fund distribution process to oversee the equitable distribution of funds to local agencies.

Fund Distribution

Just as funds are raised from within the local community, they are also distributed to health and human service agencies within the community. Each year, nine committees of approximately ten volunteers each allocate funds to thirty local agencies known as "member agencies." (see Figure G.3). The process is often referred to as

Figure G.3.   United Way allocation.

Agency	Amount Received 1992 ($)
American Heart Association	130,625
American Red Cross	343,678
Association for Retarded Citizens	36,486
Big Brothers/Big Sisters	49,929
Boy Scouts	75,111
Boys & Girls Club	127,551
Casa Otonal	56,363
Catholic Family Services	151,294
Clifford Beers Guidance Clinic	139,007
Community Children & Family Services	25,971
Continuum of Care	37,005
Coordinating Council for Children in Crisis	31,663
Cornerstone, Inc.	17,000
Dixwell Community House	161,989
Domestic Violence Services	44,912
Easter Seal Goodwill Rehabilitation Center	82,485
Family Counseling	213,278
Farnam Neighborhood House	118,185
Fellowship House	17,839
Girl Scouts	61,129
Infoline	47,180
Jewish Community Center	65,979
Jewish Family Service	75,139
Latino Youth Development	22,741
Legal Assistance Association	100,803
Leila Day Nursery	58,839
Regional Visiting Nurses Association	35,734
Sage Services	28,201
Urban League	94,086
Visiting Nurses Association	57,481
West Haven Community House	147,574
YMCA	139,235
YWCA	116,922

Source: United Way documents.

Figure G.4. United Way of Southern Connecticut Moratorium on Agency Admissions (Highlights)

In March 1986, the board of directors voted to close the new member admissions process and appointed a committee to review and revise the policies and procedures governing the admission of new member agencies. This action was taken due to concerns that the United Way was adding new member agencies at a faster pace than campaign growth could absorb. A new admissions policy was developed to address this concern.

The policy calls for the board of directors to determine by December of each year whether new admissions will be considered for the following calendar year. In preparing a recommendation for the board regarding the admission of new members, the following should be considered:

1. The amount raised in the annual campaign.
2. The amounts allocated to member agencies in recent years, as well as current year estimates.
3. Any changes in current member funding relationships that might make funds available for redistribution.
4. Based on community needs, and in order to improve the network of human services, is it critical to develop a relationship with a nonfunded agency?

Source: United Way documents.

the "Citizen Review Process" because community citizens volunteer to help make funding decisions.

The fund distribution process is very thorough and involves the review of detailed financial and descriptive information on each agency. Site visits are conducted so that volunteers can see the agency's operations first hand. Finally, each agency makes a formal presentation to the committee, during which it provides detailed substantiation for its funding request.

United Way professionals often argue that the fund distribution process is central to the United Way's mission. The United Way sees itself as the convener of social service funds to the local community. The United Way not only ensures that funds are channeled to meet the most pressing community needs, but that recipient agencies meet high standards of performance and accountability before receiving funds.

In New Haven, with the exception of Latino Youth Development, Casa Otonal, and Coordinating Council for Children in Crisis (CCCC), all other agencies have been funded continuously for at least the past 25 years. Latino Youth Development and Casa Otonal were admitted as member agencies in 1985 and 1981, respectively, in response to the needs of a growing Hispanic community. CCCC was admitted in 1986.

Since that time there has been a moratorium on new agency admissions. The rationale for the moratorium is due, in part, to sluggish growth in annual fund raising campaigns. Annual increases have barely kept up with inflation. Therefore, funding additional agencies would mean slicing the pie into even smaller pieces. Allocations in smaller amounts could greatly reduce the efficacy of grants. The moratorium was also enstated in order to meet member agencies' needs for long-term, stable funding in an increasingly unstable funding environment (see Figure G.4 for excerpts from the moratorium).

As community needs have continued to grow at a rapid pace, so have the number of local health and human service agencies. An increasing number of these new agencies have sought funding from the United Way, but have been turned away due to the moratorium.

Critics of the moratorium argue that changing community needs require a change in the composition of member agencies funded by United Way. They argue that traditional agencies such as the Girl Scouts should be replaced by agencies that address more contemporary issues. However, United Way officials state that traditional agencies like the Girl Scouts have successfully adapted to changing times. They cite examples of how the Girl Scouts has shifted its focus to meet the needs of inner-city girls, and addresses issues such as substance abuse and teenage pregnancy. Most of the directive for these radical changes in the Girl Scouts came from its national office. However, the United Way fund distribution committee has also played an important role in bringing about a shift to more contemporary issues. The committee made several specific recommendations to the Girl Scouts regarding a shift to inner-city programs.

Despite the changes made by the Girl Scouts over the past few years, there is still a perception among the public that the agency is an exclusively white, middle class organization. This perception often makes fund distribution a challenge for both the United Way and the Girl Scouts.

Since United Way funding covers only a portion of member agencies' budgets, these agencies must conduct their own fundraising efforts as well. However, they are required to comply with the United Way's Supplemental Fund Raising Policy Guidelines (see Figure G.5).

Needs Assessment

Every three to five years the United Way of Southern Connecticut conducts a Community Needs Assessment. It is part of the United Way's ongoing effort to better understand the health and human service needs of the community and enhance the delivery of social services in the area. The Needs Assessment is one of several criteria used by fund distribution volunteers to make allocation decisions. It is also used by United way volunteers to develop recommendations that can lead to coordinated community responses to high-priority needs.

The process is conducted by a committee of volunteers, with staff support, over a three to four month period. The four major components include: (1) A key informant survey, (2) a general population survey, (3) demographic data, (4) demand data.

Key Informant Survey

The committee identifies local community leaders within city and state government, the private sector, the health and human service field, and organized labor, as "key informants." Each individual is asked to complete a survey that ranks a broad range of local human service needs. Both qualitative and quantitative information is provided (see Figure G.6).

General Population Survey

A similar survey is sent to a random sample of community residents. Residents are also asked to provide their perceptions of community needs, both qualitatively and quantitatively.

Figure G.5. United Way of Southern Connecticut Member Agency Supplemental Fund Raising Policy Guidelines

BACKGROUND

The United Way system is built on the concept of a single communitywide fundraising campaign on behalf of member agencies to support programs that meet the human service needs of the community. Support for this single, communitywide campaign is based on a recognition of the benefits it provides to the community at large and to the different groups whose cooperation make it a reality—agencies, businesses, givers, volunteers. The United Way system and the single communitywide campaign offer:

Agencies—a relatively stable source of funds, the opportunity to compete for the larger pool of funds generated by the access to the work place afforded to a single campaign, and lower fund raising costs.

Businesses—an efficient method of providing funds to address the community human service needs (one request/one gift) with assurance of the effective use of funds due to United Way's assessment of community needs and the Citizen Review Process for distributing funds.

Givers—an easier way to give (payroll deduction), as well as cost effective, community-based, representative method of distributing funds.

Volunteers—more efficient use of their time in fundraising.

In order for the single consolidated campaign on behalf of all members to remain successful, all participating groups must continue to realize the benefits they expect from this process and must see these benefits as significant enough to warrant continued participation.

POLICY

This policy recognizes the need for fundraising by member agencies while reaffirming commitment to the single communitywide campaign on behalf of all United Way member agencies, and defines the parameters within which fundraising activities by member agencies should be done.

1. *Suggested sources of self-supporting income* Member agencies are encouraged to raise funds through fees for services, private foundations, government grants, service related memberships, the Neighborhood Assistance Act, bequests, memorial funds, fees for program activities and use of facilities, sustaining memberships, benefits, special events and merchandise sales.

2. *Workplace solicitation is restricted* Member agencies may not solicit funds from company in plant federations or employees in the workplace.

3. *Soliciting corporate supporters of the annual campaign is restricted* Member agencies may not solicit funds from those corporations or businesses that support the United Way campaign.

4. *Fundraising restricted during annual United Way campaign* Member agencies may not conduct fundraising activities or events from Labor Day through Thanksgiving. Exceptions may be made for incidental or traditional fundraising activities.

(*continued*)

Figure G.5. *(Continued)*

PROCEDURES

1. Member agencies should submit plans for fundraising for the coming year to the United Way with their budget materials.

2. Member agencies should inform the United Way, in writing, of any changes to the submitted plans.

3. The United Way will review all agency fundraising plans to notify an agency, in writing, of any activity that is not in compliance with this policy.

4. Agencies are required to identify themselves as United Way affiliated organizations in all approved fundraising activities.

COMPLIANCE

Noncompliance with this policy on the part of some member agencies could reduce the level of funds raised in the consolidated campaign for all members. Therefore, fairness requires that all members adhere to this policy and that failure to comply carry a penalty. Fundraising activity beyond the scope of this policy may result in a reduction of the member agency's United Way allocation. Repeated noncompliance with this policy may be grounds for termination of the United Way–member agency relationship.

Source: United Way documents.

Demographic Data

Secondary data, consisting largely of studies done by state and city departments, are utilized. This information is used to identify affected populations in terms of race, gender, ethnicity, socioeconomic status, and so on.

The Needs Assessment committee utilizes data from Infoline, the state of Connecticut's telephone information and referral service. Infoline acts as an information clearinghouse for social services throughout the state of Connecticut. Community residents call Infoline to collect information on issues such as affordable day care, finding a homeless shelter for the night, and other social service needs.

Infoline employees who answer the phone are trained social workers who also provide counseling to callers. Every fifth call is tracked for data gathering purposes. This information consists of demographic data on the caller, as well as the types of services requested. The Needs Assessment committee utilizes this data as an approximate gauge of service demand.

Once all primary and secondary data are collected, tabulated and analyzed, a written report is produced (see Figure G.7).

The Donor Choice Program

Ten years ago, due to an increasingly competitive fundraising environment, and pressure from donors and nonmember agencies, the United Way of Southern Connecticut initiated a Donor Choice program. Through this program, contributors may choose one of four options: (1) allow the Citizen Review Process to allocate their contribution, (2) designate only a subset of member agencies as recipients of their donation, (3) designate all or part of their contribution to one or more *non*-member agencies within the state of Connecticut, (4) make a negative designation

South Central Connecticut United Ways

Community Needs Assessment -- Your Opinion Counts

Dear Community Resident:

The United Ways of Greater New Haven, Meriden and Wallingford, Middlesex, Milford and the Valley are working together to determine the needs of people in their communities and in South Central Connecticut. As part of this community and regional needs assessment, we would like to have your opinion. The following "Problems/Needs" section occasionally contains more than one element in each numbered description. Please circle any elements that apply to your rating of the problem or need. Then, indicate your rating by placing an X in one of the categories, one through five.

    1 - This is not a problem here at all; very few people have a difficulty
    2 - This is a slight problem; there are some people in need
    3 - A somewhat serious problem; a significant number of people have
    4 - A very serious problem; many people are significantly affected
    5 - I am unable to classify this issue

EXAMPLE:

	1 Not a Problem	2 Slight Problem	3 Somewhat Serious	4 Very Serious	5 Don't Know
I. Problems/Needs					
1. Abuse or neglect (children, spouse, elderly)	___	___	___	___	___

	1 Not a Problem	2 Slight Problem	3 Somewhat Serious	4 Very Serious	5 Don't Know
I. Problems/Needs					
1. Abuse or neglect (children, spouse, elderly)	___	___	___	___	___
2. Adoption or foster care	___	___	___	___	___
3. Adult day care and home care	___	___	___	___	___
4. AIDS (prevention, medical care, shelter)	___	___	___	___	___
5. Alcohol/Drug Abuse (children, adolescents, adults)	___	___	___	___	___
6. Child care (infant, preschool, school age)	___	___	___	___	___
7. Crime	___	___	___	___	___
8. Economic development or decline	___	___	___	___	___
9. Financial Assistance	___	___	___	___	___
10. Education (elementary, secondary, adult basic)	___	___	___	___	___
11. Emergency services (fire, police ambulance, disaster)	___	___	___	___	___
12. Environment (pollution, land use, zoning)	___	___	___	___	___
13. Family issues (stress, divorce, single parent families, dual career couples)	___	___	___	___	___
14. Health and Dental care (affordability, quality, catastrophic illness)	___	___	___	___	___
15. Housing and shelter for all incomes, including the homeless (affordability, availability)	___	___	___	___	___
16. Hunger/nutrition	___	___	___	___	___
17. Isolation/loneliness	___	___	___	___	___
18. Jobs/and job training	___	___	___	___	___
19. Legal services (affordability, accessibility, quality)	___	___	___	___	___
20. Mental health (affordability, accessibility, quality)	___	___	___	___	___
21. Racial or ethnic relations	___	___	___	___	___
22. Recreation/leisure (affordability, accessibility, quality)	___	___	___	___	___
23. Support services (counseling, life skills, advocacy, disability, crisis intervention)					

Figure G.6. Southern Connecticut United Way Community Needs Assessment. *Source:* United Way documents.

	1 Not a Problem	2 Slight Problem	3 Somewhat Serious	4 Very Serious	5 Don't Know
24. Teen Pregnancy and Family Planning	___	___	___	___	___
25. Transportation (affordability, accessibility, quality)	___	___	___	___	___
26. Other (please specify)	___	___	___	___	___

Optional

II. Of those problems/needs you scored with a "4" -- in other words you see them as
VERY SERIOUS - Can you describe specifically what the problem is?

1. Problem/Need_____
_____
_____

2. Problem/Need_____
_____
_____

3. Problem/Need_____
_____
_____

III. Please tell us about yourself

1. Are you ... Male ... Female?

2. How would you describe your race or ethnicity?

(1) - Asian   (4) - White

(2) - Black   (5) - Other (which?)

(3) - Hispanic   _____

3. Which of the following categories describes your occupation?

1. Executive, administrative, or managerial
2. Professional
3. Technical
4. Sales
5. Administrative support (e.g., clerical, secretarial)
6. Services
7. Industrial
8. Homemaker
9. Unemployed
10. Other_____

4. Within what range is your total household income?

(1) - under $10,000   (5) - $40,001-50,000

(2) - $10,001-20,000   (6) - $50,001-$100,000

(3) - $20,001-$30,000   (7) - over $100,000

(4) - $30,001-$40,000

5. What is your age?

(1) - under 14   (6) - 51-60

(2) - 14-20   (7) - 61-65

(3) - 21-30   (8) - 66-80

(4) - 31-40   (9) - over 80

(5) - 41-50

6. My town of residence_____ Zip _____

7. The social services serving my town are

(1) - Excellent   (4) - Very inadequate

(2) - Adequate   (5) - Don't know

(3) - Inadequate

8. The information available about social services serving my town is

(1) - Excellent   (4) Very inadequate

(2) - Adequate   (5) Don't know

(3) - Inadequate

THANK YOU   YOUR PARTICIPATION COUNTS!

Please return this survey to the United Way of Greater New Haven, One State Street,
New Haven, CT 06511.

Figure G.6. (*Continued*)

Figure G.7.   The United Mission.

Key Informant *Top 10 Needs*	General Pop. *Top 10 Needs*	Aggregate *Top 10 Needs*
1. Housing & Shelter	Substance Abuse	Sustance Abuse
2. Substance Abuse	Crime	Housing & Shelter
3. Crime	Housing & Shelter	Crime
4. Abuse/Neglect	AIDS	AIDS
5. AIDS	Teen Pregnancy	Abuse/Neglect
6. Jobs/Job Training	Health & Dental	Teen Pregnancy
7. Teen Pregnancy	Abuse/Neglect	Jobs/Job Training
8. Child Care	Education	Health & Dental
9. Transportation	Economic Development	Child Care
10. Financial Assistance	Jobs/Job Training	Education

Source: United Way documents.

to one or more agencies. This option indicates which member agencies the donor does *not* want his/her gift to include.

These four options are printed on a separate Donor Choice brochure and pledge card. LEs are trained to distribute Donor Choice materials only upon request. If in the course of an employee presentation, an individual specifically asks about designating his/her donation, the LE would then provide the Donor Choice materials.

Designated contributions are counted as follows: (1) designations to nonmember agencies are taken off the top and checks are sent to those agencies; (2) designations to member agencies are counted using a method called "first dollars in." This means that if the amount designated to a particular agency *exceeds* the allocation it receives through the Citizen Review Process, then the agency would receive the designated amount over and above its regular allocation. If, however, the designated amount is less than the regular allocation, the designated dollars would count as the "first dollars in" and would not change the agency's final allocation. The following is a hypothetical example to help illustrate this point:

Agency *X* receives $10,000 through the Citizen Review Process.

Agency *X* receives $1,000 through the Donor Choice program.

Since its designated (Donor Choice) dollars are less than its regularly allocated dollars, the $1,000 counts as the "first dollars in" and the agency receives a final allocation of $10,000. If Agency *X*'s Donor Choice dollars equaled $12,000, the agency would receive a total of $12,000 since its designated dollars exceeded its regular allocation.

Competitive Environment

The number of charitable organizations in the Southern Connecticut area has grown considerably over the past twenty years. This is due, in part, to growing human service needs. The competition for charitable dollars has also intensified. The United Way has a near monopoly in workplace solicitation at most of the largest employers in the area in that it is the only charitable organization allowed to

FOCUS

ON SOUTH CENTRAL CONNECTICUT

A STUDY OF
CRITICAL HUMAN SERVICE NEEDS
1990

Conducted by:

Middlesex United Way
United Way of Greater New Haven
United Way of Meriden & Wallingford
United Way of Milford
Valley United Way

WHY A COMMUNITY
NEEDS ASSESSMENT?

By making available an accurate and timely assessment of critical needs, United Ways will enable social service agencies, local government, and employers to:

- understand emerging community needs

- plan effectively to meet those needs

- understand and work to solve the problems that affect all communities in the region.

The data will also help United Ways in south central Connecticut to take an active role in solving community problems through the allocation of funds, coordination of services, and provision of grants to innovative programs that address current problems.

THE UNITED WAY MISSION:

TO INCREASE THE ORGANIZED CAPACITY OF PEOPLE TO CARE FOR ONE ANOTHER

United Way

United Ways are making public the results of the Community Needs Assessment to raise awareness of community trends, emerging issues, and community problems. To obtain a copy of the report summarized in this brochure, contact your local United Way.

Middlesex United Way	346-8695
United Way of Greater New Haven	772-2010
United Way of Meriden & Wallingford	235-4403
United Way of Milford	874-6791
Valley United Way	735-9331

CRITICAL ISSUES IN SOUTH CENTRAL CONNECTICUT

In 1990, the United Ways in south central Connecticut conducted a comprehensive study of human service needs and a review of the services that exist to meet those needs. The following issues surfaced as the most critical needs in the region.

1. Substance Abuse
2. Housing and Shelter
3. Crime
4. AIDS
5. Child Care
6. Abuse and Neglect
7. Health and Dental Care
8. Teen Pregnancy
9. Mental Health Care
10. Education/Literacy

SUMMARY OF SERVICE AREA FINDINGS

The Community Needs Assessment is part of the United Way's ongoing commitment to solving community problems. Each United Way is a community-based organization that provides funding and works to ensure that a high quality network of human services is available to all who need help.

The most pressing issues identified in each United Way service area were as follows:

MIDDLESEX UNITED WAY

1. Housing and Shelter
2. Substance Abuse
3. Crime
4. Abuse and Neglect
5. Mental Health Care
6. Child Care
7. Environment
8. Family Issues
9. Transportation
10. AIDS

UNITED WAY OF GREATER NEW HAVEN

1. Substance Abuse
2. Housing and Shelter
3. Crime
4. AIDS
5. Abuse and Neglect
6. Teen Pregnancy
7. Jobs/Job Training
8. Health/Dental Care
9. Child Care
10. Education Transportation

UNITED WAY OF MERIDEN & WALLINGFORD

1. Housing and Shelter
2. Substance Abuse
3. Child Care
4. AIDS
5. Abuse and Neglect
6. Crime
7. Teen Pregnancy
8. Education
9. Health/Dental Care
10. Youth Services

UNITED WAY OF MILFORD

1. Housing and Shelter
2. Substance Abuse
3. Crime
4. Child Care
5. Mental Health Services
6. Health/Dental Care
7. Abuse and Neglect AIDS
9. Environment
10. Youth Services

VALLEY UNITED WAY

1. Substance Abuse
2. Housing and Shelter
3. Crime
4. Child Care
5. Abuse and Neglect
6. Youth Services
7. Crime
8. Jobs/Job Training
9. Family Issues
10. Systemwide Issues

HOW THE STUDY WAS DONE

The Needs Assessment examined three major sources of data to obtain the results.

COMMUNITY SURVEYS polled community leaders in government and business, service providers, and local and state legislators. In an effort to survey people of a wide range of ages and socio-economic backgrounds, surveys were also distributed to a representative cross-section of the population.

SERVICE PROVIDER DATA was examined to assess demand for various services. Data was gathered from INFOLINE, a statewide information and referral service funded by Connecticut United Ways and the State of Connecticut.

DEMOGRAPHIC AND SOCIOECONOMIC DATA was analyzed for each United Way service area to track broader trends.

The results detailed in this report were achieved through the analysis of over 2,400 surveys which where correlated with provider and demographic data.

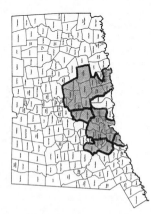

283

conduct employee solicitations at these work sites. This monopoly position is being threatened by other charitable organizations that feel that the monopoly puts them at an unfair disadvantage.

One of the United Way's fastest growing competitors is the Combined Health Appeal (CHA). CHA is an umbrella organization of eighteen health-oriented agencies. Many contributors are attracted to CHA because of its broad appeal. Not only are its agencies widely known to the public, but most people know someone who has suffered from one of the afflictions addressed by CHA agencies.

A new executive director had recently been named to the local CHA chapter. Ed Rogers was a highly motivated individual who believed strongly in the work of CHA and its agencies. He had already begun an aggressive effort to gain access to workplace solicitation. He had spoken with several of the largest employers in the area, and was told that they supported the United Way. Rogers responded that he also believed in the United Way, and simply wanted to give employees the opportunity to make an additional contribution to CHA if they so desired. He would be satisfied to use only ten minutes of United Way's half-hour presentation to make his pitch. At the conclusion of the presentation employees would receive both United Way and CHA materials, and would have the choice of giving to either or both organizations.

A week after Rogers began the effort to gain access to local companies, Doug Higginbottom received a phone call from Harold Berry, CEO of Central Bank, the largest bank in town, and one of United Way's largest contributors. The conversation proceeded as follows:

BERRY: "Listen, Doug, we've been getting hounded by this Rogers guy over at CHA. He keeps insisting that we run side-by-side workplace presentations involving both United Way and CHA."

HIGGINBOTTOM: "Harold, I know you are a strong supporter of United Way. As you know Central Bank comprises 10% of our annual fund raising proceeds. It could be a major threat to us if you allowed CHA in. The recession in this area has greatly weakened our fundraising effort over the past three years, and we just can't afford another big hit."

BERRY: "I understand that, but there are those who feel that United Way's monopoly position in the workplace is unfair, and that other worthwhile agencies should be allowed equal access."

HIGGINBOTTOM: "Well that's why we have the Donor Choice program—so that employees can designate their gifts."

BERRY: "I realize that, but this Rogers guy insists that CHA have equal time at the presentations. And frankly, I'm having a hard time arguing against him. Look, I'm not interested in allowing other agencies in, because it would just increase the administrative burden on us. I would much rather funnel all donations through you guys, rather than deal with multiple organizations. If I let CHA in, then where do I draw the line? How many organizations do I let in?"

HIGGINBOTTOM: "And that's what the United Way concept is all about—one efficient, centralized clearinghouse for health and human service donations. It's efficient for you and for the community. And don't forget Harold, that United Way performs an important accountability role in terms of ensuring that donor dollars are allocated wisely and equitably. . . ."

BERRY: ". . . Doug, I know that, and that is precisely why I've been committed to United Way for all these years. However, I've been getting pressure from a lot of my employees who want to give to CHA because their brother had cancer or because they know a co-worker who quit smoking with the help of the Lung Association. I just can't keep putting Rogers off. Doug, I need your help to come up with a plan by which I can accommodate you both. Our annual fund drive is three months away. Talk to your volunteers and staff, and come back to me with something concrete, or I'll be forced to accept Rogers on his terms."

As Higginbottom hung up, he knew that Berry was right. This was not a problem that would go away. The United Way had to take a proactive stance with respect to the threats of CHA and other agencies. The United Way could no longer take its monopoly position for granted. He decided that a brainstorming session should be scheduled, at which all interested parties could voice their opinions.

The Brainstorming Session
Meeting attendees included:

Joe Johnson	president of the board, and CEO of a large manufacturing company.
Mark Chaney	volunteer chairman of the United Way's annual fund drive, and executive vice president at Nationwide Bank.
Patricia Lawrence	executive director of Farnam Neighborhood House, a United Way member agency.
Jim Riley	executive director of the Boys & Girls Club, a United Way member agency.
Mary Ann Serino	executive director of Harrison House, a local homeless shelter, and nonmember agency.

Higginbottom began the meeting by relating his recent conversation with Harold Berry. Since that conversation, he had received similar calls from other CEOs who had been long-time supporters of the United Way. Higginbottom further explained that United Way was no longer fulfilling one of the primary functions it was created to perform 100 years ago—to be an umbrella fundraising organization for all local health and human service agencies. It was becoming increasingly difficult for United Way to justify its monopoly position when it funded fewer than 30% of the agencies in the local area.

Joe Johnson jumped in at this point to echo Higginbottom's concerns. As CEO of one of United Way's most supportive companies, he expressed concern that a large number of worthwhile agencies were not currently included in the United Way umbrella. It was his feeling that most of his employees were unaware of the current Donor Choice program. Those that were aware tended to be skeptical of the "first dollars in" concept. They felt that it was a farce, and that their money was not really going to their designated agencies.

At this point, Mark Chaney chimed in. He echoed Johnson's sentiments, and went one step further. He believed the existing Donor Choice program should be expanded. The "first dollars in" concept should be eliminated. All designations should be taken off the top, and the remaining funds should be subject to the Citizen Review Process. In addition, Donor Choice should be actively marketed and used as a marketing tool to gain access to businesses that did not support United Way.

Chaney believed that active marketing of Donor Choice would increase the total pool of contributions by offering donors a wider range of giving options. United Way would become more donor-driven and responsive to its customers. It would also allow United Way to be more inclusive and to respond to a broader range of community needs. Finally it would force member agencies to take their membership less for granted, and to play a more active role in marketing themselves.

At this point, Pat Lawrence joined the discussion to voice her concerns about

Chaney's plan. Her biggest concern was that United Way's accountability role would be undermined. Agencies that were inefficient, ineffective, or had exceedingly high administrative costs may not be screened out. Funds would be allocated according to the whims of donors, rather than according to the most pressing needs in the community. Issues that received the most media attention would receive the most dollars. Programs of a more preventive nature may not be funded because they were less "sexy." Such programs may be vital long-term approaches to addressing social problems, but may not capture the attention of donors.

Furthermore, Donor Choice could result in larger agencies receiving an unfair advantage. Agencies with the largest marketing budgets would prevail by providing the most media coverage. Finally, the effectiveness of agency programs would be threatened by dividing the pool of available funds into even smaller pieces. Member agencies that counted on United Way as a source of long-term, stable funding would suffer. Many of these agencies would be forced to adopt a short-term perspective because a large percentage of their funding was short-term and varied from year to year. This would make long-term planning and budgeting a real challenge.

Jim Riley agreed with Lawrence's apprehensions, and further argued that broadening donors' choices would not be an effective means of addressing growing community needs. If United Way wanted to enhance its efficacy as a community problem solver, it should encourage its existing member agencies to shift their programs into identified high-need areas.

Mary Anne Serino was skeptical as to whether member agencies were equipped to shift or refocus their programs to high-need areas. She felt strongly that the United Way's mission has shifted from a comprehensive approach to addressing local health and human service needs, to supporting the same small group of agencies year after year. She argued that the United Way needed to recommit itself to raising funds for all worthwhile social service agencies.

Having heard all opposing viewpoints, Higginbottom decided that the best way to address the issues would be to somehow modify the existing Donor Choice program. The challenge would be to modify it in such a way as to satisfy local companies and donors, member agencies, nonmember agencies, and United Way staff and volunteers. Once the modifications were made, it would have to be marketed effectively to all those constituent groups.

As he pondered these questions, Higginbottom knew that he would soon have to deal with the Boy Scout issue. He wondered if a revised Donor Choice program could somehow be a solution to the Boy Scout issue as well.

CASE H

The Solomon R. Guggenheim Foundation (A)

When Thomas Krens was appointed director of the Solomon R. Guggenheim Museum in 1988, four tasks demanded his immediate attention: (1) the ambitious and controversial expansion program begun in 1982 by his predecessor would not be complete until the summer of 1991; (2) the financial resources of the museum were inadequate to support the expansion (see Figure H.1); (3) the post–World War II portion of the museum's permanent collection was comparatively weak; and (4) the museum was hampered by the public's perception of it as the Guggenheim family's private museum. As Krens described it, the Guggenheim was "basically a startup venture in a saturated market."

The U.S. Museum Industry

The 1980s marked the third consecutive decade of explosive growth in the U.S. museum industry (defined to include aquaria, botanical gardens, historic sites, nature centers, and zoos, as well as history, natural history, and art museums). Figure H.2 summarizes the historical growth of the industry.

Museums are a post–World War II phenomenon. Since 1950, a total of 5,273 museums were founded—almost 65% of all existing museums. After World War II the U.S. government invested heavily in educating its citizens through the GI bill. This increased the demand for culture, and cultural institutions were founded to satisfy that demand. Soon the government began to subsidize culture, too, through the National Endowment for the Arts (NEA). Demographics played a part in continuing the expansion. The "baby boom" generation grew up even more educated than their parents, and they became heavy consumers of culture, devoting more of their disposable income to museums. Tax laws fueled the growth of museum collections, allowing donors to declare the appreciated value of a work of art rather than its cost, as a charitable contribution.

From 1979 to 1988, the total number of museums increased by 14.2%, while the number of art museums increased by 20%. Museums increased their interior space over 15%, to 221.7 million square feet (14.9% of it art museums), and their exterior space almost 4%, to 22.7 million acres. Also, during that time, 59.1% of museums reported undergoing major renovations, while the number of art museums reporting the same was only 46.8%.

Toward the end of that decade, from 1986 to 1988, museums attracted over 1.6 billion visitors, 218 million of whom attended art museums. During that time they mounted over 132,000 exhibitions, close to 39,000 of them by art museums. For the industry, the average number of exhibitions per museum increased from 4.9 in 1986 to 6.0 in 1988; during this same period, however, art museums increased their average number of exhibitions from 9.6 to 11.5.

Mark Koening, Ruth Taylor and Robert Wayne prepared this case under the director of Professors Sharon Oster and Stan Garstka of the Yale School of Organization and Management as the basis of class discussion, May 21, 1993.

Figure H.1. Solomon R. Guggenheim Foundation Statement of Revenues, Support, and Expenses Statement of Changes in Funds Balances Fiscal Years 1985–88

	1985		1986	
	Operating	Art	Operating	Art
Statement of Revenues, Support, and Expenses				
Current Funds				
Revenues and Support				
Support and Revenue:				
Exhibition Fees & Other Service Income	423,397		331,986	
Admissions	1,163,552		1,336,293	
Membership Fees	287,265		354,505	
Grants and Gifts	2,130,350	150,900	2,286,217	191,786
Investment Income	1,927,409	33,338	1,989,834	
Wet Realized Gain (Loss) on Investments		24,707		
Other	100,000	421,031		
Auxiliary activities:				
Restaurant	329,232		366,767	
Catalogues Merchandise	1,197,215		1,421,419	
Total Revenues & Support	7,558,420	629,976	8,087,021	191,786
Current Funds Expenses				
Museum Operations:				
Salaries & Benefits	2,755,093		3,056,546	
Exhibitions	725,135		1,137,504	
Maintenance and Guards	562,666		419,513	
Materials and Supplies	351,434		340,754	
Packing, Shipping, & Storage	203,450		257,062	
Insurance	174,976		179,750	
Telephone & Utilities	543,894		440,927	

Special Programs	74,000	102,800		
Rent				
Amortization of Discount			153	
Other	850,840	839,084		
Total Museum Operations	6,241,488	6,773,940	153	
Supporting Services:				
Management and General	420,215	459,388		
Fundraising	188,387	189,310		
Cost of Sales and Expenses of Auxiliary Activities:				
Restaurant	400,260	400,529		
Catalogues Merchandise	669,095	845,055		
Total Expenses	7,919,445	8,668,222	153	
Excess (Deficit) of Revenues and Support over Expenses	(361,025)	(581,201)	629,976	
Statement of Changes in Current Funds Balances				
Fund Balance (Deficit) Beginning of Year	(3,881,401)	(4,413,670)	0	(1,665,769)
Excess (Deficit) of Operating Revenues and Support over Expenses	(361,025)	(581,201)	629,976	
Transfer from (to) Plant Fund	(174,194)	(600,365)	197,000	
Deaccession (Accession) of Art for collection, net		(37,791)	(2,492,745)	
Currency Translation Adjustment	2,950			191,633
Transfer from (to) Endowment Fund		5,633,027		1,970,306
Fund Balance (Deficit) End of Year	(4,413,670)	0	(1,665,769)	496,170

*Fiscal Year ends December 31st.

Figure H.1. Solomon R. Guggenheim Foundation Statement of Revenues, Support, and Expenses Statement of Changes in Funds Balances Fiscal Years 1985–88 (*Continued*)

	1987		1988	
	Operating	Art	Operating	Art
Current Funds				
Revenues and Support				
Support and Revenue:				
Exhibition Fees & Other Service Income	499,196		498,431	28,131
Admissions	1,700,208		2,027,664	
Membership Fees	330,244		431,069	
Grants and Gifts	2,262,036	582,198	2,131,446	194,063
Investment Income	1,546,094	39,581	1,364,996	582,316
Wet Realized Gain (Loss) on Investments				
Other				245,000
Auxiliary activities:				
Restaurant	447,516		476,935	
Catalogues Merchandise	1,858,510		2,269,893	
Total Revenues & Support	8,643,804	621,779	9,200,434	1,049,510
Current Funds Expenses				
Museum Operations:				
Salaries & Benefits	3,240,848		3,748,116	
Exhibitions	1,696,962		1,541,162	
Maintenance and Guards	473,414		514,597	
Materials and Supplies	388,804		446,356	
Packing, Shipping, & Storage	233,594		396,613	
Insurance	136,935		95,275	
Telephone & Utilities	475,089		504,354	
Special Programs	131,400		130,900	

Rent				
Amortization of Discount				
Other	868,719	18,814	1,163,209	381,396
Total Museum Operations	7,645,765	18,814	8,540,582	381,396
Supporting Services:				
Management and General	538,885		603,536	21,840
Fundraising	174,638		241,066	
Cost of Sales and Expenses of Auxiliary Activities:				
Restaurant	457,456		498,259	
Catalogues Merchandise	1,058,185		1,299,663	
Total Expenses	9,874,929	18,814	11,183,106	403,236
Excess (Deficit) of Revenues and Support over Expenses	(1,231,125)	602,965	(1,982,672)	646,274
Statement of Changes in Current Funds Balances				
Fund Balance (Deficit) Beginning of Year	0	496,170	0	1,156,802
Excess (Deficit) of Operating Revenues and Support over Expenses	(1,231,125)	602,965	(1,982,672)	646,274
Transfer from (to) Plant Fund	(2,434,049)	57,667	(2,329,153)	5,034,197
Deaccession (Accession) of Art for collection, net	(49,166)			
Currency Translation Adjustment	3,714,340		44,010	
Transfer from (to) Endowment Fund			4,267,815	
Fund Balance (Deficit) End of Year	0	1,156,802	0	6,837,273

(continued)

291

Figure H.1. Solomon R. Guggenheim Foundation Statement of Revenues, Support, and Expenses Statement of Changes in Funds Balances Fiscal Years 1985–88 (*Continued*)

Balance Sheet	1985	1986	1987	1988
Assets				
Current Funds				
Cash	876,997	330,726	845,701	6,980,721
Investments (at cost)	243,845	194,086	200,000	199,812
Receivables:				
Dividends and Interest	357,478	375,842	250,980	249,282
Grants, donations and bequests	690,375	655,668	853,750	354,886
Other	1,385,146	714,720	885,233	1,942,407
Art Collection	1	1	1	1
Inventories	833,938	1,224,591	1,387,972	1,144,598
Prepaid Expenses	343,638	178,422	399,740	1,036,961
Deferred Costs				
Total Current Funds	4,731,418	3,674,056	4,823,377	11,908,668
Endowment Fund				
Cash				
Investments (at cost)	22,814,296	23,322,066	25,906,912	24,954,432
Other Assets	275,000	917,932	187,500	187,500
Total Endowment Fund	23,089,296	24,239,998	26,094,412	25,141,932

Plant Fund				
Cash			24,072	8,581
Investments (at cost)				
Property, equipment, & leasehold improvements, net				
Solomon R. Guggenheim Museum	4,990,116	4,781,170	4,710,326	11,027,426
Palazzo Venier dei Leoni	1,077,952	1,210,821	1,349,996	1,418,698
Deferred Expenses	807,524	1,826,881	4,464,980	
Prepaid Expenses				
Loan Issuance Costs				
Receivables				
Total Plant Fund	6,875,592	7,818,872	10,549,374	12,454,705
Campaign Fund				
Cash	913,416	172,396	35,820	4,565,065
Investments (at cost)		718,933		
Grants and Donations receivable	1,373,490	2,104,119	2,396,119	2,194,619
Other Assets	67,187	99,629	600	600
Total Campaign Fund	2,354,093	3,095,077	2,432,539	6,760,284
TOTAL ASSETS	37,050,399	38,828,003	43,899,702	56,265,589

(continued)

293

Figure H.1. Solomon R. Guggenheim Foundation Statement of Revenues, Support, and Expenses Statement of Changes in Funds Balances Fiscal Years 1985–88 (*Continued*)

Balance Sheet	1985	1986	1987	1988
Liabilities and Fund Balances				
Current Funds				
Accrued Expenses and Other Liab.	591,911	935,133	1,397,107	2,676,151
Due to (from) other funds, net	6,818,676	1,378,803	1,207,618	263,768
Demand Loans Payable	2,732,000	232,000	232,000	1,132,000
Note Payable				
Deferred Income:				
Grants, donations and bequests	665,270	631,950	829,850	999,476
Exhibition fees	3,000			
Fund Balance	(6,079,439)	496,170	1,156,802	6,837,273
Total Current Funds	4,731,418	3,674,056	4,823,377	11,908,668
Endowment Fund				
Accrued Expenses and Other Liab.				
Deferred Income	275,000	275,000	395,903	473,243
Due to (from) other funds, net			(886,164)	640,597
Fund Balance	30,034,578	25,715,829	26,584,673	24,028,092
Total Endowment Fund	30,309,578	25,990,829	26,094,412	25,141,932

Plant Fund				
Accrued Expenses and Other Liab.				
Due to (from) other funds, net	103,578			
Deferred Income				
Mortgage Loan Payable				
Loan Payable				
Fund Balance	6,772,014	7,818,872	10,549,374	12,454,705
Total Plant Fund	6,875,592	7,818,872	10,549,374	12,454,705
Campaign Fund				
Accrued Expenses and Other Liab.	197,682	356,838	81,459	14,424
Due to (from) other funds, net	298,028	372,028	(321,454)	(904,365)
Deferred Income	1,373,490	2,079,119	2,396,119	2,224,619
Fund Balance	484,893	287,092	276,415	5,425,606
Total Campaign Fund	2,354,093	3,095,077	2,432,539	6,760,284
TOTAL LIABILITIES AND FUND BALANCES	44,270,681	40,578,834	43,899,702	56,265,589

Source: Annual Report, 1989.

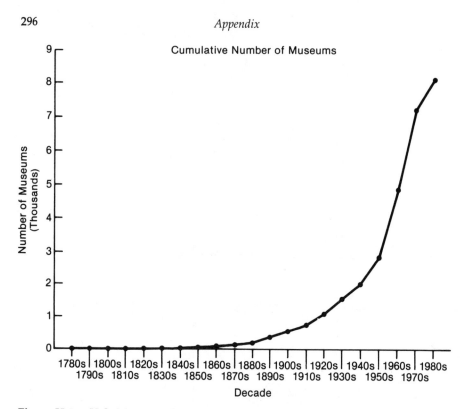

Figure H.2. U.S. Museum Growth by Decade. *Source:* American Association of Museums, internal study.

In 1988, the industry took in a total of $4.395 billion in operating revenue and support against a total of $4.017 billion in operating expenses. Art museums accounted for about 25% of both totals, at $1.184 billion in revenue and support and $1.113 billion in expenses, even though they totalled only 15% of all museums. Table H.1 outlines the sources of revenue and support for the art museum sector of the industry in 1988. Museums had 148,223 paid employees, of which 91,954 worked full-time. In addition, the industry benefitted from another 376,374 volunteers. Art museums employed 22.1% of all paid full-time museum employees, more than any other type.

Along with this tremendous growth, there have been some fundamental changes in the industry in recent years. The Tax Reform Act of 1986 stipulated that donated artwork could no longer be deducted at its appreciated value, except under very specific circumstances. A patron could make a larger donation by selling the piece, paying the capital gains, and giving the organization the remaining cash. However, museums were usually priced out of the market, and these works were usually sold to other private collectors, many of them from outside the United States. Thus, the supply of donated museum-quality art decreased.

Other factors affected the revenue and support side of the industry. The NEA had less and less money to distribute during the Reagan years. After the stock market crash of October 1987, the baby boomers reevaluated their spending patterns. Many of them chose not to renew their museum memberships (or not to donate as much money as in the previous year).

Table H.1. Art Museum Industry
Revenue and Support Mix (1988)

Government Sources	25.8%
Private Sources	26.3%
Investment Income	19.6%
Earned Income	28.3%
Total	100.0%

Source: American Association of Museums.

On the expense side, the increase in the number of exhibits (especially those that required artwork to be loaned out or borrowed) caused an increase in security and insurance costs. Artwork purchased by museums was much more expensive to acquire due to the booming art market, which also contributed to higher insurance premiums. As collecting became more difficult and collections aged, museums changed their focus from collecting to conserving, which had become a technically advanced, and therefore expensive, science. Like most complex organizations driven by information, the museum evolved into an institution driven by technology. The capital outlays associated with adopting computer equipment rose rapidly. The biggest operating expense for museums, however, was labor, and the best curators, directors, and other key personnel commanded higher and higher salaries.

The Guggenheim Foundation and Museum

In the late 1920s, Solomon R. Guggenheim, heir to a vast mining fortune, traveled to Europe, where he had his portrait painted by Baroness Hilla Rebay von Ehrenwiesen. Their friendship blossomed, and she persuaded him to acquire modern paintings for his art collection. Over the next few years, with her guidance, he purchased approximately 200 paintings and sketches by Vasily Kandinsky, forming the nucleus of his collection of nonobjective paintings.

The Solomon R. Guggenheim Foundation was chartered in New York in 1937 as a nonprofit "educational corporation for the promotion and encouragement of art and education in art and enlightenment of the public, especially in the field of art." Two years later, a facility to be owned, operated, and maintained by the foundation was established to contain Guggenheim's private art collection. Hilla Rebay was named the director and, in an automobile showroom on East 54th Street, the Museum of Non-Objective Painting held its grand opening.

In 1943, Guggenheim commissioned architect Frank Lloyd Wright to design an original building to house a contemporary art museum. Before he died in 1949, Guggenheim approved the plans and purchased a plot of land on Fifth Avenue. It was another ten years, however, before the building opened, shortly after Wright's death. Wright's design had two purposes: to break up the Upper East Side's endless skyline of high-rise apartment buildings, and to present modern art in a hostile, nonconventional setting. Many despised it.

Meanwhile, Hilla Rebay was succeeded by James Johnson Sweeney in 1952, and the museum was renamed as a memorial to its founder, signifying a shift in acquisition and exhibition policies to reflect a broader view of modern and contemporary art. In 1961, Thomas Messer became director of the museum, and he continued to expand the collection. During his tenure, two significant collections were donated to the museum: Justin K. Thannhauser donated a portion of his collection of nine-teenth and twentieth century art, Impressionist and Post-Impressionist works; and Solomon's niece, Peggy Guggenheim, donated her collection of twentieth-century surrealist and abstract art, along with her Palazzo in Venice, Italy. Together with other gifts, bequests, and purchases, the Foundation's collection came to represent most of the modern period's major artistic movements.

During Messer's tenure, two additions were made to the museum building. An annex of additional gallery, storage, and work space was completed by Wright's successor, William Wesley Peters, in 1964. A restaurant and bookstore were added in 1974.

In spite of these additions, the museum outgrew the Wright building by the early 1980s, haphazardly expanding its support operations throughout the city. The Foundation began to consider expansion plans to deal with its rapidly growing staff and collection. In 1982, Gwathmey Siegel and Associates were retained to develop an addition to the Frank Lloyd Wright building that would accommodate the muse-um's staff and collection without sacrificing its architectural intricacies.

The development of the plans for the annex progressed quietly until 1986, when the plans were submitted to the NYC Board of Standards and Appeals and Com-munity Board. This constituted a formal announcement that the Foundation in-tended to alter the Wright building. The proposal was seen by many as a desecra-tion of Wright's work, and it sparked a public outcry. Gwathmey Siegel's plans continued the conflict with New York, and indeed even clashed with Wright's building. Many of the arguments surrounding the opening of the building in 1959 were repeated. The opposition formed a rallying cry, "don't wrong Wright!"

The Foundation's ensuing battle with the public and the zoning committee was a public relations nightmare. A constant dialogue with the media and the public resulted in many changes to the original proposal. As the conflict wore on, Wright's building approached its thirtieth birthday, at which time it would likely be placed on the historic register, making additions or modifications almost impossible.

At the end of 1987, Thomas Messer formally announced his retirement, naming Thomas Krens his successor. Krens was appointed the new director of the founda-tion and the museum in January 1988. At the end of the month, the expansion proposals were finally approved, placing Krens, and his role in the museum's imminent expansion, even more in the spotlight.

Krens' background was typical of many museum directors. After graduating in 1969 from Williams College with a degree in Political Economy, Krens went abroad, where he explored more artistic pursuits. Upon his return to the United States, he earned a masters degree in art from the State University of New York at Albany and began teaching. Shortly thereafter, he was named director of the Williams College Museum of Art.

Krens was considered a "new breed" of museum director in spite of this tradi-tional background. At forty-one, he was younger than most directors. In addition, Krens held a management degree, an entirely foreign concept in the art world. During his tenure as director of the Williams College Museum, he attended the Yale School of Organization and Management, graduating in 1984 with a Master's in Public and Private Management. While at Yale, Krens concluded that "if cultural institutions did not address the problems of how to survive, they would not sur-vive." He also became convinced of the importance of the emerging computer technology in the management of the arts, and began compiling a record of the financial history of thirty major North American art museums. This database con-firmed his belief that an industry crisis was near (see Figure H.3).

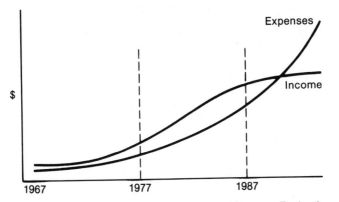

Figure H.3. Art Museum Industry: Income versus Expense Projections. *Source:* Guggenheim Museum internal documents.

Further analysis of these data led Krens to the conclusion that increasing the Guggenheim's share of visitors to New York City art museums was the key to surviving the crisis. Data on visitors to New York City museums are contained in Table H.2. He defined his principal competitors as the other three large art museums in New York—the Metropolitan Museum of Art, the Museum of Modern Art, and the Whitney Museum of American Art. Figure H.4 details the operating statements of these three museums in 1988.

Table H.2. Selected Operating Statistics, New York City Art Museums, 1985–1988

	FY 1985	FY 1986	FY 1987	FY 1988
GUGGENHEIM				
Number of Visitors	444,700	442,330	539,173	587,303
Number of Members	2,480	2,242	3,036	3,882
Exhibition Space (sq. ft.)	31,679	31,679	31,679	31,679
Total Interior Space (sq. ft.)	59,244	59,244	59,244	59,244
WHITNEY				
Number of Visitors*	454,679	613,148	786,267	722,928
Number of Members	3,993	4,718	6,546	6,544
Exhibition Space (sq. ft.)*	36,100	36,100	42,100	42,100
Total Interior Space (sq. ft.)	n/a	n/a	n/a	n/a
MoMA				
Number of Visitors	1,679,263	1,386,582	1,594,070	1,345,394
Number of Members	50,500	52,200	56,693	53,920
Exhibition space (sq. ft.)	112,000	112,000	112,000	112,000
Total Interior Space (sq. ft.)	352,200	352,200	352,200	352,200
MET				
Number of Visitors	4,085,080	3,474,583	4,859,529	3,973,059
Number of Members†	33,859	32,199	32,154	30,425
Exhibition Space (sq. ft.)	n/a	n/a	n/a	n/a
Total Interior Space (sq. ft.)	n/a	n/a	n/a	n/a

Source: Case Researchers Compilations.

*Figures include branch locations; †Does not include family members; n/a Not available

Figure H.4. The Metropolitan Museum of Art Balance Sheet

| | 1988 | | | | | 1987 |
	Operating Fund	Funds for Specified Purposes	Endowment Funds	Elimination of Interfund Receivables and Payables	Total	Total
Assets:						
Cash	$810,966	$426,682			$1,237,648	$1,915,744
Investments, at market (Notes B & J)	2,194,194	28,512,874	$394,384,100		425,091,168	444,762,386
Receivables, including dividends and interest	7,152,463	12,378,266	6,581,660		26,112,389	13,697,322
Interfund receivables, net (Note C)	6,121,834	7,573,118		($13,694,952)		
Merchandise inventories (Note D)	13,110,043				13,110,043	10,848,449
Fixed assets, at cost less total accumulated depreciation 1988, $4,147,750; 1987, $3,671,131 (Note E)	8,140,114	440,370			8,580,484	8,548,091
Deferred charges, prepaid expenses and other assets (Note L)	3,542,397	17,562	1,340,954		4,900,913	4,510,822
Total assets	$41,072,011	$49,348,872	$402,306,714	($13,694,952)	$479,032,645	$484,282,814

Liabilities and Fund Balances:						
Accounts payable	$9,158,199	$6,207,086	$8,561,356		$23,926,641	$16,527,236
Notes payable (Note J)	10,400,000				10,400,000	8,000,000
Accrued expenses, primarily payroll, annual leave and pension (Note L)	9,636,881				9,636,881	6,003,065
Interfund payables, net (Note C)			13,694,952	($13,694,952)		
Deferred income, principally memberships and grants	8,716,301				8,716,301	7,533,288
Loan payable (Note F)			48,260,000		48,260,000	44,990,000
Total liabilities	37,911,381	6,207,086	70,516,308	(13,694,952)	$100,939,823	83,053,589
Fund balances (Notes G & H)	3,160,630	43,141,786	331,790,406		378,092,822	401,229,225
Total liabilities and fund balances	$41,072,011	$49,348,872	$402,306,714	($13,694,952)	$479,032,645	$484,282,814

The accompanying notes are an integral part of the financial statements.

June 30, 1988, with comparative totals as of June 30, 1987

Figure H.4. Statements of Changes in Fund Balances: Metropolitan Museum

	1988			1987		
	Operating Fund	Funds for Specified Purposes	Endowment Funds	Operating Fund	Funds for Specified Purposes	Endowment Funds
Balances (deficit), beginning of year	$2,116,194	$45,276,269	$353,836,762	($1,932,715)	$41,635,125	$321,974,899
Additions:						
Return from restricted endowment funds (Note 1)		4,597,318			4,350,385	
Investment income		2,524,188			2,649,166	
Increase (decrease) in net investment appreciation		(258,015)	(22,010,679)		(345,153)	33,301,853
Gifts, bequests, and grants (Note H)		23,749,301	11,971,801		13,064,146	14,027,324
Proceeds from sales of art (Note G)		1,757,304			223,460	
Return from invested loan proceeds (Note F)		1,220,406			2,793,511	
Excess of revenue and support over expenses	10,239,993			4,048,909		
	10,239,993	33,590,502	(10,038,878)	4,048,909	22,735,515	47,329,177

Deductions:

Acquisitions of art (Note O)		15,845,522			7,000,695	
Construction, renovation, and other capital expenditures (Note P)		30,504,681			21,956,495	
Fellowships, reference books, expenditures, and other		1,605,021			1,473,383	
Interests and other loan related expenses (Note F)		3,150,296			4,131,112	
Premium and other related costs of loan refinancing (Note F)		5,822,500				
		56,928,020			34,561,685	
Interfund transfers (Note K)	(9,195,557)	21,203,035	(12,007,478)		15,467,314	(15,467,314)
Balances, end of year (Notes G & H)	$3,160,630	$43,141,786	$331,790,406	$ 2,116,194	$45,276,269	$353,836,762

The accompanying notes are an integral part of the financial statements.

For the years ended June 30, 1988 and 1987

Figure H.4. MoMA Statements of Activity of the Operating Fund

	1988	1987
Revenue and support:		
Admissions	$3,500,900	$4,682,500
Membership	4,314,900	4,349,400
Income allocated from Endowment and		
Restricted Funds (Note 4)	4,596,100	3,786,300
Annual Fund contributions	3,250,500	2,669,400
Program grants and subsidies from Restricted		
Funds (Note 1)	1,732,000	1,527,000
Other grants and subsidies	1,730,000	2,077,500
Government support	1,139,400	966,400
Exhibition fees	721,500	868,200
Other	1,493,200	1,568,600
Revenue of auxiliary activities	13,000,800	12,614,700
Total revenue and support	35,479,300	35,110,000
Expenses:		
Curatorial and related support services	5,750,700	5,387,400
Exhibitions	2,547,300	3,396,900
Membership and development	2,293,800	2,117,900
Public information	434,100	351,800
Administration	2,637,200	2,732,900
Facilities, security, and other operating costs	6,971,600	6,828,900
Programs	1,732,000	1,527,000
Other	1,295,400	1,365,800
Cost of sales and other expenses of auxiliary		
activities	12,489,200	12,020,000
Total expenses	36,151,300	35,728,600
Excess of expenses over revenue and support	($672,000)	($618,600)

The accompanying notes are an integral part of these financial statements.

For the years ended June 30, 1988 and 1987

Figure H.4. Whitney Museum of American Art Balance Sheet

	1988				1987
	General Fund	Land. Building and Equipment Fund	Endowment Fund	Total All Funds	Total all Funds (Note 10)
Assets					
Current Assets:					
Cash and temporary cash investments	$ 1,055,909	$ —	$ —	$ 1,055,909	$ 1,284,286
Accounts receivable	595,302			595,302	385,896
Pledges and grants receivable	1,230,287	389,499	785,563	2,405,349	1,359,693
Accrued interest and dividends receivable	309,119	47,701		356,820	271,092
Museum store and publications inventory (including work-in-process of $552,745), at lower of cost or market	977,558	—	—	977,558	1,038,297
Prepaid expenses	707,431	—	—	707,431	482,618
Interfund advances (Note 4)	222,213	(222,213)	—	—	—
Total current assets	5,097,819	214,987	785,563	6,098,369	4,821,882
Other Assets:					
Pledges and grants receivable—noncurrent	897,750	3,233,133	610,000	4,740,883	4,888,741
Investments in marketable securities, at quoted market (Note 3)	14,686,205	1,502,725	4,106,741	20,295,671	21,254,756
Land, building and equipment at cost net of accumulated depreciation of $3,196,760 (Note 6)	—	5,450,155	—	5,450,155	5,665,536
Deferred expansion costs (Note 4)	—	2,579,158	—	2,579,158	2,295,961
Net investment in real estate held for expansion	—	2,197,731	—	2,197,731	2,276,495
Art collection (Note 1)	—	—	—	—	—
Total other assets	15,583,955	14,962,902	4,716,741	35,263,598	36,381,489
Total assets	$20,681,774	$15,177,889	$5,502,304	$41,361,967	$41,203,371

(continued)

Figure H.4. Whitney Museum of American Art Balance Sheet (Continued)

	1988				1987
	General Fund	Land. Building and Equipment Fund	Endowment Fund	Total All Funds	Total all Funds (Note 10)
Liabilities and Fund Balances					
Current Liabilities					
Accounts payable and accrued expenses	$ 2,086,789	$ 46,747	$ —	$ 2,133,536	$ 2,087,140
Deferred traveling exhibition and other fees	584,701	—	—	584,701	321,747
Current portion of deferred restricted support (Note 5)	1,353,138	289,499	580,563	2,223,200	1,725,726
Total current liabilities	4,024,628	336,246	580,563	4,941,437	4,134,613
Deferred Restricted Support less current portion (Note 5)	1,109,295	4,840,492	610,000	6,559,787	6,960,454
	5,133,923	5,176,738	1,190,563	11,501,224	11,095,067
Fund Balances (Note 11)					
Unrestricted, designated by the trustees for investment (Note 1)	15,547,851	—	—	15,547,851	17,115,822
Land, building and equipment	—	10,001,151	—	10,001,151	10,136,361
Endowment	—	—	4,311,741	4,311,741	2,856,121
Total fund balances	15,547,851	10,001,151	4,311,741	29,860,743	30,108,304
Total liabilities and fund balances	$20,681,774	$15,177,889	$5,502,304	$41,361,967	$41,203,371

Figure H.4. (*Continued*)

	General Fund			Land, Building and Equipment Fund	Endowment Fund	Total All Funds	Total All Funds (Note 10)
	Operations	Investment (Note 1)	Total				
Expenses:							
Program services—							
Collections and exhibitions	2,561,171	—	2,561,171	151,727	—	2,712,898	2,820,880
Building operations and security	1,881,681	—	1,881,681	80,846	—	1,962,527	2,119,931
Branch programs	1,633,073	—	1,633,073	—	—	1,633,073	1,106,522
Public education program	308,087	—	308,087	4,331	—	312,418	255,500
Film and video program	277,362	—	277,362	6,609	—	283,971	256,849
Independent study program	301,024	—	301,024	9,498	—	310,522	293,833
Publications and sales desk	361,061	—	361,061	17,209	—	378,270	302,581
Library services	181,920	—	181,920	4,904	—	186,824	170,478
Net purchases of art for collection (Note 1)	751,100	—	751,100	—	—	751,100	1,554,886
Total program services	8,256,479	—	8,256,479	275,124	—	8,531,603	8,881,460
Supporting services—							
Management and general	$1,368,553	$ —	$ 1,368,553	$ 140,640	$ —	$ 1,509,193	$ 1,774,878
Fund raising	689,893	—	689,893	57,942	—	747,835	719,095
Total supporting services	2,058,446	—	2,058,446	198,382	—	2,257,028	2,493,973
Loss from real estate held for expansion (net of operating expenses of $549,954)	—	—	—	275,601	—	275,601	44,050
Total expenses (Note 6)	10,314,925	—	10,314,925	749,307	—	11,064,232	11,419,483

(*continued*)

Figure H.4. Whitney Museum of American Art Balance Sheet (*Continued*)

	1988						1987
	General Fund			Land, Building and Equipment Fund	Endowment Fund	Total All Funds	Total All Funds (Note 10)
	Operations	Investment (Note 1)	Total				
Excess (deficiency) of support and revenue over expenses before capital additions	71,213	(1,177,602)	(1,106,389)	(696,901)	—	(1,803,290)	940,078
Capital Additions:							
Contributions	—	—	—	100,109	1,498,086	1,598,195	1,753,303
Net gain (loss) from securities sales and changes in market prices of endowment investments	—	—	—	—	(42,466)	(42,466)	(12,092)
Total capital additions	—	—	—	100,109	1,455,620	1,555,729	1,741,211
Excess (deficiency) of support and revenue over expenses after capital additions	71,213	(1,177,602)	(1,106,389)	(596,792)	1,455,620	(247,561)	2,681,289
Fund Balances beginning of year (Note 1)	—	17,115,822	17,115,822	10,136,361	2,856,121	30,108,304	27,427,015
Investment allocation (Note 1)	89,142	(89,142)	—				
Property acquired and loss from real estate held for expansion financed with unrestricted funds	(160,355)	(301,227)	(461,582)	461,582			
Fund Balances end of year	$ —	$15,547,851	$15,547,851	$10,001,151	$4,311,741	$29,860,743	$30,108,304

The accompanying notes to financial statements are an integral part of this statement.
Source: Metropolitan Museum of Art, *Annual Report*, 1988. Whitney Museum of American Art, *Annual Report*, 1988.

In 1988, the Guggenheim had only 3,882 members, and had counted 587,303 visitors, mostly foreign. Only 31,679 square feet of the Frank Lloyd Wright building was exhibition space. Table H.2 compares the Guggenheim with its competition based on these operating statistics. No money had ever been appropriated for preventive maintenance work on the building, so the planned expansion included a great deal of renovation. While these plans were well under way, the resources had not yet all been acquired to pay for it. (The endowment totalled $24 million—the same amount as in 1959.) The construction would make it difficult to maintain, let alone increase, attendance levels.

Krens believed the Guggenheim had four assets working in its favor. Though it had its weaknesses, the permanent collection, built around the world's largest collection of Kandinskys, was still outstanding. The Frank Lloyd Wright building, which the museum called its home, was, according to Krens, "perhaps the greatest piece of sculpture in New York City." Many visitors were attracted to the museum solely to experience the architecture. In addition, the museum's location, at Fifth Avenue between 88th and 89th Street on Manhattan's Museum Mile, was ideal. Finally, unlike the other three New York museums, the Guggenheim was a truly international institution, with its Peggy Guggenheim collection housed in the Palazzo Venier dei Leoni on the Grand Canal in Venice, Italy. "I ought to be able to make Vasily Kandinsky, Frank Lloyd Wright, Fifth Avenue, and the Grand Canal work," said Krens.

The question was . . . how?

CASE I

LEEWAY, INC. (A)

As Catherine Kennedy awoke on the morning of June 30, 1988, she tried to concentrate on the task immediately before her: to get through the Connecticut state and federal examinations she was scheduled to take that day in order to become a licensed nursing home administrator. No matter how hard she tried, however, she could not fight back the feeling of depression that seized her. When she had registered for the exams six months ago, her plan to establish LEEWAY, Inc., an innovative and desperately needed long-term care facility for AIDS patients, had seemed certain to succeed. As she had served the required internship at area nursing homes, Catherine had become increasingly aware that the costs of her facility would be far higher than she had originally anticipated. Now, it appeared that the Medicaid reimbursements from the state of Connecticut, which were the only form of payment available to the indigent, intravenous (IV) drug-using population she had intended to serve, would cover less than one half of LEEWAY's operating expenses.

Background

Catherine Kennedy moved to New Haven with her husband and three children from their native England in 1983. Soon after arriving in New Haven, she co-founded the More House Soup Kitchen, which provided 160–240 meals weekly during the academic year. As a result of her work at the soup kitchen, she was invited to become a board member of the Connecticut Food Bank. Although Catherine had taught economics for nine years in England, she entered Yale's School of Management in the fall of 1984 in order to learn to combine her theoretical knowledge of economics with skills gained as a volunteer to move into a new, more practical, career (see Figure I.1 for Catherine's resume).

When Catherine graduated in June 1986, she accepted a position with a major insurance company in Hartford as a consultant in the employee benefits division. Her job would be to monitor and analyze public policy relating to health insurance and pension benefits. Within her first few months, Catherine found herself frustrated in her work. At Yale, she had been made to feel that she could "make a difference." Now, however, she felt that she could not accomplish anything within the insurance company's rigidly hierarchical structure. Instead of being an agent of change, she was working to provide an intellectual underpinning for the status quo in a health care system she increasingly believed to be deeply inequitable.

As a mother of three, Catherine found it difficult to work the professional hours

Research Associate Ellen West prepared this case under the supervision of Professor J. Gregory Dees as the basis for class discussion rather than to illsutrate either effective or ineffective handling of an administrative situation.

CATHERINE KENNEDY

EDUCATION

Yale School of Organization and Management, New Haven,
Connecticut
Master of Public and Private Management (MPPM), 1986

University of East Anglia, Norwich, England
MA in Economic and Social History, 1975
BA (Hons) in Economics, 1974

University of Hull, England
Postgraduate Certificate in Education, 1978

Newcastle-upon-Tyne Polytechnic, England
Associate of the Chartered Insurance Institute, 1968

EXPERIENCE

1987-
present
Leeway, Inc. (Intermediate care/skilled nursing facility for
people with AIDS/ARC)
Founder and Executive Director

1986-1987
Major Insurance Company, Hartford, Connecticut
Consultant, Employee Benefits Division
Monitored and analyzed public policy relating to health
insurance and pensions--particular areas of expertise are
Long Term Care, Retiree Health Benefits, AIDS and Health
Maintenance Organizations

1986
Holt, Wexler and Crawford, New Haven, Connecticut and
Department of Correction
Produced feasibility study on halfway house for discharged
prisoners

1985-1986
GTE Service Corporation, Stamford, Connecticut
Economic Analyst, Department of Revenue Plans and Strategy

1981-1983
University of East Anglia, Norwich, England
Assistant Professor, School of Economic and Social Studies

1974-1978
1980-1983
Norwich City College, Norwich, England
Assistant Professor, Department of Business and Management
Studies
Taught Economics and Statistics to Business and Management
students

1969-1970
Pergamon Press Ltd., Oxford, England
Insurance Manager, Finance Division

1963-1968
Royal Insurance Group Ltd., Newcastle-upon-Tyne and Oxford,
England
Insurance Clerk, Underwriting and Claims

Figure I.1.   Catherine Kennedy; resume.

PERSONAL

1984–present	Board Member, Connecticut Food Bank Board President Chair, Personnel Committee Member, Executive Committee Member, Finance Committee
1979–1983	Board Member, St. John's First School and St. Thomas More Middle School, Norwich, England Secretary to the Board
1983–present	Co-founder, More House Soup Kitchen, New Haven
1981–1983	Marriage Guidance Counselor, Catholic Marriage Advisory Council, England

Figure I.1. *(Continued)*

required of her and have time for voluntary work, which had always been an important part of her life. One day in April 1987, she confided in the assistant chaplain at her church that she was concerned about her lack of participation in volunteer activities. The chaplain suggested that she make use of her previous experience in counseling by offering counseling to people with AIDS. Catherine's initial reaction to his suggestion was that without any understanding of the disease or the communities it affected, she lacked the empathy necessary to be an effective counselor. She did agree, however, to attend a meeting of AIDS Project New Haven later that week in order to learn more.

The Hospice Concept

AIDS Project New Haven, an AIDS support and service organization, was founded in 1983 by Alvin Novick, a biology professor at Yale. At the meeting that Saturday, Catherine was surprised to hear that the only form of in-patient care available to people with AIDS in New Haven was acute care provided in a hospital setting. Many AIDS patients could not be discharged from the hospital after an acute episode because there was nowhere for them to go. She came home that evening and mentioned to her husband that there was a tremendous need for a hospice in New Haven for people with AIDS, but that it would be an incredibly difficult thing to accomplish.

By the following Saturday, Catherine began to see the development of an AIDS hospice as a project she should undertake. After all, she had been talking about the project all week, saying that "someone" should do it. Catherine decided she could investigate the feasibility of starting an AIDS hospice while continuing to work full time.

> I had management skills and training, the foundations of an excellent network in New Haven and Connecticut—and this was the chance to do something real. I had watched the start-up of the Connecticut Food Bank and had seen how one person could make a difference and learn to master a difficult job as he went along.

Catherine took the same approach she had used the previous summer when she had conducted a feasibility study of halfway houses for the Connecticut Department of Corrections. She began by identifying and establishing relationships with people in the New Haven area who were committed to the AIDS crisis. She talked with those who provided medical care to AIDS patients. Al Novick introduced her to G. Harold Welch, the president of Yale-New Haven Medical Center.

Yale-New Haven Hospital was interested in helping Catherine develop an alternative care facility because it was losing money on almost every AIDS patient admitted. The majority of people with AIDS in New Haven were poor, IV drug users whose health care was funded through the Connecticut Department of Income Maintenance (DIM), the funding agency for the state's Medicaid and welfare programs. The DIM payment system was complex, but as Catherine understood it, the hospital was, in effect, reimbursed a per diem amount of approximately $550 for state-supported patients based on an average length of stay. The hospital could charge approximately $900 per day to private pay patients.

Catherine worked closely with AIDS service organizations and the New Haven Mayor's Task Force on AIDS, which was chaired by Al Novick. Catherine also knew that it would be important to cultivate local politicians to develop community support for her efforts. She had worked with state representative Bill Dyson, a leader of New Haven's black community, on the Connecticut Food Bank. Bill introduced her to the other New Haven state-level politicians.

The First Partnership

Throughout this period Catherine had been discussing her ideas with Elizabeth Pelz, the AIDS coordinator in the employee benefits division at the insurance company where Catherine worked. Elizabeth had a masters degree in public health from Yale and had experience in AIDS prevention education. As they talked, the prospect of a partnership arose. Initially, the idea was for them to form a consulting firm specializing in AIDS education. However, Catherine had some concerns about whether consulting alone would be a viable business. She also felt that they could add more value by creating and running a hospice. The hospice idea became the central impetus and focus of the partnership. They planned on financing their effort in part by doing consulting work. In addition to providing financial support, the consulting would also allow Catherine and Elizabeth to smooth out what they projected would be the uneven work flow involved in setting up the hospice. While Catherine balanced the demands of her job with her pursuit of the hospice project, she gained strength from her partnership with Elizabeth.

Catherine and Elizabeth discussed the project with increasing enthusiasm over the next several weeks, but several factors in Elizabeth's personal and professional life resulted in her decision not to continue the partnership. Although Catherine understood Elizabeth's reasons for ending the partnership, she was very disappointed. Not only had Catherine counted on the psychological support of a partner, she felt it would be impossible for her to follow through alone on the plan to combine a money-making consulting business with development of the AIDS hospice. She kept a path open to Elizabeth to join the venture by writing in a role for her on the management team outlined in the business plan. Privately, however, Catherine suspected that once she put her full-time efforts into the project, it would inevitably become hers alone.

Full-Time Commitment

By August 1987, Catherine was convinced that the facility was needed and that she had the support of the relevant constituencies in New Haven to make it a reality.

Implementing the project, however, and getting the necessary government approvals and financial support was not something she could do in her spare time after a sixty-hour week at the insurance company. While her husband supported her efforts, one of their three children was about to begin his senior year in high school, and they had been planning on Catherine's income to finance his college education. Catherine and her husband decided that she should take a year to see if the hospice project would fly. At the end of the year, they would evaluate the project's potential to provide sufficient income to Catherine.

After leaving the insurance company in August 1987, Catherine began to strengthen the ties she had with the various groups involved in the AIDS crisis. Already a member of the New Haven Mayor's Task Force on AIDS, she joined the Connecticut AIDS Residence Coalition, a statewide group begun in 1987 with the objective of providing residential care for people with AIDS. Members of the group provide mutual support and cooperate on applications for funds from government and foundation sources in order to avoid competing with one another.

Catherine also gave her project a name, in order to make it seem more real. She chose "LEEWAY," meaning a shelter from harsh winds, which had been the name of a battered women's shelter in England.

Developing a Model

Catherine began to look at approaches to housing for people with AIDS that had been successful in other parts of the country. The Shanti Project in San Francisco had developed a model consisting of small group homes that place four to five people within a middle class environment. Friends and family provided emotional support. Medical care, when needed, was supplied by visiting nurses. However, Catherine did not think that a middle class home environment requiring a strong support network of family and friends would work in New Haven. Many people with AIDS in New Haven were homeless before they had AIDS and for them the disease was the last straw in a long history of problems. The higher incidence of IV drug use as the risk factor for AIDS in New Haven would also require the provision of a greater level of health care than was possible in the group home setting.

Now that Catherine was moving toward a facility that would provide more comprehensive health care to people with AIDS, she turned her attention to the Connecticut Public Health Code. LEEWAY would need to conform to models of health care delivery allowed by the code. Any deviations from the models outlined by the code would need to be authorized by legislation.

Up to now, Catherine had been describing her facility as a "hospice." As she read through the code, however, she realized that there were significant barriers to entry into the hospice market in Connecticut. The first free-standing hospice in the United States had been the Connecticut Hospice in Branford. The legislation authorizing the licensing of hospices had been specifically tailored to Connecticut Hospice, down to the prescribed size of the janitor's closet.

Catherine identified two other problems with the hospice model. A basic tenet of hospice care is that the patient accept that he or she is dying by authorizing that no life-saving interventions will be made in the course of care. Catherine thought that AIDS patients, who are considerably younger than the average terminally ill patient, would be less likely to forego possible life-saving or experimental treatments. The hospice model would also pose significant financial problems. Because hospices in Connecticut were reimbursed on a per admission basis, they had an incentive to delay admission as close to the time of death as possible so that the one-time payment from the state would be sufficient to cover the costs of caring for a patient. Catherine was not comfortable with this incentive for quick patient turn-around.

Other models of in-patient health care delivery permitted by Connecticut Public Health Code were "chronic disease hospital" and "chronic and convalescent nursing home." The chronic disease hospital model initially looked very promising. This model was originally intended to address the needs of people suffering from such illnesses as tuberculosis, and its section of the Public Health Code was very short. Managers at the Connecticut DIM were very open to LEEWAY pursuing this type of license as they would also have fewer restrictions on reimbursement under this model. Unfortunately, the Connecticut Department of Health Services was very negative about the prospect of licensing the facility as a chronic disease hospital. Its official reasoning was that there were very few facilities in the state so licensed. It believed that this was an anachronistic section of the public health code. As it was hoped that eventually this section of the code would disappear, the Department of Health Services was not in favor of granting new licenses under this section of the code. In reality, the real problem seemed to be that there were insufficient statutory requirements to allow the Department to keep close control on a new, unknown entity if it were licensed as a chronic disease hospital.

As Catherine looked through other models allowed by the code, she thought that the nursing home model was best suited to the needs of New Haven's AIDS patients. Nursing homes were authorized to provide a wide range of care, serving patients who needed low levels of monitoring and help with the activities of daily living, as well as those who were extremely dependent on skilled care to manage their complex array of medical and psychosocial problems. Such a license would allow LEEWAY to provide care throughout the symptomatic stages of AIDS, through to terminal care. Statutory requirements were less strict than those for hospice care; nursing homes were reimbursed on a per diem basis, eliminating the incentive for rapid patient turnover, and each of the three state bureaucracies with jurisdication over the provision of health care in the State of Connecticut—The Commission on Hospitals and Health Care, the Department of Health Services, and the DIM—were agreed that such a plan was acceptable to them.

The Second Partnership

After Catherine began planning to structure her facility as a nursing home in the summer of 1987, she met Jim Smithson through the New Haven Mayor's Task Force on AIDS. Smithson owned a nursing home in Fair Haven, Connecticut, as well as a single room occupancy dwelling for elderly women in New Haven's Worcester Square. He planned to move the elderly women and those on the waiting list for his Fair Haven home into St. John's Nursing Home, a twenty-year-old facility that was for sale. In the fall of 1987 he proposed to Catherine that LEEWAY purchase a discrete twenty-eight-bed wing of the home.

Catherine could not believe her good fortune in having Smithson approach her with this opportunity. St. John's was ideally situated for LEEWAY, within easy reach of the major New Haven hospitals and the New Haven neighborhoods where LEEWAY's target population lived.

Smithson asked Catherine who she planned to have administrate the LEEWAY facility. Catherine had always assumed that she would do it. To do this she would first need to become a licensed nursing home administrator. When Catherine investigated licensure requirements, she discovered that it was critical that she qualify by July 1, 1988, because state law regulating nursing home administrators had recently been changed. If an applicant qualified by July 1, licensing would require the successful completion of one course in nursing home administration, 900 hours of administrative internships in nursing homes and a passing score on both state and federal examinations. If an applicant did not meet these requirements by July 1, she would need to enter a two-year program to obtain a master's degree in nursing home administration. Catherine had just enough time to enroll in the required course at the University of Connecticut and begin her internship.

Working with the Regulators

As she fulfilled her licensing requirements in the spring of 1988, Catherine worked on developing good working relationships with three state agencies whose cooperation would be critical to LEEWAY's success. At DIM she was helped by someone she had known at the insurance company. Since Catherine assumed that all of LEEWAY's patients would be on welfare, LEEWAY would have to operate within DIM's Medicaid reimbursement rate for nursing home care of $105 per day plus amortized building costs.

Harold Welch introduced her to the bureau chief of the Connecticut Department of Health Services (DHS), which was responsible for licensing facilities, promulgating public health requirements, and ensuring code compliance. Because a facility could not be licensed until it was fully staffed and ready for operation, it was important for Catherine to work with DHS staff members as she developed her operating plan to ensure that all licensing requirements would be met.

In order to avoid the appearance of discriminating against, or quarantining, people with AIDS by placing them in separate facilities, DHS advocated "mainstreaming" AIDS patients in existing nursing homes. Nursing homes were not then knowingly accepting AIDS patients, however, and even if they were, their services and programming had been designed to meet the needs of a geriatric population. The DHS therefore supported Catherine's proposal for a separate nursing home for AIDS patients, but until she developed a successful working model, the department publicly maintained its policy on "mainstreaming."

Welch also introduced Catherine to one of the commissioners of the Connecticut Commission on Hospitals and Health Care (CHHC), from which LEEWAY would need to obtain a Certificate of Need. The commissioner, who had special responsibility for consumer affairs, recognized the need for a facility such as LEEWAY. Since the CHHC also had responsibility for reviewing health care facility budgets and deciding on allowable costs for nursing homes, it quickly recognized that a subacute care facility for AIDS patients would also be cost-effective.

During this period, Catherine carefully began to assemble a board of directors to ensure representation from key groups whose support would be critical to LEEWAY's success and she continued to actively recruit for additional members in the business and minority communities (see Figure I.2 for a roster of board members as of June 30, 1988).

Problems Develop

Catherine's first internship was at The Bradley Home, a twenty-five-bed skilled nursing facility in Meriden, Connecticut, which was the facility most closely compa-

Figure I.2.   LEEWAY, Inc., Board of Directors, June 5, 1988

Anne Tyler Calabresi
–extensive experience working on programs addressing the issues of education and hunger in New Haven
William Dyson
–one of the New Haven members of the Connecticut State Legislature and a leader in New Haven's black community
Leetha Fraulino
–AIDS coordinator for Yale-New Haven Hospital
Catherine Gobes
–former AIDS coordinator for a major insurance company
Al Masciocci
–qualified actuary for a major insurance company's Health Insurance Division, working on innovative Long-Term Care insurance products
Alvin Novick
–Founder of AIDS Project New Haven, Chair of the New Haven Mayor's Task Force on AIDS and a well known expert on the AIDS problem, on both a local and national level
Douglas Rae
–Chairman of Yale's Political Science Department and leader of Yale's new program on Ethics. He serves on several socially conscious study groups and task forces

rable to LEEWAY. She used the staffing levels at the Bradley Home to determine nursing requirements for LEEWAY. Her second placement was with Arden House in Hamden, a 360-bed for-profit intermediate care/skilled nursing facility. The two nursing homes were extremely helpful and even opened their books to her.

As Catherine learned about nursing home finance, however, she began to have doubts about her intended partner, Jim Smithson. She wondered how Smithson could expect to profit from purchasing the twenty-year-old St. John's facility under Connecticut's capital cost reimbursement system. The state's philosophy was that it would only "pay" for a building once, based on a thirty-year mortgage on its original construction cost. Once the building had been "paid" for, no additional reimbursement would be paid to users of the facility for housing costs. Secondary owners of a nursing home were not reimbursed based on their purchase price for the facility, but received only the amount of the original cost of the facility not paid out to the previous owner.

By the beginning of June, Catherine had developed a business plan for LEEWAY that she felt she could use to seek funding (see Figure I.3 for excerpts from the June 5, 1988, LEEWAY business plan). She began distributing it for comments to administrators and registered nurses (RNs) at the two facilities she had interned with as well as to the AIDS Coordinator at the Yale-New Haven Hospital.

The first comments to come in from the registered nurses pointed out that while Catherine had written her plan based on staffing levels suitable in a geriatric facility, people with AIDS needed much more nursing care. The RNs were especially concerned about the increased level of responsibility involved in caring for AIDS patients who had been IV drug users. Although the RNs were content to be the only RN in the facility overnight in a standard nursing home, they all stated that they would not be willing to be the only professional accountable at any given time in a

facility for people with AIDS. To paraphrase one RN who responded to Catherine's
business plan:

> You had better always program at least three RNs on the premises because, if you have
> only two, one night someone is going to call in sick—and if I am the only RN left on
> the premises, I am going home as well. I wouldn't accept all of that responsibility.

As each business plan came back to Catherine, the comments expressed the
same concern about the levels of staffing provided for in the budget. A more
realistic plan would budget for five nurses and five nurses' assistants on duty at all
times. When Catherine revised her business plan to account for the increased level
of nursing care, she realized her costs would be far above the $105.45 pay day
maximum state reimbursement.

Figure I.3.   LEEWAY, Inc., Healthcare Facility for People with AIDS/ARC
BUSINESS PLAN (Abridged) June 5, 1988

Executive Summary

LEEWAY, Inc., is a planned 28-bed skilled nursing and intermediate care facility for
people with Acquired Immunodeficiency Syndrome (AIDS) or AIDS-Related Complex (ARC). The only AIDS/ARC inpatient care currently available in Connecticut is
acute hospital care and two beds at Connecticut Hospice. LEEWAY would be the
first long-term care unit in Connecticut for people with AIDS/ARC. LEEWAY Inc.
will be a model facility, fully documented, so that it will be reproducible as the need
arises.

By the end of the 1987, 156 cases of AIDS had been reported in New Haven out
of 601 cases in Connecticut. The Centers for Disease Control project 700 to 800 cases
in New Haven and 2,500 to 3,500 in Connecticut by 1991. Of these, between 250 to
400 patients will still be alive in New Haven and 1,000 and 2,000 will still be alive in
Connecticut. There will be, in addition to the people with AIDS, approximately an
equal number needing inpatient care due to ARC. More people are officially diagnosed with ARC than with AIDS, but a lower proportion of ARC patients need
inpatient care.

Research in Seattle and Washington suggests that about 10–15% of AIDS patients are most appropriately cared for in a nonacute institutional setting. This
would indicate that by 1991 between 50 and 120 nursing home beds will be required
in New Haven and between 200 and 750 beds in Connecticut.

As AIDS becomes less a disease afflicting white, gay men and makes its way
into other community groups—initially through those who use intravenous
drugs—the current pattern of AIDS infection in New Haven will become more
prevalent in other communities. San Francisco, Washington and other communities
have produced successful models for the treatment of gay men with AIDS/ARC,
which depend heavily on a supportive community. These models may not work as
well with an AIDS/ARC population largely made up of drug users and their families, who typically have fewer resources, less social support and lower motivation.
We have the opportunity to explore ways of cooperating with drug treatment agencies to establish replicable models for treatment of people with AIDS who have
multiple medical and social problems.

New Haven has a higher proportion of AIDS patients who are women and who
are black or hispanic than is yet experienced in most other parts of the United
States. The unique needs and experiences of these community groups need to be
addressed in order to develop effective models for their treatment.

Need for LEEWAY Health Care Facility

Present Need

Between 1981 and the end of 1987, 156 cases of AIDS were reported in New Haven.
Of these, about 60 are still living. A survey of needs conducted on behalf of the
Connecticut AIDS Residential Program in June 1987 identified 67 people with AIDS
who had been hospitalized in 18 local hospitals beyond acute care need because of
housing difficulties during the first half of 1987. A review of social service agencies
and health care clinics obtained reports of 30 people with AIDS in New Haven in

need of housing. While it is likely that some double-counting has occurred here, it is apparent that there is already a pressing need, which will become worse as people infected with the AIDS virus show symptoms of their illness.

The Connecticut Department of Income Maintenance is working on the assumption that there will be a need for 215 places in facilities providing long-term or intermittent hospital care for people with AIDS/ARC at any one time during 1988 in Connecticut. As New Haven has about one quarter of the AIDS cases in Connecticut, this suggests that 50–55 people in New Haven are currently in need of long-term care or intermittent hospital care.

Needs in New Haven by 1991

AIDS is such a new disease that all projections of its future development can only be based upon educated guesswork. These projections can, therefore, only be phrased in general terms. Epidemiologists have provided estimates of the expected number of reported AIDS cases in New Haven by 1991 that vary between 700 and 900. These figures do not take into consideration those people who are officially designated as suffering from ARC and who may be in as great a need of health care as someone who is suffering from AIDS. Reports from New York City suggest that there are three people suffering from ARC for each person diagnosed as having fully developed AIDS. On the other hand, ARC sufferers are only one-third as likely to need in patient care. It would seem realistic to assume that there will be an equal number of beds needed for ARC patients as for AIDS patients.

The impact of drugs such as AZT on the need for care by AIDS/ARC sufferers is as yet unclear. As many doctors currently treating AIDS patients believe that the use of AZT is appropriate only for those already exhibiting AIDS/ARC symptoms, it is likely that the use of drugs will prolong the period during which chronic care is necessary.

Bearing in mind these uncertainties, the lowest estimate of people needing accommodation as a result of AIDS/ARC in New Haven in 1991 is about 240, between 60 and 100 of whom would need chronic inpatient care of the type to be provided by LEEWAY.

The Department of Income Maintenance is projecting a need of 385 long-term care and intermittent hospital beds for people with AIDS/ARC in Connecticut during 1989 and 670 beds during 1990. Although LEEWAY patients will primarily come from New Haven, the absence of any other long-term facility for AIDS/ARC patients in Connecticut makes it likely that some patients will come from other areas of the state.

Levels of Care

AIDS is a relatively new disease. Treatment information and experience are limited, though growing daily. In New Haven there is a significant complicating factor of drug use. The consequence is that not much is known about the care needs of people affected by AIDS/ARC. As drugs such as AZT become more prevalent, they will affect the quality of life and therefore the level of care required for people with AIDS/ARC. One attempt to categorize the needs of people with AIDS/ARC, which may be useful, has been developed by the Seattle/King County Public Health Department in the report on "Residential Long-term Care for Persons with AIDS and Disabling ARC." In this report, the categories of care needed are outlined as follows:

- Minimum Assistance: reminders to take medicines, to go to support groups; help in setting up bathing equipment. This type of care is estimated to be needed for six months.
- Moderate Assistance: help from one person to provide standby assistance for bathing, transfer to chair, assistance with feeding. This type of care is estimated to be needed for two months.
- Total Assistance: help from one to two people with minimum amount of resident participation including feeding resident, transfer to chair, bed, bath. This type of care is estimated to be needed for one month.

There is a great deal of variation around these estimates of average times of need. LEEWAY would be appropriate for those people with AIDS/ARC who need moderate assistance or total assistance.

Responses to the AIDS Crisis

The New Haven Mayor's Task Force on AIDS has identified five levels of housing need for people with AIDS/ARC, resources currently available and responses recommended to meet currently unmet needs:

Independent Living

Many people with AIDS/ARC lose their accommodation because they cannot afford to pay the rent once they are unable to continue working, or are discriminated against by landlords. This is part of a much larger accommodation problem in New Haven, but is particularly problematic for people with AIDS/ARC. The suggested response to this problem is to provide financial subsidies to allow AIDS/ARC sufferers to remain in their own homes as long as possible. In July 1987, 18% of people in the hospital due to AIDS who required help finding accommodation before they could be discharged were capable of living alone and needed assistance to find an independent living situation.

Accommodation with Some Supervision but Minimal Care

This category of need refers to accommodation with a director or supervisor, who would notice if a resident was ill, but would not be able to offer medical care as part of the program. Existing programs include the YMCA, Christian Community Action, Columbus House and St. Joseph's Guest House. Such accommodation is clearly not designed for people who are in need of regular medical assistance. Recommendations by the New Haven Mayor's Task Force on AIDS include increasing existing programs, encouraging the development of daycare for both child and adult AIDS/ARC patients, and supporting the development of the Connecticut AIDS Residential Program (CARP) that would provide accommodation and minimal health care by contracting with visiting nurse agencies. In July 1987, 28% of people with AIDS/ARC in need of housing before they could be discharged from the hospital were in need of accommodation which would give some supervision, but minimal care.

Foster Care

Currently, foster care for children and babies with AIDS/ARC is arranged through the Department of Child and Youth Services. It is recommended that these services should be expanded and should include a program which would provide the equivalent of foster care for adults with AIDS/ARC. In July 1987, 8% of AIDS/ARC patients in need of housing were infants needing foster care.

Accommodation with Some Supervision and Contracted Health Care

People with AIDS/ARC whose disease has progressed further and who need a greater degree of medical care, although not institutional care, could benefit from the care provided by such organizations as the New Haven Visiting Nurses Association, Shared Care and Hospice Home Care. It is recommended by the New Haven Mayor's Task Force on AIDS that these services should be coordinated. In July 1987, 24% of people with AIDS/ARC in need of housing while in the hospital could have benefitted from these programs.

Institutional Care

Medical care available for AIDS/ARC patients in New Haven is, for the main part, currently provided by the Yale-New Haven Hospital and St. Raphael's Hospital. The hospital setting is only appropriate for those AIDS/ARC patients suffering an acute episode, but many patients must remain in the inappropriate and expensive hospital setting longer than their state of health requires because there is nowhere to discharge them to. During the first half of 1987, 22% of people with AIDS who could not be discharged from the hospital because they had no accommodation needed institutional care.

Hospice of Connecticut in Branford has provided two beds for AIDS patients, but has only filled one of these beds at any one time. Hospice of Connecticut is now setting up a cottage annex for terminally ill people who are homeless. This cottage will accommodate up to five patients and it is likely that some of the homeless people accommodated will have AIDS/ARC. The facility, however, is not readily accessible from downtown New Haven and most AIDS patients are not ready to concede that they are ready to die and to forego any treatment to prolong their lives, which is an integral part of hospice philosophy.

One area of care that is completely absent in Connecticut is a chronic care residential program for people with AIDS/ARC. Existing nursing homes have not yet accepted any patients with this diagnosis. LEEWAY intermediate care facility, which is being recommended in a report soon to be published by the New Haven Mayor's Task Force on AIDS, will meet this need.

A survey conducted by CARP identified 67 people with AIDS/ARC in Connecticut hospitals during the first months of 1987 who could not be discharged due to the lack of appropriate housing. The 67 individuals belonged to the following risk groups:

58% IV drug users

21% gay men

10% infants of people with AIDS

10% other

1% wife of person with AIDS

The level of care needed for these individuals was reported as:

18% independent living situations

28% some supervision/minimal assistance

8% foster home care for children with AIDS

24% supervised accommodation with contracted health care

22% institutional nursing care

In view of the high proportion of AIDS sufferers in New Haven who are IV drug users, the provision of accommodation without supervision is unlikely to be satisfactory. The preceding data lead us to believe that LEEWAY would provide appropriate care for at least 22% and possibly up to 46% of people with AIDS who could be discharged from acute care hospitals if appropriate accommodation could be found, representing approximately 6–11% of living cases of AIDS in New Haven. There would be an equivalent number of patients who were equally as ill, but officially diagnosed as suffering from ARC. These estimates are not too far removed from the Seattle estimates of 10–15% of people with AIDS/ARC needing in-patient care.

Description of the LEEWAY Facility

LEEWAY will be located in St. John's Nursing Home on Whalley Avenue, New Haven. St. John's is a 90-bed nursing home, built in 1970 and currently fully equipped, although in need of refurbishment. St. John's is designed in four discrete wings, one of which would be occupied by LEEWAY. LEEWAY would, therefore, initially have about 28 beds at its disposal.

The size of the LEEWAY facility has been chosen for the following reasons. The Connecticut Department of Income Maintenance will reimburse for services rendered in a licensed nursing home on a cost basis, up to a limit of $105.45 per day plus an amount for fair rent of the premises. There are fixed costs associated with running a facility (e.g., salaries and costs of maintenance and utilities). These fixed costs produce an approximately "break-even" point at an average daily census of 25 patients at maximum reimbursement levels. If more patients were accepted and the average daily cost fell, this would not be reflected in profit, but in a reduction of Department of Income Maintenance reimbursement.

Department of Income Maintenance reimbursement is made on the assumption of 90% average occupancy, a reasonable assumption for nursing facilities. LEEWAY has therefore agreed to use a 28-bed wing of St. John's Nursing Home, which would give sufficient flexibility to enable a 90% average occupancy at a census of 25 patients to be met.

The facility will be licensed to provide a mixture of skilled care and intermediate care, including terminal care of patients. The exact mix of care will not be clear until the facility is running. The basic services to be provided include safe and healthful living accommodations; personal assistance and care, observation and supervision, food and laundry service, and nursing, social work, appropriate recreation and volunteer services. The approach taken by LEEWAY will be palliative rather than curative, using modern pain relief and system management techniques to keep patients comfortable and alert. Support will also be offered to family members and friends through the bereavement period.

The Connecticut Public Health Code makes minimum staffing requirements for skilled nursing and intermediate care facilities. It is generally recognized that these minimum requirements are not adequate for good patient care. Staffing above minimum levels is of particular importance in the LEEWAY facility because of the many medical and social problems many LEEWAY residents are likely to have. In order to offer a high quality of patient care, the following staff will be employed:

Executive Director (C. Kennedy)

- To be in charge of the day-to-day operation of the facility in accordance with current applicable federal, state, and local standards, guidelines and regulations and as directed by the governing board.
- To assure that the highest degree of quality patient care is maintained at all times, in conjunction with the Commissioners for Hospitals and Health and the Department of Income Maintenance.
- To raise funds to meet the shortfall between third-party payments and the costs of running the facility.
- The executive director of LEEWAY will also serve as administrator of St. John's Nursing Home and her salary will be shared by the two institutions.

Director of Education and Public Relations (E. G. Pelz)

To set up AIDS education programs for staff, volunteers, and the general public. The purpose of these programs would be:

- To provide positive public relations for the facility.
- To improve public awareness of AIDS.
- To train staff, in cooperation with the director of nurses, in infection control and psychosocial aspects of dealing with AIDS patients.
- To recruit and train volunteers to provide recreation and psychosocial support for residents.

Director of Nurses

- To plan, organize, develop and direct the overall operation of the nursing service department in accordance with current applicable federal, state and local standards, guidelines, and regulations.
- As guided by the executive director, to assure that the highest degree of quality patient care can be maintained at all times.
- The Director of Nurses shall be a nurse registered in the State of Connecticut with at least one year of additional education or experience in hospice, psychiatric or substance abuse care and one year of nursing service administration.

Shift Nursing Supervisor

LEEWAY will operate the Baylor Plan with three shifts from 7 A.M. to 3 P.M., 3 P.M. to 11 P.M. and 11 P.M. to 7 A.M. Monday through Friday and two shifts from

7 A.M. to 7 P.M. and 7 P.M. to 7 A.M. Saturday and Sunday. The Baylor Plan will be used because it has been found to minimize absenteeism and staff turnover and to make it easier to recruit weekend staff. In this way, five registered nurses will be needed in addition to the Director of Nurses.

The primary purpose of nursing supervisors is to assist in the planning, organizing, developing and directing of nursing service in accordance with current applicable federal, state and local standards, guidelines and regulations and, as may be directed by the director of nurses and the executive director, to assure the highest degree of quality of patient care can be maintained at all times.

A nurse supervisor shall be a nurse registered in the State of Connecticut. Nursing supervisors should have experience in working in hospice, psychiatric or substance abuse care.

The Connecticut Public Health Code requires a skilled nursing facility the size of LEEWAY to have one registered nurse on duty at all times. The LEEWAY facility will meet this requirement and will have an extra registered nurse on duty during the daytime shift, Monday through Friday.

Nursing Assistant

Provides routine nursing care in accordance with established policies and procedures, as directed by the shift nursing supervisor, director of nurses or executive director, to assure that the highest degree of quality patient care can be maintained at all times.

Each Nursing Assistant will have completed 75 hours of training including 25 hours of classroom training and 50 hours of clinical training. Classroom training will have covered the following subject areas: patient rights, the progression of AIDS as a disease, patient environment and reality orientation, patient psychosocial needs, infection control, basic patient care procedures, emergency procedures and fire safety, food service and dietary policy, and special care needs (such as dementia and patients with a history of drug use). Clinical training will have included demonstration and supervised experience in the following areas: patient care, comfort and daily living; monitoring of patient condition; and patient safety and emergency procedures.

Nursing Assistants will also operate under the Baylor Plan and will be staffed as follows:

Monday through Friday
7 a.m. to 3 p.m.	Three nursing assistants
3 p.m. to 11 p.m.	Two nursing assistants
11 p.m. to 7 a.m.	Two nursing assistants

Saturday and Sunday
7 a.m. to 7 p.m.	Three nursing assistants
7 p.m. to 7 a.m.	Two nursing assistants

The Connecticut Public Health Code requires a skilled nursing facility of the size of LEEWAY to supply 39.2 hours of total nursing and nurse's aide personnel between 7 A.M. and 9 P.M. and 14 hours of total nursing and nurse's aide personnel between 9 P.M. and 7 A.M. each day. LEEWAY will supply 58 hours of nursing and nurse's aide personnel between 7 A.M. and 9 P.M. (54 hours on the weekends) and 30 hours between 9 P.M. and 7 A.M.

Constant Adequate Nursing Supervision

LEEWAY will use nursing pools, overtime, temporary, and intermittent staff or whatever means necessary to maintain more than adequate nursing staff at all times. A total of $35,000 has been budgeted under "additional personnel" to cover the possible costs of pool staff.

It is well known that there is currently a nursing shortage in Connecticut and this is likely to be a problem for LEEWAY in the same way that it is for other facilities. LEEWAY may also find it difficult to recruit staff because of the fear that AIDS produces. On the other hand, when the first AIDS hospice was opened in London, management was inundated with offers from prospective staff members who were attracted by the prospect of an innovative program. LEEWAY management has already been approached by interested nursing staff. In addition, those community groups who have been hardest hit by AIDS in New Haven (lower-income black and Hispanic communities) have traditionally been the source of highest recruitment of nursing aide staff. There may be people within these communities who feel a compassionate commitment to the AIDS cause because of personal loss.

Medical Director

The medical director shall be a physician licensed to practice medicine in Connecticut and shall serve on the facility's active organized medical staff, shall have at least one year of prior clinical experience in adult medicine, and shall be a member of the active medical staff of a general hospital licensed in Connecticut.

The medical director shall have powers and responsibilities as set out in the Connecticut Public Health Code that will include, but not be limited to, the following:

- Enforce the facility's bylaws governing medical care.
- Assure that quality medical care is provided by the facility.
- Serve as a liaison between the medical staff and administration.
- Approve or disapprove a patient's admission based on the facility's ability to provide adequate care for that individual in accordance with the facility's bylaws. The medical director shall have the authority to review any patient's record or examine any patient prior to admission for such purpose.
- Assure that each patient in the facility has an assigned personal physician.
- Provide or arrange for the provision of necessary medical care to the patient if the individual's personal physician is unable or unwilling to do so.
- Visit the facility at least once every seven days to assess the adequacy of medical care provided in the facility.

Psychiatric Medical Director

Will have the same qualifications, powers and responsibilities as the medical director, except that he or she will have responsibility for the psychiatric care of residents.

Bookkeeper/Receptionist

This position will be shared with St. John's Nursing Home. The purpose of the job will be to perform reception duties in an efficient manner and to maintain accounts for the facility in accordance with current applicable federal, state and local standards, guidelines, and regulations as directed by the administrator.

Recreation Director

The purpose of the job will be to assist in the planning, developing, organizing, implementing, evaluating and directing of activity programs, including (in cooperation with the director of education) the recruitment and training of volunteers to assure that recreational and social needs of the residents are met and maintained on an individual basis. The Connecticut Public Health Code requires a facility of LEEWAY's size to employ a recreation director for at least 20 hours per week. Given the special problems and youth of LEEWAY's residents, however, the job is likely to be much more demanding than in a nursing home catering to elderly patients. A full-time position has therefore been budgeted.

Dietician

Since there is only one kitchen on the premises, food will be prepared by St. John's Nursing Home and subcontracted for LEEWAY residents. LEEWAY will employ its own dietician who will work one half hour per patient per month to plan, organize, develop, and direct diet plans for each individual patient.

Housekeeping/Laundry Staff

All laundry will be done in-house. Housekeeping and laundry staff will be employed at an approximate ratio of one full-time equivalent member of staff for each ten patients.

Maintenance/Security

A maintenance/security staff person will be employed around the clock and the costs will be shared with St. John's Nursing Home.

Social Worker

The social worker will ensure that the medically related spiritual, emotional, and social needs of the residents are met and maintained on an individual basis. One social worker for up to 28 patients is more than is normally provided, but the special needs of LEEWAY's residents make this higher ratio necessary.

Occupation therapy and physical therapy will be provided on a contractual basis when the need is indicated by an individual resident's physician.

Marketing

The future need for chronic care beds for AIDS patients has already been described. As yet, there is no supply of this type of health care in Connecticut. Rather than have to market the facility, it is more likely that the program will be forced to grow faster than planned, because people with AIDS/ARC from other parts of Connecticut also need help.

Contact has already been made with the Yale-New Haven Hospital and St. Raphael's Hospital, both of which are eager to cooperate with LEEWAY. People who have had an acute episode due to AIDS/ARC may be discharged to LEEWAY if they are too sick to be discharged to their homes.

The Connecticut AIDS Residence Program (CARP) is planning to provide accommodation for AIDS patients in a rooming house in New Haven. The Connecticut Public Health Code does not allow health care to be provided without a license, but residents in the CARP facility may engage visiting nurses or arrange for other care themselves. When this level of care is no longer sufficient, residents may be referred to LEEWAY.

AIDS Project New Haven has a well established counseling service and will be able to counsel suitable clients of the existence of LEEWAY.

The New Haven Mayor's Task Force on AIDS has recommended the implementation of a case manager system for people with AIDS/ARC. When this program is operational, LEEWAY will be an option for people to be referred to by their case manager.

The Connecticut Public Health Code requires that people only be admitted to a nursing home as a result of the recommendation of their physician. Wherever an initial recommendation for admission to LEEWAY comes from, each individual must be referred by his or her physician.

Financing

Appendix A outlines the costs of setting up the facility.
Appendix B gives five years of operating budgets for the facility.

Assumptions

1. No cash flows exist prior to January 1, 1989 other than projected start-up costs outlined in Appendix A.
2. Catherine Kennedy works pro bono from September 1987 to January 1, 1989.
3. For the three months following January 1, 1989, staff will be recruited and equipment set in place. LEEWAY will begin to incur costs, but these will not be reimbursable by the Department of Income Maintenance.
4. The first patients will be accepted on April 1, 1989 and the census built up to an average of 25 patients by July 1, 1989.
5. Department of Income Maintenance reimbursement will be made three months in arrears.

Facility

The building can be bought for $2 million of which LEEWAY's share is $500,000. The Department of Income Maintenance will pay $281,000 for the first two years and then $230,000 for the following ten years as a fair rent for the whole building. LEEWAY will be entitled to one-quarter of these payments. This flow of funds can probably be exchanged for a lump sum of about $400,000 with an organization that makes socially conscious investments, leaving a sum of $100,000 which must be raised towards the building. The Department of Housing and Urban Development will give credit insurance for 0.5–1.0% of the debt if necessary.

The facility is currently equipped, but as it is eighteen years old, much of the equipment will have to be replaced. Total replacement costs would be approximately $180,000. In addition, about $50,000 is needed to bring the building up to the current requirements of the Connecticut Public Health Code and to make a physical separation between LEEWAY's facility and St. John's Rest Home/Home for the Aged.

Other Start-Up Costs

Fees for engineers, consultants and lawyers will amount to about $35,000. This amount may actually be lower as Yale Law School is providing legal services as part of its clinical program under the guidance of Professor John Simon and Catherine Kennedy will do most of the tasks usually allocated to consultants.

Department of Income Maintenance Reimbursement

LEEWAY must assume that it will have all Medicaid (DIM-reimbursed) patients because most of its residents will be inner-city poor and because health insurance does not cover long-term care. The Department of Income Maintenance will reimburse running expenses up to a maximum of $105.45 per patient per day plus a fair rent for the building beginning July 1, 1988.

LEEWAY estimates that running costs will be in the region of $105 per patient per day in 1989 dollars. Budgets have been derived from actual running costs of the Bradley Home in Meriden, a beautifully run skilled nursing facility licensed for 30 patients. Other nursing home budgets for larger facilities confirm that the budget projections are realistic.

Fair rent would add about another $7 per patient per day at full occupancy giving a total per diem of about $112. There are nursing homes in Connecticut currently receiving more than $112 per person per day, due to higher building costs.

DIM reimbursement is based on a nursing home's historic costs, with reimbursement rates increased each year by an inflation factor based on the consumer price index. Over recent years, health care inflation has been far in excess of general inflation levels and many nursing homes finding it difficult to make ends meet, have reduced service levels. A new facility has the advantage of having no history and the opportunity to start out with high levels of care, which should give it some "cushion" against future reductions in real levels of reimbursement.

It is the typical experience of nursing homes in Connecticut that the Department of Income Maintenance reimburses costs about 90 days after they are incurred. LEEWAY will need about $450,000 to cover expenses during the period needed to prepare the facility and recruit staff, build up patient census and receive reimbursement from the Department of Income Maintenance.

Figure IA.1. Appendix A Leeway Inc.,
Start-up Costs

Building[a]	$100,000
Building renovation	50,000
Legal and consulting costs	35,000
C. Kennedy expenses[b]	5,000
Beds	70,000
Carpet/floorcovering	20,000
Office equipment	8,000
Linen	7,500
Chairs	7,000
Century tub	7,000
Closets	5,000
Chests of drawers	5,000
Bedpan hopper	3,500
Wheelchairs	3,000
Medical record holder	2,000
Overbed tables	1,500
Mattresses	1,500
Showers/commodes	1,000
Nurses' gowns, etc.	1,000
Crockery	800
Tablecloths, napkins	500
Vacuum cleaner	500
Flatware	200
Other medical goods	5,000
	$340,000

[a] Difference between net present value of DIM's fair rent reimbursement over 12 years and the cost to LEEWAY of purchasing a discrete wing of St. John's Nursing Home.

[b] Includes $3,215 to pay for tuition and examinations involved in acquiring licensure as a nursing home administrator.

Figure IA.2. Appendix B Leeway, Inc. Budget

Expenses	1989–90	1990–91	1991–92	1992–93	1993–94
Salaries					
Administrator[a]	$ 20,000	$ 21,600	$ 23,328	$ 25,194	$ 27,210
Director of Education	35,000	37,800	40,824	44,090	47,617
Director of Nurses	35,000	37,800	40,824	44,090	47,617
RNs	150,000	162,000	174,960	188,957	204,073
Nursing assistants	180,000	194,400	209,952	226,745	244,888
Housekeeping/laundry	37,500	40,500	43,740	47,239	51,018
Social worker	25,000	27,000	29,160	31,493	34,012
Recreation	25,000	27,000	29,160	31,493	34,012
Bookkeeper/receptionist	10,000	10,800	11,664	12,597	13,605
Maintenance/security	30,000	32,400	34,992	37,791	40,815
Subtotal	$ 547,500	$ 591,300	$ 638,604	$ 689,692	$ 744,867
Benefits[b]	$ 109,500	$ 118,260	$ 127,721	$ 137,938	$ 148,974
Other personnel	$ 35,000	$ 37,800	$ 40,824	$ 44,090	$ 47,617
Total Salaries	$ 692,000	$ 747,360	$ 807,149	$ 871,720	$ 941,458
Medical Expenses	$ 75,500	$ 81,540	$ 88,063	$ 95,108	$ 102,717
Maintenance	23,500	25,380	27,410	29,603	31,971

Figure IA.2. Appendix B Leeway, Inc. Budget (*Continued*)

Expenses	1989–90	1990–91	1991–92	1992–93	1993–94
Utilities	21,000	22,680	24,494	26,454	28,570
Administration	17,500	18,900	20,412	22,045	23,809
Food service	73,000	78,840	85,147	91,959	99,316
Housekeeping/laundry	16,500	17,820	19,246	20,785	22,448
Recreation	6,250	6,750	7,290	7,873	8,503
Insurance	66,133	71,423	77,137	83,308	89,973
Rent	70,250	70,250	57,500	57,500	57,500
Total Expenses	$1,061,633	$1,140,943	$1,213,848	$1,306,355	$1,406,265
Income					
Maximum DIM patient reimbursement	$1,000,721	$1,080,778	$1,167,240	$1,260,620	$1,361,489
Rent allowance	$ 70,250	$ 70,250	$ 57,500	$ 57,500	$ 57,500
Total Income	$1,070,971	$1,151,028	$1,224,740	$1,318,120	$1,418,963
Excess Cash Flow	$ 9,338	$ 10,085	$ 10,892	$ 11,763	$ 12,704

Assumptions
8% annual inflation
26 patients

[a]Cost shared with St. John's Nursing Home.
[b]Benefits estimated at 20% of salary.

Notes

Chapter 1

1. The best source for data on nonprofits is Virginia Hodgkinson, et al., *Nonprofit Almanac*, 1992–93. San Francisco: Jossey Bass, 1992.
2. Thomas Stewart, "Turning Around the Lord's Business," *Fortune*, September 25, 1989, pp. 116–28.
3. For an excellent review of the early history of nonprofits, see Peter Hall, "A Historical Overview of the Private Nonprofit Sector," in W. W. Powell, *The Nonprofit Sector: A Research Handbook*. New Haven: Yale University Press, 1987, pp. 3–26.
4. An excellent current survey of the law governing nonprofits in the United States is Note, "Developments in the Law: Nonprofit Corporations," *Harvard Law Review*, Vol 105, 1992, pp. 1578–1699; the classic discussion of nonprofit tax rules is John Simon, "The Tax Treatment of Nonprofit Organizations: A Review of Federal and State Policies," in W. W. Powell, *The Nonprofit Sector: A Research Handbook*. New Haven, Yale University Press, 1987, pp. 67–98.
5. Peter Drucker, "What Can Business Learn from Nonprofits," *Harvard Business Review*, July–August 1989, pp. 88–93.
6. Giandomenico Majone, "Professionalism and Nonprofit Organizations," *Journal of Health Politics, Policy and Law*, 8, 1984, pp. 639–59.
7. William Newman and Harvey Wallender, "Managing Not-for-Profit Enterprises," *Academy of Management Review*, 3, January 1978, pp. 23–31.
8. John Simon, "The Tax Treatment of Nonprofit Organizations: A Review of Federal and State Policies."
9. Drucker, "What Can Business Learn from Nonprofits?" p. 89.
10. *Ibid.*
11. There has been some recent movement in the direction of establishing uniform standards, as FASB has established a number of study projects to try to design common standards for the nonprofits. We discuss this further in Chapter 9.

Chapter 2

1. Frances Hesselbein, cited in John Byrne, "Profiting from the Nonprofits," *Business Week*, March 26, 1990.

2. The arguments developed here about the efficiency of organizational forms were begun by Ronald Coase, "The Nature of the Firm ," *Economica* #4, 1937, pp. 386–405, for which he won the Nobel Prize in Economics. It has been continued by A. D. Chandler, *Strategy and Structure*, Cambridge, MA: MIT Press, 1962, and Oliver Williamson, *Markets and Hierarchies*, New York: Free Press, 1975.

3. Richard Nelson and Michael Krashinsky, "Two Issues of Policy: Public Subsidy and the Organization of Supply," in Dennis Young and Richard Nelson, eds., *Public Policy for Day Care of Young Children*, Lexington, MA: D. C. Health, 1973; Henry Hansmann, "The Role of Nonprofit Enterprise," *Yale Law Journal*, 89, 1980, pp. 835–901; David Easley and Maureen O'Hara, "The Economic Role of the Nonprofit Firm," *Bell Journal of Economics*, 14, 1983, pp. 531–38; and Avner Ben-Ner, "Nonprofit Organizations: Why Do They Exist in Market Economies?" in Susan Rose-Ackerman, ed., *The Economics of Nonprofit Institutions: Studies in Structure and Policy.* New York: Oxford University Press, 1986.

4. Avner Ben-Ner, "Nonprofit Organizations: Why Do They Exist in Market Economics," 1986.

5. Burton Weisbrod, "Toward a Theory of the Voluntary Nonprofit Sector in a Three-Sector Economy," in Edmund Phelps, ed., *Altruism, Morality and Economic Theory*, New York: Russell Sage, 1974.

6. James Douglas, "Political Theories of Nonprofit Organizations," in W. W. Powell, *The Nonprofit Sector.*

7. Estelle James, "The Nonprofit Sector in Comparative Perspective," in W. W. Powell, *The Nonprofit Sector.*

8. *Ibid.*

9. This argument has been made most forcefully by Lester Salamon, "Partners in Public Service: The Scope and Theory of Government-Nonprofit Relations," in W. W. Powell, *The Nonprofit Sector.*

10. Michael Krashinsky, "Management Implications of Government Funding of Nonprofit Organizations." *Nonprofit Management and Leadership.* Fall 1990, 38–54.

11. Dennis Young, "Entrepreneurship and the Behavior of Nonprofit Organizations: Elements of a Theory," in Michelle White, eds., *Nonprofit Firms in a Three-Sector Economy*, 1981.

12. Michael O'Neill, *The Third America: The Emergence of the Nonprofit Sector in the United States.* Jossey Bass: San Francisco, 1989.

13. Anne Preston, "The Nonprofit Worker in a For-Profit World." *Journal of Labor Economics*, vol. 7, No. 4, 1989, pp. 438–63.

14. P. Kotler, *Marketing Management: Analysis, Planning, Control*, Englewood Cliffs, NJ: Prentice Hall, 1980, pp. 50–53.

15. Joseph Schumpeter, *Capitalism, Socialism, and Democracy*, New York: Harper and Row, 1942.

16. Carl Milofsky, "Not for Profit Organizations and Community: A Review of the Sociological Literature." PONPO working paper #6. Yale University, 1979.

17. Melissa Middleton Stone, "The Propensity of Governing Boards to Plan," *Nonprofit Management and Leadership*, vol. I, no. 3, 1991, pp. 203–16.

18. See, for example, John Pearce and Fred David, "Corporate Mission Statements: The Bottom Lines," *Academy of Management Executive*, May 1987, pp. 109–16.

19. Theodore Levitt, "Marketing Myopia," *Harvard Business Review*, July, August 1960, p. 45.

20. Carl Milofsky, "Not for Profit Organizations and Community."

Chapter 3

1. Thomas, quoted in *Business Week*, "Profiting from the Nonprofits," March 26, 1990, p. 48.
2. Michael Porter, *Competitive Strategy*, New York: Free Press, 1980.
3. Garth Saloner, "Applied Game Theory and Strategic Management." Paper presented at Napa Valley Conference on Strategy, November 29, 1990.
4. Franklin Fisher, *Industrial Organization, Economics and the Law*. MIT Press: Cambridge, 1991, p. 43.
5. See Sharon Oster, "Nonprofit Organization as Franchise Operations," *Journal of Nonprofit Management and Leadership*, March 1992.
6. Judith Blau, Laurie Newman, and Joseph Schwartz, "Internal Economies of Scale in Performing Arts Organizations," *Journal of Culture Economics*, June 1986, pp. 63–76.
7. U.S. Small Business Administration, *The State of Small Business*, Washington, D.C., 1986.
8. James Gapanski, "The Lively Arts as Substitutes for the Lively Arts," *American Economic Review*, May 1986, pp. 20–25.
9. The distinction between donative and commercial nonprofits comes from H. Hansmann, "The Role of Nonprofit Enterprise." Many nonprofits are a mixed type.
10. Christopher Edley, *Wall Street Journal*, June 12, 1987, p. 1.
11. V. Hodgkinson, *Nonprofit Almanac*.
12. L. Salamon, "Partners in Public Service."
13. D. Netzer, "Dance in New York: Market and Subsidy Changes," *American Economic Review*, May 1986, pp. 15–19.
14. This technique was first suggested by George Stigler, "The Economies of Scale," *Journal of Law and Economics*, October 1958, pp. 54–71. It has been applied many times in the industrial organization literature. One early example of application is Leonard Weiss, "The Survival Technique and the Extent of Suboptimal Capacity," *Journal of Political Economy*, June 1964, pp. 246–61.
15. Garrison, quoted in *Business Week*, "Profiting from the Nonprofits," March 26, 1990, p. 73.

Chapter 4

1. Myron Weiner, *Human Services Management*. Homewood, IL: Dorsey Bess, 1982; Richard Bush, "Survival of the Nonprofit Spirit in a For-Profit World," *Nonprofit and Voluntary Sector Quarterly*, Winter 1992, p. 410.
2. David Wilson, "The Strategic Challenge of Cooperation and Competition in British Voluntary Organizations," *Nonprofit Management and Leadership*. Spring 1992, pp. 239–54.
3. Sharon Oster, *Modern Competitive Analysis*, New York: Oxford University Press, 1994. Second edition.
4. Avinash Dixit and Barry Nalebuff, *Thinking Strategically*, New York: W. W. Norton, 1991.
5. R. Bush. "Survival of the Nonprofit Spirit in a For-Profit World."
6. Armand Laufer, *Understanding Your Social Service Agency*, Newbury Park, CA: Sage, 1984, p. 78.
7. R. Bush, "Nonprofit Spirit in a For-Profit World."

8. Frank Fisher, "On Donor Sovereignty and United Charities," *American Economic Review,* September 1977, pp. 632–38.
9. Robert Axelrod, *The Evolution of Cooperation,* New York: Basic Books, 1984.
10. Carl Milofsky, *Community Organizations: Studies in Resource Mobilization and Exchange.* Oxford University Press: New York, 1988; and Judith Blau and Gordana Rabrerovic, "Interorganizational Relations of Nonprofit Organizations," *Sociological Forum* v. 6, 1991, pp. 327–47.
11. I. MacMillan, "Competitive Strategies for Not-for-Profit Agencies," *Advances in Strategic Management,* VI, 1983, pp. 61–82.
12. E. James and Susan Rose-Ackerman, *The Nonprofit Enterprise in Market Economies,* Harwood Press: New York, 1986, p. 51.
13. Susan Rose-Ackerman, "Altruistic Nonprofit Firms in Competitive Markets: The Case of the Day Care Centers." *Journal of Consumer Policy,* 9, 1986, pp. 291–310.
14. *Ibid.*
15. B. Weisbrod, *The Not-for-Profit Sector,* 1985.
16. See, for example, E. Greenberg, "Competing for Scarce Resources," *Journal of Business Strategy,* Vol. 2, no. 3, Winter 1982, pp. 81–87; and Israel Unterman and Richard Davis, *Strategic Management of Not-for-Profit Organizations,* New York: Praeger, 1984.
17. Alan Houghton, cited in "Doing the Lord's Business," *Fortune,* 1989.
18. Jon Van Til, *Critical Issues in American Philanthropy: Strengthening Theory and Practice,* San Francisco, CA: Jossey-Bass, 1990, p. 278.
19. David Wilson, "The Strategic Challenges of Cooperation and Competition in British Voluntary Organizations."
20. John Lammers, "The Effect of Competition on Labor Management in Nonprofit Organizations," *Nonprofit and Voluntary Sector Quarterly,* Summer 1990, pp. 171–87.

Chapter 5

1. Hodgkinson, et al., *Nonprofit Almanac: Dimensions of the Independent Sector.* Independent Sector: Washington, D.C., 1993.
2. *Ibid.*
3. For an introduction to the idea of stakeholders, see E. Freeman and D. Gilbert, *Corporate Strategy and the Search For Ethics.* Prentice Hall: New Jersey, 1988.
4. Charles Perrow, *Complex Organizations.* Third edition. New York, 1986.
5. Dennis Young, "Performance and Reward in Nonprofit Organizations," PONPO working paper #79. Yale University, 1984; and Ben Cole, "Compensation," *Modern Health Care,* December 1982, pp. 67–90.
6. Richard Freeman, "The Job Market for College Faculty," in Daniel Lewis and William Becher, eds., *Academic Rewards in Higher Education,* Cambridge: Ballinger, 1979.
7. Burton Weisbrod, "Nonprofit and proprietary sector behavior: wage differentials among lawyers," *Journal of Labor Economics* vol. 4, 1983, pp. 246–63.
8. For a review of these data see Anne Preston, "The Nonprofit Worker in a For-Profit World," *Journal of Labor Economics,* vol. 7, 1989, pp. 438–63.
9. Anne Preston, *Ibid.*
10. Anne Preston, "Women in the White Collar Nonprofit Sector: The Best Option or the Only Option," *Review of Economics and Statistics,* 1990, pp. 560–68.

11. Preston, *Ibid.*

12. Philip Mirvis and Edward Hackett, "Work and Work Force Characteristics in the Nonprofit Sector," *Monthly Labor Review,* April 1983, pp. 3–12.

13. Estelle James, "The Nonprofit Sector in Comparative Perspective," 1986.

14. Dennis Young, "Executive Leadership in Nonprofit Organizations," in W. W. Powell, *The Nonprofit Sector,* pp. 167–79.

15. Dennis Young, *Ibid.*

16. Sharon Oster, *Modern Competitive Analysis.* Second edition. New York: Oxford, 1994, esp. Ch. 8.

17. B. Cole, "Compensation," *Modern Health Care,* December 1982, pp. 67–90.

18. Richard Steinberg, "Profits and Incentive Compensation in Nonprofit Firms," *Nonprofit Management and Leadership,* Winter 1990, pp. 137–51.

19. *Ibid.*

20. Jeffrey Pfeffer, *Organizations and Organizational Theory,* Houghton Mifflin: Boston, 1982.

21. William Newman and Harvey Wallender, "Managing Not-For Profit Enterprises," *Academy of Management Review,* January 1978, pp. 24–31.

22. Mark Pauly, "Nonprofit Firms in Medical Markets," *American Economics Review,* May 1987, pp. 257–62.

23. J. Schumpeter, "Developments in Nonprofit Law," *Harvard Law Review,* 1992.

24. Dennis Young, "Performance and Reward in Nonprofit Organizations."

25. Paul DiMaggio, "Nonprofit Managers in Different Fields of Service," in M. O'Neill and D. Young, *Educating Managers of Nonprofit Organizations.* San Francisco: Jossey Bass, 1989, pp. 51–69.

26. Henry Mintzberg, "Strategy Making in Three Modes," *California Management Review,* 1973, 16(2), pp. 44–53.

27. Jeffrey Pfeffer, *Organizations and Organizational Theory.* Boston: Houghton Mifflin, 1982.

28. Israel Unterman and Richard Davis, *Strategic Management of Not-For-Profit Organizations,* New York, 1984.

29. Jeffrey Pfeffer, *Organizations and Organizational Theory.*

30. H. Mintzberg and A. McHugh, "Strategy Formulation in an Adhocracy." *Administrative Science Quarterly.* 1985, 30, 160–97.

31. Paul Menchik and Burton Weisbrod, "Volunteer Labor Supply," *Journal of Public Economics,* 32, 1987, pp. 159–83.

32. Peter Drucker, cited in "Turning Around the Lord's Business," *Fortune,* September 25, 1989, p. 116.

Chapter 6

1. See, for example, recent work by R. Abzug, et al., *Study of Nonprofit Boards,* Yale Program on Nonprofits, 1994.

2. Paul Hirsch and Thomas Whistler, "Reforming the Corporate Board," University of Chicago working paper, September 1979.

3. Israel Unterman and Richard Davis, *Strategic Management of Not-for-Profit Organizations.* Boston: Harvard Business School Press, 1984.

4. E. Fama and M. Jensen, "Separation of Ownership and Control," *Journal of Law and Economics,* June 1983, pp. 301–26.

5. *Ibid.*

6. Note, "Developments in the Law: Nonprofit Corporations," *Harvard Law Review,* Vol. 105, 1992, pp. 1578–1699.

7. J. Price, "The Impact of Governing Boards on Organizational Effectiveness and Morale," *Administrative Science Quarterly,* 8, 1963, pp. 361–77.

8. Melissa Stone, "Nonprofit Boards of Directors: Beyond the Governance Function," in W. W. Powell, ed., *The Nonprofit Sector,* 1986.

9. Richard Cole, "Constituent Involvement in Nonprofit Organizations," PONPO working paper no. 18, Yale University, 1980.

10. An excellent review of current law on nonprofit directors is given in Note, "Developments in the Law: Nonprofit Corporations," *Harvard Law Review,* vol. 105, 1992, pp. 1578–699.

11. E. Fama and M. Jensen, "Separation of Ownership and Control," 1983.

12. Note, "Developments in the Law: Nonprofit Corporations."

13. I. Unterman and R. Davis, *Strategic Management of Not-for-Profit Organizations,* 1984.

14. J. Blau, et al., "Interorganizational Relations of Nonprofit Organizations," *Sociological Forum,* vol. 6, no. 2, 1991, pp. 327–47.

15. *Ibid.*

16. E. Sturckhoff, cited in Stone, 1986.

17. Jeffrey Pfeffer, "Size, Composition and Function of Hospital Boards of Directors," *Administrative Science Quarterly,* vol. 18, 1973, pp. 349–64.

18. B. Bittker and G. Rahdert, "The Exemption of Nonprofit Organizations from Federal Income Taxation," *Yale Law Journal,* vol. 85, 1976, pp. 336–42.

19. See, for example, Richard Chait and Barbara Taylor, "Charity: the Territory of Nonprofit Boards," *Harvard Business Review,* January 1989, pp. 44–54; and C. Houle, *Governing Boards: Their Nature and Nurturing,* San Francisco: Jossey Bass, 1989.

20. See, for example, R. Herman, "Methodological Issues in Studying the Effectiveness of Nongovernmental and Nonprofit Organizations," *Nonprofit and Voluntary Sector Quarterly,* 19, 1990, pp. 293–306.

21. D. Fenn, "Executives as Community Volunteers," *Harvard Business Review,* vol. 49, 1971, pp. 156–57.

22. Clarkson, cited in P. DiMaggio. *Nonprofit Enterprise in the Arts.* New York: Oxford Universitiy Press, 1986.

23. T. Odendahl and E. Boris, "A Delicate Balance: Foundation Board: Staff Relations," *Foundation News* vol. 24, 1983, pp. 34–45.

24. B. O'Connell, *The Board Member's Book,* New York: Carlton, 1985, p. 52.

25. R. Chait and B. Taylor, "Charting the Territory of Nonprofit Boards," *Harvard Business Review,* January–February 1989, pp. 44–54.

26. Miriam Wood, "The Governing Board's Existential Quandary: An Empirical Analysis of Board Behavior in the Charitable Sector," PONPO Working Paper #143, Yale University, May 1989; p. 4.

27. R. Augsburger, Notes on Nonprofit Management Session 5, Stanford University Notes, Autumn 1992.

28. P. Bradshaw, V. Murrage, and S. Wolpin, "Do Nonprofit Boards Make a Difference? An Explanation of the Relationship Among Board Structure, Process and Effectiveness," *Nonprofit and Voluntary Sector Quarterly,* vol. 3, 1992, pp. 227–50.

29. Cited in C. Houle, *Governing Boards,* 1989, p. 24.

30. A good example of studies which use self-reportings include R. Herman and P. Tulipiana, "Board-Staff Relations and Perceived Effectiveness in Nonprofit Organizations," *Journal of Voluntary Action Research,* vol. 14, no. 4, 1985, pp. 48–59.

31. B. Taylor, R. Chait, and T. Holland, "Trustee Motivation and Board Effectiveness," *Nonprofit and Voluntary Sector Quarterly,* Summer 1991, pp. 207–224.
32. P. Bradshaw, V. Murray, and J. Wolpin, "Do Nonprofit Boards Make a Difference? An Exploration of the Relationships Among Board Structure, Process and Effectiveness," *Nonprofit and Voluntary Sector Quarterly,* Fall 1992, pp. 227–49.
33. An excellent broad statement of this is given in R. Herman and R. Heimovics, *Executive Leadership in Nonprofit Organizations.*
34. Taylor, et al., "Trustee Motivation and Board Effectiveness," 1991.
35. Taylor, et al., "Trustee Motivation and Board Effectiveness," 1991.
36. Peter Hall, *The Organization of American Culture, 1700–1900: Institutions, Elites and the Origins of American Nationality,* New York: New York Universitiy Press, 1982.
37. See M. Stone, "Nonprofit Boards of Directors," 1986.
38. Bradshaw, et al., "Do Nonprofit Boards Make a Difference," 1992.
39. J. Carver, *Boards that Make a Difference,* San Francisco: Jossey Bass, 1990.
40. Robert Greenleaf, cited in C. Houle, *Governing Boards: Their Nature and Nurture,* San Francisco: Jossey Bass, 1989.
41. R. Herman and R. Heimovics, "The Effective Nonprofit Executive: Leader of the Board," *Nonprofit Management and Leadership,* vol. 1, no. 2, 1990, pp. 167–80.
42. C. Houle, *Governing Boards: Their Nature and Nurture.*
43. K. Fletcher, "Effective Boards: How Effective Directors Define and Develop Them," *Nonprofit Management and Leadership,* Spring 1992, pp. 283–93.
44. R. Greenleaf, quoted in C. Houle, *Governing Boards: Their Nature and Nurturing,* 1989, p. 1.

Chapter 7

1. John Byrne, F. Hesselbein, cited in "Profiting from the Nonprofits," *Business Week,* March 26, 1990.
2. For an interesting discussion of the use of commercial enterprises in religious organizations, see P. LaBarbera, "Enterprise in Religious-Based Organizations," *Nonprofit and Voluntary Sector Quarterly,* Spring 1992, pp. 51–67.
3. C. Lovelock and C. Weinberg, *Marketing for Public and Nonprofit Managers* (Second edition) New York: Wiley & Sons, 1989.
4. *Ibid.*
5. J. Crimmins and M. Kiel, *Enterprise in the Nonprofit Sector,* New York: Rockefeller Brothers Fund, 1983.
6. Paul Firstenberg, *Managing for Profit in the Nonprofit World,* Washington: The Founditon Center, 1986.
7. R. Clark, "Does the Nonprofit Form Fit the Hospital Industry?" *Harvard Law Review,* May 1980, pp. 1416–89.
8. Estelle James, "How Nonprofits Grow," *Journal of Policy Analysis and Management,* vol. 2, no. 3, 1983; p. 353.
9. *Ibid.*
10. R. Nielsen, "Piggybacking Strategies for Nonprofits," *Strategic Management Journal,* May 1986, pp. 201–16.
11. Robert Clark, "Does the Nonprofit Form Fit the Hospital Industry," 1980, pp. 1416–89.
12. E. James, "How Nonprofits Grow."
13. Nielsen, "Piggybacking Strategies for Nonprofits."

14. E. Skloot, "Enterprise and Commerce in Nonprofit Organizations," in W. W. Powell, *The Nonprofit Sector: A Research Handbook,* New Haven: Yale University Press, 1987.

15. *Ibid.*

16. For a review of tax policy on this and other issues in a number of countries, see B. Weisbrod, "Tax policy toward nonprofit organizations: An eleven country survey," *Voluntas,* vol. 2, no. 1, 1991, pp. 3–25.

17. For a discussion of the Mueller case, and the history of the unrelated business income tax, see S. Rose-Ackerman, "Unfair Competition and Corporate Income Taxation," *Stanford Law Review,* May 1982, pp. 1017–39; and H. Hansmann, "Unfair Competition and the Unrelated Business Income Tax," *Virginia Law Review,* vol. 75, 1989, pp. 605–35.

18. Internal Revenue Code Section 512 (a)(1), West Supplement, 1991.

19. For a review of the current U.S. law in this area, see Note, "Developments in the law: Nonprofit Corporations," *Harvard Law Review,* Vol. 105, 1992, pp. 1617–19.

20. B. Weisbrod, "Tax Policy Toward Nonprofit Organizations."

21. T. Haake, quoted in "Competition in the Nonprofit," *Association Management,* August 1986, 31.

22. *Ibid.*

23. Note, "Developments . . .." 1992, p. 1619.

24. M. O'Neill and D. Young, "Educating Managers in Nonprofit Organizations," in O'Neill and Young, ed.

25. P. Firstenberg, *Managing for Profit in a Nonprofit World,* Washington, D.C.: The Foundation Center, 1986.

26. Hodgkinson, et al., *Nonprofit Almanac,* 1992.

27. R. Anthony and D. Young, *Management Control in Nonprofit Organizations,* Homewood: Irvin, 1984; Chapter 4.

Chapter 8

1. A simple regression of real private contributions against a constant and national income for the period 1960–1990 yields the following result. (t - statistics in parentheses).

Real Contribution = −2.21 + .03 Nat Inc.
$$(-.54) \quad (14.8)$$
$$R^2 = .88$$

2. *Chronicle of Philanthropy,* June 30, 1992, p. 10.

3. V. Hodgkinson, *Nonprofit Almanac.* p. 82.

4. *Ibid.*

5. G. Williams, "Charitable Giving Up in 1991," *Chronicle of Philanthropy,* June 30, 1992, p. 1.

6. S. Boyle and P. Jacobs, "The Economics of Charitable Fundraising," *Philanthropy Monthly,* May 1978, pp. 21–27. A modified version of the production function approach is R. Steinberg, "Should Donors Care about Fundraising," in S. Rose-Ackerman, ed., *The Economics of Nonprofit Institutions: Studies in Structure and Policy.* New York: Oxford, 1986, pp. 347–64.

7. Note, "Developments in Nonprofit Law," 1992.

8. S. Rose-Ackerman, "Charitable Giving and Excessive Fundraising," *Quarterly Journal of Economics*, May 1982, pp. 193–212.

9. B. Weisbrod and N. Dominquez, "Demand for Collective Goods in Private Nonprofit Markets," *Journal of Public Economics*, June 1986, pp. 83–96.

10. R. Steinberg, "Should donors care about fundraising?" 1986.

11. C. Jencks, "Who Gives to What?" in W. W. Powell, *The Nonprofit Sector*, 1986.

12. M. Feldstein and C. Clotfelter, "Tax Incentives and Charitable Contributions in the U.S.," *Journal of Public Economics*, vol. 5, 1976, pp. 1–26.

13. C. Clotfelter and E. Steuerle, "Charitable Contributions," in H. Aaron and J. Pechman, eds., *How Taxes Affect Economic Behavior.* Washington, D.C.: Brookings, 1981.

14. A. Greeley, *The American Catholic: A Social Portrait.* New York: Basic Books, 1977.

15. Study cited in C. Jencks, "Who Gives to What."

16. E. Carson, "The Evolution of Black Philanthropy: Patterns of Giving and Voluntarism," in R. Magat, ed. *Philanthropic Giving: Studies in Varieties of Goals.* New York: Oxford, 1989.

17. C. Clotfelter and M. Feldstein, "Tax Incentives and Charitable Contributions in the U.S."

18. C. Jencks, "Who Gives to What?"

19. *Ibid.,* p. 324.

20. See, for example, A. Adnati and M. M. Perry, "Joint Projects Without Commitment," *Review of Economic Studies*, April 1991, pp. 259–76; and J. Miller and J. Andreoni, "Can Evolutionary Economics Explain Free Riding in Experiments?" *Economic Letters*, May 1991, pp. 9–15.

21. K. Teltsch, "Charitable Giving Rose to $124 Billion in 1992," *New York Times*, May 26, 1993, p. A17.

22. For an excellent review, see C. Clotfelter, "Federal Tax Policy and Charitable Giving," in Ragat, 1989.

23. G. Williams, *Chronicles of Philanthropy*, "The Ups and Downs of Charitable Giving," June 30, 1992, p. 21.

24. P. Anderson, "Corporate Generosity is Greatly Depreciated," *Business Week*, November 2, 1992, p. 118.

25. J. Logsdon, M. Reinder, and L. Burke, "Corporate Philanthropy: Strategic Responses to the Firm's Stakeholder," *Nonprofit and Voluntary Sector Quarterly*, Summer 1990, pp. 93–109.

26. M. Useem, "Market and Institutional Factors in Corporate Contributions," *California Management Review*, vol. 39, no. 2, 1988, pp. 77–88.

27. J. Logsdon, et al. "Corporate Philanthropy," 1990.

28. P. Caesar, "Cause-Related Marketing: The New Face of Corporate Philanthropy," *Business and Society Review*, vol. 59, 1986, pp. 15–19.

29. See F. Fisher, "On Donor Sovereignty and United Charities," *American Economic Review*, September 1977, pp. 632–38; and S. Rose-Ackerman, "Charitable Giving and Excessive Fundraising," *Quarterly Journal of Economics*, May 1982, pp. 193–212.

30. R. Steinberg, "Economic Perspectives on Regulation of Charitable Solicitation," *Case Western Law Review*, 39, 1989, pp. 775–782.

31. Note, "Developments in. . ."

32. G. Williams, "Charitable Giving Up in 1991," *Chronicle of Philanthropy*, June 30, 1992, p. 19.

33. M. Bilodean, "Voluntary Contributions to United Charities," *Journal of Public Economics,* June 1992, pp. 119–133.
34. T. Odendahl, "The Culture of Elite Philanthropy in the Reagan Years," *Nonprofit Voluntary Sector Quarterly.* Fall 1989, pp. 232–40.
35. J. Pfeffer and G. Salancik, "Organizational Decision Making as a Political Process," *Administrative Science Quarterly,* vol. 19, 1974, pp. 135–51.
36. Salamon, "Partners in Public Service," in W. W. Powell, *The Nonprofit Sector,* p. 114.
37. W. W. Powell and R. Friedkin, "Organizational Change in Nonprofit Organizations," in W. W. Powell, *The Nonprofit Sector,* 1986.
38. Wilson, "The Strategic Challenges of Cooperation and Competition in British Voluntary Organizations."

Chapter 9

1. For a comprehensive discussion of nonprofit accounting, see R. Anthony and D. Young, *Management Control in Nonprofit Organizations,* Homewood: Irwin, 1984.
2. R. Anthony, "The Financial Information that Nonprofit Trustees Need and How They Can Get It." *Nonprofit Management and Leadership,* Summer 1991, pp. 371–88; and R. Herzlinger, "Why Data Systems in Nonprofit Organizations Fail," in P. Kotler, ed., *Cases and Readings for Marketing for Nonprofits.* New Jersey: Prentice Hall, 1983.
3. There is an interesting question about what is meant by maintaining a gift in perpetuity. Suppose a donor gives $200 in 1850 to Yale University. The real value of that $200 is considerably higher than $200 by 1992. Is Yale committed to save the real value of the bequest or only its nominal value? At present, the case law in this area suggests that only the nominal sum forms the "corpus" of the gift, and thus, in this case, only $200 needs to be protected.
4. R. Anthony, "The Financial Information that Nonprofit Trustees Need and How They Can Get It," p. 387.
5. Anthony and Young, *Management Control in Nonprofit Organizations.*
6. Anthony and Young, *Management Control in Nonprofit Organizations.*
7. W. J. Scranton, "A Theory of the Nursing Home Market," *Inquiry,* Spring 1980, pp. 25–41.
8. H. Tuckman and C. Chang, "Nonprofit Equity: A Behavioral Model and its Policy Implications," *JPM,* vol. 7, 1992, pp. 76–87.
9. For a review of this work see H. Tuckman and C. Chang, "Nonprofit Equity: A Behavioral Model and its Policy Implications."
10. Tuckman and Chang, "Nonprofit Equity."
11. Anthony, "The Financial Information That Nonprofit Trustees Need and How They Can Get It."
12. M. O'Neill and D. Young, *Educating Managers in the Nonprofit Sector.*
13. R. Herzlinger, "Why Data Systems in Nonprofit Organizations Fail," in P. Kotler, ed., *Cases and Readings for Marketing for Nonprofits.* Englewood Cliffs: Prentice Hall, 1983, pp. 47–66.
14. Under FASB ruling, depreciation is required on all assets. Noncompliance with this ruling is widespread and appears to have no impact on an organization's bond rating. Anthony has argued that depreciation on contributed capital as-

sets serves no purpose. See R. Anthony, "The Financial Information That Non-profit Trustees Need and How They Can Get It."
15. R. Anthony and D. Young, *Management Control in Nonprofit Organizations.*

Chapter 10

1. For a discussion of profit centers in a university setting, see C. Manns and J. March, "Financial Advertising, Internal Competition and Curriculum Change in a University," *Administrative Science Quarterly,* December 1978, pp. 541–52.
2. J. March and P. Olsen, *Ambiguity and Choice of Organizations*, Bergen, Norway: Universitesforlaget, 1976.
3. R. Anthony and D. Young, *Management Control in Nonprofit Organizations.*
4. P. Drucker, *The Age of Discontinuity.* New York: Harper and Row, 1968, p. 196.
5. R. Kanter and D. Summers, "Doing Well While Doing Good: Dilemmas of Performance Measurement in Nonprofit Organizations and the Need for a Multiple Constituency Approach," in W. W. Powell, *The Nonprofit Sector.*
6. J. March and P. Olsen, *Ambiguity and Choice in Organizations*, 1976.
7. C. Perrow, "Three Types of Effective Studies," in P. Goodman and J. Lennys, *New Perspectives on Organizational Effectiveness.* San Francisco: Jossey Bass, 1977, pp. 96–105.
8. J. Pfeffer, *Power in Organizations.* Boston: Pitman, 1981; and C. Perrow, "Goals and Power Structures: A Historical Case Study," in E. Freidson, *The Hospital in Modern Society.* New York: Macmillan, 1963, pp. 112–46.
9. C. Perrow, "Goals and Power Structures," p. 144.
10. R. Kanter and P. Summer, "Doing Well While Doing Good."
11. R. Anthony and D. Young, *Management Control in Nonprofit Organizations,* p. 556.
12. B. Staw and J. Ross, "Behavior in Escalation Situations," in *Science* vol. 246, 1989, pp. 216–20.
14. R. Herzlinger, "Why Data Systems in Nonprofit Organizations Fail," 1977.

Chapter 11

1. V. Hodgkinson, *Nonprofit Almanac,* 1992.
2. P. Selle and B. Oymyr, "Explaining Changes in the Population of Voluntary Organizations: The Roles of Aggregate and Individual Level Data," *Nonprofit and Voluntary Sector Quarterly,* Summer 1992, pp. 147–79.
3. An interesting study of the history of nonprofits in the United States is Peter Hall, "A Historical Overview of the Private Nonprofit Sector," in W. W. Powell, *The Nonprofit Sector.*
4. Among the most prominent of the population ecologists writing in the organizational area are M. Hannen and J. Freeman. See, for example, M. Hannen and J. Freeman, "Structural Inertia and Organizational Change" *American Sociological Review,* April 1984, pp. 149–64.
5. For a discussion of the important role of rules of thumb in organizations, see R. Nelson and S. Winter, *An Evolutionary Theory of Economic Change.* Cambridge: Harvard University Press, 1982. Similar discussion of the role of habit in organi-

zations is C. Gersick and R. Hackman, "Habit formation in organizations," Harvard Working Paper, 1992.

6. M. Hannen and J. Freeman, "Structural Inertia and Organizational Change."

7. P. Dimaggio and W. W. Powell, "The Iron Cage Revisited: Institutional Isomorphism and Collective Rationality in Organizational Fields," *American Sociological Review,* vol. 48, 1983, pp. 147–60.

8. The data underlying Table 11.1 come from V. Hodgkinson, et al., *Nonprofit Almanac,* 1992.

9. N. Churchill and U. Lewis, "The Five Stages of Small Business Growth," *Harvard Business Review,* May–June 1983, pp. 30–51.

10. A. Chandler, *Strategy and Structure.* Cambridge: MIT Press, 1982.

11. C. Perrow, "Goals and Power Structures."

12. C. Jenkins, "The Radical Transformation of Organizational Goals," *Administrative Science Quarterly,* vol. 22, 1977, pp. 248–67.

13. See, for example, Pfeffer and Salancik, "Organizational Decision Making as a Political Process," *Administrative Science Quarterly,* vol. 19, 1974, pp. 135–51.

14. For a review of this literature see Powell and Friedkin, "Organizational Change in Nonprofit Organizations," in W. W. Powell, *The Nonprofit Sector.*

15. National Committee for Responsive Philanthropy, "Nontraditional Giving," September 1990.

16. P. Dimaggio and W. W. Powell, "The Iron Cage Revisited."

17. M. Zald, *Organizational Change: The Political Economy of the YMCA.* Chicago: University of Chicago Press, 1970.

18. S. Oster, "Nonprofits as Franchising Operations," in *Nonprofit Management and Leadership,* Spring 1992, vol. 2, pp. 223–38.

19. T. Marmor, M. Schlesinger, and R. Smithey, "Nonprofit organizations and health care," in W. W. Powell, *The Nonprofit Sector.*

20. A. Ginsberg and A. Bucholtz, "Converting to For Profit Status: Corporate Responsiveness to Radical Change," *Academy of Management Journal,* vol. 2, no. 3, 1990, pp. 445–57.

Index

Abzug, R., 161 n1
Accrual principles, 127–28
ACLU. *See* American Civil Liberties Union
Admati, A., 165 n20
Affiliate structure, 33
Agency problems, 67–69
Agency theory, 67–69
AIDS, 25, 34, 92
Altruism, 49, 57, 63
American Civil Liberties Union, 20
American Heart Association, 39, 98
American Red Cross, 3, 21, 34, 38, 74, 101, 218–32
Anderson, P., 165 n24
Andreoni, J., 165 n20
Annenberg, W., 118
Anthony, R., 123, 125, 128, 143, 164 n27, 166 n1, n2, n4, n5, n6, n11, 167 n3, n11
Apley, G., 83
Aramony, W., 36, 67
Archdiocese of San Diego, 88
Arts, 21, 37. *See also* Museums
  management of, 37
  support for, 111, 118
Augsburger, R., 82, 162 n27
Axelrod, R., 59, 160 n9

Balanced budget, 127
Barriers to entry. *See* Entry barriers
Becker, W., 160 n6
Ben-Ner, A., 158 n4
Best School, 54–56
Bilodeau, M., 166 n33
Bittker, B., 162 n18
Black United Fund, 39, 57
Blau, J., 159 n6, 162 n14, 160 n10
Board of trustees, 14, 75–86

effectiveness, 83–86
function, 76–83
Boisture, R., 95
Boris, E., 162 n23
Boston Symphony Orchestra, 91
Boundary functions of mission statements, 22–23
Boundary-spanning, 77–78
Boyle, S., 111, 164 n6
Boys and Girls Club of America, 44–45, 49–50, 125–26
Bradshaw, P., 82, 84, 85, 162 n27, 163 n38
Braille Institute, 75
Brand name value, 33–34
Break even calculation, 103
Bright Horizons, 61
Bristol-Myers, 75
Bucholtz, A., 155, 168 n20
Budgeting systems, 127–38
Bureaucracy, 69–72
Burke, L., 165 n25
Bush, R., 159 n1, n5, n7
Buyer power, 38–40
Byrne, J., 163 n1

Caesar, P., 165 n28
Canada, nonprofits in, 20, 107
Carson, E., 115, 165 n16
Carver, J., 85, 163 n39
Case guide, 157–59
Categories of nonprofits, 7–10
Catholic Charities, 41
Catholic Relief Services, 129
Cause related marketing, 119
Centralization, 69–72
Certificates of need, 34
Chait, R., 81, 83, 84, 162 n19

Chandler, A., 152, 158 n2, 168 n10
Chang, C., 129, 166 n8, n9, n10
Change, 149–55
  difficulty of, 121, 154–55
  sources of, 84, 121, 151–54
Charitable contributions, 107–22
  case on, 272–86
  causes of, 114–18
  corporate giving, 118–19
  sources of, 107–11
  trends in, 107–11
Chicago Art Institute, 38
Child care, 61–62, 144–45
Children's Television Workshop, 90–97
Church of Latter Day Saints, 24
Churchill, N., 152, 168 n9
Clark, R., 90, 163 n7, n11
Clarkson, 162 n22
Cleveland Salvation Army, 79
Cleveland Symphony Orchestra, 134, 135
Clotfelter, C., 115, 165 n12, n13, n17, n22
Coase, R., 158 n2
Coca-Cola, 11, 47
Cole, B., 66, 160 n5, 161 n17
Cole, R., 77, 162 n9
Combined Health Appeal, 26, 39, 120
Compensation, 66–69
Competition, 13, 31–32, 47–64
  case on, 197–217
  dangers of, 63, 119
  with for-profits, 61–63
  utility of, 62–63, 119–20
Competitive analysis, 29–45
Composition of the field, 4–6
Constituencies, multiple, 22–27, 78–79,
  140–42, 164–65
Contract failure, 18–20
Contributed capital fund, 124
Cooperation, 31, 47, 57–61, 119–20
Core business, 87–88
Corporate giving, 118–19
Cost allocation, 104–6, 132, 139
Council on Foundations, 79
Creative Arts Workshop, 26–27
Credible commitment, 58–59
Crimmins, J., 163 n5
Cross elasticity of demand, 37
Cross subsidization of programs, 14, 90–92,
  131
Current fund, 124

Dalton Books, 118
Dance in America, 121
David, F., 158 n18
Davis, R., 76, 162 n13, 160 n16, 161 n3, n28

Decentralization, 69–72
Decision tree. *See* Game tree
Demographic profile of donors, 114–15
Depreciation, 128
Diagnostic Related Groups, 140, 145
Dimaggio, P., 121, 150, 154, 161 n25, 162
  n11, 168 n7
Distribution, access to, 33, 36
Diversification, 87–94
  advantages of, 87–92
  comparison of nonprofit and for-profit,
  87–92
  types of, 92–98
Diversity issues, 19–20, 62, 83
Dixit, A., 50, 159 n4
Dixwell Community House, 8–10
Dominant strategies, 56–57
Dominquez, N., 165 n9
Donations, 7–8, 107–11. *See also* Charitable
  contributions
Donor characteristics, 40–41, 114–16
Donor choice, 153, 272–86
Douglas, J., 19, 158 n6
Drucker, P., 12, 28, 73, 141, 157 n5, n9, 161
  n32, 167 n4

Easley, D., 158 n4
Easter Seal. *See* National Easter Seal Society
Ecology. *See* Population ecology
Economies of scale, 32–34
Economies of scope, 88, 91–92
Edley, C., 38, 159 n10
Education, 19–20, 39, 42, 56, 61, 83, 90, 100
Educational Testing Service, 37
Edwards, A., 81
Elasticity of demand, 38–39, 104–5
Endowment fund, 124, 130
Entrepreneurship, 24–25, 310–32
Entry barriers, 32–36
Equitable Life Insurance Co., 118
Escalation, 143
Ethiopian relief, 129
Evaluation, 139–47
Expected value, 54
Externalities, 57, 100

Failure of nonprofits, 34–35
Fair division, 51–52
Fama, E., 78, 161 n4, 162 n11
Farm Workers Union, 152
FASB. *See* Financial Accounting Standards
  Board
Federal Express Co., 24
Fee-for-service, 98–102
Feldstein, M., 115, 165 n12, n17

Fenn, D., 81, 162 n21
Financial Accounting Standards Board, 15, 124, 125, 128
Financial reporting systems, 15, 123–38
First mover advantage, 53
Firstenberg, P., 97, 163 n6, 164 n25
Fisher, F., 159 n4, 160 n8, 165 n29
Five Forces Diagram, 29–30
Fletcher, K., 85, 163 n43
Ford Foundation, 29
Foster Parent Plan, 48
Foundations, 11, 107, 108
Franchises, 33, 154–55
Free rider, 116
Freeman, E., 160 n3
Freeman, R., 66, 150, 160 n6, 167 n4, 168 n6
Friedkin, R., 121, 166 n37, 168 n14
Fund accounting, 124–27
Fund balance, defined, 124
Fund-raising, 30–31, 57–59, 107–22

Game theory, 48–56
Game tree, 50–54
Gapinski, J., 37, 159 n8
Garrison, J., 45, 159 n15
General Motors, 11, 41, 139
Gersick, C., 168 n5
Getty Museum, 40
Ginsberg, A., 155, 168 n20
Girl Scouts, 17, 87, 88
Girls, Inc., 23–24
Goal congruence, 57, 67–68, 72, 84–85
Good Faith Fund, 25, 233–50
Government buyers, 40–41
Government regulations, 34–35
Great Britain nonprofits, 47, 107, 110
Greeley, A., 165 n14
Greenberg, E., 160 n16
Greenleaf, R., 163 n40
Greenpeace, 37, 63
Guggenheim Museum, 8–10, 118, 141, 287–369

Haake, T., 95, 164 n21
Habitat for Humanity, 154
Hackett, E., 66, 161 n12
Hackman, R., 168 n5
Hall, P., 84, 157 n3, 163 n36, 167 n3
Hannen, M., 150, 167 n4, 168 n6
Hansmann, H., 158 n3, 159 n9, 164 n17
Harvard University, 83, 87
Health care, 99. *See also* Hospitals
Health care reform, 99
Health maintenance organizations, 155
Healthco, 142

Heimovics, R., 85, 163 n33, n41
Herman, R., 85, 162 n20, 163 n33, n41
Herzlinger, R., 166 n2, n13, 167 n14
Hesselbein, F., 17, 157 n1, 163 n1
Hierarchy, 69–70
Hirsch, P., 76, 161 n2
History of nonprofits, 4
Hodgkinson, V., 7, 109, 111, 157 n1, 159 n11, 160 n1, 164 n26, 164 n3, 167 n1, 168 n8
Holland, T., 83
Hospitals, 42, 67–68, 79, 90, 95, 103, 136, 142
Houghton, A., 63, 160 n17
Houle, C., 85, 162 n19, 163 n40, n42
Human resources, 65–74
  case on, 233–50
  management of, 65–74
Human services sector, 63
Humana, 75, 76

IBM, 3, 88
Ideology, role of, 20, 25–26, 67, 100–101
Incentive compensation, 67–69
Industry analysis, 29–46
  case on, 176–96, 287–309
Inertia, 149–50
Innovation, 143–44
Institutional isomorphism, 154
Internal Revenue Service
  categories of nonprofits, 10–11
  rules of tax exemptions, 68, 80, 94–96, 114, 117
Iron cage theory, 150

Jacobs, P., 111, 164 n6
James, E., 6, 61, 66, 158 n6, 160 n12, 161 n13, 163 n8, n12
Japan, nonprofits in, 6, 107
Jencks, C., 114–15, 165 n11, n15, n18
Jenkins, C., 152, 168 n12
Jensen, M., 78, 161 n4, 162 n11
Johnson & Johnson, 119
Joint costs, 103
Joint ventures, 48, 57–58
Julius Rosenwald Foundation, 121
Junior Achievement, 118

Kanter, R., 142, 146, 167 n5, n10
Karami House Theater, 79
Kennedy, C., 25
Key success factors, 42–44
Kiel, M., 163 n5
Kinder Care, 61
Kotler, P., 158 n14

Kraft General Foods, 118
Krashinsky, M., 20, 158 n3, n10
Krens, T., 141

LaBarbera, P., 163 n2
Labor intensity, 7–8, 65–66
Lammers, J., 160 n20
Land, E., 24
Laufer, A., 57, 159 n6
Law, Bernard, 3
Lear, N., 25
Learning curves, 33–34
Leeway, 34, 310–32
Leonardo Museum, 113
Levi Strauss and Co., 43
Levitt, T., 27, 158 n19
Lewis, D., 152, 160 n6
Lewis, U., 168 n9
Licenses, role of, 34–35
Life cycle of nonprofits, 82
Lincoln Center, 153, 251–71
Logsdon, J., 119, 165 n25, n27
Lovelock, C., 89, 163 n3
Luther, M., 38

MacMillan, I., 60–61, 160 n11
Magat, R., 165 n16
Majone, G., 157 n6
Management audit, 140–43
Management control systems, 123–38
Managerial control, 123–38
  case on, 287–309
Manns, C., 167 n1
March, J., 141, 167 n1, n2, n6
March of Dimes, 41
Marginal tax rate, effect on contributions, 117–18
Market definition, 30–31, 37
Markup pricing, 102–3
Marmor, T., 168 n19
McHugh, A., 161 n30
Menchik, P., 161 n31
Miller, J., 165 n20
Milofsky, C., 28, 158 n16, n20, 160 n10
Minimum efficient scale, 44
Mintzberg, H., 69–70, 161 n26, n30
Mirvis, P., 66, 161 n12
Mission, 12–13, 17–28
  breadth of, 27–28
  cases on, 160–75
  centrality of, 20–23
  choice of, 22–24
Mission statements, 24
Mortality, organizational, 34–35, 149–51
Motivation, 65–69

Mueller Macaroni Co., 94
Murray, V., 84, 162 n27
Muscular Dystrophy Association, 47
Museums, 9, 40, 41–42, 81, 87, 89, 90, 95, 113, 141
Mutual benefit nonprofits, 10–11

Nalebuff, B., 50, 159 n4
National Charitable Information Bureau, 113
National Council of Churches, 152
National Easter Seal Society, 24, 45
National Endowment for the Arts, 40, 81, 121
National Public Radio, 90
National Resources Defense Council, 145
National Urban League, 70
Nature Conservancy, 63
Nelson, R., 158 n3, 167 n5
Networks, 33, 35, 36, 59, 79
Netzer, O., 159 n13
New York Children's Health Project, 23
New York University, 94
Newman, L., 159 n6
Newman, W., 157 n7, 161 n21
Nielsen, R., 163 n10, n13
Noisy boards, 76, 78, 82
Nondistribution constraint, 4–5, 77–78
Nonprofit venturing, 93–98
Norwegian nonprofits, 149, 151

O'Connell, B., 81, 162 n24
Odendaul, T., 121, 162 n23, 166 n34
O'Hara, M., 158 n4
Olsen, P., 141, 167 n2, n6
O'Neill, M., 158 n12, 164 n24, 166 n12
Operations analysis, 140–41
Optimal level of fund raising, 111–14
Oster, S., 159 n3, n5, 168 n18
Oxfam, 31, 98
Oymyr, B., 151, 167 n2

Paley, W., 118
Patents, 34
Patterson, F., 57
Pauly, M., 68, 161 n22
Payoff matrix, 54–56
PBS, 197–217
Pearce, J., 158 n18
People for the American Way, 25, 28, 91, 160–75
Pepsi Cola, 47
Performance evaluation, 139–48
Perrow, C., 142, 152, 167 n7, n9, 168 n11
Perry, M., 165 n20

Pfeffer, J., 68, 69–70, 79, 121, 142, 161 n20, n27, n29, 162 n17, 166 n35, 167 n8, 168 n12
Phelps, E., 158 n5
Philanthropic Advisory Service, 113
Philanthropy. *See* Charitable contributions
Phillips, J., 79
Pigeon holing, 70
Planned Parenthood, 14, 24, 87, 92
Polaroid, 24
Population ecology, 149–51
Porter, M., 29, 159 n2
Powell, W. W., 121, 150, 154, 157 n3, n4, 162 n8, 164 n14, 166 n37, 168 n7, n13, n16
PPBS, 130
Preston, A., 66, 158 n13, 160 n8, n9, n10, 161 n11
Price, J., 77, 162 n7
Pricing, 98–105
Prime School, 54–56, 102, 127–28, 132–38
Prisoner's Dilemma, 56–58
Product bundling, 91
Product competition, 60–63, 99–100
Product matrix, 60–61
Product mix, 87–98
Product portfolio, 90–94
Production function, defined, 111–13
Professional bureaucracy, 69
Profit-centers, 139
Program budgeting, 127, 130–31
Program effectiveness, 140–41
Program evaluation, 139–47
Public Broadcasting Service (PBS), 197–217
Public goods, 19, 100
Public partnerships, 20–21, 40–41

Rabrerovic, G., 160 n10
Rahdert, G., 162 n18
Red Cross. *See* American Red Cross
Reiner, M., 165 n25
Relief and development organizations, 31. *See also specific organizations*
Religious organizations
    charitable giving, 115
    education, 20
    human resources, 66–67
    as ideological organizations, 20–21, 25
    market power, 38
    revenues, 107
Rent-seeking behavior, 120
Reputation, 33–34
Reputational effects, 33
Residual ownership, 76–77
Resource dependency theory, 152–53

Resource-attracting activities, 90, 93
Revised Model Nonprofit Corporation Act, 77
Rings of nonprofits, 10–11
Role of nonprofits, 4–8, 17–22
Roman Catholic Church, 3
Roos, J., 167 n12
Rose-Ackerman, S., 61, 62, 158 n4, 160 n12, n13, 164 n6, n17, 165 n8, n28

Salamon, L., 121, 158 n9, 159 n12, 166 n36
Salancik, G., 121, 166 n35, 168 n12
Saloner, G., 30, 159 n3
Salvation Army, 8
Sanger, M., 24
Santa Fe Opera Company, 8, 30
Save the Children
    board, 75
    competition, 48
    fund-raising, 114, 116, 119
    mission, 18, 21, 31
    product mix, 95
Schlesinger, M., 168 n19
Schumpter, J., 25, 158 n15
Schwartz, J., 159 n6
Scope of nonprofits, 17–27
Scranton, W., 166 n7
Security Exchange Commission, 78, 123
Self-dealing, 80
Selle, P., 151, 167 n2
Sensitivity analysis, 54
Sequential move games, 50–54
Sigler, A., 41
Simon, J., 10, 157 n4, n8
Simultaneous move games, 54–56
Six Forces Diagram, 29–42
Skloot, E., 92, 164 n14
Smith, J., 24
Smithey, R., 168 n19
Smithsonian Museum, 90
Social service agency, 69, 70–72, 87, 93
Span of control, 69
Specific assets, 34–35
Spending rules, 130
Stages of growth, 152
Stakeholders, 27, 65
Statue of Liberty, 119
Staw, B., 143, 167 n12
Steinberg, R., 68, 114, 161 n18, 164 n16, 165 n10, n30
Steuerle, E., 165 n13
Stewart, T., 157 n2
Stigler, G., 159 n14
Stock options, 67–68
Stone, M., 26, 158 n17, 162 n8, 163 n37